**BLACK
CRUSADER**

Black Crusader

A BIOGRAPHY OF ROBERT FRANKLIN WILLIAMS

by Robert Carl Cohen

LYLE STUART, INC. / SECAUCUS, NEW JERSEY

Acknowledgment

My appreciation to Professor David Fine for his comments and editorial assistance, Charles B. Bloch for his guidance and criticism, my wife Helene for her patience, and my daughters Dianna and Julia for helping me to keep smiling.

The prospect of peaceful integration is dead. White sanity is dead. The American Dream is dead and the cringing nigger is dead. All were killed by the White man's satanic hatred and violence.

> —Robert Franklin Williams, Peking, May, 1968 (commenting on the assassination of the Reverend Martin Luther King, Jr.)

CONTENTS

**BLACK
CRUSADER**

INTRODUCTION

Neither at the head of an army nor stealthily by night, in September, 1969, knowing it would mean certain arrest, Robert Franklin Williams decided to return to the United States of America. But when he attempted to change planes in London, Trans World Airlines, claiming the FBI had warned them that he was "extremely dangerous," refused to honor his air ticket. And the British detained him as an unadmittable alien.

During the week that followed, while Williams went on a hunger strike, the world press marveled that any man should be so feared that he wasn't permitted to enter the most powerful nation in history to surrender himself to its police. Faced with a growing wave of protests, TWA allowed him to board one of their flights. However, the airline's insistence on the logic of its initial caution led to the unprecedented spectacle of a giant jetliner flying from England to the United States with Robert Franklin Williams as the sole passenger. Eight years after fleeing to Havana and Peking, Black America's leading advocate of urban guerrilla warfare and a Socialist revolution was coming home.

I first met Williams in Cuba in 1963 when my wife and I went there to produce a documentary film for educational television in the United States. Despite the notoriety which his Radio Free Dixie propaganda broadcasts beamed at the South had already achieved, I knew very little about him. The more I learned the more interested I became.

Tall, and rather stockily built, he looked more like a football player or boxer than a revolutionary. Though he was usually soft-spoken, when he became engrossed in discussing injustice, the intense emotion stored up within him quickly revealed itself. The vitriol of *The Crusader,* the newsletter he was publishing in Havana and sending to his supporters in the States, was so searing that reading it invoked the image of an enraged zealot of Biblical times calling down damnation upon his people's oppressors.

The metamorphosis of Robert Franklin Williams from an

easily contented youngster who dreamed of being a poet into an archenemy of the U.S. power structure was neither quick nor easy. In 1955, he wandered the streets of his hometown in North Carolina unable to earn enough to feed his wife and two little boys. Like so many contemporary Blacks, his unwillingness to play the role of either mute "field hand" or bootlicking "house nigger" had already damned him at the age of thirty to the economic rubbish heap. But instead of sinking into the bottomless pits of crime, narcotics, or schizophrenia, which claim so many who find themselves in similar straits, he had joined the struggle for civil rights. His subsequent experiences, from battling the Ku Klux Klan, to evading an international FBI dragnet to reach sanctuary in Cuba, were startling, to say the least.

At the conclusion of that 1963 visit to Havana I told Williams of my decision to write a magazine article about his adventures. I scoffed when he suggested that no major U.S. journal would publish an objective report about him. But he was right. Every editor to whom it was submitted turned my story down flat. The basis for rejection was always the same: They didn't want to be accused of providing a platform for what they considered unsubstantiated claims about a coming Black uprising. My argument—that it was their responsibility to help inform the public before the situation reached the boiling point—failed to convince anyone.

Back in Cuba the following year to complete work on my film, I interviewed Williams once more. By then his predictions of civil strife in the United States had become quite specific. In the April–May, 1964, issue of *The Crusader* he had written that the "storm" would reach "hurricane proportions by 1965 and the eye of the hurricane will hover over America by 1966." Once again, the national magazines weren't interested. Ostrichlike, they seemed to think hiding Williams' thoughts from the public would prevent what he foretold from taking place.

The fact that his predictions were based on a real awareness of his people's growing frustration was brought out with dramatic force by the explosion of the Watts ghetto in August, 1965. "Burn, baby, burn!" became the catch phrase of similar outbursts across the nation.

By mid-1967, with Detroit ablaze and smoke from the Newark ghetto blackening the skyscrapers of Manhattan, and with President Lyndon B. Johnson personally demanding that *The Cru-*

sader be banned from the mails, the message finally got through that Robert Franklin Williams had something important to say. Several major publishing houses approached me about doing a book on his life, but by then he had become almost impossible to reach. The year before, following serious disagreements with certain high Cuban officials, he had left Havana and moved to Peking.

In November, 1967, learning that he had been invited to lecture at universities in Sweden, I went to Stockholm hoping to meet Williams there. My trip was for naught because the Swedish government refused to issue him a visa; and he remained in China.

Then, unexpectedly, in June of 1968 Williams sent me a cable announcing he was in Tanzania, East Africa. Jetting halfway around the world, I landed at the Dar es Salaam airport on July 4th to find him waiting.

The five weeks that followed were spent tape-recording his life story. The fifty hours of dialogue which resulted were later transcribed to more than fourteen hundred pages of manuscript. I also had a crew of bearded, turbaned Sikhs flown down from Nairobi to film an interview for television in the United States.

When he learned that I planned to send the film and tapes to New York by the next available jet, Williams warned me that the CIA might try to hijack the shipment. Seeing no reason for the U.S. government to steal something that would soon be available in every bookstore, I didn't take his suggestion very seriously. But, knowing that the ridiculous or the unforeseen is always possible, I'd already taken the precaution of copying the tapes.

The next afternoon my publisher cabled to say the package wasn't aboard the plane when it arrived. TWA claimed it had accidentally been taken off during a refueling stop in Athens, and wouldn't get to New York for at least a week.

Suspicious, I checked the flight schedules and discovered that the airline had *daily,* rather than weekly, flights from Athens to New York. My apprehension deepened when I telexed the Athens airport with the waybill number and was told they had no record of such a parcel having been there.

Upon learning this, I telephoned my publisher and suggested he call the president of TWA and tell him that unless the package was found by the following noon a press conference would be called to announce its mysterious disappearance. Less than thirty minutes after this was done, TWA called to say that due to an innocent oversight the package had been in their possession in New York for several days and was being rushed over by messenger at once.

During the approximately seventy-two hours when the package was missing, the cans of film hadn't been opened. That would have destroyed the visual part of our interview. However, the seals I'd placed on every box of tape had been cut, and the tapes appeared to have been hastily rewound. I've no way of knowing if the CIA was involved, but it seems evident that someone with lots of connections had been very much interested in what Williams had to say. Another one of his predictions had been proven correct, but at least the material had finally gotten through.

This book is primarily based on those African tapes. It also contains information from my talks with Williams in Cuba; various editions of *The Crusader*; his speeches, radio broadcasts, articles, interviews, and personal letters; *Negroes With Guns,* a small book he wrote in 1962; and anecdotes related by people who have known him.

Although a good deal of what follows is quoted verbatim, where Williams' thoughts were expressed in a fragmentary or not-readily-understood manner I have taken the liberty of reconstructing them in the style of his other remarks. Throughout, I have tried to present his ideas accurately, but caution the reader that when someone has written, said, and done so much for so many years, a certain amount of misinterpretation is always possible.

Robert Franklin Williams' story is more than an account of the first Black American to advocate armed self-defense or to live in both Cuba and China; it is a dynamic example of the rapidly developing political self-awareness of a people held down for centuries. The crisis facing the United States is too severe, the danger of devastating civil war too great, for us to remain ignorant or complacent a moment longer. I have written this book because I am convinced that unless White America is capable of understanding how it not only gave birth to such a man, but is daily creating countless more like him, and unless we accept the responsibility of ending, once and for all, the twin evils of intolerance and exploitation, the continued existence of our nation is in serious doubt.

Chapter One

HAPPY DAYS

Back in the mid-1920's, about one-third of the eleven thousand inhabitants of Monroe, North Carolina, were Black. Following the usual southern pattern, they lived on one side of the railroad tracks while the Whites lived on the other. Everything in the Black part of town revolved around the "Seaboard," the Seaboard Airline Railway Company, which was the major source of jobs for Blacks in that part of Union County.

The houses in Monroe were predominantly built of lumber, which was abundant and inexpensive because of the nearby woods and sawmills. Being bisected by the rail yards, it was a smoky town, and a light rain of cinders constantly fell on the white and yellow frame houses near the tracks, tinting them a uniform dirty gray.

John Williams was a quiet, medium-sized man who worked as a boilermaker's helper for the Seaboard. His salary of thirty to forty dollars a week wasn't great, but it sufficed to support his family and to buy a house at 14 Boyte Street, a seven-room, two-story wooden building which stood on a hill near the rail yards. It was in this house that his youngest son, Robert Franklin Williams, was born on February 26, 1925.

When Robert was a child the pavement and sewage lines ended where the Black residential areas began. After Franklin Delano Roosevelt became president in 1933, the Work Projects Administration (WPA) extended the sewage lines to the Black part of town. But it wasn't until years later that the authorities compelled the landlords—most of whom were White—to install plumbing and indoor toilets in the houses they rented to Blacks.

The streets of Monroe were lined with elm and chinaberry trees. Many of the poorer people, Whites as well as Blacks, planted small vegetable gardens wherever they could find unused land. Little patches of corn, peas, tomatoes, and other crops grew everywhere.

The bus and railway stations, courthouse, and hospital were segregated. In general, the attitude of the Whites toward the Blacks was typical of most small southern communities.

The shortest route from the Black community to the White part of town was directly across the rail yards. Every morning the Black women and girls employed by the Whites as domestics could be seen stepping carefully over the rails as they went to work. Among the White railroad men were a few who made it an almost daily practice to stroll outside their wash house in the nude in order to exhibit themselves to the Black women who were passing by. And, whenever within earshot of a Black man, these types would loudly brag about how many Black women they had fornicated with.

Although the Black workers were furious over these provocations, they could do nothing about them for fear of losing their jobs. Positions with the Seaboard being hard to come by and paying better than most, they swallowed their anger and pretended not to see or hear what was going on.

But when John Williams would come home after work, he could no longer restrain his fury, and would sit for hours discussing the latest degradations which he and the other Black railroad workers had been forced to endure. Robert was too young at first to understand most of what was being said, but his father's helpless rage burned itself into his memory.

Robert Franklin Williams' grandparents on his father's side were born into slavery but, being very young at the end of the Civil War, they remembered little about pre-Abolition days. After being freed they had both been able to go to school; and Grandfather Sykes Williams had continued on to college. In the 1880's he and Grandmother Ellen Elizabeth Williams were among the first Black teachers in Union County.

Around the turn of the century Grandfather had been as active as a Black was allowed to be in southern politics. He was considered somewhat of a radical because of his efforts to get Black people to register to vote. Despite this, the Whites never gave him any serious trouble because it was known that he was related to some of them through his mother, who was either White or part-White.

Williams' mother, a devout Baptist, was an honest and kind woman, always ready to help those in need. When he was little she would take him with her to the Elizabeth Baptist Church, which functioned as both the religious and social center for the Blacks of Monroe. Along with her fellow churchgoers, she was known as one of the "good people" of the community. She wouldn't permit tobacco or alcohol in their house. Even playing cards were taboo. As a result, when they were teen-agers, Robert and his two older brothers avoided pool halls and bars. When he entered the Army, the fellows in his unit were amazed that he didn't know how to shoot craps.

Williams' father was one of ten children, so the young boy had many aunts and uncles. The uncle he liked best was Charlie Williams, a World War I veteran who ran a rural school for Blacks near Monroe.

Uncle Charlie was considered very controversial because of his atheism. While Williams' father wasn't religious either, he was diplomatic enough to excuse himself from the revival meetings at the Baptist church by telling his wife he was "too tired" to go. Uncle Charlie, on the other hand, got her and the other "good people" angry by saying, "You church niggers are always down on your knees praying. If the God you believe in is so good, why doesn't he answer your prayers and set you free?"

But while many looked upon him as little less than an outlaw, to others Uncle Charlie was a good friend and benefactor. He would frequently help people fill out their relief forms, and was always available when anyone needed assistance in legal matters. Even his detractors admitted that he was highly intelligent, but Robert's mother tried to keep the youngster from associating with him because she was afraid Charlie might make her son an atheist too. When she discovered that he was letting her "Baby Rob" drink "home brew," a bootleg whiskey prepared in crude stills, she really turned against him.

Uncle Charlie's closest friend was the Reverend Perry, whose occupational problems were similar to his own. Although he had attended Boston University and Andover Theological Seminary, the only job the Reverend could hold onto was running a rural school. He was unable to keep a congregation because, whenever one of his parishioners asked a question which he felt was stupid, he couldn't resist answering sarcastically. Both he and Uncle

Charlie were far too well educated and outspoken for their provincial environment.

While Robert's father wasn't as learned as the Reverend Perry or Uncle Charlie, by his hard work and dedication to his family he set a good example for the young boy. The railroad company had a rule that only Whites could be boilermakers, but some of the Black helpers, like John Williams, had been at it longer and knew the work better than their bosses did. The boilermaker himself would often spend the day boozing in those houses in the Black community where home brew was sold, while Williams' father did the job for both of them. His skill kept him on the payroll all through the Depression, when a great many other people in town were unemployed.

In 1932, when Robert was seven, he started attending the Winchester School, the only one they had for Blacks in Monroe. It encompassed all the grades from first through senior high.

His grandmother had specialized in history when she taught school, and she still spent much of her time reading about it. She would tell the children about Hitler's coming to power in Germany and what was happening in other countries. Robert was so fascinated by such events that by the time he was eight or nine years old he had become somewhat of a neighborhood expert on world affairs.

There was a small general store on the block, where the men gathered after work to play checkers. Many of them were illiterate, and those who weren't had never been encouraged to take an interest in reading the papers or listening to news broadcasts. Whenever little Robert passed by, they would ask him to explain the latest world events, and would jokingly call him "The News Man."

In addition to history, Williams liked geography, though he was very unhappy when the teacher first told him that Brazil, the Soviet Union, Canada, and some other countries were larger in area than the United States.

He also enjoyed reading about great war victories and valiant heroes, and would daydream about being in one of the Black cavalry units that had captured San Juan Hill under Teddy Roosevelt's command back in 1898.

Robert was still too young to understand that being dark-skinned placed him in a special category that was systematically discriminated against. He saw racism only as a characteristic of bad individuals. There were some people who were mean, and others who weren't. The White Georgian who ran the railway's general store would always greet him pleasantly, saying to the other Whites in the store, "That's John Williams' boy. I can tell how long I've been here in Monroe by how tall he's getting." As there were quite a few other Whites who didn't seem to have any hatred toward Blacks, it was normal for young Robert not to see them all as being bad.

The textbooks he was given at the Winchester School presented slavery in an almost pleasant light. According to them, although there may have been a few cruel masters, most of the plantation owners were good people, who taught their slaves to read and write, gave them wholesome food and warm lodgings, and never whipped or worked them too hard. They made the old days sound rather attractive to Black children whose parents were unemployed and couldn't provide them with decent shoes to wear or food to eat.

But Williams didn't believe the stories of "good masters" in those textbooks. He'd already heard first-hand accounts about what slavery was like from an ex-slave woman on his block who people said was 105 years old. She would often tell the children how cruel many of the slave owners had been. And how, when they heard that the Union Army was approaching Monroe, the wealthy Whites had become frightened and hurriedly hid their money and valuables. A number of them had then run wild, murdering every slave who might tell the northern soldiers where they had cached their wealth. They had also killed several slaves who had dared to express jubilation over their coming freedom. These included members of her own family.

Robert Franklin Williams first began to understand the real relationship between Whites and Blacks when he was around ten years old. He was walking down the main street of Monroe when he saw a White policeman dragging a screaming Black woman by her feet. The cop was grinning as he pulled her by the heels, her dress up over her hips and her back being scraped by the concrete pavement. The White shopkeepers and passers-by were laughing at the sight. Those Blacks who were near—especially the men—

were quickly leaving the scene. Since they didn't have the courage to protest against the cop's cruelty, the best thing they could do was walk away and pretend not to see it.

Young Robert didn't leave. He watched until the woman was dragged off to jail. The worst part of it for him was the laughter of the White onlookers, men and women alike. And he couldn't accept the idea of Black men seeing something like that and being so afraid they would run away.

Another aspect of the system which burned itself into Robert's youthful consciousness was the chain gang. There were chain gangs throughout the Monroe area, and he thought that the men on them—especially those who wore striped uniforms—were very bad. Indeed, in his childish view they were almost like wild animals, who would tear you apart if they ever got loose. The Williams house being close to the prison farm, he and the other children often went there in the evening to watch the prisoners being herded into their barracks after working all day at the nearby rock quarries, swamps, road projects, and farms.

Each man had a short chain connecting his legs at the ankle so he couldn't escape, and some of the prisoners were chained to each other. The law at that time prohibited Whites under eighteen from being sentenced to the chain gang, but the minimum age for Blacks was only sixteen, and there were even fifteen-year-old Black boys on it. After he grew up, Williams realized that many of the prisoners—White as well as Black—far from being savage criminals, were the innocent victims of a system of involuntary servitude.

Although lynchings were common in other parts of the country during the Depression, none had taken place in Monroe for many years. Whenever the religious Blacks heard about a lynching they would say "how shameful" it was, and that "God was some day going to punish the White folks for doing such things." Robert's father told him that the Ku Klux Klan had tried to stage a parade in Monroe some years before he was born. But a large number of the Black men of the town had stood out in front of their homes holding rifles and shotguns. Seeing this, the Klansmen had decided the climate wasn't too healthful in that area, and hadn't tried to parade there again.

The value of demonstrating a willingness to fight to defend oneself first became evident to Robert when he was ten years old.

A group of Black boys had started bullying him whenever he walked past their block on his way home from school. He didn't tell his family about it but one morning woke up early and went to the Seaboard's general store, where he bought a pocket knife and charged it to his father's account.

He kept the knife in his pocket all day at school. That afternoon, on his way home, three of the boys were waiting by a telephone pole. As he walked past, they came at him. But when he pulled the knife out of his pocket and snapped the blade open, they turned tail and ran off down the street.

He had no more trouble from them; in fact, they became his best friends. Years later they asked him, "Were you really going to cut us with that knife?"

"Yeah," he said. "I was going to cut you all right. Did you think I was going to let somebody beat me, and not do anything about it?"

Among young Robert's close friends were his cousin Arthur Williams, who was called "Bro," short for brother; Perry Little, the son of a local Baptist minister; and Thomas Roddy, "Tad." The four of them roamed the nearby woods together—fishing, hunting birds, and rafting. One day they were on their way home from playing in the woods when they came upon some White hunters sitting in a pickup truck on the side of the road. As they walked past, the Whites suddenly pointed their rifles at them and said, "Okay, you little niggers, let's see you dance."

Though frightened, Robert and his friends looked at each other, and realized they weren't about to do as the hunters wanted. First one, then the others, answered, "No, we won't dance. We don't know how to dance. Leave us alone."

Cocking their rifles, the White men began shouting, "You damned niggers better start dancing or we are going to start shooting." But the four boys stood there without moving. Finally, seeing they couldn't bully them, the hunters said, "Get out of here, then, goddamn you!"

A few years later Williams' father bought him his first rifle, a .22-caliber single-shot. If he'd had it with him that day when the White hunters tried to make him dance, he would have used it.

The idea of standing up and fighting for your rights as a human being was something Robert and the other Black children weren't being taught in the schools, or anywhere else for that mat-

ter. They were told it was good to fight for flag and country, but
the only examples of bravery they were shown were those of
Whites. The concept that Blacks could also be heroes first came to
Williams' attention in the fifth grade. One of his teachers, a Miss
Carter, started telling her class stories that weren't in their textbooks. The one that meant the most to young Robert had to do
with a Black man who, as a result of having had a fight with a
White, was about to be lynched. When he heard the mob approaching, he grabbed his rifle and fled to the woods. The Whites
finally tracked him down, but he refused to surrender and killed
several of them before being killed himself. The children would
bubble with excitement when Miss Carter told them that story,
and then were saddened by its tragic ending. Robert's sadness,
though, was allayed by pride that the Black protagonist had died a
hero.

The absence of Black heroes in his textbooks was also true in
the comic books he read and the movies he saw. The good guys
were always Anglo-Saxon types—never people of color, or even
Whites of central or southern European ancestry.

When he was eleven, Williams first came to understand that
those who were against Blacks were not merely some mean individuals—but included the White authorities who ran the town of
Monroe. For years, Black parents had vainly pleaded with the
school board to replace the aging, broken-down main building of
the Winchester School. The school board had refused to do anything about it, though they hadn't hesitated to build a new addition to a nearby White school. The matter took a dramatic turn
one night when the old school building caught fire and burned to
the ground.

It took about eighteen months, but the town finally did con-
struct a new school building for the Blacks. However, the Whites
didn't believe in spending any more tax money on Blacks than
they absolutely had to, and the new building was overcrowded
and inadequately equipped.

When Williams was twelve, Mrs. Pauline Barber, one of his
sixth-grade teachers, praised a story he had written about going
fishing. It was the first time a teacher had gone out of her way to
compliment him. Although he normally disliked homework, he
began looking forward to each new prose or poetry assignment.

The idea of being a writer wasn't completely new to young

Robert. A few years before he was born, his father and a man named Darling Thomas had unsuccessfully tried to publish a newspaper for the Blacks of Monroe. Their small printing press, rusting and gathering dust in a corner of the barn, had fascinated him even before he knew what it was for.

At fourteen Robert was large for his age. There were other boys in the neighborhood who were taller and heavier, but he was faster, stronger, and a better fighter than any of them. Although he was on the boxing team at Winchester, he couldn't go out for football because all the uniforms had been destroyed when the old school building burned down. Rather than replace them, the school board had discontinued the sport.

About this time a group of Black teen-agers formed a street gang which they called the "X-32." Williams, as their leader, was referred to as "Captain X." World War II was beginning, and everyone was interested in military matters. The teen-agers, following the trend of the times, made uniforms for themselves and played at war in the woods.

Armed with slingshots, air rifles, bottles, and bricks, they would patrol the Black community at night, watching for those Whites who crossed the tracks to try to pick up Black women. When they spotted a White man sitting alone in a car, the X-32 would quietly surround it and suddenly emerge from the darkness to kick and pound on its roof and fenders. Then they would disappear into the shadows before the police arrived.

The cops assumed that the gang was made up of delinquents from a nearby Black area called "The Neck," which was known as a bad district. They never thought of questioning Robert and his friends because they were the sons of "good niggers." Even the minister's son was in their gang.

In addition to conducting night raids on tomcatting motorists, they often got together to discuss how the Whites were mistreating Blacks in general. Many of the Black schoolchildren had to walk past a section of town inhabited by White mill workers, and the boys from that area often chased and beat them just for the hell of it. Williams' X-32 gang started finding out which Whites were involved in the attacks. Whenever they spotted one of them in the Black part of town, they would run him out in retaliation.

By maintaining strict discipline, they managed to keep the

X-32 gang going for several years without being caught by the police. It finally broke up when most of them left high school and started working.

The greatest tragedy Williams felt as a youngster was when his Uncle Charlie passed away. It wasn't that he didn't know about death—one or another of his many aunts or uncles seemed to die almost every year—it was the way Charlie died that stayed in his memory.

The morning they heard that Uncle Charlie had suffered some sort of stroke, Williams' entire family rushed over to his house. Charlie's wife, who had been one of his high school students, and all of her relatives were there. He was lying in bed, struggling a little bit but steadily growing weaker. During the hours the family sat waiting, young Robert had the impression that his uncle was looking straight at him, staring as though desperately trying to tell him something. The boy looked into his uncle's eyes until they finally closed in death.

When she saw he was gone, his wife cried out, "Oh God! You took Charlie, now take me too." Then the relatives started closing down the house and packing away all of his clothes and other belongings. Robert was surprised at the large number of books he had. The house seemed full of them.

Those were sad days for a lot of people. Despite the reforms of the New Deal, the Depression was still on, and there were quite a few "Hoover Carts" on the streets. These were horse- or mule-drawn wooden carts which used the axles, metal wheels, and pneumatic tires of automobiles whose owners were too poor to keep them running.

Since very few Monroe Blacks had enough money to buy a car even when times were good, most of the "Hoover Carts" were owned by Whites. The reason they were called this was that many people blamed President Herbert Hoover and his Administration for having brought on the Depression.

One of the diversions that softened those hard times was an old White engineer whom everyone called "Happy Days." He became sort of a legend on the Seaboard because he was able to play the melody from the song "Happy Days Are Here Again" on the steam whistle of his locomotive. Sometimes late at night Williams would be awakened by the cheerful tooting echoing over the hills.

The next morning he would think he'd only dreamed it, but then everyone he met would say, "Did you hear it, Rob? Happy Days passed through last night again." It was only a little thing, but it helped many people keep smiling despite the distress of the Depression.

Back then, many Black hobos from the Deep South stole rides on the freight trains heading north. Some were talented, self-taught musicians. They would exchange performances on the harmonica, guitar, or washboard for a place to sleep and something to eat; and were frequently invited to play their blues and barrelhouse music in those houses in the Black community that had pianos. Williams' mother and the other "good" people denounced the hobos as "riffraff," and said their music was a bad influence, but he and the other Black boys were fascinated by them. Sometimes they would sneak out at night to go where they were putting on a show. The sessions would often last all night. Red-eyed from lack of sleep, young Robert would creep back into the house at dawn, hoping his parents wouldn't awaken and discover where he had been.

The December 7, 1941, Japanese attack on Pearl Harbor took place as Williams was about to enter the eleventh grade. While not yet seventeen, he was close to six feet tall, and people were already asking why he wasn't in the Armed Forces. Many of his friends who were only slightly older began to drop out of school to go to work in the war plants being built all over the country. They didn't do this for patriotic reasons, but because the growing manpower shortage was making an unprecedented number of good jobs available for Blacks.

In those first few months the war seemed to Williams like something make-believe happening far, far away. Of course he'd heard about such things as Hitler's invasion of Russia, but, despite his personal interest in History and Geography, Communism and Fascism were still only words to him. The newspapers in Monroe, North Carolina, didn't bother to explain very much about the conflicting philosophies of the various combatants; nor did they discuss the competition for control of eastern Asia which had led to the war in the Pacific.

All that Robert and his buddies knew was that the United States had been badly hurt at Pearl Harbor, and the local Whites were frightened. Sometimes, when they heard a large number of aircraft passing overhead, the Black teen-agers would jokingly say, "Here come the Japs. Whitey is going to get it now."

As more and more of the young men in the neighborhood left school for war jobs or to enter the service, Williams' mother became afraid that he would also drop out. "Once you leave," she would tell him, "you won't ever go back. And that will make you the only one of my five children without a high school diploma." Her fears were well-founded. The New Deal had established a National Youth Administration (NYA), and one of its functions was to train young people for skilled jobs. Though Williams enjoyed living with his parents, he felt the time had come to go out into the world and prove his manhood. So, in 1942, soon after turning seventeen, he followed the example of several of his friends and signed up with the NYA to learn the trade of machinist.

The seeds of self-awareness and discontent planted in him hadn't yet begun to sprout. Having been raised in a community where almost everyone unquestioningly accepted segregation, lower wages, and a denial of their rights, he was largely unaware of what being Black meant. Had he been born in a big-city ghetto, he would most certainly have been wise to the harsh realities of prejudice and discrimination at a much earlier age. The next four years, however, were to increase his understanding very rapidly. Robert Franklin Williams was about to experience the first of his many head-on collisions with the less savory aspects of the "American Way of Life."

Chapter Two

TENT CITY

The NYA camp was located near the town of Rocky Mount, North Carolina, about 150 miles north of Monroe. Food, clothing, lodgings, and classes were free of charge, and each trainee was given $32.00 per month to spend as he saw fit.

One of Williams' favorite teachers was an elderly White man who owned a big machine shop in town. With so much war work available, he could have made more money there, but he preferred teaching at the NYA camp. "Learn all you can," he would tell the trainees. "You are being given an opportunity few colored boys have ever had before."

Although all of the trainees were Black and all of the instructors White, Williams didn't experience a single incident of discrimination at the NYA camp. The instructors treated him fairly; and he once again began to think racism was limited to certain bad individuals.

When the Rocky Mount camp became overcrowded, he was among those sent to another training center at the all-Black State Teachers' College in Elizabeth, North Carolina. A few classrooms were set aside for the NYA trainees, but they shared dormitories and eating facilities with the regular students.

In contrast to the good meals at Rocky Mount, the food the school served was bad. Sometimes there was nothing but beans for breakfast, and at other times only dried apples. They hardly ever saw meat or butter; everyone was hungry. It became so unbearable that some of the trainees complained to their families, and an investigation resulted.

The federal investigators told the trainees that the United States government had been paying the North Carolina state officials in charge of the college extra money so that they would be given eggs, butter, milk, meat, and other foods required for good health. Instead of doing this, the officials had put the federal money into their own pockets. The Black president of the college, fearful of losing his job, hadn't dared complain.

The state authorities were compelled as a result of the investigation to honor their contract to feed Williams and the others properly. But, instead of providing everyone with decent food, they set up a separate table for the NYA trainees. The regular college students were forced to watch them being served butter, meat, milk, and eggs, while they had only beans and dried apples. Williams considered it a disgusting situation, but it didn't occur to him or any of the others to do anything about it.

In the beginning of 1943, having completed the training course, Williams went to Detroit, where his oldest brother Edward lived, and started working at the Ford Motor Company as a boring-mill operator, turning out armor plate for tanks. He was earning over $300 per month—about five times as much as he could have gotten in Monroe, but a family crisis forced him to send $50.00 of his pay home every week.

Things had first begun to go badly for Williams' father in 1939, when he went into debt to buy a 1936 Dodge. Then he took on the expense of sending two of his children to college, which forced him to borrow against the family house. Everything would have been all right, except that, just as Robert was turning eighteen, his father suffered a stroke while working on top of a locomotive and was injured severely as he fell to the ground. Since his father was no longer able to meet the installments on the mortgage against the house, Robert had to help pay the approximately $500 that remained. He was able to manage only because his brother let him stay in his house in Detroit rent free, and he spent as little as possible on his personal needs.

Tension was building in Detroit in those days. There were a lot of "hillbillies" coming to the city—poor Whites from the rural areas of Kentucky, Tennessee, and other parts of the South who, like the Blacks, were attracted by the high-paying jobs available in the war plants. Many were just as antagonistic toward Blacks in the North as they had been back home. Quite a few of the servicemen stationed in the area were also from the South, but the most anti-Black of the Whites in Detroit were the Polish-Americans who lived in Hamtramck, a district near Williams' brother's home in MacCormack Gardens.

Late one Sunday afternoon, Robert, his brother Edward, Edward's wife, and another couple were coming home from a picnic when their car was caught in a traffic jam on the Belle Isle bridge. At first they assumed it was due to the usual weekend rush, but then they saw that the bridge was blocked by a crowd watching a gang of White sailors beating a single Black man.

The other two men both carried pocket knives, but all Williams had was a pipe he'd started smoking recently. So he held it clenched in his fist with the stem sticking out as if it were a knife too. Without discussion, the three of them climbed out of their car. Suddenly, a White girl in the crowd started shouting, "Look out for those niggers! Look out for those niggers!" As soon as she said, "They got knives!" the crowd opened up, and the White sailors started backing away from them.

The moment the Black who was being beaten saw what was happening, he ran off without saying a word. Williams and the others returned to their car, thinking there had been only that one fight. But, as they drove on, they found that groups of sailors were attacking Blacks all along the bridge. Telling his wife to drive, Edward sat behind her with his knife sticking out of the left rear window. His friend sat by the right front door with his knife out as well. They slashed at those White sailors who tried to jump onto the running board and pull them out of the car.

They were able to fight their way off the bridge—only to find a large mob of Whites blocking the street and trying to break the windows of every car with Blacks in it. Whenever the mob caught somebody who hadn't locked his door, they dragged him out and beat him. There were several White policemen standing just a few feet away, but they pretended not to notice anything. Fortunately, Williams and the others managed to get home without being hurt.

He went to bed that night thinking some sort of minor riot, perhaps over a traffic dispute, had taken place at the bridge. But the next morning his brother told him, "You can't go to Ford today, Rob. What we saw was only the beginning. They've been rioting in Detroit all night long." The newspapers reported how someone had run down to the Black community shouting that the White mob had thrown a Black woman and her baby off the bridge. The rumor had spread, knives and guns had appeared, and soon mobs of both Blacks and Whites were running amuck through the streets.

A lot of people—the majority of them Black—were killed

during those 1943 race riots. Because relatively few Blacks in Detroit owned guns, groups of armed Whites were able to go to isolated Black residential areas and shoot them up without reprisal.
The Detroit police stood aside during most of the fighting, seem-
ing to intervene only when the Whites were getting the worst of it.

The moment word reached them that the Poles from Hamtramck were getting ready to burn down MacCormack Gardens,
Williams, his brother, and their neighbors started organizing to
defend the area. Before the attack could take place, however, President Franklin D. Roosevelt ordered thousands of Army troops
into the streets with jeeps carrying .50-caliber heavy machine
guns, and the rioting quickly came to a halt.

Williams often wondered about the Black man on the bridge.
His thought had been only of himself when Williams and the others had risked their safety to rescue him. Had he joined with them,
he would certainly have escaped, but running away alone perhaps
led to his being beaten or killed.

Nevertheless, Williams reflected that he would do the same
thing again in a similar situation. For him and for other Blacks,
the Detroit riots provided a useful education. The sight of White
mobs running through the streets attacking everyone with a dark
skin compelled many normally disorganized Blacks to join forces
in order to survive.

Williams was convinced that, had the Detroit auto factory
owners ordered the cops to stop the hillbillies and sailors from
mobbing Blacks, there wouldn't have been any trouble in the first
place. But, once the "poor White trash" saw they could lynch
Blacks with impunity, they concluded that the Establishment
wanted it done, and went wild. It appeared to be only when the
rioting began to seriously interfere with war production that FDR
sent in the troops.

The 1943 riots in Detroit didn't turn Williams against White
society as a whole. He continued to believe that there were good
as well as bad elements within it. In those days many Blacks referred to all of the various liberal and leftist organizations as the
"Communists." They didn't say this in order to criticize them, but
only because, in their naïveté, they thought that everyone who
preached such things as socialized medicine and an end to racial
discrimination had to be a "Red."

The U.S. Communist Party was the largest and most active of

the leftist groups at Ford and other factories. Russia and the United States were allies in the war. Pictures of Roosevelt, Churchill, and Stalin were widely displayed, and the Communists refrained from preaching revolution or attacking the government directly. They would make speeches on street corners, pass out leaflets at factory gates, and leave pamphlets in washrooms where the workers could find them.

Williams wasn't especially interested in politics, but when he heard that the Communists were for equal rights, he decided to attend their rallies. The speakers he heard called for an end to the exploitation of man by man, and exhorted against allowing any small group to hog everything. He saw them less as members of a political party than as friends who wanted to abolish racism.

The Communists were pushing the local and federal authorities for more and better housing for Blacks, and they were constantly raising money for lawyers to defend Blacks who were in trouble down South. Another thing Williams liked about the Communist Party was that it had a number of Black officials, such as Henry Winston. What Winston and the others had to say impressed Williams a great deal, though he was never asked to join the Party or attend cell meetings.

After Williams had worked in Detroit for some eighteen months, a recruiter from the Kaiser Shipyards offered him a job on the West Coast. With hundreds of other Blacks, he accepted, but when they got to California, the all-White Machinists Union refused to admit them as members. Kaiser had to give them their travel expenses back to their hiring point.

This was an important lesson for Williams. The Detroit Communists had preached that the working class was good and that it was the capitalists who maintained racism. But, when the capitalists in their hunger for profits were willing to give Blacks good jobs, the White workers wouldn't accept them.

When he heard he didn't have to be a union member to work there, Williams took a job at the Mare Island Navy Yard near San Francisco. He signed up for six months, after which he had an option to go to the Navy Yard at Pearl Harbor, and was assigned to work on paravanes (special devices used by minesweepers).

The Navy housed its Black and White workers together in wooden barracks at a place called Hillside Dormitories. There were a lot of drunks, gamblers, and other bad types staying there, and hardly a night went by without a fight. The California State Troopers would use even minor disturbances as excuses to raid the place, beating and arresting people at random. Williams didn't like it at all, and remained at Mare Island only long enough to pay off the mortgage on his family's house. He considered going to Pearl Harbor, but heard that dormitory conditions there also were very bad, and that there was constant trouble between Blacks and Whites in the area. So he quit his job and took the train back to Monroe.

As soon as he got home, he enrolled in Winchester School and spent a couple of months completing the subjects he needed to graduate from high school. Then he went to New York to look for work. But the draft board there said his deferment as an essential war worker would be terminated unless he went either to the Mare Island or Pearl Harbor Navy Yards at once. "Williams," the head of the draft board told him, "make up your mind. It's either work or fight." Williams chose to be drafted.

Following his induction, he was sent to Fort Bragg, South Carolina, for processing. Having scored high on the Radio Aptitude Test, he was assigned to a Signal Corps Training Battalion at Camp Crowder, Missouri.

When his troop train arrived in Birmingham, Alabama, there were Red Cross women serving free coffee and doughnuts on the station platform. The White soldiers got out of the train and lined up, but when the Blacks, who were segregated into the last two cars, attempted to do the same, they were stopped by the conductor. "Where in the hell are you nigger boys going?" he demanded incredulously. "Do you think these White women are going to serve you?" Some of the Black GI's had begun to argue with him, when one of their officers rushed over and shouted, "Shut up and get back to your cars!" Williams was shocked. The idea that the U.S. Army could go along with discrimination hadn't occurred to him.

At Camp Crowder, he reported to his unit, the all-Black Company C of the 29th Training Battalion. Instead of being trained as a radio operator, he discovered that he'd been assigned to the School for Telephone Linesmen. He was going to become a "pole monkey," as linesmen were called.

While all of his commissioned officers were White, Williams' sergeants, corporals, and other noncommissioned officers were Black. First, he was put through eight weeks of basic combat training, which he didn't mind at all. When he'd chosen to be drafted he'd wanted to see some front-line action, and he was disappointed when he realized he wasn't going to learn how to handle weapons heavier than the .45-caliber pistol and .30-caliber carbine.

They really did make monkeys out of them in that Telephone Linesmen School, Williams concluded. They had to climb up and down splintery old telephone poles all day. "Where else could you colored boys be trained as linesmen?" the officers would shout as the GI's tried to hang onto the tops of the poles and throw rolls of wire to each other. "After the war they're going to have to open this field up to Negroes, there'll be so many of you who know how to do it!" But Williams soon learned the real reason so many of them were being trained as linesmen was that the Army preferred to have Blacks in service companies rather than combat units.

At Camp Crowder, Blacks were discriminated against in almost every way possible. They were housed in a barracks area referred to as "Shanty Town." While the White GI's lived in solid, two-story buildings, the Blacks' barracks were wood frames with tar-paper walls and swing-type hatches instead of windows. They were also given less technical training than the White telephone linesmen received. While the Whites did most of the wiring and circuit testing, the Blacks spent their time digging holes, hauling poles, and hoisting them into place. The worst outrage was that they had to go around picking up the garbage cans for the White units as well as their own, while the White soldiers lounged about on their bunks.

The commanding officer of Company C was an Englishman who had volunteered to train an all-Black unit because he refused to believe they didn't make good soldiers. He resented the Army's treating them as inferiors, and asked Williams and the others to cooperate with him to prove that they could do as well as anyone else.

The second lieutenant in charge of Williams' platoon was Jewish. Because he had a good attitude toward them, whenever the Black soldiers passed him in the company area, they would say, "Hi spook," instead of saluting. By using that slang term for

Blacks they were showing they considered him one of them. The lieutenant, rather than taking offense, would answer, "Hi spooks," in return.

One day their Jewish "spook" lieutenant called Williams and the other GI's together and asked, "How do you guys feel about having to haul your poles and those of the White units as well?" When they answered that they didn't like it, he said, "I'm not telling you what to do, but those White troopers have just as much right to get up a sweat as you do. If you consider yourselves men, the next time they try to get you to haul their poles, you might just not go." After he left, the Black soldiers talked it over and decided on a plan of action.

The next time the trucks came to pick them up to go move poles for a White unit, they boarded them as usual. But at the first traffic signal, they all quietly jumped off and returned to their barracks.

When the battalion commander asked Williams' English commanding officer why his men hadn't shown up, he answered, "My men resent being used as unskilled laborers, and I agree with them. I volunteered to train soldiers and technicians, not ditchdiggers." As a result, the 29th Battalion decided to stop using Blacks as pack mules for the White units.

In addition to combat and signal training, Williams was given a course in how to withstand enemy propaganda. One of the training films used showed Germans firing artillery barrages of propaganda leaflets which said, "Negro soldiers, back home you are segregated and discriminated against. You are not wanted in America! So why die fighting for it?"

Although few of Williams' Black service buddies knew a great deal about the Nazis, they laughed at this because most were aware of Hitler's racist policies. But their attitude toward the Japanese was different: Nobody Williams knew really disliked the Japanese. They were always meeting veterans of the Pacific Theater of Operations who told them that the Japanese often tried to be friendly to Blacks. Some even said that their snipers wouldn't fire at Blacks unless they shot first.

Then there were the propaganda posters which showed the Japanese as being rather dark-skinned with big white teeth and bulging eyes. Such illustrations, although designed to inspire hatred, actually made Williams sympathetic toward the Japanese because they were similar to the caricatures the racists in the United States used to insult Blacks. There was one poster that showed a swarthy Japanese soldier trying to rape a blonde White woman. Every time Williams saw it he speculated that the war with Japan might really be based on racism.

While the Nazis didn't stand a chance, if the Japanese had appealed to the Black GI's as their "brown-skinned brothers," they might have stirred up some real trouble for Uncle Sam, Williams thought. But, just as most Black Americans were ignorant of the Fascist nature of the Japanese system, so the Japanese didn't understand the seriousness of racism in the States.

While Williams was still in training, the atomic bombing of Hiroshima and Nagasaki brought the war to an end in August, 1945.

Before he was able to complete the course for telephone linesmen, he developed a series of migraine headaches so severe that he was transferred to Clerk Typists School. He enjoyed learning how to type and, upon completion of the eight-week course, was assigned to a new unit as its Company Clerk.

Williams' new company commander, a White lieutenant from Ohio named Tillsberry, was known as a tough guy. One of his pet tricks was to come into the barracks as soon as the whistle blew in the morning and kick over the beds of whomever he caught lying down.

With the war over, morale at Camp Crowder grew worse every day. Once again the Blacks spent a good part of their time on garbage detail. They resented being used as domestics, and several were punished for refusing to work.

The good impression Williams had gained of the U.S. government at the NYA camp was rapidly eroded by the officially endorsed discrimination practiced at Camp Crowder.

What really made him angry was the way Lieutenant Tillsberry kicked their beds over every morning. Williams was always out of bed on time, but one day he decided he was fed up. Several of the other men felt the same way, and they all stayed in the barracks instead of making formation.

It wasn't long before they heard Lieutenant Tillsberry shouting, "What are those goddamn troops doing in the barracks this time of day?" When he came storming into the room, the others jumped to attention, but Williams remained sitting on the edge of his bed.

The CO seemed shocked that he wasn't trembling in his presence. He stood silently looking down at him for a moment. Then he shouted, "Just who do you think you are?"

Williams answered, "I'm a man like you. If you don't believe it, just try me."

The CO knew the men were watching to see if he would try to kick the bed over, but he changed his mind when he realized Williams didn't intend to let him get away with it. Shouting at him to report to the Orderly Room, he turned and stamped out of the building.

In the Orderly Room, the executive officer began to speak in an almost confidential manner. "Williams, we don't really blame you. Everyone gets fed up sometimes. The problem is, if we let you get away with it, pretty soon nobody will follow orders. There won't be any discipline left, and we won't have an Army."

"What you say is true," Williams answered, "but I can't help it, because this is not my Army. It's a White man's Army, and we Blacks are being used as garbage collectors and laborers."

The officer kept calm and said, "Soldier, you know we must punish you. The other men will lose their respect for us if we don't."

"You mean they'll lose their fear of you," Williams retorted.

As a demonstration to the other men not to step out of line, Williams was put on full-time KP. He spent day after day peeling potatoes, mopping floors, cleaning garbage cans, and doing other unpopular jobs. One afternoon, just as he had completed his work and was going off duty, the mess sergeant complained the kitchen floors hadn't been cleaned properly. Since the GI assigned to mop the floors had already left, the sergeant ordered Williams to do it. When he refused to do someone else's job after working a full day, he was called up before a special court martial.

He was found guilty of insubordination and sentenced to sixty days at hard labor in the Stockade.

The Camp Crowder Stockade was surrounded by a high fence, guard towers, and machine guns. Discipline was harsh. Prisoners who got out of line were placed in a solitary confinement cell with no windows and a naked light bulb that stayed lit night and day. They received no mail and were given only a loaf of bread and a pitcher of water per day. Like the rest of the camp, the Stockade was segregated—with the Black prisoners compelled to work in a wood lot sawing logs. In command of the whole operation was one Major Stonebreaker, a man reputed to be so mean he could crack a rock just by staring at it.

Williams was proud of being in the Stockade because he felt he was there for resisting an unjust system—not for committing a crime. Some of the other Black prisoners felt the same way. While their refusing to be submissive wasn't organized, they did encourage each other, and it became a status symbol among them to stand up to the White guards and tell them how they really felt.

One winter afternoon, the Black prisoners, fed up with the bad conditions in the Stockade, refused to return to their barracks after working all day in the wood lot. The guards didn't know what to do, and night fell before Major Stonebreaker came out to see what was wrong.

When the major reached the fence that enclosed the wood lot and saw the prisoners sitting around the fire, he shouted, "Now hear this. Unless you come out of there immediately, all of you are going to be charged with mutiny!"

At this, one of the Black prisoners approached the fence and said, "Major Stonebreaker, sir, did you say something to us?"

Stonebreaker became furious and shouted, "Goddamn it. I said come out of there, and I mean it!"

But the Black prisoner said, "Excuse me, sir, I couldn't hear you. What did you say?"

"I'll give you one last chance to come out of there!" Stonebreaker screamed. "If you don't, I'll have the MP's go in and get you!"

But the Black GI continued to claim he couldn't hear him, while Williams and the other prisoners sat around the fire, saying nothing.

Stonebreaker finally calmed down and said, "Look, if you men have problems, I'll let you send two representatives to discuss them with me, and we'll try to work things out." He waited a minute, then asked in a low voice, "Did you hear what I said?"

At that, all of the prisoners shouted back, "Oh yes, sir. We heard you. We heard you good."

Williams was chosen to be one of the two representatives.

When he and the other prisoner went in to see Stonebreaker, the major accused them of having instigated the sitdown. The strike resulted in the Blacks being given better food and more heat in their barracks, but Williams and the other man were separated from the other prisoners and were put to work cleaning the guard-house, with an armed civilian guard assigned to watch them all day.

Their guard was a big Missourian who had recently been discharged from the paratroops. He used to strut around with a .45-caliber "grease gun," and was constantly trying to provoke them. One day when they were alone, he said to Williams, "You don't talk much, do you?" Williams didn't answer. As he continued silently mopping the floor, the guard grew angry, and said, "If you don't want to talk, then let's see you dance, Nigger!" cocking his machine gun and pointing it at his feet.

Williams put the mop down and said, "If you want to shoot me you'd better do it, but I'm not dancing." The guard stood there, seemingly unable to believe that any Black would rather die than do as he said. Then he turned and walked away cursing.

Although sleeping was forbidden during the lunch break, some of the prisoners would sneak under their beds to nap on the floor. One afternoon Williams failed to wake up when the whistle blew. At roll call, thinking he'd escaped, the guards sounded the alarm. When they searched the barracks and discovered him on the floor, Major Stonebreaker sentenced him to fourteen days' solitary confinement in "Tent City."

Tent City was a special compound in the woods. It was surrounded by a double fence, plus the usual watch towers and machine-gun-toting guards. Each prisoner there was given a shelter-half to use as a one-man pup tent, a sleeping bag, and some straw for flooring. The guards threw K-rations over the fence each day, but they wouldn't enter the area except in an emergency.

This special outdoor area was used only when it was very cold. The prisoners were convinced that the authorities did this because the unventilated solitary-confinement cells indoors, which in summer were suffocatingly hot, were warm and cozy in winter. During his two weeks out there Williams was hard put to avoid being frostbitten.

There's nothing quite like prison for stimulating a man's thinking. During those seemingly endless nights Williams felt that the true nature of things was becoming clearer and clearer. He didn't see it as a coincidence that almost all of the prisoners in Tent City were Black; they were there because the Army was their enemy. If they weren't willing to bow their heads and submit, the Army was ready to torture and kill them. Being Black, they were considered lower than the lowest beasts of the field.

A day finally came when, after it had snowed for hours, half-burying the tents, a freeze set in. As night fell, Tent City became covered with ice. The camp doctor told Major Stonebreaker that, if the prisoners didn't get out of the cold by morning, they would all be dead. But when the guards came to take them back to the Stockade, they found the locks on the gates frozen shut and had to send for blowtorches to thaw them out. Williams and the others didn't get into a heated building until after 2:00 a.m. It was a miracle that no one died.

Around this time the Army set up a special Military Review Board to listen to soldiers' complaints. When the Board came to Camp Crowder, Williams was among the prisoners selected to appear.

The first thing the officers on the Board asked him was why he had been making so much trouble. He answered that he was unhappy because of the Army's racist policies. Then they asked if he didn't feel his position was highly unpatriotic.

"Unpatriotic!" he answered. "How can I be unpatriotic when I don't have a country? You men are White. You represent the Whites who own and run this country. Since the Army is racist, the government that created it must be racist as well. If the people of this country elected such a government—a government which segregates me and discriminates against me just because I was born with black skin—then how can I be patriotic?" Williams went on to declare that, in return for expecting Blacks to fight and die in its defense, the government was obligated to guarantee and defend their rights as citizens. He completely agreed that a person would be unpatriotic, even a traitor, if he failed to defend to the death a government which provided justice for all. But he contended that the U.S. government had given up its right to support from its Black citizens because it hadn't honored its constitutional obligations to them—that any system which forces its citizens to fight for it, but doesn't defend their rights, is no government at all, only a tyranny.

Williams doubted that the officers on the Review Board were used to having such issues raised by the soldiers they were interviewing, especially the Black ones. He searched his memory to see if any of the points he'd made came from his brief exposure to the Communists in Detroit, but decided that he hadn't been that greatly influenced by them. Rather than the Communists, the U.S. Army itself was responsible. From the first moment he'd been in uniform, his officers had told him about his responsibility to serve his nation. What they hadn't bothered to define, however, was the nation's responsibility toward its citizens. That had popped into Williams' head on its own, once they'd started him thinking about the general subject.

He completed his sentence without any further problems. Following his release from the Camp Crowder Stockade he was reassigned to Fort Lewis, Washington, for about six months. Then in 1946, as part of the postwar demobilization, it was announced that GI's with one year or more of service could ask to be discharged immediately.

Although Williams was disillusioned with the Army, he knew some Blacks who were enthusiastic about it. Many of them, especially those from really poor families, literally "never had it so good." They weren't interested in it for the fighting, but because they saw it as a pretty easy life. The Army was offering all those who reenlisted a bonus, various types of extra pay, and a two-month leave. Some men, unable to resist the temptation, signed up for six more years, got a fistful of money, and drove home in a new car. Many changed their minds after seeing civilian life again, but they were already hooked. They had to return to the Army at the end of their leave, often after having blown all of their reenlistment money on girls, booze, and fancy clothes.

Surprisingly, even Williams was encouraged to reenlist! Instead, he asked to be let out as soon as possible. They gave him an honorable discharge, but not the Good Conduct Medal, which every GI who has kept his nose clean and mouth shut usually receives. Convinced that he, for one, would never go near the military again, he boarded the train for home.

Being placed in direct, everyday contact with racism in the Army had been an important lesson for him. Back home in Monroe he'd been brought up to take it for granted that the Whites had everything "figured out and wrapped up in a bag"—that they

really were superior. But now he knew they weren't all-powerful—
that their running the world wasn't the only way things could be.
Many of the Whites he'd met in the Army couldn't think on their
feet when they encountered a situation they hadn't been taught to
expect. If anything changed or went wrong, they had to ask someone for new orders. Not only weren't all Whites superior, many
seemed to Williams to be both his mental and physical inferiors.

He'd also discovered that certain actions could keep the machinery of authority from functioning properly. The more he and
the other Blacks had resisted, simply stopped obeying orders, the
more confused their officers had become. His thinking wasn't yet
revolutionary, but Tent City had moved it a long way from his
childhood daydreams about charging up San Juan Hill for the
glory of Teddy Roosevelt and the Red, White, and Blue.

Chapter Three

NOTHING TO LOSE

Robert Franklin Williams returned home in the fall of 1946 to find many changes. Monroe was still a sleepy, dusty town, but the Seaboard's steam locomotives had been replaced by diesel engines. His father, partially paralyzed, was collecting a small retirement pension. Fortunately, he was still able to get around by himself. Also living in the house on Boyte Street were his mother, a younger sister, and his older brother John, who had become a member of the "52-20 Club."

The 52-20 Club was what many people called the federal unemployment insurance to which all World War II veterans were entitled. If you couldn't find a job after being discharged, the government gave you $20 a week for a maximum of fifty-two weeks. Like millions of other veterans, Williams' brother was using up this money while readjusting to civilian life. He decided to apply for it himself.

Several of his buddies warned him that the clerks at the State Employment Office were endeavoring to prevent Black vets from getting this money. Many White ex-officers were going into business on their own, and needed low-paid laborers. They disliked the fact that so many Blacks could now get $20 a week unemployment compensation because it was driving salaries up. Before the war they'd been able to hire them for $15 a week—or less.

At the employment office an elderly White woman clerk offered to send Williams out to be interviewed for an unskilled job paying $18.75 a week. When he refused to go, she said, "The sooner you niggers stop thinking the world owes you a living, the better off you'll be. That federal money is just spoiling you."

He answered, "Lady, I'd have to pay for bus fare, lunch, and work clothes out of that $18.75, not to mention taxes, and would be lucky to clear $13 a week. Why don't you just give me the $20 I've got coming?"

"Don't you sass me," she replied. "I don't have to take this from any nigger. I'll call the chief of police." She didn't carry out her threat, but that wasn't the end of it. Those Black veterans who couldn't be pressured into working for less than $20 a week were frequently disqualified from collecting their unemployment insurance. One tactic was to insist on their listing every place where they'd inquired about work during the week. In a small town like Monroe one quickly exhausted the limited number of possible employers, and had to keep naming the same companies over and over again. When an applicant did this, the clerks at the employment office would accuse him of not really trying to find work and say, "If you can't get a job here, why don't you go to some other town, like Charlotte?" They knew full well that most local Blacks could neither afford to commute that far each day, nor undertake the expense of moving there. In Williams' case, they refused to accept his claim that he was a writer by profession; and he couldn't get any unemployment money at all.

After a group of Blacks wrote a letter of complaint to the Veterans' Administration in Washington, D.C., a federal investigator came to see Williams. When asked why he was claiming to be a writer, he told the investigator of having taken an off-duty course in writing at Camp Crowder, and displayed some of his recently published works.

Williams' poetry and prose, chiefly dealing with love and nature themes, had already appeared in such publications as *The Hearth Songs Journal* and *The Westminster Magazine.* A poem of his used by the latter, "Time and Passion," had won one of their annual prizes. He also had a weekly verse column in the local newspaper, *The Monroe Enquirer.*

Convinced that he was telling the truth, the investigator told the officials at the employment office: "This man is a self-employed writer. There's nothing in the law that says he has to work at anything else." This so angered the clerks that they would make Williams wait for hours every time he went to pick up his 52-20 check. But he didn't permit himself to be provoked, and would sit patiently until closing time, when they would finally have to give him his money.

Although most of Williams' work in those years concentrated upon lyrical impressions of life in the South, he did some writing of a social-protest type—attacking such things as lynching and discrimination. But he confined himself to expressing a dislike of bad conditions, without suggesting what could be done to change them.

Back then in the late 1940's, most of the members of Monroe's Black bourgeoisie were either teachers or preachers. Many belonged to the National Association for the Advancement of Colored People (NAACP).

Although they did little more than hold meetings and solicit funds, the Black professionals looked upon their membership in the NAACP as a status symbol. They used to criticize Blacks who weren't members as lacking in "race consciousness." For all their talk, their militancy was limited to occasionally hiring a local White lawyer to defend a poor Black in a rape or assault case. In most instances the accused would have been as well off with no lawyer at all, because, once the authorities had decided to try him, he was inevitably found guilty and sent to prison. By using only White lawyers who were part of the local power structure, the NAACP members made certain they weren't offending those who controlled the schools, offices, and other places where they worked. Williams saw them as trying to pose as heroes to their Black brothers, but not fooling anyone but themselves.

A case which received some national attention took place shortly before Williams came home from the Army. It involved a former high-school classmate of his named Benny Montgomery who had been seriously wounded in the fighting in Europe. After a long hospitalization, he was sent back to Monroe with a steel plate in his head. People noticed that his behavior wasn't quite normal, but he was able to get a job on a dairy farm.

One day he ended an argument with another man by pulling a knife and stabbing him to death. When the police arrived, they found Benny in a restaurant drinking beer. His clothing was covered with bloodstains, but he sat there as if nothing had happened.

At the trial, the NAACP provided the usual local White defense lawyers. They neglected to raise the point that the Army had kept Benny under psychiatric care for a long time before discharging him. Although he was a disabled veteran with a steel plate in his head, the defense lawyers didn't suggest that he was mentally disturbed or should be institutionalized. An all-White jury found him guilty, and he was sentenced to death.

By the time Williams came home from the service, Benny was

awaiting execution. Despite many pleas for clemency, the governor of North Carolina refused to stay the sentence, and he died in the gas chamber.

Benny's family wanted to bring his corpse home to be buried, but the chief of police visited the Black undertaker and told him there would be trouble if he tried to bury Benny in Monroe—especially in his Army uniform—because the Whites wouldn't stand for it.

As soon as the chief of police left him, the undertaker went to see Williams and several other Black vets. "What do you fellows think about it?" he asked. "I don't want my funeral parlor torn up. Will you support me if I bring Benny back here?"

They all felt very strongly when they heard this. Benny had won medals for bravery, while the chief of police had stayed home during the war. They felt that Benny had paid his debt to society for killing the other man, and saw no reason that he shouldn't be given a decent burial like any other veteran. So they told the undertaker they would support him all the way.

Many of the Black vets owned souvenir guns—such as German automatic pistols—and they went out and bought ammunition for them. Several local tough guys volunteered to join the vets. One of their group lived next door to the undertaker, and a guard post was set up in his house. Armed patrols were organized and they began to circulate through the neighborhood.

The undertaker picked up Benny's body at the state prison, brought it back to Monroe, and prepared him for burial in his Army uniform with all his medals on it. Then a Black preacher went to the police chief and told him, "I have come here as a concerned citizen to warn you against permitting any attempt to interfere with the burial of Benny Montgomery. The Black veterans have armed themselves and are walking the streets ready to kill."

They buried Benny without incident.

The readiness of the Black vets to defend such a minimal right as being buried was a new thing. But they weren't ready to take the next step and form a permanent armed organization. The lesson wasn't completely lost on them though. Some ten years later, several of the same men would set up the first Black self-defense group in the history of the United States.

During the war, many of the Monroe girls had married. As a result, some homecoming vets found themselves looking for new women friends. Williams had dated a girl called "Snooky," who'd later married an old friend of his. One night they invited him to go driving with them. When they stopped in front of Snooky's house, a girl who looked familiar came out to the car. It was Snooky's sister, who'd been a child of thirteen when Williams last saw her. In only three years, she had blossomed into womanhood.

"Aren't you Snooky's little sister?" he asked her.

"What do you mean, 'Snooky's little sister'? My name is Mabel," she answered.

"Oh," Williams said, "I thought you were still a little girl."

Mabel, who was sixteen, was attending high school. Williams began escorting her home from school every day. She lived with her mother and stepfather, Mr. Farmer, who worked for the Seaboard and knew Williams' father.

So many veterans were getting married around this time that the Black community appeared to be having a virtual epidemic of weddings, even of men who'd been known as confirmed bachelors. Mabel and Robert didn't buck the trend. They were married in a Baptist preacher's house in the summer of 1947.

Not only was that year important for Williams because it witnessed his marriage, it also saw the unexpected death of his beloved mother. She was only forty-nine when she died of a hemorrhage, and it was a great shock to him. Her short life had been devoted completely to her family, and her dedication and sacrifice to provide her children with an education had, Williams was certain, hastened her death. He would cherish her memory for the rest of his life.

The following year, 1948, shortly after his first son, Robert, Jr., was born, Williams returned to Detroit to seek work in the automotive industry. After getting a job buffing chrome strips at the Cadillac plant, he had his wife and baby boy join him.

A short time after Williams arrived in Detroit, he bought a 9-mm luger pistol from a White worker at the Cadillac factory. After the race riots back in 1943, he'd decided that, if he ever lived in Detroit again, he was going to have a weapon handy.

Though the Cold War was already in full swing, the U.S. Communist Party was still active around the auto plants. As it was back in 1943, the Party newspaper, *The Daily Worker*, was sold on the newsstands and in the plant washrooms. Williams frequently read it because, unlike the other Detroit papers, it often carried stories about how badly Blacks were being treated in the South.

When he noticed that *The Worker* had a Detroit edition, he submitted one of his short stories to the local office. Called "Some Day I Am Going Back South," it dealt with a Black who had gone to work in the North, but planned to return home one day to change things among his people. They published it in full.

After several months, he decided to go to college. Having a wife and child entitled him to around $120 per month living allowance from the GI Bill but, as this wasn't enough to pay for rent and food in Detroit, he couldn't go to school there. It was decided that Mabel and the baby would live with his father in Monroe, and he would enroll in a school that wasn't too far away.

Since he'd been in the Army for eighteen months, Williams was eligible for approximately two years of educational benefits. It wasn't enough time to get a degree, but he could pick up some of the basics. Once he'd learned how to do research, he thought he could acquire whatever additional information he desired without having to be in a classroom situation.

Moving back to Monroe in early 1949, his wife completed high school, graduating with her old classmates, while Williams studied the catalogues of several nearby colleges to see what they had to offer.

The two areas he was primarily interested in were writing and psychology. Despite his already published works he knew that his writing needed polishing. He had become interested in psychology while browsing around bookstores and libraries in Detroit. A knowledge of why people think and behave as they do seemed essential if he were ever to write meaningfully about life.

Williams saw nothing extraordinary about wanting to get a higher education. Throughout the United States, Black mothers scrub floors and Black fathers work long hours at low-paying jobs in order to put their children through college. They make great personal sacrifices because they are convinced that Blacks are treated as inferiors only because so many have been poorly educated. They dream that their children, once educated, will be integrated into the American way of life and freed from bondage.

But racism, Williams found, is so deeply imbedded in the thinking of many Whites that they cannot conceive that those whom they consider lower than the dirt under their feet are really trying to raise themselves up. For years, when Black university graduates applied for professional positions with White corporations, they were looked upon with amazement and offered only menial jobs. Some Blacks do secure jobs as schoolteachers, and a few even become minor businessmen, but all too many of those who struggle for years to earn a degree are frustrated in their attempts to gain employment on the level their educational achievements warrant.

E. Franklin Frazier, in his book, *Black Bourgeoisie,* observes that there is more hatred of Whites among educated middle-class Blacks than among the uneducated poor of the ghettos. It is the bourgeois Blacks—those who've tried the hardest to make themselves acceptable—who finally realize how profound and insane racism is. No matter what they achieve in science, the arts, literature, the military, or any other field, millions upon millions of Whites continue to treat them as their inferiors.

Although he subsequently was to become convinced of the futility of trying to gain the respect of the racists merely by getting an education, back in the summer of 1949 it was one of Williams' chief reasons for wanting to go to school.

He decided to enroll in West Virginia State College. It had a good scholastic reputation, and offered courses in both psychology and creative writing.

For the physical examination required for admission, he went to the Monroe Clinic. The White doctor there, noticing where the college was located, asked him, "Boy, why would you want to go to a school way up in West Virginia?"

He knew that there were local colleges for Blacks, and appeared to be probing to see if Williams would say anything negative about North Carolina. Realizing the doctor could cause a lot of trouble by writing something derogatory on his medical form, Williams didn't give him an argument. "Well, I guess I just thought it would be nice to see what it's like up there," he answered.

It wasn't that he was afraid of him—there just wasn't any point in standing and fighting when there was no real principle involved. As Williams saw it, one had to distinguish between times when it's important to resist and times when it's a needless waste of energy to make an issue of something.

West Virginia State College is located near the town of

Charleston. Back in 1949, the faculty was integrated, but all the students were Black.

When they discovered that he was studying writing and psychology, most of Williams' classmates were surprised. The majority were education majors who planned to become schoolteachers. They would ask him, "Rob, do you think you'll be able to eat, buy a car, or own your own home on what you'll earn from your writing?" Even psychology was considered too chancy a field by most of them. When they did take a science major, it tended to be in the physical sciences or sociology. Their primary concern was in acquiring a degree that would best guarantee them a good job after they graduated.

Some students were planning to go on to law or medical school, but they were far more adventurous than the general run. Even Williams' classmates in the creative writing course were insuring themselves by simultaneously working toward teaching certificates. While they used to talk about some day writing a bestselling book, most made certain they could get school jobs in case their dreams didn't come true. Those few who were devoted to a literary career hoped to work for Afro-American newspapers or magazines.

The attitude of his fellow students caused Williams to review his decision to study writing. He analyzed himself as having two primary interests: the desire to express his personal feelings about life, and to contribute to the development of Black literature. After serious consideration, he decided to stick to his decision because he felt that Blacks needed to be able to communicate both among themselves and with the peoples of the world. Only through their own writers would the world learn of their sufferings, joys, and dreams.

In retrospect, he realized that he must have seemed hopelessly naïve to his more pragmatic classmates. If he'd known more about the obstacles facing professional writers, White as well as Black, he might not have been so sure he was doing the right thing.

During his first few days at college, Williams was afraid that the superior educational backgrounds of most of his fellow students would make him appear ignorant. After a short time, however, he found that he could do as well, if not better, than many of them. When it came to writing assignments, they were so concerned with style that they hardly had time to say anything meaningful. He, on the other hand, was primarily concerned with telling a story, and saw formal considerations as secondary to communication. Despite the limited education he'd received in Monroe, and his childhood dislike of homework, he did well in college—far better than in high school.

One of Williams' favorite instructors was a Dr. Herman Kennedy, a Black professor of psychology who worked at the nearby West Virginia State Hospital. He often used to tell his students about his undergraduate days at Northwestern University in Chicago, where, as the only Black on campus, he'd worked his way through school by waiting on tables.

One of his favorite anecdotes dealt with the university swimming pool. In those days, despite Illinois being a northern state, the campus authorities wouldn't let Black students go into the pool when the Whites were using it. One day he had put on his only suit, walked into the gymnasium, and, pretending to lose his balance, thrown himself into the pool fully clothed. Williams and the other students would go into hysterics when Dr. Kennedy related how the Whites, panic-stricken, had started jumping out of the water. They hadn't minded sitting next to him in class or having him serve them their food, but when a "nigger" fell into the pool, they behaved as if the water had turned to fire.

From time to time, Dr. Kennedy would interrupt his lectures to ask, "If anybody questions you students about what I'm teaching, what're you going to tell them?"

"You are teaching psychology!" they would shout.

"Yes, I'm teaching you psychology," he would say, "the type of psychology you're going to have to live with. In this classroom we're going to talk about the real, everyday problems we Blacks have to contend with here in the United States."

Dr. Kennedy constantly discussed the question of racial discrimination. "Now look at you darkies," he would say, "just look at you. You are the dregs of the Black people of the world. You are the descendants of the Uncle Tom nigger-slaves, the ones who survived. The great African warriors never got here. They died fighting the slave traders and their stooges. The independent Blacks, the ones who wouldn't let themselves be chained, were killed off in Africa or on the boat coming over. No, you are the offspring of the submissive ones. We have to realize this, and be patient with you until we can once again breed the type of Blacks who won't submit."

While he felt that most of the students at West Virginia State probably weren't fully aware of what Dr. Kennedy and some of the other teachers were doing, it was obvious to Williams that they were trying to stir up their anger against racism, and create pride in them as Blacks.

But the college was no hotbed of militancy. The dominant attitude among the students was an almost compulsive obsession with mimicking the way of life of the White middle class. Dr. Kennedy would frequently denounce these bourgeois urges by saying, "It's shameful, absolutely shameful, that after every one of our dances there are tens of thousands of dollars worth of empty liquor bottles bulging out of the campus garbage cans. Why you niggers seem to want nothing but to be able to wear white top hats and tail coats. You are closing your eyes to the slave chains still hanging out from under your pants! If you want to copy Whites, then copy their industry and productivity, not their conspicuous consumption."

Williams soon began contributing to *The Quill*, the school's literary magazine; which used some of his poems as fillers, but didn't say who had written them. When a Scottish poet named Edward G. Davidson, who was on campus to give a series of lectures, discovered that Williams was the author, he asked to meet him. After reading some of his other work, he offered Williams a scholarship to attend a writers' seminar at the University of Colorado.

"Your writing is very powerful, and I'm convinced a great career awaits you," Davidson told him. "But you have a tendency toward political themes, and I suggest you make an effort to eliminate such ideas from your work." When Williams responded that he didn't believe he'd expressed any real political concepts in his poems, the Scottish poet said, "Perhaps you don't think so, but I can detect them there all the same. You can't mix art and politics if you want to be a successful writer."

To insure that they wouldn't be distracted from their studies, freshmen weren't allowed to participate in extracurricular activities. But after Davidson praised his poems, Williams was allowed to join the staff of *The Quill* and to take creative writing without having completed the prerequisites. He was also given special permission to join the staff of *The Register,* the official newspaper of the college, and of a magazine called *The Creole.*

His new stature on campus soon attracted the fraternities, and he was asked to join one. The thing that repelled him the most about them was the way they delighted in harassing their pledges. The upper classmen would beat the freshmen with wooden paddles, forcing them to run to the nearby river and back all night. When Williams said he didn't have the hundred-dollar initiation fee which they required, the fraternity boys replied that, if he kept quiet about it, they would put up the money themselves. He finally had to tell them that he wasn't interested in joining because their hazing system was degrading. "If anybody hits me with a wooden paddle," he said, "I won't consider it a joke, and will respond accordingly."

The fraternity men assured Williams that such sought-after pledges as himself didn't have to worry about being mistreated. Then they began to talk about "fraternal brotherhood"—how all the members would stick together after college and help each other to get good jobs. That really turned Williams off. "What can you do for your brothers?" he asked them. "You don't own Ford, General Motors, or U.S. Steel." After that they left him alone.

Williams remained at West Virginia State College for one year, during which time his second son, John, was born. In 1950 he transferred to North Carolina College at Durham. He didn't follow up on the scholarship offer from the University of Colorado because, with a wife and two children, he couldn't afford to move to a school that far away from home.

Although Williams was only a sophomore, the chairman of the English Department at North Carolina College allowed him to audit his graduate class in literature. In addition to poetry and the classics, he read several political publications. Junius Scales, one of the Black leaders of the U.S. Communist Party, was active in Durham. He and some Blacks working with him came on campus to distribute Party literature. They gave Williams *The Works of Lenin, The Communist Manifesto* by Marx and Engels, and some books by Stalin.

The Korean conflict began that summer, and Williams was soon involved in arguments about it. One day his current affairs instructor declared, "There's good news this morning, students. For the first time, the Communist advance has been stopped, and it was done by an all-Black unit, the brave men of the 24th Regiment. Now everyone can see just how well we Blacks can fight."

Some of the students applauded, saying it was a great day for their race, but Williams voiced disagreement. Standing up, he asked, "Why do we have to go all the way to Korea to convince the Whites we can fight? You niggers can't even buy a hamburger in most of the eating places right here in Durham, yet you cheer this as a victory for our race. Are we in Korea to liberate Blacks, or are we just helping our oppressors to enslave another colored nation?"

His questioning caused the class to split. Some students felt as he did about Korea, while others agreed with their instructor's position. After the class was over, he approached Williams and, almost pleading, asked, "Why didn't you give me a break? After all, most of us haven't had the same sort of bad experiences with Whites you've suffered. Can't you take it easy?" It saddened Williams to see a Black teacher behaving that way.

In the fall of 1950, he transferred to Johnson C. Smith, an all-Black Presbyterian college located in Charlotte, North Carolina. This enabled him to live in Monroe with his family. He commuted twenty-five miles by bus each day. It was the same college his grandfather, Sykes Williams, had attended after he was freed from slavery. They offered no courses in writing, so he studied English literature instead.

Except for required authors, Williams read very little contemporary fiction. His reading tended toward philosophy, especially classical authors such as Plato. Reading the *Dialogues* helped him understand his conflict with the Army. It was an important insight when he realized that the relationship of the citizen to the state had been considered in antiquity. When he first questioned the Army's responsibility to its Black soldiers, he naïvely thought such matters had never been considered before. Once he discovered that such issues had been pondered through the ages, he began to read as much as he could on the subject.

He soon concluded that the situation faced by Blacks in the United States was far more complex than merely one of citizen versus state. As he saw it, American Blacks were, in effect, noncitizens. On the one hand, they were no longer slaves—at least, no

laws made them the private property of other men. But they
weren't protected from exploitation, segregation, discrimination,
beatings, and murder by the racists. While the Constitution guaranteed equal rights to all U.S. citizens, he saw that, where the
rights of Blacks and other non-Whites were involved, the Constitution was not enforced.

When his GI benefits ran out, in 1952, Williams was forced to
leave college and look for work in order to support his family. The
job possibilities in Monroe were unlikely, and he decided to go to
New York. That part of the country had always fascinated him.
There were many myths among the Blacks in Monroe about it, especially about the Jews.

In Williams' childhood, whenever the Black children saw
White Northerners driving past on the highway to Florida, they
would say, "There go the Jews." They did this because many of
the people in cars with New York license plates spoke with a
Brooklyn accent. Since someone had once told them that all the
people who spoke this way were Jews, they assumed everyone
from New York who wasn't Black was Jewish.

There were probably some Jews living in the Monroe area
but, since they spoke with the same accent as the other southern
Whites, as a child, Williams didn't know how to identify them.

Many adults believed another myth—that if a Black could
only work for the Jews, his troubles would be over. People would
say, "The Jews treat you as if you were White. They make you sit
down and eat with them like one of the family. And they let you
use their car on your day off." Such stories being almost legend
among southern Blacks, when he decided to try his luck in New
York, everybody said, "Rob's going North to work for the Jews."

Arriving in New York by bus, he moved in with Esther Williams, his aunt, who lived on 117th Street in Harlem. There were
jobs available for machinists at the Curtiss-Wright aeronautical
plant across the river in Woodbridge, New Jersey. The Korean
conflict was in full swing, and workers were needed to turn out
military aircraft. Williams got a job operating a radial drill. The
pay was $110 a week and, when he was lucky enough to get over-
time, it often went up to $125.

In New York he soon became acquainted with a group of
White intellectuals to whom he was introduced by some Black

friends. They invited him to their homes for parties and get-to-gethers. They called themselves "progressives," and talked of such things as "the need to build unity between workers and intellectuals, and between Negroes and Whites." A Black factory worker who was trying to be a writer was considered very exotic among their set.

When Williams mentioned to some White acquaintances active in the American Labor Party that he was looking for living quarters closer to his work than his aunt's place in Harlem, they said there was a nice top-floor apartment available in Yorkville. It belonged to friends who were planning to move to Long Island. Rather than give up their old place, they would sublet it to Williams, and even leave their furniture for him to use. The motivation behind their generosity was that this group of left-wingers had always wanted to integrate that all-White area, which was also known as Germantown, but hadn't been able to find any Blacks who were willing to do it for them.

After they had explained this to him, Williams accepted their offer. The apartment wasn't expensive and was much closer to his job. As he was away at work most of the day, it was some time before the Whites in the building realized he was living there. It was when Mabel came up from Monroe and moved in with him that the trouble started.

Williams was taking out the garbage one day when he saw a group of White women staring at him. An old lady with a thick German accent started whining, "Oh my, I don't know what this building is coming to. They'll let anything live here now—even niggers."

After that he and his wife were harassed. Whenever he put his name on the mailbox, it would be scratched off. Garbage and trash would be dumped in front of their door. The lights would be turned off at the fuse box. The telephone would ring in the middle of the night, and the caller would hang up the moment they answered. Someone would pound on the door, then run away before they could get it open. Mabel, who had left the boys with her mother in Monroe, would sit in the apartment alone and frightened until Rob came home from work each day.

Williams didn't know if there was an organization involved, but his antagonists did everything they could think of to get him and his wife to move out. Once a man telephoned in the middle of the night and said, "We hear you have niggers living there, and we are coming to get you."

"You do just that," Williams answered. In case anyone tried it, he had his 9-mm luger and five hundred rounds of ammunition waiting for them.

Then the owner of the building started complaining that their being there was in violation of the contract with the people who had sublet the apartment. Williams' left-wing acquaintances contacted a lawyer from the American Labor Party, who offered to fight the matter out in court at no cost, but he had already decided to leave. Although the idea of integrating the area seemed worthwhile, Williams wasn't interested in living in the same building with people who knew nothing about him, yet treated him as if he were a leper or a criminal. He had gone out of his way to be as courteous and quiet as possible, but his behavior made absolutely no difference to them.

Intellectually, Williams knew that the people harassing him were individuals, but, emotionally, he found it increasingly difficult to avoid feeling hatred whenever he met someone with light skin. He knew it was time to leave when, entering the building one day, he responded to an elderly White woman's mutterings about, "How can they let black niggers live here?" by angrily turning and telling her, "Lady, what I can't figure out is how they let you pale-faced dogs from Europe get here in the first place."

After he'd said it, Williams felt ashamed at having lost his self-control. Rather than remain in a situation where he might end up killing someone, he had Mabel return to Monroe. He moved back to his aunt's place in Harlem.

During this period, Williams was getting more and more involved with the leftists. They encouraged him in his writing, and offered him a scholarship to attend an evening class in poetry at the Jefferson School. He turned down the offer because, after working a radial drill all day, he didn't want to sit in a classroom at night.

Every time Williams read in the papers how J. Edgar Hoover of the FBI was warning the public that the leftists were trying to overthrow the country, he would laugh. The ones he knew were about as far away from anything resembling revolution as you could get. Rather than trying to change bad conditions, they spent their time telling each other how, once the workers realized its advantages, they would create a Socialist society by themselves. Williams couldn't accept that line of reasoning because he'd seen nothing among his fellow workers to indicate that they would ever spontaneously overthrow the capitalist system.

Another point upon which Williams disagreed with the leftists he knew was their attitude toward religion. He felt that they were wrong in referring to church-goers in a demeaning manner; and tried to explain that by doing so they were cutting themselves off from millions of good people. Most Black Americans, even if they didn't go to church, resented hearing it criticized. The church for them was much more than a place of worship. It was their traditional meeting place, and functioned as the social and welfare center of most rural communities. He felt that the Left should be trying to establish friendly relationships with the church, sending people to work with the ministers and priests to help alleviate the plight of the poor. But the group he knew said they could never cooperate with an institution based upon mysticism. In doing so, they were going against the announced policy of the U.S. Communist Party, but Williams wasn't fully aware of the various schisms on the Left at that time.

Despite their talk about being friends of the poor, many of the "progressives" seemed to spend most of their time drinking cocktails in richly furnished Manhattan apartments. Their greatest pleasure was telling Williams what they thought everybody else really wanted. They were always saying, "Comrade, how honorable it is for you to be part of the working class," but he didn't see them rushing to join him in Harlem and share the "honor" of cockroach-ridden tenement life. He began to feel revulsion every time he heard a wealthy "progressive" use the term "working class."

During the early 1950's the American Left was hounded by Senator Joseph McCarthy and other witch hunters. Williams would listen to his friends complaining about what was going on, and he tried to keep up with news accounts of the hearings. He did this more out of curiosity than from any great interest. At the time he wasn't sophisticated enough to see the relationship between the power structure's attack on civil liberties and the problems faced by Blacks. Knowing that, because of race, millions were prevented from going to a decent school, earning a decent living, and receiving decent medical aid, he found it hard to get excited when those who enjoyed all those things were blacklisted from well-paying jobs because of belonging to the wrong groups or saying the wrong things. Civil liberties were indeed important, but Williams knew it was possible to survive without them.

Still, he instinctively disliked the witch hunters. It was obvious to him that the rightists were trying to discredit many Whites who were the Blacks' best friends. He felt that, if Congress really was interested in exposing un-American activities and subversion of the Constitution, it should have investigated the KKK and the racists, instead of throwing mud at the leftists—who had already lost much of the popular influence they enjoyed during the Depression.

The single incident of the McCarthy era that most frightened New York left-wingers was the Rosenberg case. Most of Williams' White friends were circulating petitions and organizing protests against the Rosenbergs' execution for supposedly conspiring to give the Russians the plans for the atomic bomb. But he didn't like the way some of them went about it. They appeared more concerned with the Rosenbergs as symbols than as living human beings. Williams knew that the leftist organizations (including the U.S. Communist Party, to which the Rosenbergs were accused of belonging) had refused to help them during their trial. It was only after their death sentence that the Left involved itself—along with many others of all sorts of political persuasions who feared that, if the Rosenbergs could be killed, so could everybody else the government didn't like.

As time passed, Williams' differences with his leftist companions grew deeper. They said he was too concerned with individuals, and told him, "Our object is to change the system which allows inequities to develop. The revolutionary is the only true humanitarian."

His response was, "If you don't have concern for each and every individual, you become nothing but ruthless machines. A new system based on Socialist political and economic relationships, but lacking in love for its citizens, will not be a humane society."

The leftists finally began to refer to Williams as a "sentimentalist," and stopped trying to involve him in their projects.

As the Korean fighting slowed down, aircraft production ta-

pered off, and Williams lost his job at Curtiss-Wright. In mid-1953
he left Harlem and returned to Monroe. When he sought work
there, one of the local hotel bellhops told him a wealthy White
textile-mill owner was looking for a Black chauffeur and general
assistant. His name was Robert Spillman. Since he had been an
officer in the U.S. Army, people usually called him "Colonel Spillman." When the colonel heard that Williams was a veteran, he
gave him a job driving his new Cadillac. The pay was only $25 a
week, but the colonel took care of hotel bills and other expenses as
they traveled around visiting his mills. It was far less than Williams had made at Curtiss-Wright, but the job was easy. He wasn't
required to wear a uniform, open the door for the colonel, or do
anything servile. If there was something he needed, such as shoes
or clothing or some extra money to pay the doctor for Mabel or
the boys, the colonel gave it to him without hesitation. Whenever
Colonel Spillman had to go so far away that he preferred to take
an airplane, he left his Cadillac for Williams to use.

The colonel had recently purchased a textile mill in Shelby,
North Carolina, and he had Williams drive him there. As a Black,
he had to get a room in a different hotel from the "Whites Only"
one the colonel stayed in. And when he went to the colonel's hotel
to pick him up, Williams had to use the side entrance because
Blacks weren't allowed to enter by the front door or wait in the
lobby. Noticing this, the colonel called the hotel manager over
and said, "I don't want you to bother this man. He's working for
me, and he will use the front entrance and wait in the lobby from
now on." And that was the end of it.

One morning Williams was driving the colonel and an associ-
ate to a mill outside of town. In the Shelby business district, a
White man tried to make a right turn from the wrong lane, and
smashed into the left side of the Cadillac. Shelby was a town
where Blacks were beaten or lynched with little provocation, and
Williams was apprehensive. He got out to see how badly the Cadillac had been damaged. The other driver knew he was at fault
and said little, but a crowd of belligerent Whites soon gathered.

Soon a policeman arrived and said to Williams, "Boy, let me
see your driver's license."

Someone in the crowd shouted, "I saw it all. It was the
nigger's fault." Others joined in, saying, "The nigger did it, make
the nigger pay," and so on. After checking the other man's driving

permit, the policeman turned back to Williams and asked, "Boy, is this your car? Where did you get it?"

At that moment, Colonel Spillman opened the rear door of the Cadillac and stepped out. The crowd was surprised; they hadn't noticed there was someone else in the car. "What's all this trouble out here?" he asked the policeman. "This is my car, and it's covered by insurance." Then he took out his wallet, showed his identification to the driver of the other car, and said, "I am Colonel Robert Spillman. Would you be so kind as to tell me where you work?"

When the other driver answered, "I work out at the textile mill," the colonel said, "Well, I happen to own that mill."

At this, the other driver turned red and started talking fast: "Oh there won't be any problem with me, sir. No, sir, you won't have any trouble on my account, no trouble at all."

The colonel turned to the policeman and said, "And what the hell do you think you're doing? Do you know my cousin is the mayor of this town? Are you trying to lose your job?"

The policeman blurted out, "I didn't mean any harm, sir."

Then the colonel said to him, "I'm getting too old to go around looking for problems, but if I'm pushed I'll make trouble. This man who hit us with his car says he has no complaint, so why don't you get the hell out of here?"

Instructing Williams to deliver the Cadillac to a garage to be repaired, the colonel and his friend hailed a taxi to take them to the mill. Seeing the crowd of Whites still standing around, he turned and shouted at them, "Go on, you people, you-all get the hell out of here, too." Starting the car, Williams stepped down hard on the gas, causing the wheels to spin and screech. The crowd had to jump out of the way as he shot off in a cloud of exhaust and burning rubber.

Working for a wealthy White Southerner was educational for Williams. It showed him dramatically how those who own the mills control the police; and that, when they want to do so, they can eliminate segregation and discrimination with ease. Commanded by their masters to leave a Black in peace, even the most racist poor Whites swallowed their hatred and followed orders. At the same time, being employed by the colonel convinced him that Blacks are being held down by the specific intent of those who run the economy. The colonel's paternalistic benevolence toward Williams as an individual didn't apply to all Blacks. He behaved no differently from other mill owners in his hiring practices. Like the others, his mills employed Blacks primarily as janitors. They had no training programs to help them develop other skills.

When Colonel Spillman sold out most of his interests in the United States and moved to Puerto Rico, Williams was once again unemployed. Hearing that Eastman was hiring in Rochester, he took what little money he'd saved and went to New York. He covered the Kodak plant inch by inch, but there were no jobs to be had.

The only work readily available in that part of New York State was picking fruit and vegetables. As his savings were almost exhausted, and he lacked money to get back to Monroe, he was forced to take a job as a bean picker on one of the large farms near Rochester.

After awakening at 4:00 a.m. and spending the entire day stooping over in the hot sun, Williams could hardly stand up in the evenings. There were a few poor Whites, but most of the bean pickers were Blacks—many of whom came from as far away as Florida, Georgia, or Alabama. Hired down there by contractors who supply northern farmers with cheap labor, they were packed like cattle into semi-trailer trucks, and transported more than a thousand miles to upstate New York.

The big industrialized farm Williams worked on was run much like an Army prison. The entire place was ringed with an electrified barbed wire fence studded with guard towers and searchlights. A special pass was required to get in or out, and a small army of private police in radio-equipped cars patrolled the area. The workers were told that such precautions were necessary both to prevent theft and to keep out "subversive agitators," which Williams soon learned meant union organizers.

It was supposed to be possible for a fast field worker to earn as much as twelve dollars a day but, despite being strong and in good health, Williams seldom could pick enough beans in ten hours to make more than three or four dollars. The best he ever did was five dollars—only a little more than enough to cover room rent, food, and the cost of getting out to the farm. There were days when he earned so little that it actually cost him money to go to work.

After picking beans for three weeks, he was transferred to

gathering apples and cherries. It was better work, both because he didn't have to stoop over all day and because he could save money on meals by eating some of the fruit he was picking—apples and cherries being considerably tastier than raw beans.

Sharing the lot of those migrant farm workers proved to Williams that exploitation isn't limited to the cotton fields of Dixie or to Blacks. In the North as well as the South, Americans of all colors are viewed, not as human beings, but as "cost factors." To the investors and administrators of that industrialized farm in upstate New York, Williams and his co-workers were no different from machines or beasts of burden—a means of production to be herded, confined, regulated, and paid only enough to keep them from starving. Like surplus fruit and vegetables, they could be dumped without a second thought the moment market fluctuations made retaining them unprofitable.

Williams had to continue working until the end of the harvest season to save enough money for bus fare back to Monroe. Returning home, he spent most of his free time in the latter part of 1953 and the beginning of 1954 writing poetry and prose. He also tried composing song lyrics. A typical song of his was titled "Autumn's Call." One of his romantic ballads, "At the End of Every Rainbow," was accepted for recording by Signature Records. A publishing company in Denver also printed a limited sheet-music edition of several of his lyrics.

But his writing wasn't providing an income. After months of being unable to find steady work in Monroe, he once again considered going elsewhere. Having seen ads offering jobs for machinists in aircraft plants in the Los Angeles area, he raised the money for bus fare to California by selling his typewriter, phonograph, an old car, and most of his other personal possessions.

Arriving in downtown Los Angeles a few days later, he checked into a small transient hotel not far from the railroad station. Early the next morning, he began making the rounds of the aircraft plants.

He applied at a different factory each day for almost six weeks, but there were no jobs to be had. The post-Korean Recession was in full swing and, while the aircraft companies kept running full-page want ads in the newspapers, they were laying off thousands of skilled workers.

The clerks at the California State Employment Office urged

Williams to hold on until the aircraft companies completed switching over to civilian production, and started hiring again. But, since he was from out of state, he was ineligible for unemployment compensation. When he realized that he had only enough money left for two days' rent, provided he didn't eat, and had no way to get back to Monroe, he became desperate.

Near Williams' hotel, there was a Marine Corps Recruiting Station, which had a poster in its window that said, "Join Today— Leave Tomorrow." At first he had paid it little attention but, as day after day went by and his savings dwindled, he became very much aware of it. One day he walked over to the window and saw a second sign which said that all those who enlisted in the Marines would be eligible for thirty-six months of university education under the new Korean GI Bill.

Williams stood in the street and considered what to do. There he was, eager to work and twenty-nine years old, but unable to support his family. If he went into the Marines for three years, he would be able to send most of his pay home to Mabel and the boys. Then, after he got out, he would have enough GI-Bill time coming to be able to return to college and earn at least a Bachelor's degree. He knew that there was a possibility they wouldn't accept him because of his problems with the Army. And he'd heard that you were ineligible to enlist if you had children. On the other hand, if he didn't tell them he'd been a soldier and was married, they might not throw him out once he was in. Another positive point was that the Armed Forces were no longer segregated.

Driven by his inability to find any other means of support, Williams suddenly walked into the Recruiting Station, telling himself that he only wanted to see what the Marines were prepared to offer.

Saying it wouldn't obligate him in any way, the recruiting officer had Williams take an aptitude test. He then said that the test results, plus his college background in writing, indicated he was well suited for training as an information specialist. "If you enlist," he said, "I'll recommend you for the Information Services School at Quantico, Virginia, which isn't too far from your home. You'll be trained in newspaper and script writing, producing and directing films as well as radio and TV shows, and all the other duties of an information specialist. After leaving the Marines," he continued, "you'll easily be able to earn a degree in Journalism,

Radio, Television or Motion Pictures, and your income will be assured."

He made it sound so attractive that Williams could hardly resist. "If I can really get into the Information Services, and can leave for boot camp tomorrow," he impulsively told the recruiting officer, "I'll sign up on the spot."

"I'm sorry," the officer answered, "but those who sign up for three years are only *recommended* for the specialty of their choosing. In order to be *definitely assigned* to the Information Services School, you have to join for the full four years. Also, four-year enlistees are the only ones we ship out the day after enlisting. Those who sign up for three years usually have to wait a couple of weeks before we can take them."

By this time Williams was grasping at straws. He'd seen the penniless bums begging for handouts and sleeping in doorways down on Skid Row. If he didn't do something to save himself, he would be down there in a few days. All it had taken to make him forget his elaborate philosophical objections to military service was several months of unemployment. He grabbed the recruiting officer's pen and signed up for four years as a U.S. Marine.

That evening Williams spent his last two dollars on supper at an inexpensive downtown Los Angeles restaurant. The next morning he checked out of his hotel and reported to the Recruiting Station for a physical examination. That same afternoon he was on a bus with a group of other recruits heading for the Marine Corps Recruit Depot at San Diego.

Chapter Four

A MARINE NEVER RETREATS

The moment Williams and the other enlistees were inside the fence of the Recruit Depot all hell broke loose. They were screamed off the bus—screamed across the field—and screamed into their barracks. "This is the Corps! This is the Corps!" the drill instructors shouted as they forced them to run through the darkness. What really shocked Williams was that the "DI's" were hitting and kicking recruits who didn't move fast enough to suit them. He had never seen anything like it.

The recruits were pushed into a loose formation and made to empty their pockets on the ground. The DI's inspected each man's belongings, confiscating and throwing away cigarettes, candy bars, and other personal items. Midnight was long past when the recruits finally crawled into bed. It was more like a prison than a training camp.

The next morning the drums began at dawn. The new men fell out to a drum beat, had their heads shaved to a drum beat, drilled to a drum beat, and moved their bowels to a drum beat. The DI's were screeching windup toys that never slowed down. It seemed the only way they could communicate was by bellowing at the top of their lungs, and their only purpose in life seemed to be to push, punch, and torment the recruits until they collapsed from exhaustion.

Like Japanese officers from World War II, they wore ceremonial swords. Their old-fashioned, wide-brimmed campaign hats were pulled so low they had to tilt their heads back in order to see anything, resulting in a characteristic jutjawed expression. The shadow of the hat's brim hid their eyes, making them appear all the more threatening and inhuman. Even though many were only corporals or privates, the recruits had to address them all as "Sir."

Harassment was an integral part of the training, and went on at all hours. Forced marches at night were common. A few minutes after the men had wearily fallen onto their beds after a forced night march, the DI's would rush in blowing their whistles, and make the exhausted recruits run outside and march again.

One of the favorite places for harassment was the food line outside the mess hall. When it was raining the DI's would order the recruits to leave their caps and overcoats in the barracks, then mark time in ankle-deep water before they could enter to eat.

A typical stunt would be for one of them to sneak up behind a recruit in the food line and shout in his ear, "Marine, you like the Corps, don't you?"

"Yes, sir!" the recruit would answer as loudly as he could, having already learned that responding in a normal tone of voice could get him a fist in the stomach. Then the DI would say, "Marine, your girl friend is home shacking up with your buddy, but you don't care, because you would rather be here, wouldn't you?"

"Yes, sir!" the recruit would shout once more.

"Marine, you love the Corps more than you do your own mother, don't you?" he would demand, and once more the recruit would answer in the affirmative.

Finally he would ask, "Marine, suppose you were out on the battlefield and two enemy soldiers came at you, one from the left and one from the right. Which way would you retreat?" If the recruit was unfortunate enough to answer, "I'd retreat to the rear, sir!" the DI would step back and kick him in the buttocks with all of his might, push him out of the food line, and scream, "A Marine never retreats! A Marine never retreats! You will go forward!"

In addition to the general harassment, any recruit the DI's felt was learning too slowly was taken late at night into the "head," as they called the barracks toilet, and beaten bloody by three or four of them. If asked the source of their injuries, the recruits were warned to answer, "I got up in the middle of the night and stumbled over my footlocker." This would always produce a knowing smile, since everyone, including the officers and doctors, knew what it really meant.

After a few days it was Williams' turn to be a victim. Among his DI's was a White corporal from Georgia. It didn't surprise Williams when he came over and pushed him in the back. Unlike most of the recruits, though, Williams didn't hesitate to tell the DI to take his hands off.

"What do you mean, take my hands off?" the corporal screamed. "Don't you know we are going to take you in the head tonight and kick the shit out of you for saying that?"

"No," Williams answered. "If there's any kicking done it'll be in both directions, because this Marine isn't going to stand still and let anybody hit him."

At this, the platoon sergeant, a hulking Texan, came over and told the corporal, "Leave him alone. He looks like an ex-dogface to me, and doggies don't make good Marines anyway." Realizing that they would find out about his Army service sooner or later, Williams said, "Yes, I'm an ex-doggy, and I know you've got no right to beat me."

That night the sergeant sent for him. "Williams," he said, "I could tell you'd been in the Army by the way you handle yourself in training. But don't worry, the Corps is kind of like the Foreign Legion. We don't care what you did before becoming a Marine—so long as you become a good one. I know they don't beat trainees in the Army, but we've been doing it in the Corps for almost two hundred years, and we're not going to change."

"That may be well and good for the Corps, sir," Williams answered, "but, even if it's a thousand-year-old tradition, I'm not going to let anyone hit me without hitting back." The sergeant looked at him for several moments, then said, "I'll tell you what I'm going to do. I've been a DI for more than fourteen years, and my training platoons have always been the best. You seem to know how to take care of yourself, so I'm going to make you a squad leader."

To say that Williams was pleased would be an understatement. He'd always been interested in military matters, and was happy at being given the opportunity to show that a Black could do a good job commanding other men. The sergeant had made a wise decision in giving him authority instead of trying to break him. That would only have forced him to resist. Once the shock of the harassment wore off, the fact of the matter was that Williams liked being in the Marines.

The Army had been entirely different. First of all, he'd been a soldier only because he'd been drafted, while he had volunteered for the Marines. Also, he looked upon the Corps as having saved him from unemployment. And he was enthusiastic about the specialized training they were going to give him in the Information Services. Most important, the Corps was integrated.

The first time Williams' battalion commander spoke to the recruits, he said, "Listen carefully, because I am not going to repeat myself. This is the word: There will be no discrimination of any kind in here. Whoever engages in harassment based on color, religion, or national origin will have to deal with me. This is the Corps, and in the Corps we have only one type of man—the fighting man."

When he heard that, Williams knew it was Uncle Sam himself speaking. Whereas in 1945 he had been segregated into Camp Crowder's "Shanty Town" section, he now slept on the bottom bunk, while a White recruit from Mississippi had to sleep on the top one. The White may have disliked being in the same building with Blacks, but this was 1954, and he was afraid even to say anything about it. His Uncle Sam had told him that was the way it had to be.

Most of the men in Williams' squad were of American-Indian or Mexican-American ancestry, and they got along well. The first thing he told them was, "Ours is going to be the best squad in the whole boot camp. If you don't want to be in it, speak up right now, because I don't want anybody here who's not ready to follow me all the way. If you stay, but refuse to obey my orders, I won't have the DI's gang up on you in the head, I'll give you a chance to outfight me man to man."

One day Williams had to get his squad up at 4:00 a.m. to do KP. There was a White from San Francisco who resented his being the leader. Instead of dressing, he just lay in his bed. When told to get up like the others, he opened one eye, sneered, and said, "Williams, if you don't get away from my bunk I'm going to kick your ass." For an instant Williams' mind flashed back to a somewhat similar scene in Camp Crowder in 1945—only there he'd been the one who wouldn't get up.

Just as eight years earlier the GI's had watched Lieutenant Tillsberry, to see what he would do when Williams called his bluff, so the Marines in his squad were now waiting to see if he would back down. Without hesitating, he grabbed the White from San Francisco by the front of his t-shirt, pulled him out of his bunk, and hit him in the mouth.

Williams' blow didn't hospitalize him, but it did persuade him to get dressed and go to work. Then Williams got word he was spreading the lie that he'd hit him with an iron bar. When they returned to the barracks that night he took him on again, barehanded, in front of witnesses, and beat him badly. After that they became good friends.

During boot camp in San Diego and advanced training at Camp Pendleton, Williams was instructed in the use of rifles, pistols, carbines, grenades, rocket launchers, machine guns, mortars, mines, and the various other infantry weapons. He qualified in all of them, and missed winning his Sharpshooter's Medal by only one point. He was also given extensive training in night operations and the type of hill fighting which had characterized the Korean conflict.

Williams' squad became one of the best. His platoon was honored, and his company graduated as the most outstanding unit in the training battalion. The DI's told him that he, as an individual, had made one of the finest showings in field exercises of anyone who had come through Camp Pendleton.

Being in the Corps developed a feeling of pride Williams hadn't known he was capable of. It didn't matter what color a man was. If he did something well, he was recognized and rewarded for it. Everything was spit and polish, not sloppy, as it had been in the Army.

The romantic illusion was assisted by having a full drum and bugle corps serenade the trainees every time they marched on the drill field. Rather than interpreting the opening lines of the Marines' hymn, "From the halls of Montezuma to the shores of Tripoli . . . ," as a description of the role played by the Corps in imposing U.S. imperialism from Latin America to Africa, Williams convinced himself that he, the Black descendant of slaves, was somehow the inheritor of "a glorious, centuries-old, fighting tradition." With the flag flying and the drums beating, had he been ordered by Uncle Sam to do battle on some foreign shore, he would have done so with a hearty "Yes, sir!"

The zenith of glamour was reached when Warner Brothers sent a crew down from Hollywood to Camp Pendleton to film some scenes for *Battle Cry,* a cinemascope feature starring Van Heflin and Aldo Ray. Williams was one of a group of trainees of Japanese, Mexican, Indian, and Afro-American descent chosen to appear in the movie as extras. They were taken to a section of the

southern California coast that was supposed to resemble the
Pacific island of Saipan, and dressed in World War II Japanese
Army uniforms. They then pretended to defend the beach against
a landing by the U.S. Marines. The Blacks were used only in the
extreme long shots so that the audience wouldn't see their skin
color clearly. Under Van Heflin's heroic leadership, the Marines
wiped them out.

Then they took off their Japanese uniforms, dressed themselves as Marines, and began to assault themselves. As they
charged out of the landing craft onto the beach, each of them was
filmed in close-up. In the completed film, however, the scene cut
away every time a Black was about to appear. They were told that
this was done because there were hardly any Blacks in Marine
fighting units back in the 1940's.

Some twenty years had passed since young Rob sat day-
dreaming in elementary school about storming San Juan Hill, and
here he was, leading his own squad of U.S. Marines onto a make-
believe invasion beach to reenact America's conquest of the
Pacific. Had things worked out differently, Williams conceivably
might have remained in the Marines and ten years later wound up
charging onto the beaches of the Dominican Republic or Vietnam. But the contradictions of the "American Way of Life" were
such that, just as he'd been among the Black and Brown trainees
chosen to play the role of the Japanese defenders in the film, a few
short years later he was to find himself in Havana, ready to help
protect Cuba against a real invasion by his former buddies in the
U.S. Marines.

Toward the end of the training cycle, anticipating that they
wouldn't throw him out after having spent so much time and
money on his training, Williams admitted to having a wife and
two sons, and the government began sending Mabel a monthly al-
lotment check.

The seemingly idyllic relationship between Blacks and Whites
at Camp Pendleton was strained by the controversy surrounding
the 1954 Supreme Court integration decision. Along with several
others, Williams was watching television in the company day
room when a newscaster announced that school segregation had
been declared unconstitutional. At first everyone let out a cheer,
but then the TV began showing southern senators such as Strom
Thurmond of South Carolina and Richard Russell of Georgia de-

claring their opposition to the decision. They were threatening, "The people of the South will never let the niggers be shoved down their throats by a Communist-controlled Supreme Court." They said such things as, "Before we let our children be forced to attend the same schools as niggers, the streets of America will flow with blood."

Williams became so angry that he left the day room. Entering the head, he found several other Black Marines. "Man, did you hear that goddamn shit about blood in the streets?" they asked him.

When some White Marines tried to join them in the toilet, one of the Blacks asked them, "What the hell you crackers want in here? You better split before we knock you on your ass."

"Why are you fellows acting like this?" one of the Whites asked. "We're not against Blacks. We're all in the Corps together."

At this another Black retorted, "Those are your senators, and they're expressing your feelings. So why should we have anything to do with you?"

"But those people are from down South," the White said, "and we don't agree with them at all."

The Black answered, "We don't give a damn where they're from. They're White, and they run the U.S.A. If they're not speaking for you, then why don't you stop them?"

In the weeks that followed, the situation grew so tense that there were several fights between Black and White Marines on the base.

Williams' romance with the Marine Corps ended when he completed mountain warfare training at Camp Pendleton and was told that, instead of being sent to the Information Services School, he'd been classified a combat engineer. He was stunned. They wanted him, in effect, to be a laborer. It was just like back in 1945 at Camp Crowder, when the Black GI's, instead of being given technical training, had to dig holes for telephone poles.

Certain that there had been some kind of administrative error, he went to his CO to get it straightened out. The lieutenant listened, half-smiling, as Williams told of having enlisted for four years only because the recruiting officer had promised that he would be trained as an information specialist. Then he laughed in his face and said, "Marine, you're no better than anyone else in the Corps. You don't tell us what you want. We tell you. You came in here as a ditch digger, and the Corps has decided you'll leave here as a ditch digger."

In desperation, he went to the chaplain, who said he would check into the matter. Three days later the executive officer called him in and said, "Williams, you sure are lucky. We're going to give you a break. You won't have to be out in the mud all day digging holes after all. Instead of combat engineer, we've reclassified you a supply clerk."

"But I don't care whether I'm out in the mud or not," Williams said. "I was promised Information Services School, and that's the only assignment I'll accept."

"Do you mean you don't want to be a supply clerk?" the officer demanded. "Why that's the best job in the Corps. All you do is sit in a nice clean supply room all day. There are a lot of Marines who'd give their left nut for a job like that."

Williams returned to the chaplain, who said, "Just between the two of us, you're wasting your time. You might as well know the truth. The Corps doesn't allow any colored men in the Information Services. Since you have a good record as a trainee, there is a possibility that, by being patient, you might some day be the first Negro to be allowed into that specialty. But, by insisting on it this way, you'll get nothing but a lot of trouble."

There it was again, the same old racist lunacy. The Corps was integrated, but only on the killing and ditch-digging levels. No Blacks in jobs where they could think or be seen by the public. And he was expected to swallow their lies and hypocrisy without gagging, to bow his head and wait for "massa" to throw him a bone. Well, they had the wrong man. Despite the chaplain's advice, Williams kept on pushing.

What seemed like a break came one afternoon as he was walking across the parade field. An old Black staff sergeant, his chest covered with campaign ribbons and his sleeve striped with hash marks, approached him and said, "Hey, Marine. Are you the one making so much trouble about getting into Information Services?" When Williams answered that he was, the sergeant said, "I've been hearing about you over in Battalion Headquarters where I work. Let me tell you something. Seventeen years ago, when I joined the Corps, all they would let us niggers do was shine shoes, cook, and push around wheelbarrows full of mule shit. I'm a career man, and have been on Guadalcanal, Iwo Jima, everywhere else. When I get out in three years I'm in line for a fat disability pension, so I can't afford trouble. But I know you're not planning to make a career out of the Corps, and don't give a damn. If you really want to push them, here's the way to do it: As Marines, we constitute the elite troops of the president of the United States, and can 'Request Mast' from him if we want to. That means you, as an individual Marine, can present a petition to the commandant of the Corps, stating that you have a problem which your officers are unable to solve, and which you want to discuss with President Eisenhower and no one else. If you stick to your guns, they might even have to fly you to Washington."

"Supposing I'm ready to do it," Williams told the old Black NCO. "I wouldn't know the first thing about preparing that petition."

"Don't worry," he said. "I'll help you with the details. But remember one thing: You can't tell anyone where you found out about this. In fact, you can't even admit you know me. If they suspected I'd told you how to do it, they'd really mess me up."

With his guidance, Williams prepared the request. When it was ready, the old sergeant said, "Now take it to your orderly room, hand it to your first sergeant, and tell him, 'This is addressed to the commandant of the Marine Corps.' Once you do that they are duty bound to pass it on to him. I won't see you any more, but I'll be watching what happens. It's about time one of us gave them the business."

The next day Williams walked into the orderly room and did as he'd said. His first sergeant jumped up from his desk so fast he almost hit the ceiling. "What, what, what?" he stammered. "You, you don't really want to see the commandant?"

"Yes, I do," Williams insisted.

His CO then told him, "Now Williams, you don't have that kind of problem. Let's be sensible and work it out here in the unit." The next day the Battalion CO assured him, "We can take care of whatever is bothering you. Just withdraw your request and everything will be okay." Williams refused. Two days later his request landed on the desk of Major General Good, commander of the entire installation. Those few words typed on a small piece of paper had Camp Pendleton shivering and shaking. Williams felt as if he'd pushed some sort of magic button that had turned a pack of snarling wolves into frightened rabbits.

His company commander called him into his office and said, "Well, you've really messed us up. Tomorrow morning report here in your dress uniform. I've been ordered to take you to see General Good."

When Williams entered the base commander's office, the general didn't look up. Sitting at his desk writing, he kept him standing at attention for almost fifteen minutes. Then, having demonstrated his ability to make him uncomfortable, he ordered Williams to stand at ease and said, "Marine, just who is helping you stir up all of this trouble?"

"Nobody, sir," Williams answered.

But the general insisted, "Oh, yes there is. It's impossible for any one man to make things so difficult for us. There has got to be someone helping you, and you are going to tell me who it is."

When Williams insisted that he had prepared the "Request Mast" by himself, General Good switched tactics and, adopting a more conciliatory tone of voice, asked, "Marine, do you know that if this goes through to Washington, it will reflect badly on the competency of the entire staff of Camp Pendleton? What exactly is your problem?" Williams answered that all he wanted was to go to Information Services School, and the general said, "Well, if that's the case, I'm prepared to bend over backward to see you get everything that's coming to you. There's no need to go to Washington for a little problem like that, now is there? If you'll just sign this release form rescinding your 'Request Mast,' I guarantee you'll get the special training for which you're best suited."

That sounded fine to Williams so, with the general smiling and nodding his head in encouragement, he signed a release form which had already been prepared. No sooner had he done so than the pleasant, almost pleading expression on General Good's face turned into a fierce scowl. "Goddamn you!" he shouted. "You are nothing but a troublemaker. You want the training you deserve, and by God you are going to get it. Now, get the hell out of this office."

The next morning Williams was arrested by the military police—charged with having refused to march in a parade a month or so earlier, and also with refusing to salute the flag. The charges were based upon signed statements from his noncoms.

There was a man in his company who'd actually done those things—a Jewish man who had renounced his faith, become a Jehovah's Witness, and refused to salute the flag or participate in parades. The officers claimed he was really trying to get out of the Marines by pretending to be insane. Since he and Williams had discussed his belief in Jehovah's Witnesses and other topics, Williams conjectured that the officers might have assumed they were plotting something together. Whatever their reasoning, he felt that the charges against him were an absurd frame-up.

"Do you think I'm crazy?" he asked the prosecutor at his preliminary hearing. "Why should I refuse to salute the flag or march in a parade at the very time I'm trying to get assigned to the Information Services?" But his protests were of no avail; and he was ordered to undergo a special court martial.

Before they could put Williams on trial, he had to be interviewed by the Camp Pendleton psychiatrist. The psychiatrist told him that he also, being Jewish, had suffered discrimination in the Corps. He tried to convince Williams that, since he couldn't possibly win against General Good and the other officers, the best thing to do was stop pushing and take it easy.

At the court martial, the officer appointed to conduct Williams' defense made no attempt to discredit the testimony given against him by his sergeant and corporal, but asked for leniency. Williams was found guilty as charged, and sentenced to 180 days in the "brig," as the prison is called in the Marines. He was told by the court martial that he had the right to appeal, but decided it would be a waste of time. After all, to whom would he be appealing? The reality of the situation seemed to him to be that he was a powerless Black soldier who was being punished for having dared to disturb the great General Good.

Williams saw himself as just another gullible "nigger," whose hunger for integration into the "American Way of Life" had let him be fast-talked, first by the recruiting officer into signing up for four years, and then by General Good into surrendering the only protection afforded him by the regulations. It wasn't the first time he'd tried to give the U.S. system the benefit of the doubt, nor was it to be the last. He seemed compelled to keep trying to find the honesty and integrity in White America that he'd read about in his schoolbooks as a child. The leftists in New York had labeled him quite correctly: He was a "sentimentalist."

Life in the Camp Pendleton brig was hard, but at that time there weren't many beatings. Shortly before Williams' imprison-

ment several incidents took place which tended to discourage the
guards from sadistic practices. A guard who had beaten several
prisoners went AWOL and, after being caught and put in the brig
himself, was stabbed to death by a prisoner in the mess hall. In another instance, according to the grapevine, a group of men recently released from the brig waylaid and killed some of the worst
guards while they were off duty in the nearby town of Oceanside.

In the most sensational incident of all, a particularly sadistic
guard was badly beaten and bound to a pole under a pier so that
the incoming tide would drown him. He was rescued in time, but
the episode had great impact on the other guards. As a result,
when the prisoners went out on work details the guards would
offer them cigarettes and act very friendly. As soon as they saw
officers approaching, however, they would shout and curse as if
they were really giving them a hard time.

Although the over-all percentage of Blacks at Camp Pendleton was rather low, perhaps as little as 2 or 3 percent, Williams observed that they made up 30 to 40 percent of the prisoners in the
brig.

After getting to know the other men, he concluded that his
case wasn't unique, and that their being there in such dispropor-
tionate numbers was the result of a hidden, but real, racist policy.
So he resolved to start actively resisting again.

Williams decided to write to President Eisenhower, protesting
both what had been done to him and the racism that he felt still
existed in the Marines. He had the letter smuggled out of the
prison, and before long it produced some action. General Good
called all of the prisoners out and read them a message which had
been sent down through channels from the White House. In it the
president acknowledged Williams' letter, assured him that the
government wouldn't tolerate racial discrimination in the Corps,
and promised that his case would be reviewed.

"Williams must be a senator," his fellow prisoners said afterward. "What else could make old General Good read him a letter
from Eisenhower?" Furious, the officers tried to force Williams to
tell them how he'd gotten the letter mailed, but he refused.

Williams didn't know for certain if his letter was the cause,
but a short time later he was taken before a Court Martial Review
Board. They told him that, since he had one of the best records of
any trainee at the camp, they were going to release him from the

brig and put him in a special company to see how he got along. Knowing how they felt about him, he wasn't enthusiastic, and suspected that prison was preferable to what they had planned.

He was assigned to a unit heading for a place in Nevada called Pickles' Meadow to receive "cold weather indoctrination." Packed into busses, they began the long ride across the Mojave Desert, past Death Valley, and up into the Rocky Mountains.

Part of the unit's mission was to test various types of sub-arctic gear. Frostbite and other cold-weather problems had been encountered by the Marines in Korea, and the men of the unit were to be guinea pigs so solutions could be found for the future.

As the caravan of vehicles climbed higher and higher into the Rocky Mountains, it began to snow. The cold penetrated the heated busses and their winter uniforms. After a while they left all signs of human habitation and drove through an endless waste of rock and ice.

When the busses had gone as far as they could, the Marines had to get out and march through the snow, carrying all of their gear on their backs. As they walked, it got colder and colder, and they sometimes had to push through snowdrifts as high as their chests. Just when they were so tired they couldn't go another step, they were ordered to stop and set up camp. There were no barracks. Williams and the others had to dig trenches, foxholes, and bunkers on the spot in order to shelter themselves from the cold. The temperature went way below zero that night.

Early the next morning the DI's started their harassing. Claiming that the men were being trained to withstand "Chinese-type psychological warfare," they would prevent them from sleeping by blowing whistles and beating drums all night long. Besides everything else, they were forced to take cold showers in the snow every evening after training.

The special winter boots they had been issued were the worst travail of all. While the men were walking in them their feet got so hot that the boots quickly filled with sweat. Then, when they stopped to rest, the sweat would turn to ice and freeze their toes off. It wasn't long before the men started dropping like flies from frostbite, flu, and pneumonia. The only building nearby was a small infirmary about two miles down the mountain from where they were dug in. When a man collapsed, the others would drag him there through the snow on a stretcher. At one time so many

Marines were coming down with pneumonia that a special convoy
was organized each day to ship them to the nearest military hospital.

After they thought the men were acclimated to the cold, the
DI's started taking them on long marches. Marching, ceaselessly
marching through the snow, with men collapsing all around, Williams had never seen such suffering.

He'd thought Tent City at Camp Crowder was bad, but the
cold weather in Missouri seemed balmy compared to the high-altitude, wind-whipped frozen hell of Pickles' Meadow. The Marine
spit and polish were gone. There was no drum and bugle corps to
serenade them on those frigid marches. Pickles' Meadow convinced Williams that the real purpose of the Marine Corps was to
provide unquestioning, unfeeling, dehumanized machines which
could be hurled at whoever opposed the interests of the U.S.
power structure. The only thing the Corps knew how to do was
kill, and since no war was on at the moment, the next best thing
was to torture and exterminate its own men.

Strangely enough, while almost everyone else came down
with frostbite or pneumonia, Williams didn't even get a cold during the time he was at Pickles' Meadow. Although hating every
minute of it, he was in as good health as he'd ever been. One day a
White sergeant major told him, "Williams, I've been in the Corps
for almost thirty years, and I think they're doing you an injustice.
There's a special indication on your record that says you're a bad
guy. And it looks like they're trying either to break your spirit or
kill you outright before you ever see the end of your four years.
But don't think that everybody in the Marines is against you. I'm
going to try to get you out of here."

Shortly after their conversation, Williams was sent back to
Camp Pendleton. But before he could get the chill out of his
bones, he found himself running through the surf and digging foxholes in the hot sand, practicing amphibious landings. The contrast in weather conditions between the ice of Pickles' Meadow
and the roasting southern California beaches was staggering. Had
he then been sent to rot in some equatorial jungle, he wouldn't
have been surprised.

Then he received orders to go to Korea.

The moment Mabel learned he was being sent overseas, she

took the bus all the way from North Carolina to California to see him. When Williams asked for a pass so that he could meet her in town, his commanding officer had him placed in the brig. Fortunately, he was able to get word about it to the chaplain, who had him released and given permission to go into Oceanside to spend one last night with his wife before leaving for Korea.

A day or two before his unit was scheduled to board the troopship, Williams was working with some other men on a garbage detail around the barracks. Noticing that his CO was standing nearby, he pretended not to see him. Then, in a rather loud voice, Williams turned and said to the Marine next to him, "Man, if I make it up to the 38th Parallel,* do you know what I'm going to do? I'm going to go, go, go."

At this the lieutenant came running over and demanded, "Marine, what did you just say?"

"I'm sorry, sir," Williams answered, "but I wasn't speaking to you, sir."

"I know you weren't," the lieutenant said. "But I'm ordering you to repeat the statement you just made to this man."

"Well, sir, if you really want to know," Williams said, "I was telling him that, if I ever got to the 38th Parallel, I would be going."

"Going where?" the officer demanded.

Williams smiled at him, shrugged his shoulders, and answered, "Just going, sir. Just going wherever there is to go."

A couple of days later Williams' Korean-bound unit was driven to San Diego and loaded onto the boat. He'd already made up his bunk, when the same White sergeant major who had befriended him at Pickles' Meadow came into the compartment and called his name. "Williams, you sure are a lucky son-of-a-gun," he said. "The word just came from Washington to take you off this ship. Pack up your gear and come with me." Since the gangplank had been raised, they had to lower it. As the sergeant major escorted Williams back down to the dock, it seemed as if every one of the thousands of men on the troopship crowded alongside the rail and started hooting, "Oh, my, look at that lucky Marine. He's going ashore. He's really going ashore."

A truck had been brought all the way from Camp Pendleton

_____
* The frontier separating North and South Korea.

to get them. On the way back, the sergeant major said, "Williams, the reason you've been pulled off the ship is because they're going to try to kick you out of the Corps. You've a right to be defended by any counsel you choose, but you have to tell them who you want."

"I don't know any lawyers out here in California," Williams told him. "And even if I did, I couldn't afford to pay the fee."

The sergeant major thought for a moment, then leaned close and said, "Why don't you ask the NAACP in San Diego to help you?"

Although imprisoned in the brig again, Williams was able to follow his advice. He also wrote a letter to Adam Clayton Powell, the Black congressman from New York; and had it smuggled into town and mailed to Washington.

When called up for his preliminary hearing, he asked to be represented by a lawyer the NAACP was getting for him. This seemed to disturb the officers, one of whom said, "Marine, we know you don't like it here. So why not make it easy on all of us? Forget this lawyer business. You're only going to be separated administratively and will still be entitled to receive all of your veteran's benefits."

"That sounds all right," Williams answered, "but I still want to be represented by counsel."

About two weeks had passed when a captain came to the brig and said, "Okay, Williams, your discharge papers have been prepared. You're leaving for home today."

"How can I be discharged when I haven't had my hearing yet?" Williams asked.

"Now, don't get excited," the captain answered. "We've decided not to give you a hearing because this isn't a dishonorable discharge. All you have to do is sign these papers. We'll give you your discharge pay, and you'll be a free man."

As soon as Williams signed, he had to turn in all of his uniforms and other gear. He was allowed to keep only one set of clothing—a shirt, trousers, shoes, and socks—but had to cut off the insignia from the shoulder of the shirt. Then the captain took him out of the brig and turned him over to three military policemen in white uniforms.

The four of them left Camp Pendleton and drove to the Oceanside Police Station. There one of the local cops told Williams, "Your kind isn't wanted in this town. If you aren't on the next train out of here, we'll arrest you as a vagrant."

"You don't have to worry about me loitering on your streets," he answered. "I don't ever want to see this place again."

Although Williams was legally out of the Marines, the three MP's treated him as if he still were in their custody. They took him to the railroad station, and waited until his train was ready to leave. Then the captain showed up again; and led Williams to a private Pullman compartment complete with its own bed, toilet, and sink. "This is where you'll be riding, and here's your ticket," he said.

Williams was surprised when he saw that the ticket was for Monroe. "You mean you're sending me all the way back to North Carolina?" he asked.

"That's right," the captain answered. "We've decided to do you a favor. Also, here are your meal tickets—more than enough to last you for the trip. If you need anything, just push this button, and the porter will bring it to your compartment."

As the train pulled out of Oceanside for its long journey across the United States, the people on the station platform pointed and stared at Williams. It was obviously unusual for them to see a Black riding alone in an expensive private compartment. Williams couldn't help wondering why the Marine Corps had suddenly become so generous. Why should General Good, who'd had him thrown in the brig, then sent off to be frozen at Pickles' Meadow, now appear to be in such a rush to get rid of him? And why should he provide him with such luxurious transportation all the way home, rather than just back to Los Angeles where he'd enlisted?

Williams reflected upon his military career. His efforts to learn a profession had resulted only in being taught how to march, fight, and keep from freezing to death. The one important thing he did know was that nobody could make him turn tail.

As the train approached Monroe, he considered what to do next. Since he'd been in the Marines for about a year, he estimated that he would be eligible to receive educational benefits for two or three semesters under the GI Bill. If he didn't go to school, and couldn't get work, at least he could collect the unemployment money the bill authorized. It would be some compensation for what he'd gone through.

Williams felt that he had sincerely attempted to become part of the American system, but had been betrayed and rejected. Still, he didn't suspect that his later role in life would be to advocate its destruction.

Chapter Five

A FULL-TIME AGITATOR

The first thing Williams did after returning home in October, 1955, was to apply for his GI Bill eligibility certificate. The Veterans' Administration informed him, however, that he couldn't receive any benefits because his discharge from the Marine Corps had been under "dishonorable circumstances." When he protested that this was impossible, since he'd never had a hearing or been represented by counsel, the local VA officials advised him to file an appeal to the Review Board in Washington. Not having the money to hire a lawyer, he requested legal aid from the NAACP.

While his appeal was pending, he had to find employment, but the national economy was in a slump. Even his brother Edward, who'd worked for the same Detroit auto plant for twenty years, had lost his job. This being the case, Williams was pleased at hearing that Douglas Aircraft needed machinists for its new Nike factory in nearby Charlotte.

When he told the interviewers at the missile plant about his experience, they became enthusiastic. They were having difficulty locating skilled men because there had previously been no demand for aircraft machinists in the area, and suggested they could use Williams to train other workers.

But when he arrived at the plant to go to work the next Monday morning, he was informed that he couldn't be hired. The FBI considered him a "security risk." Since the normal security check takes weeks or even months, and his clearance had been denied in less than seventy-two hours, and over the weekend to boot, it seemed obvious to Williams that the FBI had him on some sort of special blacklist. The strange thing about it was that all through Korea, while working on helicopters at Curtiss-Wright, despite openly associating with known leftists, he had held a full security clearance.

The best job Williams could find was as a night watchman at

a textile mill. It paid $42 a week, barely enough to feed Mabel and the boys. The only thing that kept them off relief was being able to live rent-free in the family house on Boyte Street.

Around this time Williams received a response from Congressman Adam Clayton Powell's office to the complaint he'd sent him from the Camp Pendleton brig. It contained a copy of a letter written to the commandant of the Marine Corps just before Williams was discharged, requesting a special investigation into his court martial. Now he knew why they'd kicked him out of the Corps so hurriedly, and had seen to it that he was transported all the way back to North Carolina. General Good had wanted him as far from Camp Pendleton as possible before anyone from the Pentagon could come around asking questions. The luxurious private railroad compartment had been provided to overcome any hesitancy he might have shown in accepting his discharge; and it had worked. He'd been taught a lot of lessons about how the power structure manipulates "niggers," but he obviously still had a great deal to learn.

When Williams' appeal was heard in Washington, D.C., he was told that the North Carolina office of the Veterans' Administration, rather than the Marine Corps, was responsible for classifying his discharge as dishonorable. The Corps claimed it had separated him solely for administrative reasons. But the VA insisted the information it had received from the Corps, even if not specifying it, could only be interpreted as indicating that a dishonorable discharge was intended. Although his NAACP lawyer charged the entire affair was a cover-up for racism, the review board's final decision was to turn down his appeal.

Williams knew he still had the right to bring a law suit, but by that time he was disgusted with the entire matter. He didn't have the $20,000 or $30,000 required to fight a case to the Supreme Court, and neither the NAACP nor any other organization was volunteering to do it for him.

A lawyer from the Catholic War Veterans who was present in the hearing room told Williams afterward that it had been a mistake for the NAACP to raise the race issue, even if it were true. "It's not too hard to get the Review Board to give in when the only question is one of justice for the individual," he said. "But this way, had they granted your appeal, it would have amounted to admitting that the Marine Corps practices discrimination."

Charging racism was an attack on the entire system. The government simply couldn't afford to let him win.

So there was Williams, thirty years old, classified as a security risk, saddled with a dishonorable discharge, and barely able to support his family. As he saw it, the "American Way of Life" had found him undigestible, spit him up, and condemned him to a life of scrabbling around for handouts like a stray dog. But just as they couldn't make him a "nigger" in the Marine Corps, so barring him from ever holding a decent job in civilian life couldn't stop him from speaking out. He began composing short stories, poems, and articles. Most important, he launched a steady barrage of letters to the editors of every newspaper in the area.

In his letters Williams criticized the immorality of racism and the injustice of segregation, spoke of the need for Black Americans to demand equality, and pointed out the ways in which the local and state authorities were trying to get around the Supreme Court's 1954 desegregation decision. There was a growing interest in such matters in the South due to the activities of the Reverend Martin Luther King and others, and many White newspaper editors welcomed such letters as a means of increasing sales by creating controversy. The more intelligent apparently wanted to show their fellow Whites that Blacks were no longer the submissive Uncle Toms of the past, while others were trying to demonstrate that northern criticism of the segregated southern school systems was unfounded. In the strange logic of the South, the fact that a Black could read and write is sometimes held up as proof that the education they receive is adequate. Whatever the editors' reasons, they were providing Williams with a platform, and he used it to the best of his ability.

Blacks also read Williams' letters, and many agreed with what he was saying. But the Whites were the ones he was most interested in reaching, especially those on the borderline who hadn't yet become completely infected with bigotry. By opening their minds to the possibility of an intelligent dialogue with Blacks, he hoped to influence them to take a stand against racism. He knew that his letters were reaching them because more and more White readers began to send in replies. In some papers a regular exchange of pro and con opinions was started. Soon even the editorial columnists were commenting on the points he was raising.

A few of the local racists started the rumor: "Someone else,

maybe a Communist, is writing those letters and paying that
darkie, Williams, to sign his name to them." They even plotted to
devise a way of getting him to write in front of witnesses in order
to try to prove that he was incapable of authoring an intelligible
phrase. The idea that Blacks have the ability to think and express
themselves in a complex manner is so threatening to many racists
that they go to fantastic lengths to discredit it.

Williams' letters eventually attracted the attention of Mr.
Shoup, the chief supporter of Monroe's Unitarian Fellowship. The
Shoup family, one of the wealthiest in that part of the state, was
helping finance the runaway northern industry that was beginning
to move south, and had been among the founders of Monroe before the Civil War. Mr. Shoup was an intellectual and world trav-
eler who had done quite a bit of writing. After leaving the Methodist Church to found the local Unitarian group, he had
personally provided the money with which their Center was built.
He was also known as one of the most active Whites working to
improve race relations in the area.

Accepting Shoup's invitation to visit the Unitarian Center,
Williams found the people there very hospitable. Although all the
members of the congregation were White, they didn't seem to
show the slightest sign of prejudice or hostility. They told him that
the violent reactions against his letters had served a constructive
purpose by revealing the severe racism which many people had
pretended didn't exist in Monroe. There was a strong desire on the
part of the power structure to portray North Carolina as an enlightened area when it came to the color question.

Although his mother had raised him as a Baptist, Williams
liked what he saw at the Unitarian Church, and joined it. But his
wife, also raised a Baptist, joined the Catholic Church and took
their boys there instead. Williams also became a member of a
Human Relations Group, which included Catholics, Unitarians,
and Protestants. In addition, he joined the Union County Branch
of the NAACP. His entry into the field of political activity was so
peaceful because, despite the racist pushing around which he'd already been subjected to, in 1956 the idea of violence as an indis-
pensable part of the fight for Black Liberation had not yet occurred to him. What he was saying in his letters to the editor,
which consisted primarily of calls for civil rights and racial equal-

ity, may have been radical for the South, but it was pretty tame stuff so far as the rest of the world was concerned.

The Unitarians invited Williams to give speeches on the issue of civil rights after their Sunday services and then had them printed in the newspaper. In doing this, they hoped to attract more Blacks to their services, but the attendance remained almost exclusively White. Those Blacks who did come were mostly bourgeois elements from the local Baptist and Methodist congregations, checking up on what Williams was saying. Like the White bigots, some Blacks saw him as a threat to their way of life.

The Black bourgeoisie of Monroe had expanded since the 1930's and 40's. The slump in employment opportunities for manual laborers brought about by the modernization of the railroad had been somewhat compensated for by a small increase in the number of positions available to schoolteachers and other professionals. They weren't much of a bourgeoisie by big-city standards, but for a small semi-rural community they were pretty high class. They had their own cliques and clubs, and delighted in copying the Whites by putting on expensive balls and social events. The fact that Williams, like quite a few of the other veterans, refused to participate in their status-seeking scramble, turned them against him. When his letters began to be published, they said, "It isn't that we don't have the courage to oppose the racists, it's just that we have more sense. Challenging the Whites the way Rob Williams is doing will certainly get him killed."

Each Sunday after services at the Unitarian Church the congregation would usually be invited to have dinner at Mr. Shoup's house. It was a large, attractive place with its own swimming pool. Having traveled widely, he owned a collection of works of art from around the world.

One Sunday seven or eight Blacks attended the services and remained to hear Williams give a speech against racism, but when Mr. Shoup invited them to dinner they refused. Since some were rather close friends of his, Williams asked why they didn't want to eat with the others. "Man, you must be crazy," one said. "How in the world can you get up in a White church and put down White people the way you do, and then sit down to dinner with them? Why they may be planning to poison us all! Williams, you are a fool. You are a fool." They couldn't understand that Shoup and the other Unitarians saw Williams' criticisms not as a personal attack, but only a condemnation of corrupt social practices.

The small and ineffectual NAACP branch in Monroe had been tolerated for several years by the local racists, but as agitation for integration began to spread throughout the country following the 1954 Supreme Court decision, it came under attack. The Black bourgeois elements were told by their White employers that belonging to it indicated they were allied with "troublemakers and subversives." They pleaded that they were not doing anything to help the civil rights demonstrations occurring in other places, but the Whites answered, "So long as you collect money to be sent to the Communists in New York who run the NAACP, you are just as guilty as they are."

When the middle-class White Citizens' Councils joined their less sophisticated Ku Klux Klan cohorts in attacking the officers and members of NAACP branches throughout the South, the threat of economic sanctions by employers, banks, and finance companies, plus the possibility of being beaten or lynched, proved too much for many Blacks. Branch after branch lost its membership and became inactive.

The Monroe NAACP branch was already on the decline when Williams joined it in 1955. By 1956 only six members remained. The officers wanted to resign, but hesitated to admit they had caved in under racist pressure. In an attempt to escape from this dilemma, they called a meeting to elect new officers. To Williams' surprise, they nominated him for the office of president. One of the older members told him, "Rob, you've been writing so many letters to the papers that you're already in the public eye. You don't have a good job to be fired from. And you don't seem to care about what else they might do to you. You're the only person in Monroe who's a big enough fool to take it." Williams was elected president and Dr. Albert F. Perry, a Black physician who was a newcomer to Monroe, became vice president.

Williams assumed the old officers wanted him as president in order to escape the pressure being put on them by the Whites, but during the weeks that followed only Doctor Perry was willing to renew his membership. When Williams tried to argue one of the others into staying, he said, "Let's face it, Rob. The NAACP is a dead issue in this town. If you can get the others to participate, I will too, but I don't think you've got a chance." Each former member he approached said essentially the same thing. When he saw that they all were very amused at his efforts, Williams understood that they had used him as a fall guy upon whom to blame the death of their NAACP branch.

Once he realized this, keeping the organization alive became a personal challenge. Almost immediately, the idea occurred to him of approaching not the professionals to whom membership in the NAACP had been a status symbol, but the working people. Late one afternoon he entered a pool hall, placed a pile of literature on the table, and announced: "I have been elected president of the Union County NAACP Branch, and I want to tell you about it." Some of the men in the pool hall were construction workers, several were unemployed laborers, and others were the scufflers, toughs, and various other types who frequent such places. They weren't exactly what Williams' mother would have called "good people," but they did represent a sizable part of the over three thousand Black inhabitants of Monroe.

Putting down his cue, one of the pool players demanded, "Man, just what do you want? Are you really asking us to join up with the teachers and preachers?" He said this jokingly because, in all the years the NAACP had existed in Monroe, they had never before solicited the workers or the poor to join. Of course the NAACP hadn't turned down the cash contributions of these people, but they never considered making them members and giving them the right to vote and influence policy. "Not only do I want you to join," Williams answered, "I want you to help me reorganize the whole thing. And once we get it going again, I want you to help me give the KKK and the other racists in this town hell."

Out of the twelve men in the pool hall that afternoon, six signed up, and Williams knew that he was on the right track at last. In the weeks that followed he walked the streets of Monroe recruiting laborers, farmers, domestics, and the unemployed. In one month, having recruited the fifty members required in order to be considered a functioning branch, he called a meeting to elect new officers.

When he opened the floor to nominations, everyone started protesting. "Williams," they said, "you're the one who got us all here. We don't want to vote. You run the thing, and choose whoever you think can help you do it." Accordingly, Williams appointed all the officers, selecting those, mostly veterans, whom he knew to have an independent attitude. He didn't realize it at the time, but theirs was one of the first NAACP branches of primarily working-class composition.

The first segregated public facility they took on was the Union County Library. A fire having recently destroyed the branch library housed in the town's Black Community Center, Williams telephoned the White who chaired the County Library Board, told him he represented the NAACP, and said the Blacks expected to have access to the main library until their branch could be rebuilt.

"We would like to do this without having to picket or make any trouble," he told him.

"I guess it will be all right," the White official answered. "I don't see any reason why you colored folks can't use the main library. It won't bother me because I don't read anyway."

His acquiescence, however, wasn't all that was required. When Williams asked for volunteers, he discovered that it was difficult to find anyone in the Black community willing to take the risk of walking into the library. He finally had to use a bit of subterfuge to get it done.

One day a Black veteran taking a night-school course came to Williams' house to ask a question about his studies. "Why ask me?" Williams responded. "Why don't you go look it up in the main library?"

"But I didn't know colored folks could go there," the student said.

"Sure we can," Williams insisted.

"Hop in my car, and I'll let you see for yourself."

Williams waited outside and watched as the veteran entered the library, withdrew the book he wanted, and left, all without incident. When they were back in the car and on their way home he told him, "Congratulations, you made history today. You are the first Black man ever to use that library."

Staring at Williams with his jaw agape, the veteran asked, "You mean colored people never went in there before? Man, how could you fool me like that? I might have gotten killed."

"I did it," Williams responded, "because if you'd known you were the first, you might have lost your nerve and not gone through with it."

Once back in the Black part of town the young veteran went around telling everyone what he had done. His fear had given way to pride. Others soon began to follow his example, and integrated use of the library became a daily event. In contrast, the attempts to integrate libraries in other southern states, particularly Virginia, resulted in violent attacks by the racists. Although relatively minor, this first victory inspired Williams and the others, and they began seeking additional public facilities to desegregate.

While the Unitarians and some other Whites continued to support the NAACP branch, the criticism directed against Williams in the local papers began to increase. He was accused of purposely creating disharmony in a town which had supposedly never before had a color problem. Even people whom he had known since childhood started crossing the street to avoid being seen speaking with him, so that the Whites wouldn't think they were supporting his policies.

The power structure began to pressure the clique of Black professionals who had formerly run the NAACP to do something to stop Williams' activities. When they encouraged them to rejoin the NAACP branch in order to dilute its militancy, membership began to boom. But the return of the bourgeois elements was ineffectual because the rank and file shouted them down every time they tried to question the group's desegregation activities.

The local public swimming pool, built by the U.S. government back during the New Deal, and supported by municipal taxation, was closed to Blacks. As there were no other pools in the area, they were forced to swim in the nearby streams and ponds. As a result, there had been several drownings over the years. The deaths of two Black children in a swimming hole during the summer of 1956 finally made Williams' NAACP branch decide to launch a drive to obtain a pool for the Black community.

The local Whites were then complaining about the Supreme Court's having banned "separate but equal" facilities. Instead of demanding integration, the first thing Williams did was ask the Union County Recreation Department for a separate pool for the Black community. When they said they had no funds for it, he asked, "Don't you realize that unless you find the money to build two pools, two libraries, and two of everything else, you will force us to integrate all the public facilities in this town?"

In an effort to find a compromise, Williams then suggested that, instead of sharing the pool with Blacks, the Whites set aside two days out of the week for them to use it.

"No," they answered, "we couldn't do that."

"All right, then," he countered, "how about just one day per week?"

"No, that's not possible either," they said. "It would just be too expensive."

"What do you mean 'too expensive'?" he asked.

"We mean we can't afford the cost of draining and refilling the entire pool every week after you Blacks have used it," was their answer.

They weren't saying this because they thought the Blacks' skin color would somehow tint the water or that they were so dirty they would contaminate the pool. Had the Whites been that concerned about avoiding contact, Williams knew, they wouldn't have had Black domestics in their homes preparing their food, making their beds, and wet-nursing their children. The real reason they feared swimming in the same pool with Blacks was that it would endanger the arbitrary caste system upon which their dominance was based.

Williams ruminated on the vagaries of southern prejudice: In the rural areas of the South it's not unusual to see a White man showing his love for his hounds by eating off the same plate with them, but the same man would probably try to smash in the head of any Black who dared sit next to him in a restaurant. His dogs' germs concern him far less than does the threat posed by desegregation. Many of the poorer southern Whites, whose standard of living is often as low as that of the Blacks, are the most ferocious guardians of this caste system. Their poverty leaves them little in life except the delusion that they are "superior." So long as there is someone whom they can look down upon and mistreat with impunity, they appear less motivated to press for better wages and conditions for themselves. Their egos, rather than their bank accounts, are all that discrimination expands. It is from these elements that the Klan draws its most vicious hoodlums and murderers.

The middle- and upper-class southern Whites, although not as open in their racism as the poor, derive the real material benefits from segregation. They are the manufacturers, large-scale

farmers, and businessmen who profit by using underpaid labor—
White as well as Black—to compete in the national and world
markets. They cloak their dominating position in the caste system
by referring to "tradition." According to them, Blacks shouldn't
attend the same schools, eat in the same restaurants, or swim in
the same pools as Whites because "it's against the traditions of
our forefathers." They claim those Blacks who aren't "troublemakers and subversives" actually enjoy being separated. Behind
all their talk of "tradition," in order to maintain their power and
profits the middle- and upper-class Whites are responsible for organizing and directing the KKK, the police, and the White Citizens' Councils. They are the ones who really keep the racist system going.

Had the Monroe Blacks been willing to remain submissive, to
continue to accept discrimination and exploitation as their forefathers had for centuries, there wouldn't have been any trouble. But
a growing number of Blacks were tired of being oppressed, and
didn't give a damn about "traditions" which said they had to let
themselves be stepped on.

As soon as they saw that their polite requests to the Recreation Department were getting them nowhere, Williams' NAACP
branch started sending groups of young people to try to integrate
the pool physically. Every time some of them lined up to buy tickets to go swimming, the authorities would close the place for the
day. Nobody, White or Black, got to go in. As this "stand-in"
campaign continued, the Klan began to hold large meetings in the
Monroe area. At first only a few hundred Whites wearing bed-
sheet robes and carrying flaming crosses would show up, but the
numbers kept increasing as the Blacks refused to stop their desegregation activities. *The Monroe Enquirer* reported rallies with
2,000, 4,000, 5,000 and, finally, 7,500 Klansmen and supporters in
attendance.

Following each rally, hundreds of KKK cars would roar
through the Black sections of Monroe. The drunken Klansmen in
them would honk their horns, shout curses, fire pistols, hurl bricks
and whiskey bottles at passers-by, and do whatever else they could
think of to harass the Blacks.

Williams was singled out for attack on various levels. The insurance policies on his car, home, and life were suddenly canceled.
Not one company doing business in Monroe would cover him.

Their standard answer was that his being president of the local NAACP made him too great a risk. He asked the national NAACP office in New York for help in fighting this, but they answered that, not being a race matter, it was out of their area of interest. Then he was laid off. While his boss said it was just temporary, he was never called back. The $42 per week he'd earned as a night watchman wasn't much, but without it things became really rough for his family. Try as he might, he couldn't find another job in the area.

Then the Klan started a petition campaign to try to force Williams out of Union County. A card table was set up in the Courthouse Square and people were asked to come there to sign a paper which declared that, since Williams and Dr. Perry were officials of the "Communist-Inspired-National-Association-for-the-Advancement-of-Colored-People," they should be banished "never to return."

While their petition had no legal basis, the KKK claimed that 6,000 of Monroe's 12,000 inhabitants had signed it. In many places, knowing that even a smaller number of people want to get rid of him will inspire a man to leave town in a hurry. What the Klan's petition really meant was that, had someone killed Williams or Dr. Perry, he probably would have gotten off lightly by pleading that he only did it to eliminate persons considered undesirable by the community.

Unable to intimidate the Blacks with the petition, the Klan stepped up their hit-and-run raids. In one week alone a total of fourteen Black women and girls were struck by objects hurled from cars; and one woman was stopped on a deserted corner and forced to dance in the street at gunpoint. The Monroe police made no arrests, not even when several people were struck by KKK cars.

While the terror campaign couldn't stop the Blacks' efforts to desegregate the pool, the nightly harassment did hurt their children and older people. In desperation a delegation of Black ministers asked the Monroe town officials to forbid the Klan from terrorizing their sections of town. The officials denied their appeal, saying, "Why, the Klan is a perfectly legal organization. It has as much right to demonstrate with a motorcade as you NAACP people have to organize stand-ins at the swimming pool." A similar request to Luther Hodges, the governor of North Carolina, also elicited a negative response. Telegrams were sent to President Eisenhower and other federal officials asking protection, but no one in Washington bothered to acknowledge them.

Finally, Williams and a group of veterans active in the NAACP got together and told the preachers, "Get up off your knees and quit begging the authorities for help. We are going to stop the Klan ourselves."

Williams wrote to the National Rifle Association, an organization in Washington which encourages the formation of gun clubs and which lobbies in Congress against firearms-control laws, and asked them for a charter. Once it was issued, his "NRA Rifle Club" members were able to buy military-surplus weapons and ammunition at very low prices. The sixty Blacks who joined the club were also able to purchase rifles and pistols from sporting-goods stores and through mail-order firms.

When the Klan found out that they were acquiring arms, it escalated its campaign of terror. One night during an NAACP meeting, a KKK spokesman telephoned Dr. Perry's wife and said they were going to bomb his house. As soon as she called and told them about it, the Blacks in the rifle club left the meeting and got their guns. While some waited in Dr. Perry's garage, others stood guard around the neighborhood.

In the early hours before dawn a discussion began among Williams and several others in the garage about establishing a permanent defense force. "If we're going to form a regular guard unit," one of the vets said, "then we'll have to organize it and staff it with officers."

"We already have all the organization we need," said another. "Our NAACP branch can do the job, and since Rob is already president, let's make him the leader of the Guard, too."

"The NAACP has never been a self-defense organization, and some of you guys don't belong to it, anyway," Williams protested. "If I, as the head of our branch, also become head of the Guard, it will look like the NAACP is supporting our being armed, which it isn't. Why don't you choose someone else?"

"Goddamn it, Rob," one of his buddies exclaimed, "you're not going to bug out on us like the teachers and preachers always do, are you? Everybody knows you were in the Marines and know all about that military jive. Besides, you're the one the Klan is really trying to get." Faced with their insistence, Williams agreed to lead the Guard.

What he and the others were doing was in direct contradiction to the Gandhian policies of the Reverend Martin Luther King, which were then gaining support throughout Black America. But it wasn't in Williams' make-up, or in those of the working people and veterans he knew, to permit themselves and their families to be brutalized. The idea that a tormentor will eventually become so tired and disgusted with beating his victim that he will drop his club and embrace the mutilated corpse in remorse just didn't seem logical to them. The veterans among them had taken an oath in the Service to defend the Constitution against its enemies, both foreign and domestic. Since neither the North Carolina authorities nor the U.S. government seemed prepared to defend their constitutional rights, they saw no choice but to do it themselves.

Those with military experience began developing the Guard's mission and structure. They started training the nonvets among them in elementary tactics and procedures, including the digging of foxholes and slit trenches. In addition to acquiring such basic items of military hardware as sandbags, gas masks, and steel helmets, they formed special three-man combat teams to stop the most probable form of Klan onslaught: hit-and-run firing from fast-moving cars.

The first team member, armed with a 12-gauge shotgun, was to protect the others against attack at short range. The second man had a .22-caliber semiautomatic rifle. His job was to fire at exposed targets beyond the range of the shotgun. The defenders of an inhabited area must do everything possible to prevent stray bullets from penetrating houses and injuring the very women and children they are trying to protect. Standard .22-caliber long rifle ammunition is very accurate and can kill or wound at long range, but is easily stopped by plaster or wooden walls, and is thus less likely to hurt innocent people.

The third team member was given a 30.06-caliber U.S. M-1 rifle, a 6.35-mm Italian carbine, or a 7-mm German mauser. As these powerful military weapons were only to be fired directly into advancing or retreating automobiles, he had to run into the middle of the street before he could shoot. Otherwise his steel-jacketed bullets would rip through the homes in the neighborhood.

Their arsenal eventually came to over six hundred weapons. Besides rifles, it included Lugers, Berettas, and other pistols; M-1 automatic .30-caliber carbines; grenades; and various types of machine guns. They also prepared Molotov cocktails, which, although crude and limited in range, were very inexpensive, and could be effective when used properly.

In addition to acquiring arms, the Guard developed an intelligence system to enable them to know in advance when, where, and in what strength the enemy was planning to attack. It utilized the janitors and domestics who worked in the offices and homes of the Klansmen and their supporters. The racists seemed so convinced of the animal faithfulness of their servants that they often would openly discuss what they planned to do to the Blacks. What they apparently didn't realize was that many of the husbands, sons, and fathers of their maids and cooks were members of either the NAACP, the Guard, or both. Williams and his supporters were told what they were talking about almost as soon as the words left their mouths.

The Blacks' intelligence system was aided by the fact that, with the exception of those already known as militants, most of the over two hundred men who worked with the Guard didn't go around telling the Whites about it. The mayor, chief of police, and other Monroe officials never realized that some of their "good niggers"—those they considered the most servile and nonviolent —were among the most dedicated and courageous men the Black community had. While they walked around with their heads bowed all day, they spent their nights gun in hand, eagerly awaiting a chance to smash the Klan's attacks.

Counterintelligence was as important as intelligence. Had the Blacks of Monroe confined themselves to a strictly defensive role, it wouldn't have been as necessary to develop anti-espionage procedures but, since they continued their stand-ins at the swimming pool all through this period, they had to take steps to keep the racists from finding out what they planned to do. They realized that their NAACP branch was being infiltrated by informers when some of the most Uncle-Tomish Blacks in town, civil servants and fairly well-paid white-collar workers who had been opposing everything they did, suddenly switched, and started attending meetings and proclaiming how enthusiastic they had always been about fighting for desegregation.

Several times when a group went to demonstrate at the swimming pool the authorities and the Klan would get there first and harass them. To foil the informers, the branch members would be telephoned and told to report to a designated spot with their towels, bathing suits, and admission money. Once they got there, Williams would send them back home. After a couple of such rehearsals, on a day when both the NAACP members and the authorities thought they were going to practice again, Williams suddenly told the people gathered at the assembly point to get into their cars and drive to the pool. The cops and the Klan were caught by surprise. From then on they had to rush down to the pool every time Williams called a rehearsal, just in case it turned into the real thing.

Another counterintelligence tactic was to stage false discussions at the NAACP meetings for the benefit of those suspected of being spies. After pretending to decide the details of the next demonstration, Williams would adjourn the meeting. Later that evening he and the other officers would meet in secret and work out the real plans. On several occasions, following a tip from one of their spies, the police and the Klansmen spent hours waiting for the Blacks to come to the pool. Then, when they had given up and left, Williams' people would arrive in force and hold a demonstration without interference.

Some of the informers, seeing for the first time in their lives fellow Blacks willing to stand up to the racists, became conscience-stricken. One such man, who had a long record of arrests and had spent years in prison, confessed that a group of local racists, including a high police official, had promised him five hundred dollars if he would kill Williams. Once they saw that Williams and the others meant business in their fight against discrimination, quite a few of the local toughs and ex-cons became hard-working and valuable members of their organization.

As the number of his supporters grew, hardly a thing took place that Williams wasn't informed of in advance. Whites from other parts of North Carolina soon began to tease their acquaintances from Monroe by saying, "Hey, are you from Union County where the niggers are running everything?" The embarrassment of the racists reached such a high point that the local politicians began making speeches and giving interviews to the press demanding something be done to stop the desegregation demonstrations. "We have to get rid of Williams. We have to get rid of that nigger," began to echo through the streets.

The reaction wasn't limited to the racists. The state and national NAACP officials began charging that Williams was operating the Union County branch as a private dictatorship.

"Democracy is a wonderful institution," Williams declared in response to his critics, "but only when everyone is experienced in its workings, has full information about the choices available, and there is lots of time to debate. The bourgeois elements who have complained about me aren't offering constructive, alternative ways to end segregation. Their sole purpose is to weaken our resolve in order to placate their racist employers. Yes, in a sense I am a dictator, but only because the vast majority of our NAACP members want me to be one. Once my leadership becomes unacceptable, the majority can either throw me out or resign en masse."

The attack spread to the "good people" of Monroe's Black community. One minister, in particular, started sermonizing against Williams' Guard, telling the women in his congregation not to let their husbands, sons, or boy friends join its ranks. "Those people are preparing for an unholy war," he would say. "What they're doing isn't right, isn't Christian, and won't work. They're bringing bloodshed and retribution down upon us all. At the first shot, they'll flee into the woods and leave us to pay for their sins." Although his exhortations swayed some of the older Blacks, they didn't seriously diminish the widespread support the Guard enjoyed.

As each effort to weaken the desegregation campaign failed, the Klansmen found themselves in an increasingly difficult position. Everyone in town knew of their threat to blow up Dr. Perry's house. Unless they acted, and acted soon, they would lose their credibility, and with it their power to coerce. But they hesitated to try anything against Blacks they knew to be armed and ready. Caught in this dilemma, they attempted a ruse.

Around four o'clock one morning, while it was still dark, the fourteen-year-old White newsboy who delivered papers in the area came bicycling up to Dr. Perry's house and threw a rolled-up copy of *The Monroe Enquirer* at his front door. Falling short, it landed on one of Williams' men dozing in a foxhole in the front yard. Waking with a yell, the guard, who said later he thought someone had thrown a stick of dynamite at him, pulled out his .38-caliber revolver and started blasting away. Sparks flew as the bullets ripped through the newsboy's bicycle.

Fortunately for everyone concerned, the guard's aim in his half-awake state wasn't very good. The newsboy's only injury was being frightened nearly out of his wits. When asked why he was delivering the paper at that unusual hour rather than at his regular time during the day, he hysterically told the Blacks that his boss had come to his house earlier that night and ordered him to do it.

Within minutes after the shots were fired, as if they had been waiting a few blocks away for something to happen, the police drove up. Appearing disappointed at finding the boy unharmed, they took him to the station house.

That afternoon the newsboy came back and told the Blacks that the police were trying to get him to say that they had attempted to kill him. He also said that his father, a poor sharecropper, had been told by the man who owned the farm where he worked that, if he didn't swear out a warrant, he would lose his job and his family would have to leave their house.

When Williams asked the boy, "Are you and your father going to do what the police and the landlord want?" he said, "No, I'm not going to lie. I had no business being out here in the dark. You colored fellows could have killed me if you'd wanted to, and nobody would've known. My daddy says he won't do it, either. So, I guess we'll just have to find someplace else to live."

When the boy and his father refused to charge the Blacks guarding Dr. Perry's house with attempted murder, their landlord did indeed put them out, and they were forced to leave the area. The Klan, apparently having set up the boy as a cat's paw to be wounded or killed, was foiled only because he and his father were so honest. Williams reflected that his group owed a great deal to those poor southern Whites who were willing to lose everything they had rather than give false testimony.

From then on, Guard members were careful not to open fire unless fairly certain they were being attacked.

A few days later, the chief of police drove up in front of Dr. Perry's house and called out, "Look, you fellows. I know you have a right to defend yourselves. The problem is that you have the wrong type of people in your Guard. Take that guy they call 'Mule Train.' Do you know he just got off the chain gang for cutting someone? And there is another guy with you who's been in prison for stealing. They're not the kind of people you should give guns to. Everybody in town would like it a lot better if you got good church people instead of such bad types."

Williams walked over to his car and said, "Chief Mauney. The reason we have those fellows is exactly because we know who they are and what they can do. If the Klan makes it necessary for us to kill, I want killers on my side—not church people." The chief rolled up the window of his car and drove away.

The Klan held an increasing number of rallies. After each one, cars would speed through the Black neighborhoods, their occupants shooting at homes and throwing rocks and bottles at pedestrians. Since such actions were seldom planned in advance, the Blacks' intelligence system couldn't always anticipate them. It was necessary to set up an emergency alarm system.

Observation posts were established in homes on the outskirts of Black neighborhoods. Every time the lookouts spotted Klan cars heading toward a Black district, they dialed certain telephone numbers and gave the alarm. While Guard members armed themselves and rushed to their posts, their wives would telephone others. Thus they could mobilize a couple of hundred men in only a few minutes. Convinced the telephone company was cooperating with their enemies and that their calls were monitored, when the Blacks gave the alarm, all they would say was, "They're coming." They never gave any specific details as to where their defense positions were or even who was calling whom.

In instances where Klan cars managed to enter a Black district without being spotted in advance, the first member of the Guard to see them would step outside of his house and fire a designated number of shots in the air. Depending on how many were fired, the other guards in that district would either take up predetermined positions or rush to where the shots had come from.

As the Klan rallies increased in frequency, so did the number of shooting skirmishes. Unable to get at Dr. Perry's house, the racists began to set off explosives in vacant lots on the outskirts of Black residential districts. The Blacks soon became accustomed to being jolted out of bed in the middle of the night by a loud blast or two. Whenever the police were called about the explosions, they would wait until the next day before coming around to investigate. Then they would say, "It must've been some teen-agers out 'funnin' with firecrackers."

One night Williams and some of his men decided to go do a little "funnin" themselves. By telephoning the wife of a Klansman and pretending to be one of their supporters, Mabel was able to learn they were holding a rally at a place called Marchville, about fourteen miles from Monroe. Twelve men, including Williams and Dr. Perry, got their guns and drove there in two cars. They found a crowd of three or four thousand Klansmen and their supporters gathered in a field, listening to speeches being given from the back of a truck outfitted with a portable public address system and floodlights. The scene resembled a traveling circus. Many of the Klansmen wore hoods and capes, but they weren't masked, as that had been forbidden by state law some years earlier.

The main Klan speaker, a Baptist preacher, was introduced as the "Cyclops." While the other Blacks sat silently in their cars with the windows open and their rifles prominently displayed, Williams and Dr. Perry got out and stood at the back of the crowd. The Cyclops was saying, "The niggers are trying to take over the world. Unless we white folks band together and wipe them out, the day's not far off when they'll overrun us."

Since there was a lot of gossip in the papers about Ava Gardner dating Sammy Davis, Jr., he soon got around to talking about her. "Right now, right this very minute," he shouted, "one of our own girls, a white girl from right here in the state of North Carolina, a white girl who went to our Sunday Schools and was educated with our tax money, a white girl who became a big movie star, is out there in Hollywood running around with a one-eyed nigger coon. Yes," the Cyclops shouted, "she has been with so many men that no one will have her now but a one-eyed nigger coon. And sure as the sun will rise in the morning, the same God-awful thing will happen to every other white girl, to your own little daughters and granddaughters, if we ever let those nigger-loving Bolsheviks in Washington and New York integrate the schools!"

At that moment a Klan patrol spotted Williams and Dr. Perry. But when they saw they were covered by the guns of the Black men in the cars, they backed off without saying anything. One of them ran down to the speaker's platform and whispered to the Cyclops, who then announced, "I understand we have some

burr-headed niggers with us here tonight. They're out there at the
back of the crowd, and I'm glad to know they want to hear our
message. Yes, we always welcome burr-headed niggers, because
they bring us good luck."

Williams' group stayed until shortly before the rally ended,
then left without any trouble. But as the KKK's terror campaign
continued, and the police continued to refuse to do anything
about it, Williams and the others finally decided to give the Klan a
taste of their own medicine. They drove to a rally at a place called
Meadow Springs, about eight miles outside of Monroe, and
parked nearby with their lights off. The Klansmen were milling
around in their hoods and robes. While some wore white and others black, the Cyclops, Kleagles, and other high officials were
draped in gold. They were singing, preaching, and praying by the
flickering light from oil-soaked, wooden crosses. Many had
brought along their wives and children, some of whom were attired in miniature Klan robes.

One of the Black veterans had made a dynamite bomb and
placed it in a large paper bag so that no one could see the fuse
burning. As he watched the Klansmen doing their hate act, instead of setting off the bomb in a nearby field as originally
planned, he said, "Goddamn it. Let's throw it right on top of
them. And to hell with the consequences!" Williams had a hard
time arguing him out of it. "The Klan has to come after us sooner
or later," he said, "and that will be the moment to blast them, not
now." Lighting the fuse and throwing the bomb into a ditch bor-
dering the road, the Blacks quickly drove away, but it didn't go
off.

Just before dawn Williams and the others returned to the deserted field and retrieved the unexploded bomb before it was discovered. Had it been found, the police might have traced it back
to them. A puddle of water in the bottom of the ditch had caused
the fuse to go out.

Toward the end of the summer of 1957 the tension mounted
until some members of the Guard were almost at the breaking
point. Night after sleepless night of standing watch was beginning
to take its toll. Early one morning one of the men in Dr. Perry's
garage began talking. "I want them to come now," he said. "Oh,
God, how I want them to come right now, so we can kill them all."
Tears ran down his face as he continued, "My old grandmother

told me what they did to us back in slavery. I was just a little boy, but I remember everything she said—how they used to beat her, how they treated our people like animals. They did us bad for hundreds of years, and they are doing the same to us today. But now they're going to pay for their crimes. I'll kill them all, even if I have to die to do it. Please, God, let them come right now."

When the Klan finally did come, on the night of Friday, October 11, 1957, it was with the Monroe police force preparing their way. Only a small number of Blacks were stationed at Dr. Perry's house. Their job was to hold off any attack until the main body of the Guard could reach the scene. So the first thing the police did was to set up a roadblock on the main street leading to the area. The moment the Klan motorcade was observed forming in the White part of town, the Blacks' alarm system went into operation. But when the members of the Guard headed for their defense posts at Dr. Perry's, the police at the roadblock tried to stop them. One man was jogging along the street carrying a semiautomatic shotgun when a cop shouted at him, "Hey, boy. You can't go down there with that gun. Come over here and leave it with us." The Black shouted back, "Man, this is my goddamned gun. You put your hands on it and one of us is going to hell right now!" The cops at the roadblock were speechless. No Black had ever spoken to them like that before. They let him go past without any more trouble, and they said nothing as the other members of the Guard arrived.

Williams and Dr. Perry were out in one of their roving patrol cars when the news came through about the roadblock. Rushing to the scene, they asked the police why they were there. One answered, "Why, Perry, all we're doing is trying to protect you. Isn't that what you've been asking for all this time?"

At that very instant a caravan of over fifty Klan vehicles, headed by several police cars, tried to get through to Dr. Perry's house, and firing broke out. When a souped-up Ford full of Whites came roaring down the street right past the roadblock, Williams asked the cops, "If you're here to protect us, why are you letting those people through?"

The police, who hadn't made the slightest effort to stop the Ford, replied, "Well, we can't stand here talking to you and do our job at the same time."

"Okay," Williams said, "you stay here. We'll take care of

them ourselves." Four of the thirty men stationed around Dr. Perry's house jumped into a car with him, and they set off after the Whites.

The driver of the Ford, possibly being a Klansman up from South Carolina, didn't seem to know the layout of Monroe. In trying to get away, he inadvertently turned into a dead-end street. Knowing that he would have to turn around and come back the same way to get out, the five Blacks parked their car and stood in the middle of the street with their guns at the ready. Williams was carrying a .45-caliber Colt automatic and a 7-mm Luger.

When the driver of the Ford saw the Blacks' guns pointing at his windshield, he screeched to a stop. One of Williams' men walked over to the car and asked the four young Whites in it, "What in goddamn hell you doing in these parts?"

One answered, "We sure are sorry. We're from out of town and got lost."

At this another Black said, "These sons-o-bitches aren't lost. I saw their car in the Klan motorcade a couple of hours ago. They came here to shoot-up the place. Let's blast them."

"Oh, no, mister," the White who was driving implored. "We don't want to shoot at nobody. If you'll just please let us go, we promise we'll never make trouble for you again."

At this the Black slapped him hard across the face, and shouted, "Stop lying, you motherfucker, or I'll blow your brains out!" He told Williams later he had seen those very same Whites displaying rifles to the other Klansmen when the motorcade was forming.

Convinced that the Blacks had made their point, Williams decided to get the Whites out of the area before his men lost control. He told the driver, "I want to see your wheels spinning all the way up this block. If I don't, I am going to shoot you myself. Now get the hell out of here."

Stammering "Thank you, sir," the Klansman slammed his foot down on the gas pedal and tore out so fast that he laid a streak of burned rubber on the pavement behind him.

Similar scenes were taking place all over town. The Klansmen had driven into the Black areas to terrorize them, but when they suddenly found themselves surrounded by armed Blacks they started smashing into each other's cars in a rush to get away. Instead of acting like "niggers," hiding in their houses with the shutters closed and the lights out, the Blacks were roaming the streets with guns, shooting out the tires of the KKK cars, shattering their windshields with buckshot, and beating up those racists who tried to escape on foot.

While there were no reports of anyone being killed or badly wounded, the Klan suffered a severe defeat. For the first time in U.S. history a Black community had organized and defended itself with gunfire, and had won. There was an almost total news blackout in the White press about the battle. One of the few papers reporting it was the Norfolk, Virginia, *Journal and Guide,* a Black publication. It was also mentioned in the *Afro-American* and in *Jet* Magazine.

The events of the month before in Little Rock, Arkansas, where President Eisenhower called the U.S. Army to enforce school integration, had been written about and televised all over the world. The national news media, however, didn't seem anxious to publicize the fact that Blacks had demonstrated they were capable of defending themselves.

Two weeks later, when a group of armed American Indians broke up a Klan rally in a neighboring county, they got worldwide press coverage. The idea that the Indians, a tiny minority, could chase the hooded Klansmen out of their territory seemed amusing to the network television commentators. But, while it had sentimental value, it posed no danger to the status quo. What the Blacks had done in Monroe, on the other hand, appeared to impress them as a potential threat. If twenty million other U.S. Blacks followed their example, it could lead to the end of their being oppressed and exploited. Both the political and economic power structure of a large part of the nation would be unbalanced. The wire services and TV networks buried the story—as if hoping that, by ignoring it long enough, they could make the specter of Blacks with guns go away by itself.

Despite the news blackout on what had happened, the KKK got the message, and their raids and rallies ended. The Monroe city officials, who had earlier defended the Klan's right to organize terrorizing motorcades, held an emergency session and drafted an ordinance banning such demonstrations without a permit issued by the chief of police.

Despite the resistance of Kelley Alexander, a local Black mortician who headed the State Conference of Branches, many of the other state NAACP officials now came out and publicly declared that the desegregation "stand-ins" against the Monroe swimming pool had merit. They began talking about taking the case to the courts on the basis that, since both federal and municipal tax money had been used to build and maintain it, denying Black taxpayers admission to the pool was unconstitutional. The moment the Monroe town officials got wind of this, they said, "Why, if all you people want is your own pool, we'll be happy to build one for you." Winter was at hand and the pool closed until the following year, so their apparent concession to the Blacks' demands helped cool interest in the question.

Back in 1957 it had been extremely daring to try to integrate a swimming pool. Civil-rights demonstrators were being beaten and mutilated elsewhere for far less provocative actions. However, once the racists saw that the Blacks weren't begging for justice, but were ready to fight for it, they seemed to change their minds about using force. So long as Williams' Guard stood by with guns, there was less violence at the civil-rights demonstrations in Monroe than in any other area in the South.

As the news of what they were doing spread through Black America, support began to pour in. Even domestics and field hands who earned as little as $35 made weekly contributions of $5 or more. People from California and New England sent in membership applications and dues money to the Union County NAACP. They lived too far away to attend meetings, but it made them proud to be able to say they belonged to the one NAACP branch in the country that had fought off the Klan.

Williams and his followers also received money with which to buy guns and ammunition—some even sent by the congregations of White churches. It wasn't long before there was a moderate but steady income from these sources. This led the members of the NAACP branch to suggest that, since he was devoting all of his time to the organization, Williams should draw a small salary. It provided enough so that he no longer had to worry about food for his wife and children.

That year, 1957, marked a major turning point in Williams' life. Until then he had been just another isolated, powerless individual. But, like the rest of Black America, the Blacks of Monroe were awakening. They'd chosen him to be their spokesman in demanding an end to segregation and exploitation. He hadn't con-

sciously sought the role, but felt that he would have been betraying his people had he refused to accept it.

It was also a very sad year, for during it Williams' father had
died. For the first time in his life the house on Boyte Street was
empty of his brothers and sisters, all four of whom had moved far
away. He, his wife, and their boys were its sole inhabitants.

One chill winter day while shopping in the White business
district, he met the mayor on the street. "Williams," the mayor
asked, "when are you going to stop making trouble and settle
down? Your father was a good man. Why can't you be like him?"

"Mayor," he responded, "you and your people thought that
by getting me fired from my job and putting pressure on me, you
could force me to either shut up or leave town. Well, all you've
succeeded in doing is pushing me into a new occupation. You've
transformed me from an amateur, part-time critic into a paid, full-
time agitator."

Chapter Six

SEX, VIOLENCE, AND THE NAACP

Failing to halt the desegregation drive by force, the racists turned to other forms of attack. One of their prime targets was the Monroe Unitarian Fellowship, whose initial support for Williams they claimed had led to all the trouble. Its members were criticized by the other Whites, and some were threatened with loss of jobs. The economic sanctions extended even to Mr. Shoup, the wealthy founder of the Unitarian Church in Monroe. His clients began canceling contracts, and many of his business properties lost their tenants. He also received phone calls from Klan types who cursed him as a "nigger-lover," and warned him to leave town or be killed. Despite his valiant efforts to keep the Fellowship operating, it eventually lost most of its members and dissolved.

In contrast to Shoup's refusal to be intimidated, Harry Golden, the well-known journalist, who lived in Charlotte and had been a frequent speaker at the Monroe Unitarian Center, did a complete about face. When Williams and Dr. Perry went to him for support, he turned them down cold, saying, "Your involvement with guns will lose you the sympathy of White liberals. North Carolina is a civilized state, and the things you claim are going on here are little more than figments of your imagination." Ironically, a few years later when Golden's own life was threatened by the Klan, Williams heard that he went out and bought a gun.

The pressure against Williams as an individual also took the form of police harassment. Every time he exceeded the speed limit by a few miles per hour, or turned a corner a bit too sharply, the cops would suddenly appear out of the bushes and give him a ticket.

In October, 1958, he was surprised to receive a telephone call from the mayor of Monroe, who said, "Williams, you seem handy at causing problems. Now let's see how good you are at solving

111

them. A couple of colored juvenile delinquents have been jailed for molesting a little White girl. I'd appreciate it if you got their mothers to sign the authorizations so's we can send them to reform school where they belong."

When Williams went to see the mothers of the two Black boys, he found to his horror that the mayor's "juvenile delinquents" were only seven and nine years old. David Simpson, age seven, and Hanover Thompson, age nine, had been playing with a group of White children when one of them, a seven-year-old named Sissy Sutton, sat on the older boy's lap and kissed him on the cheek. When her mother heard about it, she hysterically began scrubbing the little White girl's face with soap, and her father loaded his shotgun and rushed out to kill the boys. Fortunately, the police got there first, arresting the Black children on a charge of "attempted rape."

Rather than persuading the boys' mothers to agree to send them to the reformatory, Williams telephoned the other NAACP officers. They decided to intervene.

The next day they learned that the authorities were to hold a hearing at the courthouse that afternoon. But when they tried to attend, the police kept them out, saying, "The hearing is over. All that's going on in there now is the sentencing."

"How could you have held a hearing without the boys' mothers being present?" they asked.

"Since the judge felt it better not to mix the races, we held a separate-but-equal hearing with the White girl and her parents this morning," the cops responded laughingly.

That afternoon Judge Hampton Price sentenced the two little Black boys to remain in the state reformatory until they were twenty-one—which meant terms of twelve and fourteen years.

Realizing that the local NAACP treasury would be insufficient, Williams called Kelley Alexander, the Monroe mortician who headed the North Carolina State Conference of NAACP Branches, and asked for help. Alexander refused, saying he wouldn't let the organization get mixed up in a "sex case." A similar negative response came from Roy Wilkins, the executive secretary of the NAACP national office in New York. The injustice of two children being imprisoned seemed secondary to avoiding an issue involving "sex" between Blacks and Whites.

A few days after the national NAACP's refusal to intervene,

Conrad Lynn, a Black lawyer with the New York Emergency Civil Liberties Committee, volunteered to defend the boys without charge. Then *The Nation* sent a reporter to Monroe to do a story. Articles began appearing in various other liberal and left-wing publications, and the case slowly began to attract national attention.

The major newspapers and television networks refused to carry anything about it at first, but it wasn't long before the story got overseas. When foreign newspapers began featuring headlines such as BLACK CHILDREN ARRESTED FOR A KISS, CBS, NBC, and the *New York Times* finally broke their silence. Soon correspondents began arriving from all over the globe to report on the infamous "Kissing Case."

When Joyce Edgirton, who had been sent over by the *London News Chronicle,* asked Williams' help in interviewing and photographing the two imprisoned boys, he told her it would probably be impossible for a journalist, especially one with a camera, to see them. It was decided that, instead of identifying herself as a reporter, she would pretend to be a social worker. Together with one of the boys' mothers, they drove down to the reformatory at Southern Pines. Unknown to either woman, Williams had brought along a simple box camera hidden in a bag of fruit.

Because of the bad publicity the state was receiving, the Black officials who ran the reformatory behaved very courteously, especially in the presence of a White "social worker." When Miss Edgirton suggested that she could speak to the boys more comfortably if the guards weren't present, they left the room. The moment they were alone, Williams pulled out his camera and began snapping pictures. Once she recovered from her surprise, Miss Edgirton suggested he give her the roll of exposed film. That way, should the officials discover the camera and confiscate it, the photos might be saved.

They returned to Monroe without being apprehended. Taking the film, she left for England that same day. A week or so later, her interview, illustrated with Williams' photos, appeared on the front page of her newspaper. Its publication triggered an international avalanche of criticism; protest committees were formed in various nations, and the U.S. government became so embarrassed that the Voice of America began to discuss the "Kissing Case" in its broadcasts. But not even the State Department's expert propagandists could think up a logical excuse for the jailing of seven- and nine-year-old children.

The North Carolina authorities seemed confused by the widespread publicity the case was receiving. They had been imprisoning Black children for years, and the newspapers had never bothered to mention it before. In looking for someone to blame, they turned to Williams, charging that he had created the entire affair. In a sense they were right. He was issuing press bulletins, holding news conferences, setting up interviews, telephoning the TV networks and wire services, and doing whatever else he could think of to let people know about the case. The Marine Corps had refused to train him as an information specialist because he was Black, but he was rapidly learning the techniques of propaganda and mass communication by himself.

Each day more pressure was exerted to drop the case. Williams was approached by Kelley Alexander and Charles McClain, the NAACP's state field representative. They told him that Harry Golden, in addition to being one of the NAACP's most important advisers and supporters in North Carolina, was a friend of Governor Luther Hodges. "Both the Governor and Mr. Golden," they said, "want to settle this matter. If you'll just cool it with the press, after a while the boys will be sent home quietly. The parents of the White girl will never know they aren't still in the reformatory. Everybody will be satisfied. It's the best and easiest way out."

"It may seem like the easiest way out to you," Williams responded, "but it doesn't resolve the principal issue of the case. Do you mean to say that we should stop protesting the jailing of innocent Black people, much less children, merely to keep the Whites from criticizing us? Instead of trying to get me to shut up, the NAACP leadership should be supporting our fight to expose the criminals responsible for imprisoning those two little boys." When they saw he wouldn't cooperate, Alexander and McClain left.

Williams felt it was predictable that such men would be more concerned about rocking the boat than about the fate of two little boys. Alexander, after all, had a successful funeral parlor business, lived in a big house, and drove a new Cadillac. What the working people in the NAACP branch found most ludicrous about the state and national NAACP officials was their fear of becoming involved in a "sex" case. They knew full well that sexual relations are one of the most primal elements in the entire structure of racist oppression.

Sex between Blacks and Whites is a very strange thing in the South, Williams reflected. The color line in copulation is strictly one way. So long as he doesn't marry her or flaunt her in public, the racists consider it perfectly natural for a White male to have intercourse with a Black female. The slightest suggestion of sex between a Black man and a White woman, however, sends them running for their shotguns, lynch ropes, and Klan bedsheets. Before Abolition, the plantation owners inflicted themselves on their female slaves both for sexual gratification and because the offspring of such unions, being lighter-skinned than their mothers, brought higher prices at the slave market. It wasn't unknown for commercially minded Southern "gentlemen" to then force themselves upon their own daughters, and even granddaughters, in order to breed expensive "quadroons" and "octaroons." The fornicating with and selling of one's offspring was a depravity unique to the United States. The Spanish in Latin America, the Dutch in Indonesia, and the British in India at least had the decency to accept responsibility for the mixed-ancestry children they fathered.

The White Southerners' sex habits didn't change with the end of legalized slavery. Over one hundred years have passed, but their abuse of Black women continues to this day. After four centuries of White-imposed miscegenation, few of the over twenty million Blacks in the United States are of pure African descent.

From a logical point of view, a child of mixed parentage is just as much "half-White" as he is "half-Black." However, the racist nature of American society is revealed in the laws of states like Mississippi, which define as a "Negro" anyone whose ancestry is as little as one-sixty-fourth African. The premise of such legislation is that having only one Black among your sixty-four great-great-great-great-grandparents is enough of a "taint" to make you an "inferior." Of course this specious theory can also be viewed conversely. One could make the equally foolish claim that Blacks are so "superior" that the sperm or ova of only one of them overpowers the heritage of sixty-three White ancestors.

Not only do most of the Blacks in the United States have varying degrees of European ancestry, the opposite also holds true. Some geneticists have calculated that at least 51 percent of

those Whites whose families have lived here since the beginning of
the nineteenth century or earlier have some African genes. This is
especially so in the small towns of the South, where many families
can be traced back to the Revolutionary War or even the
Mayflower. Some of the very Monroe Whites out to kill Williams
were probably his distant cousins, through his White or part-
White great-grandmother.

Since the racists don't mind sleeping with Black women, their
horror of Black men doing the same with their females must be
based on something other than avoiding intimate contact, Williams concluded. If every White woman refused to have intercourse with every White man who had ever slept with a Black
woman, there would be few, if any, White babies born in the
South. The "pure Southern belles" know full well that, after their
"gentlemen callers" gallantly kiss their hands good-night, they
usually head for the red light district to get a piece of "mulattuh
titty."

In order to rationalize the brutal treatment they visit upon
them, the racists try to treat Black women as domestic animals, fit
only for labor, illicit pleasure, and bearing new generations of field
hands. And they do everything they can think of to castrate Black
men and turn them into bootlicking eunuchs.

Nine-year-old Hanover Thompson's being sent to the reformatory for allowing a White girl to kiss him on the cheek was the
South's way of demonstrating that the one-way color line on sex is
absolutely uncrossable. And seven-year-old David Simpson's
mere presence at the scene of the "crime" was enough to jail him
as well.

In almost every one of their press releases, especially those
sent to northern liberal publications, Williams' people mentioned
the national NAACP's failure to support them in the case. This
soon created so much pressure that the national office was forced
to invite Williams, Dr. Perry, and Conrad Lynn to come to New
York for a meeting in late December, 1958. At the meeting, the
NAACP lawyers present said first that the "Kissing Case" involved no constitutional issues. "Constitutional or not," Williams
told them, "every parent in the world sympathizes with the mothers of those two boys. This is more than just a cold legal matter.
It's a question of basic human emotions, and one hell of a violation of civil rights. You have to help us free them."

In response, one of the lawyers said that, on second thought, a constitutional question might well be raised. The North Carolina Penal Code under which the boys were imprisoned permitted sixteen-year-old Blacks to be sentenced to the chain gang, while Whites had to be eighteen, thus violating the Bill of Rights' guarantee of equal justice under the law. Also, when they were first arrested, instead of being detained in a juvenile facility, the little boys had been locked up in the same cell with adult criminals. They'd told their mothers that during the six days they were held in the Monroe jail the policemen had run around with white sheets over their heads trying to terrorize them. The NAACP lawyers finally decided all of these points could be added together to prove to the federal courts that North Carolina was discriminating against Blacks both through its laws and prison procedures.

Roy Wilkins then took Williams aside and said, "Look, since our lawyers are taking over the case, get rid of this Conrad Lynn fellow. You don't need him any more."

"I'm afraid I don't work like that," Williams answered. "He was the only man we could get when nobody else would help us. Just because he isn't a NAACP lawyer, we're not going to fire him now." Wilkins lowered his voice and said, "That's not why we want him out. It's because he is a known Communist."

Lynn had already told Williams he'd once belonged to the Communist Party but was expelled from it in 1937 after refusing to go along with the Stalinists. When Williams mentioned this, Glouster B. Curtis, another NAACP official, said, "Even if he isn't in the Party any more, he's still some kind of a Trotskyite."

"His politics don't interest me," Williams retorted. "We don't care who else you bring in, Conrad Lynn stays."

Before Williams returned to Monroe, Wilkins told him, "I've been watching you, Williams. You've got a lot of drive and conviction, qualities which are pretty scarce. You're wasting your time in that small town. Why don't you move up here to New York and let us find you the kind of responsible position you deserve?"

"I like it just fine in Monroe," Williams said.

"If you aren't careful," Wilkins continued, "you may starve to death. I hear you've been having trouble finding work down there."

"No," Williams answered, "my people share their food and

cash with me, and they've stood next to me with guns in their hands. They haven't abandoned me, and I won't desert them. But maybe that's the sort of relationship you guys here in New York can't understand?" Wilkins said nothing more. Williams was certain he'd made an enemy.

The news that the NAACP national office, with its battery of lawyers, was entering the "Kissing Case" caused the North Carolina authorities to change their tactics. In an attempt to blunt the criticism directed against them, they announced, "The reason those boys are in the reformatory is because their divorced mothers are unemployed and unfit to care for them. Our only motives in this case are humanitarian."

What really got them upset was newspaper headlines about a petition calling for the boys to be freed which was signed by fifteen thousand students and faculty members at a Rotterdam, Holland, Catholic school named after President Franklin Delano Roosevelt. When the petition was sent to Mrs. Eleanor Roosevelt, his widow, it stirred up even more criticism than had existed before. The "liberal" state of North Carolina was being castigated before the entire world.

In an apparent attempt at retaliation, the police arrested Dr. Perry and charged him with "criminal abortion." The racists were convinced he was the real brains behind everything the Monroe NAACP group was doing and assumed that without the money he earned as a physician they would be unable to keep themselves supplied with guns and ammunition. Dr. Perry's accuser was Lily Mae Rape, a poor Black girl who had been doing cleanup work in the Monroe hospital. She testified that several White doctors, although refusing to give her an abortion themselves, had referred her to Dr. Perry. She alleged that he performed the illegal surgery for $25 down, with the additional money to be paid when she could get it. After the operation she developed a fever, she said, and was forced to ask a White doctor at the hospital for medicine. This doctor, who just happened to be a member of the KKK, then testified that he had examined her and found evidence of a recent abortion.

During the trial, Lily Mae Rape somehow acquired the money to buy a fine new wardrobe. She was housed in a pleasant room at the local hotel, and was even driven around and taken to dinner by the local chief of police.

One of the defense witnesses was the former head of the County Medical Department. He drove to Monroe from forty miles away to swear that, when Dr. Perry had worked for him, he had refused to issue sterilization permits for the Welfare Department on the grounds that it was forbidden by his Catholic religious beliefs.

Since Lily Mae Rape swore that no one else was present during the operation except Dr. Perry and herself, it became a matter of whose word the all-White jury would find more acceptable. Dr. Perry was convicted, sentenced to five years in prison, and deprived of his license to practice medicine.

But if the racists thought jailing Dr. Perry would stop the Blacks' activities, they soon found out how wrong they were. They fought all the harder.

As part of his efforts to free the two little boys, Williams traveled around the United States giving talks about the "Kissing Case." The international publicity had attracted both the U.S. Communist Party and the Trotskyite Socialist Workers Party. In addition to the church, college, and civil-liberties groups which invited him to speak, he made several appearances which he later learned were arranged by groups affiliated with the U.S. Communist Party and the Socialist Workers Party. He was convinced that some of them saw the plight of the boys less as a personal tragedy than as a way of highlighting the injustices of the capitalist system. Still, he welcomed their support, just as he welcomed that of everyone else who was willing to help.

Williams was eventually asked if he would consider joining the SWP, but the Trotskyites and the USCP both impressed him as being primarily concerned with organizing White workers. He felt that they looked upon Blacks as mere auxiliaries to whom they would magnanimously grant equality once their revolution came to power. But Williams was only interested in belonging to organizations whose first dedication was to the welfare of Blacks.

He wasn't against the leftists. Like so many other American Blacks, he saw them as friends. In addition to always speaking out for equal rights, the fact that they were constantly being attacked by the power structure automatically made them allies. Very few Blacks Williams knew had an opinion about the U.S.S.R. before Paul Robeson went there and was given a big reception. The resulting U.S. press attack on him, while intended to make socialism look bad, affected many Blacks in exactly the opposite manner. It's common to look upon the enemy of your enemy as your friend.

By late January, 1959, the reaction to the "Kissing Case" had so embarrassed the North Carolina authorities that they decided to hold a hearing to determine if the boys should be released. The state attorney general, Malcolm Sewell, was to be in charge of the proceedings. Considered a strong future contender for the governorship, he may have anticipated that publicity from the case would enhance his career. With reporters present from England, France, Italy, Germany, and elsewhere, it certainly was an opportunity to get into the public eye.

No sooner had the hearing begun than Sewell announced, "I want Robert Franklin Williams on the witness stand." Surprised, one of the NAACP national office's lawyers stood up and said, "I object to Mr. Williams being called to testify. He's not related to the boys, and nothing he can say is relative to the case." But his objection was overruled, and Williams had to take the stand.

The first thing the attorney general asked him was, "Do you know Carl Braden?" When he answered "Yes," Sewell went on to ask if Williams belonged to the same civil-rights group that Braden did. He answered "Yes" to that as well, it being one of several groups which he had recently joined. Then Sewell demanded, "Did you know that this same Carl Braden was convicted of sedition against the state of Kentucky?"

"I knew that he was convicted for selling his home to a Black man and that the Ku Klux Klan dynamited it while he and some Blacks were trying to guard it," Williams retorted. "But I didn't know you could call that sedition."

Being answered in such an "uppity" manner by a Black seemed to disturb the attorney general. The room grew quiet as anger flushed his face. "Isn't Dr. Perry, the vice president of your NAACP branch, also a member of the group you and Carl Braden belong to?" he asked. "And is it not true that this same Dr. Perry has been implicated in a case of criminal abortion?"

"No," Williams answered, "I would say he's been 'framed' in that case."

"So," demanded Sewell, "are you saying that the courts of the state of North Carolina of the United States of America would 'frame' a man?"

"I don't have to say they *would* do it," Williams responded. "They've already done it."

The attorney general turned an apoplectic red. Blacks just weren't supposed to answer the state's highest law officer that way. Then came the big question: "Where were you the night before Christmas of last year?"

"I was in New York," Williams answered.

"And what were you doing in New York that night?" Sewell continued, giving the impression that he considered being in New York tantamount to being in Moscow.

At last his purpose seemed clear to Williams. Rather than holding the hearing to determine the rightness or wrongness of the state's actions against the little boys, Sewell was trying to turn it into an old-fashioned, Joe McCarthy-type witch hunt to divert public attention from the real issue.

"I'll tell you what I was doing up in free New York," Williams declared. "I was up there trying to raise money to bring some freedom and justice into this social jungle called Dixie." That seemed to stop Attorney General Sewell in his tracks. He looked so exasperated that many of those in the hearing room burst out laughing. Recovering his composure, he tried to get Williams to admit that he was part of some sort of conspiracy to defame the United States, but Williams continued to parry his insinuations.

The Associated Press carried the story of their confrontation all over the world, and *The Charlotte Observer* printed it on the front page. It wasn't the first time that the authorities had tried to cover their tracks with a red scare, nor would it be the last.

Apparently afraid of further embarrassment, the state acted quickly to end the case. Around two weeks after the hearing, the mothers of the imprisoned boys were approached by the State Welfare Board and told that, if they moved to Charlotte, they would receive cash allowances and other benefits. When they accepted, instead of taking them there by bus, the Welfare Board had them driven in a new state-owned automobile. "Now that you're living in better conditions," they were told, "we've decided you're once again fit to have custody of your boys."

On February 13, 1959, after almost five months in jail, the two Black children were quietly taken out of the reformatory and returned home. Officially at least, the "Kissing Case" was over.

Despite the freeing of the boys, the fight to gain equal rights in Monroe was far from won. By showing their readiness to defend themselves against the Klan's violence and then by bringing a blatant example of racist injustice to the attention of the world, the Blacks had gained a great deal of self-respect. But the power structure wasn't ready to stop its oppression. If they couldn't frighten them by wearing white bedsheets or crying "Reds," they could still use their control of the courts to remind the Blacks that they had no legal rights.

Not long after the end of the "Kissing Case," Mrs. Georgia White, a Black mother of five, was cleaning the corridor in a local hotel when a White railway engineer named Brutus Shaw, claiming she was making too much noise, kicked her down a flight of steps. When Williams' NAACP group demanded that the chief of police arrest Shaw for assault, he said he couldn't do it because there weren't any witnesses. It was only when they threatened to bring in NAACP lawyers that he changed his mind. Brutus Shaw didn't even appear in court on the day he was scheduled to answer the assault charge, but the judge refused to indict him, and the case was dropped.

That same day a Black man known to be mentally incompetent was tried on the complaint of a White woman who testified he had looked at her in a "frightening manner." Despite the defendant's testifying that he'd knocked on the woman's door only to inquire if she had any scrap iron or other junk to give away, the judge sentenced him to six months on the chain gang.

A third case heard that day involved Mrs. Ruth Reed, an eight-month-pregnant Black woman who had been the victim of an attempted rape. A White man had forced his way into her home, beating her and tearing off most of her clothing. Struggling furiously, she had managed to run out of the house. But he had caught up to her on the highway, knocked her to the ground, and beat her again. The thing that saved her was that her six-year-old son picked up a fallen tree limb and hit the would-be rapist on the head. With her assailant's attention diverted, Mrs. Reed gained sanctuary in the home of a neighboring White woman.

In this case as well, the Monroe chief of police had been reluctant to make an arrest, but after Mrs. Reed's White neighbor courageously testified to seeing the pregnant Black woman, hysterical and half-nude, being chased down the road, the authorities were forced to issue an indictment. During the weeks preceding the trial, Mrs. Reed's brothers approached Williams and said they were going to kill her attacker. He managed to convince them not to do it, arguing that, with a White woman as an eyewitness, even the most racist jury would have to find the man guilty. "Well, then," one of the brothers asked, "how about machine-gunning his house or tossing some sticks of dynamite onto his front porch just to shake him up?"

"You can't do any of those things," Williams insisted. "The only reason we're armed is because the police won't protect us against the Klan, not so's we can go around punishing people without a trial."

"What good is a trial?" they demanded. "The judge is White. The jury is White. And the prosecutor is White. They'll never punish a White man for attacking a Black woman. The only way we can get them to stop beating on us is to let them know we'll smash them whenever they try it."

"It's going to be different this time," Williams assured them, "because I've arranged for a White woman lawyer to come down from New York to make certain the case is handled right."

His idea was to show the Monroe authorities that, unless the Blacks were given the full protection of the law, they would continue to let the whole world know about it. But shortly after the lawyer arrived, Williams realized they were going to have trouble. She was the sort of liberal who thinks there is some merit on each side of a question, and that all that is necessary is for some very wise person to arbitrate a compromise between the opposing factions.

As soon as he learned the lawyer was in town, the mayor invited her to dinner. He gave her a good stiff dose of southern hospitality, speaking softly and moderately, and telling her how sympathetic the White people of Monroe had always been toward their Negroes. Then she was invited to meet one of the prosecutors handling the case. He gave her his personal assurance that the trial would be conducted fairly.

It wasn't long before she said to Williams, "I think you've mishandled the situation. You simply don't understand the ways of southern Whites. They are extremely cordial and responsible people. They want to see justice done just as much as you do. All that your publicizing of the case does is antagonize them." He tried to explain that she was being deceived, that the politeness shown her was only a false front, but she wouldn't listen. "If anyone doesn't understand the southern Whites," he finally said, "it's you. We Blacks know what they really mean, because we have to live with them."

As soon as the attempted rape trial began, the defense attorney got the judge to allow the accused's wife to sit next to him, just as if she, too, were being prosecuted. In his appeal to the jury he said, "You see this man. This is his wife—a White woman, one of God's lovely creatures, a pure flower of life. Do you think he would have left her for *that?*" By "that," he was referring to Mrs. Reed, implying that, being Black and pregnant, she couldn't appear attractive to any White man. "This fine fellow is not guilty of any crime," he concluded. "He was just drinking and having a little fun."

The White woman lawyer Williams had brought down from New York, despite her objections, wasn't even allowed to take the floor. After deliberating for a few minutes, the jury returned a verdict of acquittal. The would-be rapist was let off scot-free.

The moment the verdict was announced, the courtroom went wild. The Black women spectators started moaning and crying. The judge banged his gavel and shouted for quiet, but their laments and protests grew louder and louder. The acquitted White man, who had been all smiles the moment he heard the verdict, had to be taken out the back door by the police to avoid being torn to bits on the spot.

The Black women then began crying, "Williams. Williams. It's all your fault. That man should be dead by now. He should have been punished like he deserved. You saved him. Now they know they can do anything they want to us, and our men won't lift a finger."

Williams knew they were right. He, and he alone, had argued Mrs. Reed's brothers out of doing what common sense told them had to be done. He had permitted their minor victory in the "Kissing Case" to convince him that public exposure could compel the Monroe power structure to give Blacks equal justice, but he had been wrong. It was one thing to embarrass the North Carolina state government into freeing two falsely imprisoned little boys, and quite another to expect a jury of small town southern Whites to convict one of their own for something so minor in their eyes as attacking a Black woman.

By calling in the White woman lawyer from New York he felt he'd built up false hopes in his people, making their suffering all the worse. Their struggle wasn't going to be won for them by middle-class liberals who dreamed of being peacemakers. She had mistakenly thought that the attack on Mrs. Reed was an isolated deed by an aberrant individual and hadn't understood that it was an integral part of the racist system. The judge and jury, by acquitting the would-be rapist, seemed to Williams to be demonstrating that they believed Whites had the right to injure Blacks at will. On the same day, in the same court, two Whites who had viciously attacked Black women had been let off without even a slap on the wrist, while a Black man was given hard labor for merely looking at a White female.

As he stood there thinking about these things, Williams became angrier and angrier. The sight of the women moaning and crying added to his fury. He felt himself completely turning over inside. Had he had a hydrogen bomb at that moment he would have set it off. Yes, he was ready to blow up the entire United States, even if he had to sit on top of the bomb to do it. For him America was through, it was finished; and the sooner it was destroyed the better off the world would be.

Turning to the lamenting women in the courtroom, he said, "From now on we won't depend on the mercy of Whites. From now on whoever injures us will face Black laws, Black courts, and Black justice. From now on we will meet violence with violence, lynching with lynching, and bloodshed with bloodshed!"

About eleven that evening he received a telephone call from the main bureau of the Associated Press in Raleigh, North Carolina. The bureau chief told him, "Mr. Williams, we haven't sent out a statement you're supposed to have made earlier today because our reporter said you were very angry when you said it. We want to know if you are being correctly quoted when you advocate that Negroes should take the law into their own hands and turn to violence?"

"What I'm advocating," Williams answered, "is that, so long as the Negro in the South cannot expect justice in the courts, he must arrest, try, and punish his attackers himself. When you live among savage beasts you have to revert to the law of the jungle."

The next morning he was quoted on the radio and in the newspapers. In the days that followed he gave several press interviews. What surprised him was the interest the communications media were showing in what he had to say. When the Guard had fired at the Klan in self-defense two years earlier, not one White newspaper he knew of had reported it, but now they were publicizing his statements so widely that they were creating a nationwide commotion. The telephone was ringing night and day with what seemed like a million inquiries from all over the country. Then came the big call: Roy Wilkins was on the phone from New York.

"Williams," he said, "I want you to know we've arranged with the news media to carry your retraction of that lynching statement."

"Why should I retract it?" Williams asked.

"You're an elected official of the NAACP," Wilkins answered, "and what you say is being construed as reflecting our policy. We are not an organization of violence. Your advocacy of Negroes taking the law into their own hands is causing us great injury. You must retract it at once."

Williams pointed out that he hadn't spoken as an NAACP official, but as a private person. He also asked Wilkins why, if the NAACP considered his personal utterances inseparable from its policies, it hadn't tried to help when his insurance was canceled and he was fired from his job as a result of being elected president of the Union County branch?

"All that is irrelevant," Wilkins answered. "This is your last chance. You will either authorize us to tell the press that, being angry, you didn't really mean what you said, and now regret and retract it, or we will be forced to take action against you."

"Yes, I was angry. I am still angry. And I will be angry from now on," Williams answered. "So you'd better take whatever action you have in mind."

About an hour after Wilkins hung up, the Monroe radio station began broadcasting a special news bulletin to the effect that, due to his advocacy of violence, Robert Franklin Williams had been suspended by the NAACP. They quoted the national office as declaring that the use of force wasn't the American way to solve social problems, and that Williams' position was a violation of the organization's principles. The same bulletin was repeated on the radio every thirty minutes. A few hours later, Roy Wilkins telephoned again. "Williams," he said. "You are hereby informed that you must immediately cease all activities connected with our organization."

The members of Williams' NAACP branch rallied to his defense. And several Whites who belonged to it, although they hadn't chosen to be involved in the armed self-defense Guard, sent a telegram to the national office protesting his suspension.

When Attorney Conrad Lynn checked and found that the NAACP's constitution and bylaws contained no provision by which Roy Wilkins could arbitrarily suspend him without a hearing, Williams demanded a confrontation. His case was scheduled to be heard at a meeting in New York in June, 1959. The moment he walked into the hearing room, Williams understood for the first time that the NAACP was something other than what he had thought it to be. Seated around a large conference table were the members of the national board of directors, several of whom were White. Every time Roy Wilkins, whom he'd always assumed was the top man, opened his mouth, he would glance at the Whites as if to see if they approved of what he was saying. The man whose approbation seemed to concern him the most was a Mr. Spingarn, who held the office of NAACP president. He sat stony-faced and silent, but Williams got the impression that when Wilkins said anything, it was really Spingarn speaking. Roy Wilkins appeared to him to be nothing more than a spokesman for a group of powerful Whites.

The hearing began with a wealthy, well-dressed Black woman demanding of Williams, "Don't you know this is a respectable organization? We can't allow ourselves to be associated with people who act like common street thugs. How dare you advocate violence in our name?"

He looked directly at her as he responded, "Lady, if I should come across a White man trying to rape you, I'd take the same position on the matter as I took for Mrs. Reed, a poor southern woman. You seem to be more concerned about me being a 'thug' than you are about Mrs. Reed's rapist. At least I have yet to hear you condemn the man who attacked her. Can't you understand that our people are not going to let themselves be beaten and killed any longer? You'd better stop calling those of us who dare to meet force with force 'thugs,' because it places you on the side of our oppressors."

His statement seemed to chill the atmosphere at the hearing, and it was adjourned rather abruptly. The board of directors decided that he was to remain suspended for a period of six months, after which he would be automatically reinstated.

When they learned what had happened, the members of Williams' branch became very angry. "We refuse to accept your suspension," they declared. "Why don't all three hundred of us just quit the NAACP?"

"Every time we do something for integration and justice we are hurting those fakers," Williams countered. "Let's not let them shake us loose."

When told that the national office had instructed them to hold a special election to choose a new president, they said, "All right, Williams. We'll stay in the NAACP on one condition: Your wife has to let us make her president, but you'll still run things." Mabel agreed, and was elected unanimously.

Paula Murray, a member of Adlai Stevenson's law firm, had been present at the national NAACP hearing. Although known as a strong NAACP supporter, she sided with Williams against Wilkins and the others. Following his suspension, she suggested that he appeal to the NAACP's 50th Annual National Convention, which was to be held in New York that July.

While waiting for the convention to take place, Williams began to publish *The Crusader,* a newsletter which he hoped would provide both Blacks and Whites with information about the desegregation struggle in Monroe. He did this because he had come to realize that Blacks were at a great disadvantage in having to depend upon the White establishment's news media. With the aid of several friends, he put out the first issue on a mimeograph machine on June 26, 1959. Little did he suspect that *The Crusader* of subsequent years would be printed in such faraway places as Havana and Peking.

At the NAACP national convention the following month, Roy Wilkins' people circulated a special pamphlet which Williams felt distorted his call for self-defense against violence into an appeal for lynch law. He also resented the sensationalized tales then appearing in various publications which accused him of agitating for the indiscriminate murder of Whites.

The night before the convention session scheduled to hear his case, Williams was invited to a special caucus with several high NAACP officials. They said that, should a debate on the issue of violent self-defense take place, it might cause a split among the delegates. "You'll be crushed," they said. "But your position can do serious damage to the unity of the organization. So please reconsider and withdraw your appeal."

"Maybe I will be crushed," he answered, "but it will have to be in public, not in a closed conference room. And, so far as unity is concerned, how can we possibly have unity in the type of organization which you people want this to remain? You don't want a National Association for the Advancement of Colored People, you want a snobbish clique for the benefit of the favored few."

The next day, when he arrived at the convention, which was being held in the New York Coliseum, he was asked to step into the hallway by Clarence Mitchell, the NAACP's lobbyist in Washington. With him were Frank Reeves, a lawyer from the national office, and a couple of other people whom he didn't know. "Williams," they said, "you can be one of the biggest men here today. All you have to do is get up and say you've decided to withdraw your appeal. We guarantee that you'll receive an ovation like you've never heard before."

"Now just one minute," Williams said. "Why is it that Daisy Bates, who has already attacked me publicly, can escape being criticized, while the most important thing in your lives seems to be to get me to shut up?" The woman to whom he referred had become quite influential in the NAACP following her involvement in the 1957 school-integration struggle in Little Rock, Arkansas. The NAACP was paying for guards to protect her house as a result of Klan threats. It seemed to Williams to be an obvious contradiction for the NAACP officials to criticize him while providing her with the very armed self-defense which he was advocating.

"Yes," Mitchell responded, "it's true she has been given protection. But that isn't the problem. We didn't suspend you for forming your Guard or for shooting back at the Klan. It was when you made your inflammatory public statements that we moved against you. All that such talk can accomplish is to cause the Whites to become frightened; and then they'll react against all of us."

"So that's the way it is," Williams said. "It's okay for Daisy

Bates to have armed guards. And it's even right for us to use guns
to defend ourselves. What isn't allowed is to let our brothers and
sisters know that they can do the same to get the racists off their
backs. You're nothing but a bunch of hypocrites. The people
whose protection interests you least are the ordinary Black men,
women, and children in this country, because you're afraid of
offending your White bosses."

"Williams, if you'll just get up on that speaker's platform and
apologize," said Mitchell, "you'll go down in history."

"Sorry," Williams answered, "but I don't want to be known
as the last of the Uncle Toms." They had done their best, but his
experience with General Good in the Marines had taught him a
lesson: Once you decide to challenge those in power, never let
yourself be seduced into retracting. If they are able to compromise
you, they will crush you without pity.

When the time came to discuss Williams' appeal, the chairman announced that each speaker would be allowed five minutes.
Leading the attack was Daisy Bates, and the majority of the others
given the floor joined her in supporting his suspension. There were
two or three delegates, however, who rose to his defense. One of
them, a White man from Pennsylvania, declared, "I'm a pacifist,
and never thought I would be taking the position of defending
someone who advocates violence, but, being a Jew, and having
lived in Nazi Germany, I must tell you that I feel Williams is right.
All of your arguments based on idealism are meaningless to the
racist criminals. The only way to stop their aggression is by convincing them that they'll have to pay with their lives if they attack
you. We European Jews refused to accept this fact until the Hitler-
ites had exterminated most of us, and only started shooting back
after it was too late. You mustn't make the same mistake here in
America."

When it was Williams' turn to take the floor, the chairman
said that, since time was running short, instead of five he would
only have two minutes in which to present his case. Williams protested that this wasn't enough, but was told to accept it or remain
silent. Rising to his feet, he said, "I didn't get into this trouble for
myself, but only because of a desire to protect our people. I'd
hoped that the NAACP national Board of Directors wouldn't
crawl on their bellies like dogs, but I was wrong. They're betraying
us to the very elements they claim to be helping us resist. The rac-

ists want my head, and they're delivering it to them on a silver platter. No matter what happens, there's one thing you'll never see me doing. I will not crawl."

The majority of the delegates voted to sustain Williams' suspension. Many people who voted against him said later that they hadn't done it as a personal reprimand, but only because they didn't want to appear to be disavowing the leadership.

The over-all effect of the debate went far beyond the question of the suspension. The delegates' growing sentiment in favor of meeting violence with violence forced the national leadership, albeit hesitatingly, to include in the preamble to the resolutions passed by the convention the statement: ". . . we do not deny, but reaffirm, the right of an individual and collective defense against unlawful assaults." Even Roy Wilkins felt constrained to tell Williams, "You know, I really agree with you. I believe in armed self-defense myself, but we just can't afford to advocate such things openly."

One Black newspaper, *The Pittsburgh Courier,* carried his appeal speech under the headline "I Will Not Crawl," but none of the major news services or TV networks discussed it. The Reverend Martin Luther King's advocacy of pacifism was what everyone was talking about. Williams felt that, rather than threatening their power, the Gandhiism Reverend King preached was welcomed by the more sophisticated racists as a way of holding the Blacks back from taking the actions necessary to gain full equality.

Chapter Seven

"WE DON'T WANT NO SHIT
OUT OF YOU"

Being temporarily suspended from the NAACP didn't stop
Williams from continuing to travel around the United States and
Canada giving lectures. He was invited to speak at such places as
New York University, UCLA, the University of Chicago, and the
University of British Columbia. And every time he was in Man-
hattan, Malcolm X had him address the members of the Nation of
Islam at their Mosque on 116th Street in Harlem.

Malcolm X would present him to the congregation by saying,
"Let's get our regular business over with fast today, because
Brother Williams, the first brother to take up arms and fight, is
here from North Carolina. He and his people are facing death for
all of us." In addition to encouraging the Muslims to raise money
for them to buy guns with, Malcolm was always curious about
what Williams and his group were doing. But he never tried to influence them in any way, and only asked how his people could
help.

Besides giving lectures, Williams continued publishing *The
Crusader* on as regular a basis as his meager supply of funds would
allow, and it slowly began to grow in circulation. Not only did he
use it to preach the advantages of armed self-defense, it also provided a platform from which he tried to counteract the distortions
about him which he felt were being spread by the NAACP national office. The proof of its effectiveness was that, with every
succeeding issue, an increasing number of contributions was being
received from all over the country. Soon jazz musicians and other
entertainers were organizing public benefits for the Monroe Defense Fund. Quite a few donations came in the mail from people
who feared to sign their names.

At this time, in addition to the general poverty under which they lived, many Blacks in the South were being fired from their jobs, evicted from their homes, and subjected to various other pressures by the racists in order to dissuade them from participating in the desegregation struggle. In reaction to this campaign of intimidation, Williams and his friends organized a project called C.A.R.E., "The Crusader's Association for Relief and Enlightenment." Unlike the already established CARE organization, which solicited money from Americans to send relief packages to refugees overseas, they were appealing on behalf of needy Blacks in the United States.

The NAACP national office, the Urban League, and various other such groups refused to support the project, claiming that Williams and his followers were only trying to get more money for arms. Despite this, a growing number of people did respond to the appeals printed in *The Crusader* by sending clothing, food, medicine, and cash. When the news media publicized the aid subsequently sent to needy Blacks in Tennessee and other places by the "responsible" civil rights groups, they neglected to mention that Williams' group in Monroe had been conducting a similar program for some time.

The next issue in which they became involved was the Urban Renewal Program. The Monroe authorities had begun tearing down houses in the Black community without either consulting with or bothering to provide quarters for those who would be displaced, both of which were violations of federal law. Also, they were planning to demolish some of the best Black-owned residential districts, while the areas where new housing was most desperately needed weren't to be touched at all.

Williams was wondering how to stop this, when he noticed a story in the papers describing Eisenhower's trip to India. The president had stated in a speech there that America should see to it that the people of Asia were provided with adequate housing. Since Ike was a guest of Nehru, who was a lifetime member of the NAACP, Williams suggested that they try to embarrass him into helping them by cabling him in care of the Indian prime minister. In a telegram signed, "The Union County, North Carolina, NAACP Branch," they asked Eisenhower, "If you are interested in homes for the people of Asia, why aren't you interested in

homes for the Black people of the U.S.A.?" And they went on to
protest the manner in which the Urban Renewal Program was
being carried out in Monroe.

Soon afterward Williams received a phone call from a member of the Federal Housing Administration, who said, "President
Eisenhower has asked us to investigate your complaints. He has
personally sent word to delay the Urban Renewal Program in
your area until it can be discussed with and approved by those
who'll be affected by it."

When Williams told his people about this, they all thought
Eisenhower had done a great thing. He hadn't flown into a rage
over their approaching him in front of a foreign leader, but had
dealt with them fairly. Once again it seemed to Williams that the
federal government wasn't all bad.

Around this time, Williams was approached by two young
men from Newark who identified themselves as "Marxist-Leninists." They said that, although good in principle, the C.A.R.E. appeal was too limited. "Rather than asking for aid only from people
in the United States," they suggested, "why not internationalize
your appeal by extending it to other nations? For example, why
not ask the people of Russia for help?"

When Williams and his group agreed that their suggestion
had merit, they said that this was a propitious moment to make
such an appeal to the Soviet Union because Nikita Khrushchev
was planning to visit the United States in a few weeks. One of
them claimed to know the Soviet premier and said that he would
be able to discuss the request for aid with him personally. He was
convinced that, if he did so, the people of the U.S.S.R. would respond in the affirmative.

The two "Marxist-Leninists" from Newark then asked to be
taken on a tour of the Monroe area so they could meet the poor
face to face. The success of their cable to Eisenhower gave Williams' group reason to believe that publicizing the bad conditions
under which so many Blacks lived would embarrass the U.S. government into doing something to alleviate poverty in the South.

At each house they were taken to, the "Marxist-Leninists"
compiled a list of the things each family requested—mostly food,
clothing, medicine, seed, and agricultural implements. The young
man from Newark who claimed to know Khrushchev personally

said that he was taking it, plus the photos and names of the people interviewed, to the Soviet premier for his approval. Once Khrushchev okayed the project, the list would be sent to the Soviet Association of Trade Unions, which would get its millions of members to donate the required materials.

A couple of weeks later, he returned to Monroe to say that the Soviet premier felt their appeal would be more legitimate if it were made to all the governments of the world, not just to the U.S.S.R. They were guaranteed that, even if the other nations failed to respond, the Russian people would send a "Friendship Ship" filled with all of the things asked for. When Williams questioned the willingness of the U.S. government to permit such a ship to unload its cargo at an American port, the man from Newark said that, should Washington refuse, it would cause a great international scandal. The United States would open itself up to charges by the world press of preventing undernourished Black children from receiving food. If the U.S. State Department tried to say that there was no need for such aid, the Russians could publish the names and photos of the poor who had asked for help. It would be a propaganda coup for the Communists because it would challenge America's claims of a high living standard as well as belie the impression made by the billions of dollars in overseas aid which the United States had been pouring into Africa, Asia, and Latin America.

Some of the Blacks in Union County, which wasn't the poorest part of the South by far, couldn't even afford milk bottles and nipples for their babies. More than once, the doctor had phoned Williams to ask, "Rob, can you send some used blankets or baby clothes out here? I just delivered a child, and had to use my shirt to wrap it in because the parents don't even own a piece of cloth."

Williams' basic reason for planning the appeal was not to injure the U.S. government, but to help his people. Cold War or not, the poverty and hunger which they faced every day was real. Even the capitalist news media occasionally had to admit that millions of Americans were suffering from malnutrition, disease, and lack of decent shelter. If Moscow was ready to help expose such suffering, and thereby pressure Washington into doing something constructive, what did it matter how much of a propaganda advantage the Kremlin derived?

Williams anticipated criticism from those "superpatriots" who fear that letting the world know what's wrong in the United States threatens the nation's very existence. But, as he saw things, when a country refused to be responsible to its citizens, to provide them with decent jobs so they were able to feed their children, that nation had already abdicated its right to exist. Those who were striving to silence the critics of the contradictions in American life by charging that they supported the Communist cause, but didn't lift a finger to alleviate those inequities, only made the criticisms more damning.

As soon as Williams' group let it be known that they were making an international appeal, the ball really started rolling: A prominent public-relations man from New York, a friend of Conrad Lynn's, volunteered to donate his services. He contacted newspapers and wire services all over the world, especially in western Europe, and got them to agree to run advertisements free of charge. Although many of the papers were conservative, a campaign asking Europeans to send food, clothing, medicine, and tools to poor American Blacks interested them immensely. In a few weeks, he'd worked out a coordinated plan whereby the appeal would be launched all over the world at the same time that it was made public in the United States.

With everything set, Williams and the others waited only to be told the best date for launching the appeal, but week after week passed with no word. Finally, after two months of silence, Williams telephoned to find out what was causing the delay. When he got the two men from Newark on the phone, they said, "We're very sorry, but there has been some trouble. We'll drive down to Monroe this weekend and tell you all about it."

"The reason no date has been set," they said after arriving, "is that we received a message from Premier Khrushchev suggesting that, since relations between the U.S.A. and the U.S.S.R. are improving, we should hold off on your appeal project for the time being. He feels that, if the U.S.S.R. were to try to send food to your people at this time, it would irritate the U.S. government and endanger his entire 'peaceful coexistence' campaign. He wants us to wait and see if the improvement in relations is going to be permanent. If it is, we'll have to forget the aid project."

That was it. The whole deal was off. As Williams saw it, Khrushchev was abandoning the poor Blacks of Union County,

North Carolina, in order to appease the capitalists. Those self-styled "Marxist-Leninists" from Newark had really put him out on a limb. Here he and his group had convinced their people that they were going to be helped, and now they had to go back and tell them it was all a mistake. Some couldn't believe it. They weren't sophisticated enough to comprehend why a lessening of international tensions would prevent the Russians from sending aid to those who really needed it.

At the same time Vice President Richard M. Nixon was vainly trying to convince Khrushchev at the U.S. Exhibition in Moscow that the average family in the United States owned a new three-bedroom home with unit-heat and an all-electric kitchen, there were families in Union County so poor that all they had to sleep on were old wooden planks laid across packing crates. By accusing Nixon of lying, Khrushchev showed that he knew very well how bad things really were for more than forty million Americans, which made the Soviet premier's reported decision to pull out of the international appeal project seem all the more cynical and callous to Williams.

Placing the increased security of the U.S.S.R. resulting from the relaxation of Cold War tensions above his commitment to help the poor Blacks of Monroe was perfectly logical when considered solely in terms of national interest. Political leaders whose machinations affect the lives of hundreds of millions of people are seldom swayed by the needs of powerless minorities. Apparently accepting the Newark "Marxist-Leninists'" account of events without question, Williams felt that Khrushchev's error was not in refusing to help them, but in having claimed to be sincerely concerned in the first place.

He was convinced that, if the Russian people were permitted by their government to see just how badly the poor lived in the United States, they would send all the help they could. For that matter, he had enough faith in the humanitarian instincts in the hearts of many Americans to believe that, were the news media to stop glossing over the facts of poverty and hunger, the U.S. public itself would insist on something being done about it.

But as Williams saw it, neither government was prepared to encourage its people to make any real sacrifices to help end human suffering. The only place he could then think of where a real effort was being made to do away with poverty was Cuba.

Williams had first heard about the Cuban Revolution from Ted Posten, a Black reporter for the *New York Post*, whom he had met during the "Kissing Case." As more and more news about what the Fidelistas were doing began to reach the United States, he became enthusiastic about their revolution. Not only were the poor given a chance to receive decent jobs and education, a Black had been made head of the Cuban Armed Forces. Toward the end of 1959, Williams began printing articles and information about Cuba in *The Crusader,* urging American Blacks to support Castro as part of their fight against racism.

His articles attracted the attention of Robert Taber, a former CBS newsman who had covered the Cuban Revolution, who wrote him from New York in early 1960 to say that he was organizing a group called The Fair Play for Cuba Committee. Taber later telephoned and asked if Williams would allow the use of his name as one of the founding members, and he agreed. The purpose of The Fair Play for Cuba organization was to counteract the growing campaign against the Castro regime then being mounted by the Cuban exiles and the U.S. government.

Nineteen sixty was the year of nationwide civil rights sit-ins, and Monroe was the thirteenth town in the state of North Carolina to join the campaign. The Monroe NAACP's stand-ins back in 1957 had ended with the false promise of a "separate-but-equal" swimming pool, but the demonstrations being staged by students all over the United States inspired Williams and the others to start agitating once again.

Their first target was the practice by the local lunch counters of serving only those Blacks who remained standing. They began by sending groups of sit-in demonstrators to Jones' Drugstore. The Blacks would enter, take seats at the fountain, and order sandwiches. Although the proprietor refused to serve them so long as they were seated, they wouldn't stand up, and waited patiently until closing time. This cost Jones' Drugstore a great deal of money because its White customers, finding all of the seats taken, would go elsewhere to eat. After a few days the White lunch-counter owners started locking their doors whenever they saw the demonstrators approaching. The Blacks would wait outside for hours for the restaurants to reopen, but the owners kept the doors bolted, preferring to lose business rather than serve them.

Certain that the loss of revenue would force the store owners to change their discriminatory practices before they would permit themselves to go bankrupt, Williams' NAACP branch demonstrated as frequently as they could. Each time they did so, the crowds of both White and Black onlookers became larger, and tempers began to grow short. In marked contrast to the brutal beatings suffered by sit-in demonstrators in other parts of the South, however, the racists didn't try to touch them. They knew that, unlike the pacifist followers of Martin Luther King, the Blacks of Monroe were ready to defend themselves against any attempt to take away their right to demonstrate peacefully.

As a result of Williams' practice of always being seen with a small shoulder bag, a rumor had started that he carried some sort of small machine gun in it, and would start shooting if ever attacked. Another rumor had it that the bag was filled with TNT, so that if anything should happen to him it would blow up most of the town. Such stories made some people rather leery of coming near him. Because of this, when Williams and several other demonstrators were arrested, everyone presumed that something would be found in his bag and he would be charged with carrying a concealed weapon. At the station a policeman took the bag, put his ear to it as if to listen for the ticking of a time bomb, then started easing open the zipper very carefully. Everyone in the building seemed to be holding his breath as he slowly reached inside. He appeared greatly disappointed when he found nothing.

The truth was that Williams did sometimes carry a weapon or two in his bag, but most of the time, as on this occasion, it was empty. He felt that giving the impression he was armed was often as effective as actually carrying a weapon—unless he had reason to believe that he might be placed in a real shooting situation.

Failing to get him on a serious charge, the judge demanded that Williams either put up a $50 bond or go to prison for the minor offense of "disturbing the peace."

"I guess you'll have to jail me," Williams told him, "because I'm not worth $50."

For some reason the authorities didn't want to lock him up at that time. The police themselves went out and found a friend willing to put up his bond.

But when Williams returned to the sit-in at Jones' Drugstore a few days later and dared to sit down on a stool and ask to be served, he was arrested and formally charged with "trespassing."

This time he was found guilty and sentenced to thirty days at hard labor on the chain gang. When he said that he wanted to appeal, the judge set his bond at $750. At this point, old Reverend Perry, the good friend of Williams' late Uncle Charlie, stood up in the back of the courtroom and said he would put up the bond, but the judge refused to accept his offer. In an apparent attempt to intimidate the Black community, the cops then chained Williams' hands and legs and forced him to hobble the three blocks or so from the courthouse to the jail, parading him down the main street of Monroe along with several manacled criminals as though he were a ferocious beast they'd finally managed to subdue.

The NAACP state headquarters filed an appeal and was able to get him released on bond. After fighting his case up to the North Carolina State Supreme Court, they said they were consolidating it with those of six college students who had been arrested on a similar "trespassing" charge during the sit-ins at Chapel Hill. But then, instead of appealing on Williams' behalf to the U.S. Supreme Court, the NAACP dropped the case without consulting with or informing him. Through sheer accident, he happened to notice in a newspaper account of the students' appeals that his name wasn't listed. With only a few days left in which to make a new plea, he asked Conrad Lynn if the Emergency Civil Liberties Committee in New York would help, and they immediately accepted the case.

The U.S. Supreme Court eventually threw out Williams' "trespassing" conviction on the grounds that it was unconstitutional to jail someone merely for sitting down in a public eating place.

In the spring of 1960 primary elections were to be held in Monroe. Disgusted with being able to vote only for the candidates of the local Democratic Party clique, Williams decided to run for mayor himself. He entered the primaries not because he thought he had the slightest chance of winning, but as an act of defiance; and to demonstrate to his fellow Blacks that they had the same right as anyone else to run for public office.

When the word got around that he had filed for the office of mayor, many Blacks in Monroe became frightened. Nothing like this had ever happened before. No one thought he would be allowed to make a fair showing. The Whites controlled the election machinery, including the counting of the ballots. And one of the city officials even went around telling people, "Williams will only get two votes in this town: his wife's and his own."

There was no Republican Party to speak of in the area, and the only other candidate was the Democratic incumbent. Consequently, although he had practically no funds, Williams' candidacy received a considerable amount of publicity. He appeared on a radio broadcast over the local station, and raised the money to run an ad in *The Monroe Enquirer.* As election day neared, the Democratic Party became concerned enough to mount an unusually large campaign to make certain he didn't slip into office by default. Several White employers told their Black workers that they would lose their jobs if they voted for him, and the police openly went around trying to frighten Blacks into staying away from the polls.

On the evening of election day, without letting his Guard know about it, Williams drove into town by himself and parked in front of the courthouse. It was jammed with Whites from all over Union County; the crowd filled the corridors and even spilled out into the yard. The Whites who saw him drive up started muttering questions among themselves as to what he might be doing there. His intention was to try to enter the building and observe the counting of the ballots—something which no Black in that county had ever done before. While Williams was sitting in his car, several of his Guard people pulled up. They said they'd seen him driving into town, and had rushed over to make sure he was protected. "I'd appreciate it if you brothers would just stay outside and let me handle this myself," he told them.

When Williams pushed his way through the crowd of Whites and entered the courthouse, everyone in the building stopped talking and began to glare belligerently, perhaps hoping to frighten him into leaving. The uneasy silence was broken when one White, who seemed to be feeling pretty good from whiskey, came over and said in a low voice, "Now Williams, we know that, by law, you've got a right to be here. But if I were you I would leave right away. A lot of folks are getting angry, and there's going to be bad trouble."

Raising his voice so everyone could hear, Williams said, "I came to watch them count the votes. If that's going to cause trouble, then I'm prepared for it."

At this, the man looked at him and said, "But you're outnumbered. You don't stand a chance."

"You don't know if I'm outnumbered or not," Williams answered. "In fact, you have no idea what my position is. If anyone wants to make me leave, let them try."

When he finished speaking, the Whites in the courthouse, not knowing how many armed Blacks might be in the streets outside, started shuffling their feet, talking about other things among themselves, and acting as if he wasn't there at all. Williams remained in the building for an hour or so without anyone approaching him again and left peacefully after watching several hundred ballots being counted.

The next day the radio announced that Williams had received ninety-eight votes. This came as a big surprise. Most Blacks hadn't expected the White election officials to admit that he'd gotten any at all. Many of his friends believed this figure to be false because, just by asking around in the Black community, they found far more than ninety-eight people who swore they had voted for him. Since the Whites had done everything short of using force to keep the Blacks from voting, Williams assumed that the figure they finally gave out was an arbitrary one designed to dissuade him from going to court and demanding a recount.

An editorial in the local newspaper commented that it was surprising he could get even that many votes. What especially caught the paper's attention was that some of Williams' support came from all-White districts. This led the more paranoid among the local racists to start talking about there being "secret Communists" among the Whites of Monroe.

Late in the spring of 1960 Williams was telephoned by Bob Taber. The Fair Play for Cuba Committee was about to invite eighteen Black writers to visit Havana, and Taber wanted to know if he'd be interested in going. The Cuban government would provide air transportation, meals, and hotels from New York to Havana and return, but Williams would have to get from Monroe to New York on his own. Also invited were such people as Leroi Jones, Julian Mayfield, Sarah Wright, Harold Crooks, and Richard Gibson.

Having been automatically reinstated to NAACP membership, Williams brought up the invitation at his branch meeting.

The members not only agreed that he should visit Cuba, they also voted to give him the money with which to go to New York.

When they heard about this, the state and national NAACP offices called and said it was incorrect for Williams to visit a country with which the United States government was having difficulties, especially when part of his trip was being financed by NAACP funds. But the members of his branch insisted on their right to send him to Cuba and said that, since the funds came from their own pockets, the national office had no right to complain about what they did with them.

Back then, before the break in U.S.-Cuban relations, it was possible to fly directly from New York. Arriving in Havana, the Black writers were housed in the Riviera, one of the many deluxe high-rise hotels erected before the revolution for the American tourist trade.

Williams' first encounter with Fidel Castro took place soon after his arrival. The Cuban leader was walking through the Riviera lobby by himself, his guards waiting just outside the hotel, when a Cuban told him that Williams was one of the American writers. When he heard this, Castro came over and started shaking his hand. His English was fair, but an interpreter helped him from time to time. Williams was both surprised and flattered when, upon learning his name, Fidel said he'd heard about his advocacy of armed self-defense, agreed with it, and was grateful for the support he was giving the Cuban Revolution in *The Crusader*.

Although his impression of him from the films shown on U.S. television was that of a short man, Williams found Fidel to be several inches taller than his own six feet. In addition to being a doctor of law, he'd been an excellent athlete, starring on both the basketball and baseball teams while a student at the University of Havana. Somewhat younger than Williams, at thirty-four he was one of the youngest heads of state in the world. All in all, Fidel impressed Williams as a very intelligent and sincere person.

During that first visit to Cuba, which lasted about three weeks, Williams was taken on a tour of one of the *barrios*—shantytown slums which used to exist all over the island. What he saw there made an extremely strong impression on him. Right in the middle of Havana, a city of almost a million people, filled with modern conveniences and luxury hotels, thousands of men, women, and children were living in incredible misery. The *barrio* was a hellhole of open sewers meandering about through a maze of tin-roofed tar-paper shacks, many of which had a dozen or more people jammed into them. Most of the shacks had no flooring except the earth, which the slightest rain quickly turned into clinging mud. There were only two water faucets for more than ten thousand inhabitants.

The spaces between the makeshift shelters were crawling with children—most of them naked and covered with sores and filth—and the air was obscured by a pall of smoke from open cooking fires and burning rubbish. "My God," Williams thought, "back in the United States we wouldn't house pigs as badly as this." The worst thing about it was the smell, a noxious amalgam of the odors of rotting garbage, excrement, and perspiration. For weeks after touring that place he found it difficult to work up an appetite. Years later, merely talking about it still turned his stomach.

Most of the *barrio* dwellers were Blacks—"Afro-Cubans"—but there were also quite a few poor Whites and people of mixed color living there. The Cuban population of over seven million is divided roughly into one-third White (primarily of Spanish ancestry), one-third Black, and one-third mixed. The general rule was that the farther east from Havana it was the greater the percentage of Blacks and the poorer the people. Before the Revolution, although a few Afro-Cubans had become wealthy, they hadn't enjoyed full equality. Even Batista had been refused membership in the elite Biltmore Yacht Club because of the color of some of his ancestors.

Although Williams had never imagined that people lived in such awful conditions, what really impressed him about the *barrio* was that, throughout the place, young university students—many of them White, middle-class types—were trying to help. They were showing the poor how to purify their drinking water, get rid of the rotting garbage and excrement, and practice other forms of hygiene. He was told that this was to prepare the *barrio* dwellers for the day when they would be moved to the new houses which the Revolution was already building for them. Even there, amidst the rubbish and the stench, the college students were teaching both young and old alike to read and write.

What really sold him on the Revolution was returning to the

same place a few months later, during his second visit to Cuba, to find nothing but a vast empty lot. The shacks were gone, and the people had moved into new clean homes. This was more than just speechmaking and promises. This was a real change.

Unlike many of the other Americans invited to Cuba, rather than spending his time meeting with intellectuals and well-known leaders, Williams went out and mingled with the people as much as he could. The poorer and harder-working a man was, unless he had suffered so much that he had become vicious or withdrawn, the easier Williams had always found it to strike up a close relationship with him. His knowledge of Spanish was nil at that time, so interpreters had to help bridge the language gap. But the main thing was that, having lived and worked among such people most of his life, he felt more at home with slum dwellers, farmers, and factory workers than with politicians and theoreticians. It was what he saw in the streets and on the back roads, not what was told him at cocktail parties, that convinced Williams Fidel Castro's Revolution was good.

Wherever he went, people would come up and say, "Williams, you shouldn't go back to the United States. It's a bad place, and they hate you Black people. Until they have a revolution like ours over there, stay here and live with us."

He got along so well with the Cubans that they invited him to remain on the island for the 26th of July Celebration. When he told them he couldn't afford to be away from Monroe that long since his NAACP branch was planning to accelerate the desegregation demonstrations that summer, they said, "Okay, go home, but if you want to come back in July, we'll buy your airplane ticket and take care of everything."

Williams returned to Monroe to continue his work there. Then, in mid-July, 1960, he flew to Cuba again.

The 26th of July Celebration, which takes place every year in Santiago, commemorates the beginning of the Cuban Revolution. On that date back in 1953, Fidel Castro, together with a group of other patriots, disgusted with the injustice and brutality of Batista's dictatorship, made a vain attempt to seize the Moncada Army Barracks. Most of the men with Fidel were killed—some in the attack—but all too many by being castrated or otherwise tortured to death by the police following their capture. Fortunately, Fidel wasn't caught until several days after the attack failed. By then the world reaction to the torture murders of his comrades had become so strong that Batista was forced to keep him alive.

The events which followed—Fidel's solitary confinement on the Isle of Pines; his celebrated speech *History Will Absolve Me*,* made at his secret trial in 1953; his exile from Cuba; his group's 1957 return aboard the ship *Granma*; the fighting in the Sierra Maestra Mountains; and the victory in 1959—are all well known. But the one date which means the most to the Cubans is the 26th of July, 1953; for the example set by that attack in Santiago, although it failed, inspired them to undertake the sacrifices which ultimately led to the Revolution's triumph.

Arriving in Havana, Williams boarded a train filled with Mexican and other Latin American students who also had been invited to attend the 26th of July Celebration. As they headed eastward toward Santiago, their train was greeted at every stop by throngs of cheering Cubans. Even at 4:00 a.m. mobs jammed the station platforms, shouting salutations and singing revolutionary songs to the accompaniment of brass bands. Sometimes the people would line the tracks as far as you could see. What really got to Williams was that, along with the other slogans, the crowds kept shouting, "Solidarity with the Black people of America!"

Following the big rally in Santiago, at which Fidel and other leaders of the Revolution spoke to a crowd of two or three hundred thousand, the various foreign guests were invited to tour the rest of the country. Williams was accorded a special honor by being taken to the Air Force Academy, where visitors usually were forbidden, and asked to address the cadets training there.

When he began telling them about the conditions under which Blacks live in the United States, some of the young future pilots, Whites as well as Afro-Cubans, were deeply moved. Several approached him after his speech and said that they hoped to be able someday to join in fighting the racists.

Both during the rally in Santiago and later while touring Cuba, Williams met such leaders as Che Guevara and Raúl Castro. Often, when one or more would be attending a demonstration or other public event near where he was visiting, they would send a messenger to invite him to come and sit next to them on the

* Published by Lyle Stuart, New York.

platform. The fact that he was spending most of his time among the farmers and workers had evidently come to Fidel's attention, because one day he told him, "Williams, the Cuban people like you very much. They like you more than any foreigner who has come here."

Upon his return to Monroe from that second trip to Cuba, Williams began to receive racist hate calls at all hours. There seemed to be no point in changing his phone number. He was certain that the Whites who ran the telephone company would immediately make the new one known. He considered having the phone disconnected, but decided against it because the Guard used it as part of their defense system. Bothersome as it was, he and his wife had to answer every call, even in the middle of the night, just in case it might be a legitimate appeal for help or warning of an attack.

While both male and female voices were involved in the hate calls, those that came late at night were almost always from men. One evening a man who sounded half drunk called and kept muttering, "You Black son of a bitch. We're going to kill you. Your troublemaking days are numbered." During a pause in his tirade he forgot to put his hand over the mouthpiece, and Williams was able to hear him say to someone, "Anabelle. I've got that nigger on the phone."

Assuming that Anabelle was either the hate caller's wife or girl friend, Williams said, "First of all, you don't know what you're talking about. And, secondly, how is sweet Anabelle?"

"Goddamn your hide," he yelled. "What did you just say?"

"I was just asking about Anabelle," Williams answered. "You know, you'd better be careful when you talk about killing me, because she might not want me dead."

At that the anonymous caller started shouting, "Nigger! How do you know my wife's name?"

"Why I sometimes stop around to see sweet Anabelle when you're out of town," Williams laughed. "Why don't you ask her about me?"

"You goddamn son of a bitch!" he screamed. "I been married to that woman, goddamn it, for over eighteen goddamned years. And if I find out she's been seeing you, I'll kill her goddamn white ass just as soon as I'll kill your goddamn black one!" It sounded as if he were smashing the telephone, and Williams hung up.

Except for their hate calls, the local racists didn't try anything at that time. The most serious attack came, instead, from the NAACP National Office. Soon after Williams' return from Cuba, Roy Wilkins sent him a letter which read, in part: ". . . I wonder, however, whether you are fully aware of the dangers and disadvantages of the course of action you seem to favor.

". . . The present Cuban attempts to endear themselves to American Negroes are obviously caused by ulterior motives. (Let me just ask you how the American Negro tourist would feel in Cuba at the constant chant of 'Cuba sí, Yanqui no'!)

". . . Are you willing to forsake the important support of that section of the people who are equally opposed to suppression of Negro rights in our country?

". . . Does not the unfortunate example of the great American Negro singer Paul Robeson show you the dangers and mistakes of the road which you seem to be choosing? What has Paul Robeson with all his greatness done for the American Negro in his present struggle for equality? The answer, regrettable as it is, must be: Nothing."

Williams published his answer in the Fall, 1960, issue of *The Crusader,* telling Wilkins: "Only a fool or a mercenary hypocrite could muster the gall to call a nation and its great leader insincere in dealing with the captive blacks of North America when, in the course of their daily lives, they display the greatest measure of racial equality and social justice in the world today.

"If this is America's idea of insincerity, then heaven help this nation to become insincere like Fidel Castro and Free Cuba in granting persons of African descent entrance into the human race.

"As for my being 'used as a pawn in the struggle of Cuba' against imperialist and racist North America, I prefer to be used as an instrument to convey the truth of a people who respect the rights of man, rather than as an Uncle Tom whitewasher of black oppression and injustice and an apologist for America's hypocrisy. . . .

"On hearing 'Cuba Sí, Yanqui No!' and having lived all of my life under American oppression, I was emotionally moved to join the liberation chorus. I knew it didn't apply to me because the white Christians of the 'free world' have excluded me from everything 'yanqui.'

"You make a cardinal mistake when you fail to give the great Paul Robeson credit for making a great contribution to the American 'Negro' struggle. Paul has proven that all black men are not for sale for thirty pieces of silver. He has lit a candle that many of the new generation will follow.

"Yes, wherever there is oppression in the world today, it is the concern of the entire race. My cause is the same as the Asians against the imperialist. It is the same as the African against the white savage. It is the same as Cuba against the white supremacist imperialist. When I become a part of the mainstream of American life, based on universal justice, then and only then can I see a possible mutual cause for unity against outside interference."

Despite his dispute with Roy Wilkins, Williams still considered the NAACP an important weapon in the struggle against discrimination. But he felt that it was incorrect for national leaders like Wilkins to warn Blacks to stay away from Cuba.

Back in 1946, upon becoming twenty-one, Williams had registered Republican in protest against the Democrats' monopoly of political power in North Carolina. In 1948, again as a protest, he voted for Henry Wallace, the leftist third-party candidate. Then in 1952 and 1956 he voted for Eisenhower. The first time was a protest against Truman, whom he considered a racist from Missouri. The second time was because he felt that Eisenhower had taken some real action against segregation. But in the November, 1960, presidential election he voted Democratic for the first time. He did so not because he considered Kennedy superior to Nixon. It was because he and the other Blacks were trying to vote together in order to demonstrate their political power. After a series of discussions, the vast majority of his NAACP branch had endorsed Kennedy. Although Williams went along, he told the others they would soon find out that JFK was a hypocrite—that he was clever enough to manipulate Blacks by pretending to be a champion of civil rights but wouldn't be any different from other politicians when it came down to cases. Nixon, while by no stretch of the imagination a friend of the Blacks, seemed more firm and sincere in his position at that time to Williams.

On April 17, 1961, the Bay of Pigs invasion took place. It

confirmed for Williams the low opinion he had of Kennedy. All
the liberal speechmaking about "self determination" emerged as
part of the idealistic façade that masks the brutal reality of U.S.
power. The Cubans had dared to depose a dictatorship supported
by Uncle Sam. They had dared to nationalize the vast agricultural
tracts owned by absentee American landlords. And they had gone
so far as to seize U.S.-owned refineries. As a result, their revolution was to be drowned in blood.

Williams was pleased by the outcome of the invasion. The
CIA- and Pentagon-organized landing of fifteen hundred counterrevolutionary Cuban exiles (a motley crew including some of Batista's most vicious assassins) was a fiasco. Though U.S. news reports first boasted that Cuba would be cut in two by the invaders
within forty-eight hours, in three days everyone in the exile bri-
gade was either dead or a prisoner. Just as the Monroe power
structure could no longer make Blacks cringe by sending the bed-
sheeted cowards of the Klan to terrorize them, Williams reflected,
so Uncle Sam was shown that an armed people's government
can't be overthrown by a band of police torturers, rich boys, and
brainwashed dupes.

After JFK publicly accepted full responsibility for the Bay of
Pigs, but tried to justify it as having been done in the "cause of
freedom," Williams' NAACP branch sent Kennedy a telegram. In
it they asked that the same rationalization he had used to justify
the Cuban invasion be applied in the United States—that, in the
"cause of freedom," the federal government provide Blacks with
tanks, aircraft, artillery, machine guns, and mercenary troops with
which to defend their rights against the Ku Klux Klan in North
Carolina. As was to be expected, Kennedy neither answered their
cable nor sent them any military assistance.

On Easter Sunday, April, 1961, Williams, his wife, and a
young White woman named Dorothy, a student from Orlando
Smith College who sometimes visited them, were planning to take
a drive. When his wife chose instead to stay home with their two
boys, Williams and the White woman decided to have some fun.
They knew that the local Whites would be out driving around with
their families after church, and they planned to taunt the racists
by flaunting the fact that a Black man and a White woman
weren't afraid to be seen together.

He had recently purchased a small used English car, a Hill-

man. Between them on the front seat, in plain view, he placed a
.45-caliber Colt and a 9-mm luger. When they stopped at a red
light on the main street of town, a cop drove up and sat glaring at
them. But after a few moments, he shrugged his shoulders and
sped away.

They then drove to a local drive-in restaurant that served
Blacks only at the back door. But Dorothy, being White, could eat
in the car. Ordering an ice cream cone for herself she said, "Rob,
you lick one side of it while I lick the other." As was usual on a
Sunday afternoon, the drive-in was full of White families. When
those parked nearby saw what Williams and the young White
woman were doing, they started tumbling out of their cars in
shock. First two old women came over and stared at them as if
they couldn't believe their eyes. Then several men approached in a
group and pressed their faces against Williams' windshield, but
the moment they saw the two pistols on his front seat they jumped
back. During all this, he and Dorothy continued licking the ice
cream cone as if they hadn't noticed a thing. When they had
finished the cone, they drove off laughing.

On the way back to Williams' house on Boyte Street, they
stopped in a Black-run restaurant to get something more substantial to eat. The moment the proprietor saw them enter together he
became so frightened he dropped the pile of dishes he was
carrying. He was so terrified at having a Black man and a White
woman sitting together in his restaurant that they left without eating in order to calm him.

The following day some Blacks who worked at the drive-in
came by Williams' house and laughingly said, "Rob, what was so
funny about what you did was that the White folks came into the
kitchen and asked us if Dorothy was White or not. When we said
we didn't know for certain, they declared that you must have been
playing a trick, trying to provoke them so's you could start
shooting. And that they could tell she wasn't really White at all."

In May Williams and his wife went to New York to attend a
benefit Charlie Mingus and some other jazz musicians were giving
in a midtown night club to raise money for the Monroe struggle.
While they were there the leaders of several Black teen-age street
gangs asked Williams to speak at a big rally to be held by the
NAACP in Harlem commemorating the Supreme Court's May 17,
1954, integration decision.

"We know the NAACP hasn't asked you to speak," the gang leaders said. "That's why we're here. So far as we're concerned, if they want to hold a rally in Harlem, you're the only one who's going to be allowed to say anything."

When Williams questioned their having enough power to dictate something like that, they answered, "You stay in New York until the rally, and we'll show you how much power we have." At their insistence he agreed to delay his departure for three extra days. "I want you to know one thing," he told them. "I'll be in the crowd, but I won't go anywhere near the speaker's platform unless I receive a formal invitation."

On the day of the rally, which was held in front of the Hotel Teresa on 7th Avenue, the streets were blocked off, and the crowd numbered into the tens of thousands. Sound trucks and newsreel camera crews from the networks were there to record the speakers. Among the dignitaries on the rostrum were Roy Wilkins, the NAACP executive secretary; Daisy Bates, the woman from Little Rock who had attacked Williams before the NAACP convention in 1959; Archie Davis; the Reverend Kilgore; the New York police commissioner; and representatives from the mayor's office.

Williams and his wife were at the rear of the crowd when they heard shouting. Groups of young toughs were gathering around the rostrum. Most of them carried placards with various derogatory sayings about Daisy Bates. In addition to calling her obscene names, they declared that, since she was "living downtown with the rich White folks," she and her "mink coat" were no longer welcome in Harlem.

In an attempt to quell the excitement generated by the demonstrators, the two brass bands present struck up the national anthem. But, instead of joining in the singing, the sign carriers and their friends in the crowd began to boo. The booing soon grew so loud that it drowned out the music. Williams was astounded. It was the first time he had ever heard "The Star-Spangled Banner" being jeered at.

The police commissioner and the other dignitaries on the platform were nonplused. After several attempts to be heard over the shouts of the crowd, the musicians finally gave up and sat down.

Then Joe Williams went up to the microphone to sing, but the crowd hooted him into silence as well. "This is getting out of hand," Rob said to Mabel. "Our people have never refused to let a singer perform before."

Next, Archie Davis went to the microphone and tried to quiet the crowd by saying that he was their friend. "If you're our friend," they shouted, "then why're you up there with those Uncle Toms, instead of down here in the street with us?"

After refusing to allow Davis to speak, the crowd gave the same treatment to the Reverend Kilgore. When Daisy Bates herself stood up to say something, they shouted, "Shut up, you slut!" Then they started chanting, "We want Williams! We want Williams!"

In response, one of the NAACP officials took the microphone and said, "We're sorry, but Mr. Williams is not scheduled to speak here today."

"If he doesn't speak, nobody else will either!" the demonstrators shouted.

"How can we let him speak?" the official asked. "He isn't even in New York."

At this, the gang leaders began looking around, and spotted Williams at the rear of the crowd. "There he is!" they cried. Before he knew what was happening, people were pulling and pushing him toward the rostrum.

"This is just a mob," he shouted at Mabel, who was being propelled forward along with him. "If they get us up there and something bad happens, the NAACP will blame the whole thing on me."

Despite his protests, Williams was lifted onto the rostrum, where he reluctantly took a seat. "The way Roy Wilkins, Daisy Bates, and the others were looking at me," he said later, "one would've imagined I was the devil himself, snorting fire and belching brimstone. I've never felt more hated, even by the most rabid KKK racist."

Leaning over close to him, the NAACP national head of branches hissed, "Williams, goddamn it, we're going to let you speak, but we don't want no shit out of you. Do you understand?"

"What do you mean, you're going to 'let' me speak?" Williams demanded. "I didn't ask to be here. And now that I see how you feel, I'm going to leave."

But when he started to walk off the stage, several NAACP officials grabbed him and said, "No, no, you can't go now." With them practically begging him to stay, Williams let himself be led back to his chair.

All of this time the crowd kept chanting, "We want Williams! We want Williams!" When an NAACP big shot tried to tell them that he would be given the stand as soon as the introductions were over, the crowd shouted, "No, no. We want him to speak now!" Finally one of the officials urged Williams to take the microphone.

The moment he stepped to the podium, you could hear a pin drop. The crowd was so still that for a moment he actually became frightened. The whole thing had really turned into a mess. Figuring that the damage had already been done and he had nothing more to lose, he began to speak.

"Back in 1959," Williams said, "I was suspended from the NAACP for advocating that we Black men defend our women and children, for advocating that we defend our homes, for advocating that we defend ourselves. I was suspended then by Roy Wilkins. Well, today Roy Wilkins is here on this platform next to me, and I'm going to reiterate what I said in 1959." As he spoke, he glanced at Wilkins. The NAACP national executive secretary was staring straight ahead and wiping the sweat from his face with a handkerchief.

"I don't know what the NAACP's position may be," Williams said in conclusion, "but my position was, is, and always will be, armed self-defense. Our manhood requires us to take this stand!"

The moment he finished, the young dissidents started hooting. "No more speakers! Everybody go home! The rally is over!" Then they went wild, ripping down the banners, tearing apart the speakers' platform, disconnecting the public address system, and cutting off the power to the television cameras. While Williams and his wife were escorted out of the area by a group of the young gang leaders, Daisy Bates, Roy Wilkins, and the others had to be hurried away by a police guard.

Several things about that day impressed Williams. The number of youths involved in taking over the rally was relatively small when compared to the total crowd. What made their efforts successful, however, was that there was a general agreement with what they were saying. It seemed that many people, who had come without any conscious intention of protesting against the NAACP leadership, sided with the demonstrators once their discontent was focused.

Williams also observed the reaction of the Black policemen. The authorities had assigned a large number of them to the event; they had stood in a solid line in front of the platform, facing him as he spoke. At first their faces had been harsh and unfriendly. But after he explained his position and told why he had been suspended from the NAACP, they had begun to listen more sympathetically. By the time he concluded, several of the Black policemen were applauding along with the rest of the crowd.

The behavior of the news media was as he had expected: They either didn't report what had happened, or merely said that "extremist elements" had disrupted the rally. Instead of identifying Williams as an elected president of an NAACP-branch, they referred only to an anonymous "militant leader." Their apparent ban on the discussion of armed self-defense for American Blacks remained almost total, even when they had to cover up an event involving thousands of people taking place in the middle of Manhattan.

Most significant of all to Williams was the booing down of the national anthem. It indicated a profound change in the attitude of young Blacks. The old idea that the United States was some sort of "nigger heaven"—that only in America could a Black ever be happy—was obviously dead. The youth of Harlem no longer saw their oppressors as being only the individual cops and businessmen with whom they were in daily contact, they were beginning to become convinced that the total system, from the local officials on up through the national government, was at fault. They booed "The Star-Spangled Banner" because they saw it as a symbol of the way of life which was maintaining them and their fellow Blacks in poverty, ignorance, and disease. Williams' initial reaction to their boos was one of shocked surprise, but it wasn't to be very long before he would look back upon them as "the opening salvos of the battle for Black Liberation."

Chapter Eight

"A CHARM AGAINST POWDER
AND PAIN"

In June, 1961, after having been stalled for almost four years, the Monroe NAACP branch decided once again to try to integrate the "Whites Only" swimming pool. Every time they had raised the issue, the City Council had said that there were no surplus construction funds available. Now, however, when it was publicly known the money was on hand, all talk of building a separate pool for the Blacks had been forgotten.

Just as they had done back in 1957, the demonstrators would stand in the pool's admission line. And just as they'd done four years earlier, the authorities would close down the pool whenever the Blacks showed up. The demonstrators usually ate lunch in a picnic area near the pool. On the second day of the integration drive a group of Whites on the far side of a stream flowing past this picnic area started firing rifles in their direction, and several bullets ripped through the trees just over their heads.

Since the Monroe chief of police, A. A. Mauney, was on duty at the pool, Williams went over and asked him, "Did you hear those shots?"

"What shots?" the chief asked. "I didn't hear anything at all."

The firing continued intermittently the rest of that afternoon and resumed when they came out to the pool the next day, but the Blacks refused to be scared off.

When some of the Whites who were doing the shooting began drifting closer, Williams once again approached Chief Mauney and asked if he had heard the shots. When the chief continued to claim he hadn't, Williams said, "It's good to know you don't hear so well, because we're going to start shooting back now, and I don't imagine you'll notice that either."

"Wait just a minute," the police chief suddenly said. "If anybody's shooting around here they'd better stop right away." And he hurriedly ordered one of his deputies to tell the Whites on the other side of the stream to cease their firing.

Each day saw larger numbers of Whites coming out to shout insults at the demonstrators. As the crowds became more menacing, Williams stopped walking the picket line and took to sitting in his car with several members of the Guard. Their guns were loaded and ready, in case the racists tried anything.

The threat of violence grew so great that the Blacks sent a telegram to Attorney General Robert Kennedy asking for federal marshals to protect their right to picket. In response, the Justice Department suggested they take their problem to the FBI in Charlotte. But the agent in charge there said they had no basis for complaint because Chief Mauney had assured him the demonstrators would be given "ample protection." When Williams protested this meant "no protection at all," the FBI agent said that so far as he could see there weren't any violations of federal law taking place.

On Friday, June 23, 1961, Williams left the swimming pool and drove into Monroe in his Hillman to send another protest telegram to the Justice Department. On his way back he gave a ride to a Black high-school boy who was helping on the picket line. They were headed east on U.S. Highway 74, and had just reached the crest of a hill, when a large black 1955 DeSoto sedan suddenly roared up and rammed into their car from the rear, doing considerable damage.

The impact caused their bumpers to lock but, instead of stopping, the driver of the other car gunned his motor and started pushing them down the hill ahead of him. Every time Williams applied his brakes the Hillman would go into a skid. Fearful of losing control of his little car, he had no choice but to step on the gas to try to pull loose. As their speed increased, the other driver began swerving back and forth, threatening to run them off the seventy-five-foot drop at the side of the road. There was no doubt in Williams' mind that he was intent on killing them.

Glancing in the rear-view mirror, Williams was certain he recognized the driver of the black sedan as an auto dealer from Monroe. As his Italian carbine was on the back seat, he shouted at the teen-ager riding with him to grab it and start shooting. But the force of the initial impact had hurled forward the backrest of the rear seat, and it was jammed on top of the weapon. Although the student frantically tried to pull it out, the carbine just wouldn't come unstuck.

By this time they were approaching the State Highway Patrol Station. Hoping to attract the attention of the police, Williams began blasting on his horn. He could plainly see three cops standing in the station yard, but instead of coming to his aid they threw up their hands and started laughing. The sight of his car being pushed from one side of the highway to the other, plus the fact that both vehicles were doing seventy in a thirty-five-mile-per-hour zone, didn't seem to concern them.

As they approached the place where U.S. 74 crosses State 601, the auto dealer floored the gas pedal of his DeSoto in an attempt to ram Williams' Hillman into the cars at the intersection. Desperate, Williams made a last try to pull free. By braking and accelerating in rapid succession, he was able to induce a violent, jerking motion to the Hillman. At the last moment, less than thirty yards from the crowded intersection, their bumpers wrenched apart. Cutting sharply to the right, he was able to run his car off the road and into a shallow ditch without turning over.

As soon as they came to a halt Williams and the teen-ager pulled off the broken rear seat and freed his carbine. He was ready to kill the other driver on the spot, but he had already sped away.

Returning to the swimming pool, Williams approached Chief Mauney, pointed to the smashed-in rear of his car and said, "Do you see this?" Naming the car dealer, he said, "He did it just now when he tried to run us off the road. I've got his license number, and an eyewitness, and I want you to arrest him for attempted murder." Standing a few feet from the car, with the back all pushed-in and oil running out of the damaged wheels and brake drums, the police chief said, "I don't see anything, Williams. I don't see anything at all. How can I arrest a man when there's nothing wrong with your car?"

Coincidentally, a reporter from the *Charlotte Observer* was covering the demonstration that day. "I saw your car when you left for town a little while ago," he told Williams. "This must have just happened." At this, Chief Mauney quickly said, "Okay, Williams, come down to the police station and we'll discuss issuing a warrant."

Once they got there, however, the court solicitor, the local equivalent of a district attorney, told Williams that the man he had named "swears he's been in his office all day and didn't do anything to you. I can't indict a man just because you got his name and license number from somewhere. You and your witness go to his house. If you recognize him and bring him here, then I'll consider issuing a warrant."

Williams' assailant was a man whose face he knew well, having once bought a used car from him. But he also knew that the word of a Black wouldn't be accepted against that of a White in Union County. "It's the police, not private citizens like myself, who are supposed to arrest criminals," he told the solicitor. "I'm not about to waste time on a wild-goose chase. You just let that man know he is a very lucky man. The next time he tries anything like that, one of us is going to die."

Apparently tiring of such half-hearted attempts to get rid of Williams, on Sunday, June 25, 1961, the racists made their big move. When Williams left his house with three Black high-school students to drive to the swimming pool, he noticed a police car trailing them. Approaching the crossroads, he was surprised to see that a crowd of some three to four thousand Whites had gathered. There were so many cars in the area that several policemen were directing traffic. Just as Williams entered the intersection an old 1949 Ford, with the glass removed from its windows as if it had been used for stock-car racing, came backing toward him. Seeing that its driver appeared intent on smashing into the driver's side of his already-damaged Hillman, Williams turned sharply toward him and took the force of the collision with his front fender instead, sending both cars into the ditch.

The moment the dust cleared, the White driving the Ford jumped out waving a baseball bat. Approaching to within a few feet, he angrily shouted, "What did you hit my car for, nigger?" Williams didn't answer, waiting to see what he would do next. As if by prearranged signal, the crowd began moving toward them, shouting, "The nigger is at fault! We saw it! We saw it! The nigger ran into him!"

Spurred on by their yells, the Ford's driver came closer, gripped his baseball bat tightly, and raised it high over his head. Having brought along a Colt .45 automatic, Williams stuck it out the window into his face.

With the baseball bat frozen in midair, the man started backing away, unable to tear his gaze from the muzzle of the pistol staring him between the eyes.

Seeing this, the mob went wild. Someone fired a shot, and what sounded like a large stone smashed against the roof of Williams' car. "Kill the niggers! Kill the niggers! Pour gasoline on the niggers!" they screamed.

Telling one of the teen-agers to hand him his carbine, Williams opened the car door and stepped halfway out, displaying the weapon for all to see. Without telling him, the teen-ager had thrown a round into the chamber as he handed over the rifle. When Williams pulled back on the bolt to show he meant business, the bullet ejected, spun through the air, and fell on the ground at his feet.

At the sight of live ammunition the mob suddenly grew quiet. Two of the traffic cops at the intersection came running toward them. One grabbed Williams' shoulder and shouted, "Surrender your weapons! Surrender your weapons!" Instead, Williams hit him in the face with his left fist and knocked him down. Pointing his carbine at the policeman's head as he lay on the ground, he said, "Do you think we're crazy? We're not going to surrender to any lynch mob!"

Meanwhile, the other officer had come around on the right side of the car and was trying to unholster his pistol. Williams was within an instant of being shot in the back. At that moment, however, one of the three students in his car picked up the .45 and thrust it against the second cop's head, saying, "You pull that goddamn pistol and I'll blow your goddamn brains out!" Frightened, he fumblingly tried to reholster his gun and get away at the same time, and fell backward into the ditch.

When the mob saw this, one old White man started moaning, "Oh my God! Oh my God! What is this country coming to? The goddamn niggers have got guns, and the law can't even arrest them. Oh my God!" Still bawling, he was led away.

At that moment Chief Mauney and Steve Presson, a member of the City Council, drove up. Realizing bloodshed was imminent, Presson told the police chief, "Open up this highway and let Williams and his people out of here before someone gets hurt." When the chief complained, "But they've got guns," Presson insisted, "Clear this road. Now!"

Getting the councilman's message, Chief Mauney, with the rest of the police helping him, made a path for Williams' car through the mob. He drove the remaining few blocks to the swimming pool with his tire grinding against the fender damaged in the collision. The mob, mostly poor Whites, lined the sides of the road screaming, "No integration here! We're not going to swim with niggers! Kill them! Kill them!"

Arriving at the swimming pool, Williams found several of his people had managed to get through while everyone's attention was focused on him. As they picketed, the thousands of racists from the crossroads started surrounding them.

Every city official, including the mayor, was there. All in all, there were twenty-one Monroe cops on duty. It appeared evident that the power structure had decided to have some kind of final confrontation that day.

Rather than join the picket line, Williams and the three teenagers remained in the car. As the mob pushed closer and closer, Chief Mauney approached them and demanded, "Surrender your guns!"

"We have a legal right to these weapons," Williams answered.

"Williams," the chief declared. "If you hurt any of these White people, goddamn it, I'm going to kill you myself. Surrender your guns! Surrender your guns!" he repeated over and over, while the crowd kept screaming, "Kill them! Kill them!"

Then Steve Presson said, "Robert, I know you've got a right to picket, but the situation is getting out of hand. If you're willing to call it off for today, I'll see to it the police escort you and your people safely home."

"The police?" Williams exclaimed. "We might as well be guarded by the Ku Klux Klan. We'll leave only if you order a cop to ride with us in our car. That way, if anything happens, he will get it too."

When Chief Mauney heard what Williams was asking for, he said, "No sir. I am not about to do that."

"If that's the case," Williams said, "you'd better get ready to try and kill me, chief, because when they come at us I'm going to start shooting. Even if I only have time to get off one round, in that crowd it will kill six or eight of them. The blood of White folks will be on your hands."

With Chief Mauney and Williams glaring at each other, and the mob edging closer, Presson began to get worried. "What'll we do?" he asked in desperation.

"If the local police can't maintain order," Williams suggested, "why don't you ask for help from the State Highway Patrol?"

Presson thought that was a good idea and called the Highway Patrol, which sent over two cops, one of them a crusty old corporal. While the almost two dozen Monroe policemen present stood watching without lifting a finger to help, the old corporal started shouting, "Clear the goddamn road. I mean it! Move out!" At first the members of the mob hesitated. Some of them laughed in disbelief, apparently certain it had been arranged for the police not to intervene while they attacked the Blacks. When he saw they wouldn't move, the younger highway patrolman started wading into them with his billy club. He didn't try to hit anyone, but the sight of him swinging that long stick quickly convinced them he meant business. Sobered, they began moving back fast.

With one police car in front of him and another to his rear, Williams started to drive through the mob. Such a sight had never before been witnessed in that town. Some of the Whites were screaming, "Look how they are protecting those goddamn niggers! Look at the police guarding those Communist coons!" The police cars stayed with Williams until he got home.

Angry over not having been able to get their hands on the demonstrators, the mob began attacking every Black in sight. During the rest of that day those unfortunate enough to drive past the crossroads had their cars stoned. One Black was pulled from his auto, tied to a tree, and severely beaten. The sound of gunfire could be heard all through the night as the racists drove around firing at houses in the Black community, and the Blacks returned the fire.

As the summer grew hotter and hotter, more and more incidents of violence took place. Although the Blacks usually got the worst of it, there were exceptions. One evening a member of Williams' Guard who had gone to a restaurant with his wife was attacked by a mob of twenty-five or thirty Klansmen armed with clubs and chains. Fighting desperately, he managed to get back into his car. As the racists smashed at his car windows, he whipped out a pistol and began firing. The members of the mob ran off in all directions, but before they could get away, he managed to shoot two or three of them in the buttocks.

The Klan appeared to be embarrassed at having a large group of their men routed by a lone Black. Not one of the wounded pressed charges. It wouldn't have enhanced their public image to appear in court with their buttocks bandaged.

During the remainder of June and into July the racist attacks grew in number and intensity. It became necessary to have about twenty men headquartered at Williams' house each night. While the telephone rang every fifteen minutes or so with hate calls, they would take turns sleeping and patrolling the area.

On one occasion shots were fired at the house by a group of Whites led by a sergeant of the North Carolina National Guard. Even though the Blacks recognized him and tried to have him arrested, no action was taken by the authorities. Chief Mauney came around the next morning and said he saw nothing to indicate a shooting had taken place.

Williams printed an appeal for justice in *The Crusader.* In it he charged that the Monroe city officials, the agents of the FBI in Charlotte, and the governor of North Carolina were all involved in a conspiracy to deny the Blacks their right to equal protection under the law.

Despite a barrage of letters and telegrams to the Justice Department, Attorney General Robert Kennedy failed to take action. He remained silent even when Congressman Kowalski of Connecticut requested a federal investigation. Williams was convinced that the key to Kennedy's behavior was a Monroe lawyer named Henry Hall Wilson, Jr. Belonging to one of the wealthiest and most powerful families in Union County, Wilson had been a member of the state Senate and chairman of the North Carolina Young Democrats, and was a good friend of A. A. Mauney, the chief of police. Although not known to be a member of the Klan, Wilson had represented Klansmen in court and was reputedly one of their chief legal advisers. When Kennedy's representatives came to drum up support for the 1960 presidential elections, H. H. Wilson, Jr., was one of their leading campaigners. Despite many southerners' opposition to JFK's position on civil rights, the Klan in the Union County area didn't come out against him. Following Kennedy's victory, Wilson was apparently rewarded by being given an appointment as a White House administrative aide. Through his presence in Washington the Monroe power structure was able to exert a degree of influence on the federal government far out of proportion to that of much larger communities. As a result, when the Blacks sent protest letters and telegrams to the U.S. Justice Department and the White House, Williams suspected that they probably wound up in Wilson's hands.

Disturbed by the growing public clamor over the Klan's activities in Union County, JFK finally sent Wilson down to try to establish better race relations in the area. Instead of contacting Williams or any other Black leader, he went to see the chief of police. Williams had no way of knowing what kind of story he took back to JFK, but he did know that, unlike Eisenhower, neither of the Kennedy brothers ever responded to requests for help from the Blacks of Monroe.

Following the assassination of JFK, H. H. Wilson, Jr., stayed on at the White House under President Johnson, after which he became chairman of the Chicago Board of Trade.

In June, 1961, the federal government denied Williams an authorization to travel to Cuba, where he had been invited for the 26th of July Celebration. Their letter of denial said: "Because of the break in diplomatic relations between the United States and Cuba, the government of the United States cannot extend normal protective services to its citizens visiting Cuba."

Williams saw this as the height of hypocrisy. Would-be KKK assassins, aided by racist police and city officials, were trying to kill him on the streets of his hometown. Everyone, White as well as Black, who dared to work for civil rights in the South, was in danger. Yet the very same Kennedy Administration which refused to help safeguard its citizens in the United States, on the pretext of not being able to offer "normal protective services," was prohibiting travel to Cuba, a land where racism and exploitation were being abolished.

Encouraged by the apparent hands-off policy of the federal authorities, the Klan again began setting off dynamite charges in the middle of the night on the outskirts of the Black community. With cars roaring past with shotguns blasting, rounds from high-powered rifles whizzing overhead, and explosions rocking the area, there seemed to be a small war on almost every evening.

In reaction to the Klan's harassment, Williams' Guard began

training all those who requested it, including teen-agers. Their program included lessons in marksmanship, the handling of weapons, the operation of the three-man fire team, simple field fortifications and the use of sandbags, and the use of Molotov cocktails in urban defense.

While in the armed forces, Williams and the other vets had been shown how to use gasoline-filled bottles to attack armored vehicles in the countryside. But neither the Army nor the Marines had taught them their possible application in city fighting.

Whenever the Blacks suspected an onslaught was pending, they would have their women fill empty wine and milk bottles with gasoline. As night fell they would place them on the sidewalk near the walls of buildings. Most passers-by, including the police, thought they were only bottles someone had left on the street. Whenever forced to defend themselves quickly, especially if caught unarmed by a surprise attack, Williams' people could run to the nearest cache of these fire bombs, pick one up, touch a match to its cotton wick, and throw it. Used efficiently, the Molotov cocktail provides an inexpensive means by which even women and children can block an entire street.

About this time a mysterious series of fires broke out, mostly in the White part of town. The firemen would no sooner begin to fight a blaze on one block when a second conflagration would erupt a short distance away. After some unused Molotov cocktails were found near the scene of one such fire, the authorities decided they were purposely being set. It became so bad the White store owners hired guards to protect their businesses at night. Some Blacks suspected the Klan was setting the fires in order to make them look bad. This suspicion became stronger when the racists began saying publicly that Williams was the arsonist.

The same technique was used to set most of the fires. A window at the rear or the side of a building would be broken with a rock or a club. Then a gasoline-filled bottle would be lit and thrown deep into the structure's interior. This permitted the fire to get going inside before anyone on the street noticed the flames, frequently causing a great deal of damage. It indicated a professional was at work, for the amateur is usually content to hurl his fire bomb at the outside of a building, wasting most of its burning power on less flammable exterior surfaces, and immediately alarming passers-by.

One of the few mysterious blazes to strike the Black part of town only added fuel to the rumor that Williams was responsible. A middle-class Black woman, a teacher who also ran a small bar, had written a letter to the papers asking Blacks throughout the United States to stop sending Williams guns and other contributions. In it she had also claimed that Monroe was a peaceful town where the races had gotten along beautifully until he had started stirring up trouble. Two or three days after her letter was published, someone burned down her nightspot.

The claim that Williams was the arsonist grew so widespread that he felt compelled to tell the members of his Guard, "If any of you are setting those fires, I don't want to know about it. Arson isn't part of our self-defense program, and only increases the lawlessness which we already have in this town."

The authorities eventually brought in the FBI, the Seaboard Airline Railway detectives, the insurance company investigators, and everyone else they could think of. But whoever was responsible for the fires was never found.

The mass appeal of Williams' NAACP branch's challenges to segregation up to that time had been rather limited. Most Monroe Blacks weren't especially concerned about such things as the right to use a public swimming pool or eat at a lunch counter. In discussions among the members of the NAACP branch it was decided that in order to involve more people in the struggle they would have to deal not only with the denial of public facilities, but with jobs, welfare, and other basic economic needs.

They realized that the inequality being visited upon them was based on more than the denial of personal rights; it was founded upon economic exploitation, and could be measured in cold dollars, cents, and unemployment statistics.

Excluding children, housewives, the aged, and the infirm, more than a thousand of Monroe's population of approximately three thousand Blacks were unemployed. No matter how hard they looked, able-bodied men and women could seldom find work even as janitors, porters, or maids. Those fortunate enough to have such jobs earned, on the average, only $15 for a six-day week. Among the few types of employment available from time to time was cotton picking, which paid the grand total of $2.50 for each hundred pounds gathered. The average person had to work eight to ten hours at breakneck speed to produce that much, and a day when a worker managed to pick 150 pounds and earn $4.25 was considered a good one.

At the beginning of each summer many Blacks, including heads of families, were laid off so the local White high school and college students on vacation could take their jobs and earn spending money. With the street corners of the Black community crowded with unemployed youths just out of school, most Black graduates were forced to go elsewhere to find work.

There was a rash of new factories being established in the area. These runaway industries from the North, attracted by the low wages and weak unions in the South, received sizable concessions from the taxpayer-supported Industrial Development Commission, but they didn't hire any Blacks. On the contrary, the Commission stipulated that the new industries would be denied special concessions if they dared to employ anyone except Whites. Since the Blacks were being taxed just as much as the Whites were, they felt that this amounted to robbing them in order to provide the Whites with jobs. Being denied access to public facilities was an obvious insult, but there was no question that the lack of work was really their most basic problem.

Williams saw it as an important advance in their thinking when, on August 15, 1961, his NAACP branch presented its Ten-Point Program to the local authorities. It read as follows:

> We, the undersigned citizens of Monroe, petition the City Board of Aldermen to use its influence to endeavor to:
>
> 1. Induce factories in this county to hire without discrimination.
> 2. Induce the local employment agency to grant nonwhites the same privileges given to whites.
> 3. Instruct the Welfare Agency that nonwhites are entitled to the same privileges, courtesies, and consideration given to whites.
> 4. Construct a swimming pool in the Winchester Avenue area of Monroe.
> 5. Remove all signs in the city of Monroe designating one area for colored and another for whites.
> 6. Instruct the Superintendent of Schools that he must prepare to desegregate the city schools no later than 1962.
> 7. Provide adequate transportation for all school children.

8. Formally request the State Medical Board to permit Dr.
Albert E. Perry, Jr., to practice medicine in Monroe and
Union County.
9. Employ Negroes in skilled or supervisory capacities in the
City Government.
10. ACT IMMEDIATELY on all of these proposals and inform the
committee and the public of your actions.

> Robert F. Williams
> Albert E. Perry, Jr., M.D.
> John W. McDow

Doctor Perry's name was on the petition because he had been
released from prison after serving only eight or nine months of the
five-year sentence imposed back in 1959. When it became apparent his absence wasn't diminishing the Blacks' desegregation activities, the authorities had freed him on parole, but only on the
stipulation that he not set foot in Union County or the town of
Monroe. Despite the fact that he was without a license to practice
medicine and had to live in Charlotte, Williams and the others still
considered him one of them and consulted him on everything they
did.

A week or so before the presentation of the Ten-Point Program, Dr. Perry telephoned Williams to come see him. He said he
had been approached by a Black aide of Governor Terry Sanford,
the successor to Governor Luther Hodges, who had been rewarded by JFK for his support during the 1960 election by being
appointed U.S. secretary of commerce. This aide, a certain Dr.
Larkin, had given Dr. Perry the impression that, if he would arrange a secret meeting with Williams, he would be allowed to
move back to Union County. The meeting was to be held in Dr.
Perry's house in Charlotte.

Williams suspected Dr. Larkin wanted to see him as a result
of a phone call he had recently made to the governor's office to
ask for protection by the State Highway Patrol. On that occasion
he had managed to get through to the governor's chief aide, Hugh
B. Cannon. Cannon hadn't done anything, but his being approached so soon afterward seemed to Williams to be more than
coincidental. Wanting to help Dr. Perry, he accepted the offer.

On the designated night he carefully checked out the neighborhood around Dr. Perry's house to make certain the meeting

wasn't a ruse by the Klan to trap him. Then he walked in the front door to find Dr. Larkin already there, sitting on the sofa in the living room. Placing his rifle and two pistols on the coffee table in front of him, Williams asked, "Did you want to see me?" Glancing apprehensively at the guns just a few feet from his face, Dr. Larkin answered, "Williams, the governor has taken a great interest in you. He has decided you aren't living as well as you should be— that you deserve better. So he sent me to find out what he can do for you."

"That's very nice of the governor," Williams said. "If he really wants to help me, I suggest he push through the Ten-Point Program we are about to present to the authorities."

"Oh, no, the governor doesn't mean help you that way," Larkin replied. "He wants to know what you want for yourself, *personally.*"

"And just what would the governor expect from me in return for such *personal* help?" Williams countered.

Warming to the discussion, Dr. Larkin said, "Oh, not much, really. Just a small thing right now. You've been seen walking around town wearing guns, even right in front of the county courthouse. The governor knows there's no law against it so long as the guns aren't concealed, but he would like you to stop anyway. It sets a bad precedent and is in poor taste."

"The police are paid to carry guns so they can protect people, aren't they?" Williams asked. "So why is it in poor taste for me to be armed when the police refuse to protect me?"

At this Dr. Larkin said, "But the governor guarantees that you will get all the protection you need."

"I'm glad to hear that," Williams answered, "but how come he is only getting around to it now? As to what he can do for me— well, I am a poor man, and will certainly welcome anything he wants to give. Anything, that is, in addition to our Ten-Point Program. Until all the Blacks in our town get everything in that program, I don't see how I can accept something for myself."

The meeting ended with Dr. Larkin disappointedly saying that he didn't think the governor would be able to help them. Soon afterward, however, the authorities did give back Dr. Perry's license, and the Parole Board allowed him to return to Union County. "We are going to let you go home so's you can pull on Williams' coat-tails a bit," they told him.

Following the meeting, Williams phoned Hugh B. Cannon, the governor's aide, and said, "It seems I have just been offered a bribe by the governor's office if I will sell out my people. How would you interpret it?"

In response, Cannon said, "Oh, it's you, Williams. Do you mean to tell me you're not dead yet?"

"No, I'm not dead yet," Williams answered, "but when I die a lot of people may die with me."

To which the governor's aide said, "You may still be alive, but if you keep on agitating this way you are going to be killed soon."

Early in the summer of 1961 Williams received a phone call from Slim Brundage of the College of Complexes, a combination coffee house and militant open forum in Chicago. A pacifist, Brundage had been active in raising contributions of clothing and money for Williams' C.A.R.E. campaign. "I've been reading in the papers about all the trouble you've been having," he said. "Has it ever occurred to you that you might be using the wrong philosophy?" When Williams answered that it hadn't, Brundage went on, "Well, would you be willing to try a different approach? Would you let some people who believe in nonviolence come down there to help you?"

For quite some time Williams' self-defense activities had been severely criticized by those involved in the Sit-In and Freedom Rider Movements. They pointed to such things as the desegregation of the Montgomery, Alabama, busses following the nonviolent demonstrations led by the Reverend Martin Luther King as proof that pacifism was the best way to achieve equality. But Williams' analysis differed from theirs. It seemed to him that the power structure in Montgomery had given in because they weren't presented with a really fundamental challenge to the advantages they derived from racism.

As he saw it, fighting to ride on a desegregated bus wasn't nearly the same as demanding job equality. It might anger a poor White to share a seat with a "nigger," but it didn't mean much to those who travel only by jet and chauffeured limousine. So long as the pacifists limited their struggle to desegregating public facilities, and didn't step too hard on the racists' economic toes, they would continue to gain such small concessions.

Despite his feeling this way, Williams knew that the Gandhiism of the Reverend King and his followers was very popular. Not wanting to take the position of rejecting it out of hand, he answered Brundage, "I've no objection to anyone coming here who wants to help us. If they can show me nonviolence works, I'll become a pacifist myself. I'm looking for results, not to prove any special theories. But let me make one thing clear: I'm not going to disarm my people until I'm completely convinced we won't be attacked."

As soon as the word got out that Williams would accept pacifists, Freedom Riders all over the country began discussing coming to Monroe. But Martin Luther King's associates apparently weren't too interested in having Monroe become a focal point in the desegregation struggle. They let it be known that no funds would be made available for those who wanted to work with Williams. Despite this, a group of Freedom Riders, Whites as well as Blacks among them, just getting out of jail in Mississippi announced they were coming to Monroe before returning North. The Reverend King then decided to send the Reverend Paul Brooks, his personal representative, with instructions to work under Williams' direction. King himself was to come down the following week to help raise funds.

Learning that the Freedom Riders were definitely on their way, Monroe's Black community raised the money to rent a place for them to stay, and named it "Freedom House" in their honor. But when Williams asked his young people to cooperate, most refused. "We have to give these Freedom Riders a fair chance," he pleaded. "This will be the first time in the history of the civil-rights movement that the philosophies of nonviolence and armed self-defense will be compared in the same environment. Personally, I am not convinced racists can be changed by pacifism, but a lot of people from all over the world will be watching to see what happens here. It can't do us any harm, and might, just might, do some good." Finally, several of the Monroe young people changed their minds and agreed to work with the Freedom Riders.

When the pacifists arrived—there were seventeen of them, led by James Forman—they joined with the local youth to establish the "Monroe Nonviolent Action Committee." They then asked everyone involved in the desegregation struggle to take an oath swearing to adhere to pacifist principles and rejecting the use of any form of self-defense other than passive resistance. Williams refused to make such a pledge himself, but urged the members of his NAACP branch to support all those who chose to do so.

Besides the Freedom Riders and the Reverend Brooks, several other outsiders were in Monroe, among them Julian Mayfield, the young Black novelist. Another visitor was Constance Lever, a White exchange student from England, who had written to Williams that she was interested in observing conditions in the South at first hand before going back to Britain. In response to her offer to work with them, Williams and his wife had invited her to be their house guest. Another house guest at that time was Mrs. Mae Mallory, a Black civil rights activist from New York. They encouraged such visitors in order to overcome the press blackout on their activities, wanting as many people as possible to see for themselves what was really happening in Monroe.

The members of the Monroe Nonviolent Action Committee told Williams that they had decided to establish a picket line around the county courthouse to demonstrate for the acceptance of the Ten-Point Program. "You can picket wherever you like," he said. "I and the other members of our Guard will stay home. I promise there won't be an armed Black anywhere nearby."

On Monday, August 21, 1961, the demonstration began. That first day was so uneventful it convinced some of the Freedom Riders everything Williams had told them about the racists in Monroe was a pipe dream. One White college student from up North said, "You know, a policeman smiled at me while I was on the picket line."

"He was probably smiling at the thought of how he was going to kill you," Williams retorted.

Hearing this exchange, Constance Lever, the British exchange student, said, "Oh, I don't think these people are so bad, Rob. You just don't know how to approach them."

All of Williams' efforts to explain that the townspeople were only acting friendly in an effort to win over the strangers were to no avail. "The moment they realize they can't get you to stop picketing by being polite," he said, "is when you'll find out what they're really like."

Without consulting him, the Freedom Riders issued a press release declaring they were in Monroe to try to bring about better race relations through strictly nonviolent means. "Putting something like that in the newspapers is a big mistake," Williams told them. "For almost five years now the racists have been afraid to attack us because they knew we were armed. They are frustrated as hell. By making this kind of a public announcement, you are, in effect, challenging them to do something."

That same day a man telephoned him and said, "Robert, I am calling for the Klan. We want to know if you have become a pacifist." When Williams answered that he hadn't, the man asked, "Well then, are you and your nigger gunmen participating with those pacifists?" When Williams again responded in the negative, he said, "That's just fine. We're sure glad to know you won't be around, because we plan to give those college boys a nice warm send-off."

On Wednesday, the third day of demonstrations, the towns-people's southern hospitality turned sour. Hecklers began to taunt the pickets, and, when one of the Freedom Riders smiled back at his tormentors, two women spit in his face. A policeman knocked another picket to the ground and threatened to break his camera, and a third picket was arrested for protesting the cop's actions. The tension was beginning to mount.

On Thursday, the fourth day, one of the White Freedom Riders was attacked by three White men while walking in town, and badly beaten. But, since the cops broke up the fight and promised to arrest his assailants, even the man who had been attacked remained convinced the law was on the side of the demonstrators.

John, Williams' youngest son, who was only eight, decided to join the picket line. Both he and his ten-year-old brother Bobby were completely involved in their father's struggle. He had trained them in marksmanship and the proper handling of weapons, and they used to cry when he wouldn't let them stay up at night and stand guard with the men. But when John asked to walk with them, the Freedom Riders told him he was too young.

"I'm Black, and I'm being segregated just like everybody else," he complained. "Since you're letting even White people picket with you, you shouldn't discriminate against me just because I'm little." After he agreed to take the oath of nonviolence, they gave in and let him join the demonstration.

To try to prevent retaliation against his family, Williams didn't advertise the fact that he had a wife and children. He doubted whether more than a handful of Whites in town knew what Mabel and the boys looked like. But once the word got out that one of his sons was on the picket line, the racists showed their viciousness. On Friday, the fifth day of demonstrations, mistaking him for Williams' son, three White men savagely beat a ten-year-old Black boy named Prentice Robinson on the main street of town. Despite several witnesses to the assault, which left the child seriously injured, the police took no action.

That same day one of the White Freedom Riders was shot in the stomach by a high-powered air rifle. It happened directly in front of the courthouse, in full view of the cops, but no arrests were made then either. That was the day when the sanitation authorities had the picket line sprayed with insecticide. And it also saw the enforcement of a special local ordinance which made it mandatory for pickets to remain at least fifteen feet apart. The cops would stop one of the pickets and start talking to him. Then, when the picket behind him failed to stop walking, they would arrest him for being too close. Using this tactic, they imprisoned several demonstrators.

As part of his efforts to publicize the situation, Williams frequently telephoned news releases to the Associated Press, United Press, and other wire services. When he called the Prensa Latina News Agency at the Cuban United Nations Mission in New York, their representative said, "Williams, you know our people like you very much. If you ever have to leave the United States, you'll always be welcome in Cuba." He couldn't help but laugh as he answered, "Thanks for the offer, but I don't have any plans to leave here."

On the morning of that fifth day Williams had a rather unusual visitor. He was in the house when Mabel said there was someone outside who wanted to see him. When he asked who it was, she answered, "It's that old prophet man you helped get aid from the Welfare Department."

The old man she was referring to was an elderly self-styled preacher who lived so far out in the woods that the road didn't reach his house. The only way to get there was by mule or on foot. He and his wife had been sick and their children hungry. Williams and his group had given him some food and money from the C.A.R.E. donations they were receiving, and had gotten his wife admitted to the hospital.

Some time earlier Williams had taken a visiting Japanese exchange student to see him. She was surprised and said, "In Asia we have poverty, but everyone knows it, and we are doing our best to get rid of it. Here, in the United States I never thought to see people living so badly. You Americans hide your poor from the rest of the world." Before they had left the old man's shack she had photographed it in order to prove to her friends in Japan that she wasn't exaggerating.

Going out to see what the old prophet man wanted, Williams found him sitting in the car of a Black woman active in their NAACP branch. "I know you're busy, Rob," she said, "but please be considerate and act as though you take him seriously."

"I brought you a charm," the old man said.

"What kind of charm?" Williams asked.

"I will show it to you in a minute," he answered, "but first I am going to tell you why I brought it: Last night I had a vision. In my vision the White people were after you, the police and everybody, and were trying to kill you. So I started praying to God, and he told me to bring you this charm."

He then took a small piece of paper out of his pocket. It appeared to be some sort of Christmas stationery, having a colored painting of a decorative candle and a bit of holly printed in the upper corner. Someone, presumably the old man, had written all over it in a scratchy longhand.

"Now you take this and keep it close to your heart at all times," he said.

Williams laughingly said, "No, thanks, I don't need it."

"So long as you hold this charm they will never be able to capture or harm you," he said. "This has been revealed to me by God!"

Even the NAACP woman couldn't help but smile a bit. "Go on, Rob, take it," she urged. "He's really sincere. He walked all the way to my house and begged me to drive him here just so's he could give it to you."

When Mabel came outside to see what was going on, Williams told her, "That piece of paper won't do me any good. What I need is more bullets."

"Don't make him feel bad," she said. "Put it in your wallet. It won't hurt you." Giving in, he accepted the scrap of paper.

"Now you remember this," the old man said. "They are coming to get you in three days, but this charm will stop them from hurting you. Now write your name on it."

After he left, Williams examined the message written on the scrap of Christmas stationery. It read:

A CHARM AGAINST POWDER AND PAIN

Heavenly and holy prophet, blow every blow and misfortune away from me.
I seek refuge under the Tree of Life, which bears twelve-fold fruits.
I stand behind the Holy Altar of the Christian Church.
I commend myself to the Holy Trinity.
I, Robert F. Williams, hide myself beneath the Holy Corpse of Jesus Christ.
I commend myself unto the ruins of Jesus Christ that the hand of no man might be able to seize me, or beat me, or imprison me, or overcome me.
By God that carries all power, I beseech him to keep and be with me, to keep me in a safe place, safe from all my enemies, visible or invisible.

On the evening of that fifth day of picketing, still unconvinced of the danger of attack by the racists, several of the Freedom Riders took a drive into neighboring Macklenberg County. When they stopped for refreshments at a restaurant, they were set upon by a mob of Klansmen. In the melee, while the others managed to escape in their car, one of them was chased into the woods and was left behind.

Fearing for his life, Williams' people phoned the authorities for help, but neither the Monroe police, the Union County sheriff, the Charlotte police, nor the Macklenberg County sheriff would intervene. In an effort to save the poor fellow from a possible lynching, the Reverend Brooks called the office of Governor Terry Sanford and spoke to his chief aide, Hugh B. Cannon. But all Cannon did was complain about Williams being a "troublemaker."

"We are pacifists," the Reverend pleaded. "We believe in nonviolence."

To which the governor's aide responded, "If you're a real pacifist you'd better get the hell out of Monroe, man, because there's going to be plenty of violence there."

"Since you're so concerned about Williams," the Reverend Brooks said, "he's right here. Do you wish to talk to him?"

When Cannon said he would, Williams took the phone. "Mr. Cannon," he began, "this has nothing to do with your feelings toward me. I am appealing to you to send the state troopers to find that lost student before he gets lynched."

"You're getting just what you deserve, Williams," he answered. "You've been asking for violence, and now it's here."

"But I'm not asking you to help me," Williams said. "Besides, he's not Negro, he's White."

"I don't give a damn who he is," Cannon said.

Fortunately, the lost Freedom Rider was able to find his way back to Monroe without being hurt.

On Saturday, the sixth day of demonstrations, the Freedom Riders once again picketed the courthouse. Williams felt that he had learned an important lesson that Sunday in June when the racist mob had surrounded him at the swimming pool. The people he was trying to influence to end segregation were those who ran the community: the middle-class business and professional elements. So long as his group had confined their demonstrations to the hours when the poorer Whites were at the mills and farms they had had little difficulty. But experience had taught them that picketing either in the evenings or on Saturday or Sunday, when the workers were idle, was asking for trouble. "Stay off the streets on the weekend," Williams warned the Freedom Riders, "otherwise you will be inviting violent attack."

"But that's exactly why we have to picket on the weekend," the Freedom Riders responded. "We want the working people to see us. Instead of trying to avoid them, we will strive to change their hearts through the example of our love and nonviolence."

"You can do anything you like," Williams said, "but the worst time of all is Sunday, when the poor Whites come spilling out of church, getting drunk, and looking for excitement. It's the very moment when their kind of Christian usually falls under the influence of the devil. Love and nonviolence mean nothing to them. Racist hatred is so deeply imbedded in their souls they are little different than savage beasts."

Saturday morning was quiet, but in the afternoon, when the Freedom Riders were about to be picked up and driven back to the Black community, a mob blocked the streets and refused to let their taxicabs through. Forced to walk the mile or so back to the Black side of the railroad tracks, the pickets found themselves running a gauntlet of jeering, rock-throwing Whites. Spitting, cursing, and threatening death, the mob pursued them into the Black community. Even though Williams had ordered his Guard not to intervene, many Blacks ran into the street and began brawling with the racist mob, stoning them and their cars, and eventually forcing them out of the area.

That evening, while the usual Saturday-night drinking went on in the White districts, the Blacks quietly prepared their defenses. The Klan held off on direct attacks, being content with a few shots from long range. No one was hit, but the crack of rifles echoing from the hills and the whirr of steel-jacketed bullets overhead continued all through the hours of darkness.

As the sun rose on the morning of Sunday, August 27, 1961, reports reached Williams that the chief of police and his men were driving through Union County urging Whites to come into town. Klansmen and their supporters began arriving from neighboring counties, and the "Minutemen," an extreme right-wing paramilitary organization, also began sending people into the area. By noon there were literally thousands of racists heading toward Monroe. Carloads of them were racing around the Black community, even up and down Boyte Street in front of Williams' house.

Early in the afternoon Williams received an alert that the Klan was forming a motorcade in the Courthouse Square. There were cars in it with license plates from South Carolina and Georgia. Despite all these things, the Freedom Riders, together with dozens of local young people, were picketing as usual.

In order to get a better idea of what they would be up against, Williams and Dr. Perry decided to drive into town. They took along a semiautomatic rifle, several extra magazines, and two pistols. Dr. Perry drove, while Williams sat next to him on the front seat, his rifle standing up between his knees with its butt resting on the floor. At the sight of them, the Whites jamming the Courthouse Square began shouting and shaking their fists. But when they noticed the rifle between Williams' legs, they quieted down. Although the racists were already assaulting Blacks in other parts of town, no one made a move to try to stop the car.

The Courthouse Square looked like the site of a bizarre circus. At the head of a long line of cars was a Chevrolet convertible with a large Confederate flag covering one side of it and an equally large U.S. flag draped over the other. Standing on the rear seat, haranguing the crowd, was a tall Klan official sporting a long golden bed sheet. The cars behind it were full of Klansmen, some of them hooded, and many drinking heavily. Confederate flags and colored bed sheets were everywhere. In the middle of all this, fifty or so members of the Monroe Nonviolent Action Committee were picketing the courthouse itself. Although the crowd taunting them was growing larger and more threatening by the moment, the police seemed to be holding the racists back. As there seemed to be nothing for them to do, Williams and Dr. Perry left.

Returning to the Black community, they told their people that they might be in for a big attack that evening. Because of the extremely large number of Klansmen in town, they began distributing guns and ammunition even to those Blacks who weren't members of the Guard. The only criterion for receiving a weapon was a willingness to accept orders and, if necessary, to fight.

In mid-afternoon a lone White State Highway patrolman drove up and said that the presence of armed Blacks in front of Williams' house was stopping traffic. As he was speaking, a number of Blacks began to gather. Many carried guns, and some held fused packs of dynamite. This seemed to encourage the cop to address Williams in an unusually courteous manner. "It's perfectly all right for them to be in your front yard," he said, "but we'd sure appreciate your getting them off the street."

"I'll get everyone connected with our Guard out of the way," Williams answered, "but I'm not responsible for anyone else."

At that moment a Black woman, one of the "good people" in the community, a churchgoer who had never been known to hurt a fly, ran toward them waving a hatchet. "Let's kill him! Let's kill every White in this town and burn it to the ground!" she screamed, tears of hatred running down her cheeks. "The only thing that will stop them is death!" This set off some of the others, and they started shouting, "Shoot the son of a bitch! Hang him!" Williams had a tough job convincing them to let the patrolman leave the area in one piece.

The radio soon began broadcasting news flashes about Monroe being "an armed camp getting ready to explode!" The commentators said Governor George Wallace of Alabama had volun-

teered to send his state's National Guard to help Governor
Sanford suppress the troublemakers. While Wallace was declaring
that Alabama couldn't afford to stand by and do nothing while
"savages" overran the North Carolina forces, U.S. Attorney General
Robert Kennedy was becoming involved as well. When asked
if he would send federal troops to Monroe to maintain order, he
answered he wouldn't do so unless it became absolutely necessary.
He did say, however, that he was going to see to it that the persons
responsible for the violence in Monroe were severely punished.
Williams interpreted this as referring to the members of his Guard
and himself.

At 4:00 p.m. James Forman, one of the leaders of the Freedom
Riders, telephoned Williams that the cops were allowing the
racists to push around the pickets. He asked him to rush four taxis
to the Courthouse Square to take the Freedom Riders to safety.
But the Black cab company called to say their taxis were being
prevented from reaching the Freedom Riders by groups of Whites
blocking every entrance into town. A few minutes later a report
came in that the racist mob was out of control and beating the
demonstrators at will, shots had been fired, and the town was in
the grip of a full-scale riot.

Hearing this, several of the men in the Guard said, "Let's go.
Let's march on the town."

"No," Williams told them, "those people are pacifists. They
want to prove that love and nonviolence can work, even if it
means getting their heads smashed in. If we go there shooting,
they will say we violated our bargain with them. Besides, if we
march into town we will be leaving the Black community defenseless.
We know the Klan is getting ready to come at us. We have to
stay here."

His arguments stopped most of them, but a few part-time
members of the Guard, plus some men who weren't in it, decided
to go anyway. Julian Mayfield, the novelist, went along. With
rifles and shotguns jutting out of the windows of their cars, they
managed to force their way through the Whites blocking the
streets. Arriving at the courthouse, they saw that Constance Lever,
the White student from England, was encircled by a knot of
armed racists and being cursed and manhandled.

In an attempt to rescue her, one group of young Blacks tried
to get Constance into their car. Up until this moment the police

had been content to stand aside and let the mob do everything. Now, however, a policeman grabbed the British girl and bellowed, "No White woman is getting into a car full of niggers in this town!"

Unable to convince the policeman to let them take her away, and with the armed mob of racists edging in and threatening them as well, one of the young Blacks reached into the car and pulled out a shotgun. "Give me that gun!" the policeman started shouting; and James Forman, the Black picket captain, came over and pleaded with the youth, "Please don't make any trouble. You Williams people agreed not to bring guns near our line. The best way you can help us is to give the gun to the officer like he wants."

When the youngster surrendered the shotgun to him, the policeman handed it to a member of the racist mob, who promptly smashed James Forman over the head with it. Blood poured down Forman's face, and the members of the mob, with the cops helping them, went wild and began savagely attacking the rest of the pickets. The police disarmed the other Black youngsters, turned their weapons over to the mob, and twisted their arms behind their backs while the racists beat them. One elderly Black man, clubbed down in a pool of his own blood, continued to shout defiance as the cops dragged him away to jail along with forty-six or more of the other demonstrators.

The pickets were told they were being taken to the jail "for their own protection," but once there they were charged with such things as "disturbing the peace" and "resisting an officer." Prisoners serving sentences for common crimes were released in order to make room for them. Several men thus freed came and told Williams that the students—some of whom were severely injured— were being jammed into cells without receiving medical attention. A few were so badly hurt there was danger they would bleed to death.

To placate the growing number of his Guard who wanted to march on the town, Williams telephoned the chief of police and said, "I've been told the Freedom Riders aren't receiving medical attention and their lives are in danger. If you don't get a doctor to them in thirty minutes, we are going to have to take the jail." Although the chief's only answer was to slam down the receiver, less than fifteen minutes later James Forman telephoned from the hospital to say that all of the injured were receiving medical assistance. The chief had allowed him to call Williams in order to convince him that the Freedom Riders were being taken care of.

A few moments later, Julian Mayfield, who had managed to avoid being arrested at the Courthouse Square, returned and reported that members of the mob, including uniformed police, were on the ridge near the railroad tracks shooting at those Blacks trying to flee the White part of town.

As the warm August afternoon came to an end and darkness fell, the racists began driving through outlying sections of the community, hurling rocks and bottles from their speeding cars; and the Blacks started digging in. In front of Williams' house alone more than three hundred armed people milled about in the street, and he estimated there were at least three hundred more men with guns setting up guard posts throughout the rest of the Black part of town. Everywhere one looked, people were cleaning rifles, preparing fire bombs, and so on.

Suddenly a Black boy of about fourteen came running down Boyte Street waving a pistol, which he had taken from the Guards' stockpile without permission. He had been hanging around all day asking for a weapon, but Williams had refused, feeling he was too young. As he came up out of breath and dripping with sweat, Williams demanded, "What are you doing with that gun?"

"Oh," he answered, "this thing is no damn good. I would have been able to kill all those cops if it hadn't jammed on me. This way I didn't manage to get off but two shots into one of them." The *New York Times* later carried a story that a Monroe policeman had been shot in the leg.

By early evening Williams' telephone was ringing constantly with calls from Black parents whose children were missing, some having been arrested on the picket line, while others had been waylaid by the racist mob in Monroe. Tension grew as crowds of angry Blacks began stoning passing cars. Just as was being done to Blacks on the other side of town, those Whites caught in Black areas were being pulled out of their vehicles and beaten in the streets. The constant radio and TV news flashes about an "impending race war" were causing Blacks from other towns in North Carolina, and even from out of state, to telephone. "If it's true there's going to be a real war," they said, "then we want to come and join you." Williams warned them against trying to do so, as he had already received reports of police roadblocks on the highways leading into Union County.

He was answering one such call when he heard shouting outside. As he went to the front door, someone called out, "We got 'em! We got 'em!" Stepping outside, Williams saw a car with its doors open stopped about half a block away. Entering his front yard was an elderly White couple surrounded by a milling crowd of angry Blacks.

"They're Klan people!" someone shouted. "We saw them in the motorcade a couple of days ago! They had a big sign on their car that said, 'Open Season on Coons!' "

The crowd was on the verge of murder. Realizing that all it would take to set off their wrath was one impulsive act, Williams began trying to push them away from the White couple. The White woman indignantly complained, "We've been kidnapped! These people have kidnapped us!" Her defiance of the crowd only made it angrier. She apparently was either too confused to comprehend the seriousness of the situation or so used to dealing with servile types that she thought she could frighten the Blacks by raising her voice.

Turning to her, Williams said, "Oh, no, lady. You're not kidnapped. You can leave any time you're ready."

"We were just driving along, minding our own business, when they stopped our car and made us get out," she said. "If you are a good fellow you will take us out of here."

"Lady," he answered, "I didn't bring you here, and I'm not about to take you away. You know there has been rioting going on all day. So why did you come driving right into the colored part of town? These people are mad. Their sons and daughters are being beaten and jailed right now by your people. Your being here is your own problem."

Then the crowd started screaming, "Kill them! Kill the sons of bitches!" One old man was crying out loud, saying, "Please, somebody! Please give me a gun so I can shoot them! Please!"

Suddenly a light plane zoomed low over their heads. They had already received telephone threats that, if they couldn't get through the ground defenses, the KKK planned to bomb them from the air. As the plane circled to make a second pass, over a dozen men in the crowd opened up on it with M-1's and other high-powered rifles. At that very moment, in what appeared to be a coordinated attack, a car full of Whites came roaring down Boyte Street, guns blazing from all its windows. As it sped past, at least twenty Blacks opened up with pistol and rifle fire; flames exploded from its rear as their bullets struck. The din was so great it sounded like a full-scale battle was in progress. The elderly White woman, seeing that the Blacks were ready to kill without hesitation, lost her arrogance and began trembling and mumbling hysterically, while her husband kept his mouth shut.

Just then someone said Williams was wanted on the phone. When he walked up the steps to his front porch, the two Whites followed so closely they pressed against his back. The three of them were in almost perfect step as they entered the house. Since the living room was full of guns and ammunition, Mabel took them into the bedroom and gave them seats.

When Williams had completed answering the phone, the White woman, whose name he later learned was Mrs. Stegall, said, "If you'll just escort us out of here we'll be all right."

"Lady," he answered, "if I'd been caught in the White part of town I'd be dead by now. Our people are angry, but we're not half as cruel as you are."

As he said this, she looked closely at him and asked, "Are you that man? Are you Robert Williams?" When he said he was, she said, attempting to mollify him, "Why you're not the way everyone says you are. You seem to be a nice person. You know, my husband and I live over in Marshall, not here in Monroe. We don't agree at all with the cruel things they're doing to you colored folks. If you believe in God, and I'm certain you do, then you should help your fellow Christians by taking us out of here."

"Just be thankful you are not out there being torn to pieces by that crowd," Williams told her. "You know very well that, were our positions reversed, not only wouldn't you permit me to take shelter in your home, you'd be out with the Klan trying to kill me."

Just then the phone rang. This time it was the chief of police. "Robert," he said, "you've caused a lot of trouble in this town, but now your time is up. In thirty minutes you'll be hanging in the Courthouse Square."

"If I hang," Williams answered, "I won't hang alone. There are a couple of your Klan people sitting right here in my house,

and the only thing standing between them and death is me."
Saying he didn't believe him, the chief hung up.

Then a call came that there had been an announcement on
the television about state troops being sent to surround the town.
A few minutes later a woman called to say that a long military
convoy was already entering the White business district, and that
dozens of police cars were massing behind the jail.

"The mask is off," thought Williams. "Having failed with
bribes and threats, the racist rulers of North Carolina are turning
to open aggression against us. President Kennedy wanted to destroy the Cuban Revolution because it dared to end racism and
exploitation on its own soil, and now Governor Sanford wants to
do the same to us."

All three—the police, the military, and the Klan—seemed to
Williams to be slightly different tentacles of the same bloated
monster. He was convinced that the state troopers weren't coming
to protect the Blacks or the Freedom Riders from being lynched.
They were being sent to finish what the Klan and the cops had
started.

A few minutes after he heard that the troopers were arriving,
one of Williams' lookouts came running in and said, "The cops
are starting to surround this block! They've got machine guns and
everything!" Going outside, Williams saw that both ends of Boyte
Street were blocked by police cars. It seemed evident to him that
Chief Mauney was trying to trap them there until the state troopers could get into position for an attack.

A group of the Guard leaders came to Williams' house and
said, "Rob, things are going to be very bad tonight. We have
talked it over, and we think it would be better for you to leave
town for a week or two until this whole thing cools off. That way,
even if a lot of people get killed, they won't be able to pin anything on you."

Williams considered all the factors involved: He was the primary focus of the racists' and the authorities' wrath. With him
gone they would lack a specific target, and have to deal with the
Blacks as a whole. Also, his people were as well armed and prepared as he could get them. "Yes," he decided, "I'll leave. But
only for a few days. And when I get to New York I'll let the world
know what's going on down here."

Telling Mabel to get their two little boys ready, he began

making preparations for their departure. "Take all the guns and ammunition out of my house and to the places where they're to be hidden," he instructed the Guard. Then he armed himself with a 9-mm P-38 luger pistol, to which he attached a special thirty-one-shot spring-wound snail-drum magazine and wooden stock, thus converting it to a submachine gun. Finally, he went out to make an inspection of the Guard's defense positions.

Just as Williams was leaving the house, another car full of White men came speeding down Boyte Street, evidently having been allowed through by the police. As it passed, three of the Blacks' fire teams opened up; and lines of tracer bullets streaked into the back of it. Zigzagging back and forth down the street, riddled with holes, the car skidded around the corner and disappeared. No reports of Klan dead or wounded were ever made public, but Williams felt that it was a miracle if the men in that car got away without being hit.

He made the rounds of the Guard posts, telling the men that the state troopers were surrounding them. He asked Julian Mayfield, the author, to leave town at once so that, whatever happened, someone would survive to tell the outside world.

As Williams was walking down a side street, he suddenly saw the new police car belonging to Chief Mauney coming toward him. In a flash of anger he raised his submachine gun. A split second before his finger pulled the trigger, however, Williams saw that the chief wasn't in the car. Two local Black cops, one of them a former schoolmate of Williams', were alone in it. Williams conjectured that the chief had hoped to trick the Guard into killing them. It had almost worked.

Returning to the house, Williams was told there was a phone call waiting. "I don't have time," he said.

"But this is the Reverend Martin Luther King!" everyone started shouting.

"You tell the Reverend King he was supposed to come here last week, but he didn't," Williams told them. "Now it's too late. We are already in battle, and I don't have anything to talk to him about." He never did discover what King had wanted to say.

Going to the rear of the house, Williams told the members of the Guard assembled there, "You've got to disperse. Don't let them find everyone in one place. Get out to the defense posts in the other areas. Let them break through when they make their move, then set up roadblocks and snipers behind them. If we can trap them inside our perimeter, they'll be at our mercy." There was no doubt in his mind that, dug-in and prepared as they were, any move against them would result in heavy casualties to their foes.

Not wanting to cause panic or confusion, Williams didn't tell the rank and file of the Guard about his decision to leave. Only those closest to him were aware of it. It was almost 9:00 p.m. when he asked Mabel if she and the boys were ready.

"Please, Rob," she said, "you go without us. We'll just slow you down."

But he had no intention of leaving any of his next of kin to the tender mercies of the Klan, and insisted, "No, you're all coming along, including your mother. We're going to New York." They couldn't take any clothing or personal belongings. Time was running out.

In addition to the P-38, Williams stuck two pistols into his belt and slung a semiautomatic rifle over one shoulder in case they were fired on from long range. He also picked up a bag with several hundred rounds of spare ammo. Then the five of them—Williams, his wife, his mother-in-law, and his two little boys—headed out the back door and into the alley. To throw off the cops, he left his beat-up little Hillman standing in front of the house. It was so well known that it would have been impossible to get out of town in it anyway.

Reaching the end of the alley, Williams saw that their path was blocked. A continuous line of police cars was slowly cruising past. They were so close to one another, almost bumper to bumper, that not even a child could get through. Mabel, the boys, and his mother-in-law remained silent and uncomplaining despite the peril. The five of them huddled in the bushes at the end of the alley, waiting for an opening between the cars so they could run across the street to the next block, but none came. As more and more cops kept arriving, every minute lessened their chances of escaping. Williams had never been forced to kill before, but now there seemed no choice except to shoot their way out. If he acted at once, before the state troopers got into position, he might be able to destroy one or two of the police cars. Releasing the safety catch, he cocked the submachine gun, raised it to his shoulder, and took aim.

Chapter Nine

CHRISTMAS DINNER IN HAVANA

Just as Williams was about to blast the next police car to round the corner, something made it slow down. The path was clear. "Run, for Godsakes, run!" he whispered, and the five of them managed to get across the street and into the alley on the next block. For the moment they were out of the trap.

Moving quickly through the darkness, they reached the house of a friend. When Williams told him of his reluctant decision to leave town until things cooled down, he offered to take them part of the way. They drove out of Monroe via the back streets, avoiding the police cars and trucks loaded with troops patrolling the main thoroughfares. The entire town was being surrounded.

Their first driver took them to the house of another friend, who was to drive them the rest of the way to New York. By now it was almost 10:00 p.m. and police checkpoints were blocking all the major highways. As a result of Williams' boyhood love for the woods and his aid work with the rural poor, he had an expert knowledge of the back roads, many little more than cow paths. The going was slow and bumpy, but they were able to escape from the area.

They didn't dare use the main roads until they were well out of North Carolina. Once over the state line into Virginia, Williams disposed of his P-38 submachine gun, semiautomatic rifle, and extra ammunition in a stream in a wooded area. To make certain the weapons wouldn't be usable, he removed the bolts and firing pins and threw them away a mile or so further on. But he kept his two pistols, both because they could be easily concealed and because he had decided to shoot it out rather than surrender, at least until they got as far north as Washington, D.C. He felt certain that, were he to be disarmed by the police of North Carolina or Virginia, they would either gun him down on the spot or beat him to death in jail.

Driving all night, they reached the New Jersey side of the Hudson River and saw the skyscrapers of New York on the opposite shore silhouetted by the early morning sun. As they were about to enter the Lincoln Tunnel, they came upon a large number of policemen checking cars. It was too late to try to get away. Locked in by traffic on all sides, their only choice was to wait and see what would happen. Whatever the cops were looking for, it wasn't them; and they were allowed to enter the tunnel and drive under the river into Manhattan.

That afternoon the radio began broadcasting an all-points alarm, saying Williams was wanted by the FBI for "interstate flight to avoid arrest." He was described as "heavily armed and extremely dangerous" and possibly already in the New York area. The Union County grand jury had indicted him on the charge of having kidnapped Mr. and Mrs. Stegall.

Williams was stupefied. The last time he'd seen the Stegalls they were sitting in the bedroom of his house in Monroe. Although he later learned they had left under their own power and were unharmed, they had filed a complaint naming him as the "ringleader" of the crowd that forced them from their automobile. In one interview Mrs. Stegall told the press she and her husband had been marched into Williams' house at gunpoint and tied to chairs. In another account she said nothing about having been tied up, and admitted that Williams had criticized the crowd. In a third version she was quoted as saying: "Williams only pretended to be trying to help us."

Instead of committing any crime against the Stegalls, Williams felt that he had saved them from being lynched. Also, when he'd left North Carolina there was no indictment out for him; it wasn't issued until the grand jury met the next day. So he couldn't see how he could be legitimately charged with having fled the state to avoid arrest. He concluded that he was being charged with violating a federal law only so the FBI could be used to hunt him down in New York or wherever else he might go. As he saw it, the U.S. Justice Department had joined forces with the racists running the state of North Carolina. The debt which he believed the Kennedy Administration owed to Henry Hall Wilson, Jr., and the Klan seemed to be getting paid off.

Before the end of the day the New York television stations were exhibiting Williams' photograph, asking anyone with information as to his whereabouts to contact the police. The news reports described how a small army of police and state troopers had exchanged shots with the Guard all through Sunday night and into Monday morning. One story stated that over five thousand Klansmen and supporters had come to Monroe that weekend. The state troopers had blocked them from making a full-scale assault, not, in Williams' view, to protect the Black population, but to prevent the KKK from being massacred.

By Monday noon, the Klansmen having gone home, the Blacks had slipped away and hidden their weapons. It was at this time, under the authority of the kidnapping indictment issued by the grand jury, that a combined attack force of local, state, and federal officers armed with machine guns and tear gas rushed Williams' house. They met no resistance. The only people they found there were some of the Reverend King's pacifists. The guns and explosives the Stegalls had seen in the living room were long gone. Williams imagined that the chief of police must have been especially riled at finding that he hadn't made himself available for hanging in the Courthouse Square.

The police used Williams' disappearance as the basis for tearing apart people's homes in endless searches, conducting all-night grillings of everyone known to have been among his associates, confiscating weapons—even those which the owners had a legal right to possess—and harassing a large number of people who hadn't the slightest connection with him.

The kidnapping charge was soon expanded to include four others, including John Lowry, a White Freedom Rider from New York who had publicly declared that, even though Williams was gone, he and the other students would carry on the fight. His statement was carried in the *New York Post* and the *New York Times* that Monday, and on Tuesday he was charged with complicity in abducting the Stegalls. Two local Black teen-agers—Richard Crowder, the chairman of the Monroe Non-Violent Action Committee, and Harold Reape, who had shown leadership ability in the demonstrations—were also indicted. The fourth person charged in the kidnapping was Mrs. Mae Mallory, the Black civil-rights activist from New York who had left the state when the rioting started on Sunday. Not one of those indicted, or the "Monroe Five," as they came to be known, had been among those who had forced the Stegalls from their car.

Although Williams later heard that several people were hurt, only one incident was dealt with by the authorities. Two Monroe Blacks—Jimmie Covington, fifteen, and Albert Rorie, seventeen— were charged with shooting a police officer. Covington was sent to reform school and Rorie to prison for five years.

Inside the Union County Jail, Richard Griswold, one of the White pickets arrested at the Courthouse Square, was beaten so severely by another prisoner that he almost died. He survived only because a White demonstrator chanced to see him lying on the floor semiconscious and covered with blood, and shouted for help. Apparently unwilling to risk the trouble that could result from the death of a White prisoner before a White witness, the warden had given Griswold medical attention. But Howard Stack, his attacker, was released.

Three weeks later the cops rearrested Griswold's assailant, which made Stack so angry he wrote a confession on a piece of notebook paper and had it smuggled out of the jail. In it he swore the Monroe police had promised to drop forgery and assault charges pending against him if he would brutalize the Freedom Rider.

Conrad Lynn, the lawyer who had helped in the "Kissing Case," sent the original of Stack's confession to Attorney General Robert Kennedy and asked the Justice Department for an immediate federal investigation of the Monroe Police Department. Bobby Kennedy's office didn't acknowledge the letter, but the FBI did send agents down from Charlotte to take depositions from several people. When Lynn continued to press for legal action, he was informed that, the Union County authorities having committed Stack to a mental institution, the U.S. Justice Department considered the matter closed.

Among the weapons confiscated by the Monroe police were some Russian military-surplus bolt-action rifles. This set off the cry that Williams' Guard had been given weapons by the Communists, a charge repeated by the *New York Post*. What irked Williams was that the *Post* forgot to mention that the weapons in question were for sale in gun shops throughout the United States. Also, they failed to inform the public there was no law against owning such weapons, or that the police had also seized British, German, Italian, and U.S.-made arms from his people.

The fact that they had bills of sale from 100-percent White

American gun shops and mail-order firms for every one of those
Russian rifles didn't stop the red-baiters from getting into the act.
Williams was no longer just an "uppity nigger." As he saw it, the
U.S. government and the national press were now depicting him
as a bloodthirsty Black Bolshevik bogeyman.

Within a few hours after he arrived in New York Williams
was able to contact some friends, who then tried to get help for
him from his old left-wing acquaintances. With the alarm out for
him on radio and television, he knew better than to approach his
relatives, because the FBI would be watching them. His friends
weren't asking the leftists to shelter him or his wife, only to take
care of their two little boys. Since the FBI was probably looking
for an entire family, Williams felt it would be risky for them to
stay together.

One U.S. Communist Party member he knew told Williams
to go to his house in Manhattan and wait in front of it. He did so,
standing outside in the street for over one hour, but the man never
appeared. Later, when Williams tried to find out why he hadn't
shown up, he got a message saying that the USCP had decided
they didn't want to have anything to do with him.

It didn't take him long to discover that not one of the leftists
he knew in New York was willing to take care of his boys. They
were the same people whose greatest pleasure seemed to have
been bragging about how they supported the struggle of Blacks for
justice and equality. Williams felt that, if there was ever a way to
find out if they really meant what they said, this was it. He later
heard that those he'd once considered the most militant among
them, the Trotskyites of the Socialist Workers' Party, were actually trying to get him to turn himself in! They were approaching
his friends and asking them to advise him to have a lawyer arrange his surrender. "Tell Williams he can't possibly escape," they
were reported to have said. "J. Edgar Hoover has assigned five
hundred FBI agents to the case. The only way for him to stay alive
is to give himself up. Otherwise they will shoot him down."

Rejected by the leftists he knew, Williams tried to get help
from a prominent Black Nationalist. At first he was so enthusiastic
that he took the entire family into his home. After two or three
hours, however, with the alarm for Williams' arrest being repeated
over and over again on radio and television, he became frightened. "This thing is getting too loud," he said. "My mother is a

very scary type, and if she was to find out who you are, she might tell the police." So they had to leave his place.

Then a White doctor got in touch through a friend. "Tell Mr. Williams," he said, "that I am willing to let him and his family stay in my house on Long Island." Williams had no idea who this man was and was afraid he might be trying to get him to come to his place in order to turn him in. "He says he has been reading *The Crusader*," his friend said, "and wants to help because he believes in what you have been doing." Having very little choice in the matter, Williams decided to accept his offer.

When the little group arrived at the doctor's house, he put them up in a basement recreation room. "They won't be looking for you here," he said, "because I don't belong to any political groups. Over the years various people have tried to get me involved, and they have called me a right-winger because I've always refused to join anything. The truth is I just haven't seen a cause worth risking myself for. When I heard that some of the very people who have called me names refused to take your boys, I decided to try to get in touch with you. Helping you escape seems a really worthwhile thing to do."

Here was a total stranger, a well-to-do Jewish medical man, living in a fine home in the suburbs, who seemed ready to chance losing everything, perhaps even his life, just because he sympathized with his ideas. Williams had known *The Crusader* was being read by Whites as well as Blacks, but he'd never anticipated it would be that meaningful to someone who wasn't politically active. His general disillusionment with the New York Left was somewhat compensated for by the doctor's individual act of friendship.

After they had been holed up in the basement rumpus room for four or five days, during which time they managed to find someone to take care of their boys and a place for Williams' mother-in-law to stay, the doctor told them: "You realize you can't remain here indefinitely. I often go to Canada on hunting trips, and the officials at the border have never stopped me or searched my car before. Why don't we take the chance?" Williams and his wife agreed to try it.

Williams had only been able to take two or three hundred dollars when he fled Monroe. He'd left considerably more in the Guard's treasury in the form of personal checks, which he was unsure about being able to cash. Knowing this, the Black friend who had brought them to the doctor's went out to try to get some donations.

A few hours later he returned, handed Williams a pile of small bills and said, "I just went up to Harlem and stood on a street corner. Pretty soon, you know how it is, the hustlers and pushers started coming over and asking if I 'wanted something.' When I told them I was trying to raise money for you to escape with, they all started emptying their pockets. The word flashed around the neighborhood, and people came running. In only ten or fifteen minutes I had collected this four hundred dollars."

Support came not only from the street people of Harlem. Williams' friend had approached a Black policeman and casually asked, "Supposing you were trying to get a man some place in a car, and didn't want anybody to know about it, would it be best to hide him in the trunk?"

"Hell no," the cop had answered. "Just let him sit in the front seat like nothing unusual was happening. Unless they know he is coming in advance, nobody will pay any attention, but if they happen to make a spot check and find him in the trunk, they'll be certain something is wrong." From the confidential way he said this, Williams' friend felt certain the Black cop knew exactly whom they were discussing.

Early the next morning, Williams, his wife, and the doctor left for Canada. They looked like a typical holiday group, the doctor's station wagon piled high with golf clubs, tennis rackets, hunting gear, and suitcases. At nightfall they arrived at the bridge traversing the U.S.-Canadian border at Buffalo, New York. Following the suggestion of the Harlem cop, Williams was to ride in the car with the doctor, but first Mabel was to go over by foot. That way, even if the FBI should be waiting, they wouldn't both be caught.

A number of other people were walking across the bridge. Williams watched as his wife passed the U.S. and Canadian officials without any trouble; then he and the doctor started to drive over. At such well-traveled border points those leaving the country are not usually checked by the U.S. officials, but a Canadian immigration officer asked to see the doctor's identification papers. Looking at Williams, he asked, "Were you born in the U.S.A.?"

"I was born in Georgia," Williams answered. He had managed to borrow the passport, driver's license, and birth certificate of a Black friend from that state whom he resembled. But he didn't have to use the other man's identification, as the Canadian official let them pass without further questions.

Williams knew quite a few people in Canada. He had toured there in 1959 and 1960 while lecturing about the "Kissing Case" and for the Fair Play for Cuba Committee. Although most of his contacts were Trotskyites and Socialists, unlike the leftists he knew in New York, they were ready to help. Arriving in Toronto, he and his wife moved into a house where they were put up in an attic room reachable only by crawling through an upstairs closet.

Once he was situated, the leftists got Williams a lawyer. "You'd better have one," they said. "In case you are grabbed by the police, he can take legal steps to stop them from deporting you to the United States."

The surprising thing to Williams was that the lawyer was a member of the Canadian Communist Party. The relationship between the Communists and the Trotskyites up there was apparently far more amicable than in the United States. Since the lawyer lived in Montreal, he assigned a junior partner from his firm to go to Toronto to be nearby in case an emergency developed.

Except for sleeping in the attic room, Williams and his wife openly walked the streets, going shopping, visiting the park, attending an air show, and so on. It was his first opportunity to look calmly around Toronto, and it seemed to be a rather nice place. The people were far more relaxed than in New York or Detroit. He and Mabel began considering the possibility of remaining in Canada permanently.

Then one morning their hostess rushed in with the newspapers. The front pages carried large photos of Williams, and the accompanying stories said he was a "dangerous criminal" wanted for kidnapping by the FBI. He was believed to have fled to Canada, and the U.S. Justice Department was asking the Royal Canadian Mounted Police to arrest him.

"Oh God," Williams thought, "it isn't bad enough to have to run away from the G-men, now the Mounties are chasing me too."

When he'd been a child the teachers, history books, comics, and movies had all declared: "The Royal Canadian Mounted Police Always Get Their Man." As an adult he realized that the Mounties' infallibility was a myth, but that motto was so deeply

imbedded in his mind that he couldn't help but despair, and his
wife was perturbed as well.

He looked to see if he still had the piece of Christmas stationery the old prophet man had given him before he fled from Monroe. There it was in the corner of his billfold. "Let the Mounties
do their worst," he said. "My 'Charm Against Powder and Pain'
has kept me safe this far." As he and Mabel laughed together,
their courage returned. Many years and several continents later,
that crumpled old piece of paper was to remain in his possession.

Williams' hostess said, "You've got to move out of here right
away. This is an all-White neighborhood, and people are already
curious about you. The police are certain to be told. We have another place all arranged. Get your things together. I'll bring the
car up to the driveway at the side of the house."

When they got into her car, she said, "There's an auto with
two strangers in it that's been parked across the street from here
all morning. I think they're Mounties." Williams and his wife
stared at that car until they turned the corner, but it didn't move.

They stayed indoors at their new hideout. That night their
former hostess came by and said, "That really was the Mounties.
As soon as I got home, they knocked on the door and asked,
'Where is this Williams fellow?' Then, almost as if someone had
drawn them a map, they went straight upstairs. One of them, a police sergeant, pulled open the closet door but, instead of climbing
into the attic room, he casually glanced at it and said, 'He's not in
here, is he?' When I asked why he thought you might be in my
house, he said, 'We know you've been hiding him here. We want
you to tell him one thing: If we catch him in Canada we're going
to send him home to the U.S.A. in a pine box.' "

The Mounties gave her the impression that they weren't especially interested in what they were doing. "In fact," she said, "that
police sergeant acted as though he was afraid he might bump into
you by accident." Williams speculated that the Canadian government was reluctant to become involved in what could become a
drawn-out and controversial extradition case. Or the Mounties
themselves might not have been anxious to tangle with someone
who was being described as "heavily armed," "extremely dangerous," and "schizophrenic." That was how the Justice Department
was depicting him in the thousands of FBI WANTED circulars

on display in post offices and police stations throughout the United States.

Williams had been "heavily armed" when he fled Monroe, but had disposed of his remaining two pistols upon arriving in New York City, where it is a serious offense to possess a handgun without a special permit. He resented being described as "extremely dangerous," since he had never before been accused of an act of violence. What really annoyed him was the FBI's "schizophrenic" label. He had never been treated by a psychiatrist for a mental illness. The only source he could think of for this accusation was the Monroe chief of police.

For years, Williams had heard that Chief A. A. Mauney was telling people he had a "split-personality." He'd assumed the chief was doing this to try to convince outsiders to ignore what he was saying.

"The U.S. government," he commented later, "doesn't consider insane those poor Blacks who cower in fear every moment of their lives. The unemployed Black father who pretends not to see his family going hungry—the Black mother who slaves on her knees as a cleaning woman to send her children to inferior schools—the Black politician who mouths civil-rights slogans while knowing that his real function is to keep his people disorganized and powerless—all these, so long as they smile at their oppressors and refrain from protesting too loudly, are what Uncle Sam calls 'reasonable' people. But a man would have to be truly mad to hide from himself the insane, racist reality of the 'American Way of Life.' If saying that I was 'schizophrenic' meant I was considered abnormal in comparison to the cringing 'niggers' the U.S. power structure loves so well, then the FBI's diagnosis was correct. To those who profit from madness, sanity is an aberration."

After Williams and his wife had been moved through several different hideouts in Toronto, his lawyer suggested that he go to Montreal. "If the Mounties finally do catch you, it would be better there," he said. "In Quebec Province the chances are good we could plead your case before a French-Canadian judge, and I doubt whether any of them would permit an American Black to be shipped down South."

While Mabel stayed behind in Toronto, some friends drove

Williams to Montreal. They used two cars—the first going ahead to scout the road and the second, in which he was a passenger, following several miles to the rear. They encountered only one police checkpoint, and, after going through it, the scout car doubled back to report that the Mounties were only looking for expired drivers' licenses.

Deciding it would be too risky to get a room in a hotel and being against using another private home, Williams' friends put him up in a furnished apartment. The junior member of his lawyer's firm slept there at night, but he was alone during the day.

The apartment building had a superintendent, and one afternoon he knocked on the door. "That other fellow who is staying here is a lawyer, isn't he?" he asked Williams. "I remember once seeing his photograph in the newspaper. There was a story about him putting up somebody in a house, a witness or someone he was trying to hide. I just wanted to let you know that if you're in trouble you don't have to worry about me. No, sir. I won't tell a soul."

When the lawyer returned that evening, Williams related what had happened. "We are going to have to get out of here— fast," the lawyer said. "A nosy guy like that won't be able to resist going to the police to find out if there is a reward for you. Once he does, they'll be tipped off."

As they hurriedly packed and prepared to leave for another hideout, he said, "You know, Williams, if we were able to take your case to court and let you tell what happened from the witness stand, we could stir up the public to demand that the government allow you to stay in Canada. But we have been checking into the situation. The authorities don't want to lose public support by openly extraditing you, but they also don't want to get the U.S. government angry by giving you asylum. So it looks like, if they should catch you, the Mounties will try to secretly rush you to the border and hand you over to the FBI before we can arrange a public hearing. Because of this, we think the best thing to do is to get you out of Canada at once."

With his photograph plastered all over North America, Williams knew he didn't stand a chance of leaving by a normal route. His borrowed passport might be good enough to survive a cursory inspection, but he felt it would be foolish to try to use it to get into a country like England or France. Even if it worked, he was afraid that he would have to hide and wouldn't be able to participate effectively in the civil-rights struggle. He had to go some place where he could at least resume writing.

Some of his friends told him that Fidel Castro had ordered the Cuban embassies throughout the world to give him whatever assistance he might require. The idea of seeking asylum in Cuba was attractive to Williams. The problem was how to get there.

Leaving Montreal, he boarded a Pullman train for Newfoundland. A sizable number of Blacks lived in the Gander area. They were descendants of former slaves, and the area had the heaviest concentration of African descendants in Canada. Not only was he less noticeable up there, many of the Canadian Blacks were very militant and ready to do whatever they could to help. But his most important reason for going to Gander was that the Cubana Aviacion planes stopped there to refuel on their flights between Havana and Prague.

Shortly after his arrival, a friend went to the airport to see the Cuban mechanics. One of their planes had been delayed for several days until spare parts could be flown in from Havana. When he asked the mechanics if they could get Williams onto that plane, they answered, "Tell that guy not to come near here. The Mounties have been watching this airfield for weeks. A few days ago they questioned us, said they didn't believe our plane had really broken down, and accused us of stalling for time because we were waiting to take someone to Havana."

Every time one of the Cuban planes landed there to refuel, not only did the Mounties search it thoroughly, they even watched the runway to make certain it didn't pick up anyone while taxiing for takeoff. It seemed obvious to Williams that it wasn't going to be possible to get out of Canada via the Gander airfield. The only other avenue was the sea.

Among the friends he'd made in Newfoundland was a Jamaican-born Black who had emigrated to Canada and who resembled him. He and a Black woman friend went to the harbor to check out the situation there. If Williams could get aboard a fishing boat, it might be possible to be picked up on the high seas by a passing Cuban freighter. But the moment his friends entered the waterfront district they were grabbed by the Mounties, who demanded their identity papers. When the woman started protesting that they were being picked on because they were Black, the

Mounties became so embarrassed they blurted out that they were
only looking for a "wanted criminal from the U.S.A." They didn't
say who, but it was obviously Williams. Since it appeared just as
dangerous to try to leave Canada by sea as by air, he boarded the
train and returned to Montreal.

Then it occurred to him that the Mounties must be watching
the airfields and harbors on the east coast of Canada so intensely
because they suspected he was trying to leave for Cuba. If that
were the case, they probably wouldn't be paying too much attention to the west coast.

Deciding it was worth the risk, he took the Canadian Pacific
Railway across the country to Vancouver, British Columbia. The
gamble paid off. After checking and finding no surveillance on the
west coast, he was able to reenter the United States without even
being asked to show his borrowed identity papers. Driving down
to Seattle, Washington, he bought a ticket on a flight headed south
to Los Angeles and San Diego. While the FBI and the Mounties
were beating the bushes for him in the East, Williams was relaxing
at twenty thousand feet, watching the sunset over the California
coastline from the window of his jet.

Once in San Diego he headed for Tijuana. Having frequently
gone down to the Mexican border town while stationed at Camp
Pendleton with the Marines, he knew there was almost no danger
of being caught there. So many tens of thousands of U.S. tourists
drive across to Mexico each weekend for the bullfights, dog races,
curios, night clubs, and whorehouses that both the U.S. and Mexican immigration officials scarcely look at them on the way out of
the country.

The details of Williams' escape once he arrived in Tijuana remain secret. Many years later the FBI was still questioning people
about it. A rumor was circulated in Monroe that he had escaped
by being lifted out of his house by helicopter. Another rumor—
one that he felt might have been spread by the FBI to cover up
their inability to capture him—was that he had gotten away by
bribing the police in various countries. However it was done, in
late October, 1961, a few days after leaving Tijuana, Robert
Franklin Williams arrived in Havana.

He hadn't been there much more than an hour when, at the
first light of day, he found himself in a meeting with several of
Cuba's leaders—representatives of G-2 (the military secret police)

and MINREX (the Ministry for Foreign Relations). "Williams," they said, "this shows the United States isn't invincible. The whole world is watching this case because everyone knows how badly the FBI is trying to get you." When he asked about announcing his arrival, they said, "No, we'll let them make even bigger fools of themselves than they have already. After they've sweated for a while, we'll reveal that you've been here all the time. That way we'll show the CIA boys how little they really know about what's going on in Cuba."

Williams was given an apartment in one of the luxury high-rise buildings on the Malecon, an oceanfront district where many middle-class Cubans lived before the Revolution. From his window he could see the boarded-up U.S. embassy across the street. Fidel had nationalized it, but hadn't yet taken possession, and the American eagle was still attached to the wall.

Along with his well-furnished apartment, Williams was given a living allowance and a bodyguard. While it seemed as if half the people on the streets were wearing U.S.-Army-type fatigue uniforms and openly displaying weapons, his bodyguard, a G-2 agent, wore civilian clothes and kept his pistol concealed inside his coat.

The Cubans also placed a large black 1959 Cadillac limousine, complete with chauffeur, at his disposal. Like the apartment, it had been expropriated from a wealthy Cuban who had fled the country after Castro came to power. His chauffeur was also a G-2 agent. He carried a Czech automatic concealed under his civilian jacket and spoke English somewhat better than the bodyguard.

When Williams asked why it was necessary to give him so much protection, the chauffeur replied, "Havana is still infested with CIA agents. Your escaping to Cuba is a big insult to the imperialists in Washington. There is always the possibility they might try to even the score by kidnapping you and getting you back to the States."

After several days, Williams tried to find out what had happened to Mabel and the boys by telephoning some friends in Canada and the United States. Despite the break in Cuban-U.S. relations, it was still possible to phone from Havana, but all calls had to be paid for in dollars at the United States or Canadian end of the line.

Presuming that the CIA, FBI, or some other U.S. intelligence agency would be listening in, he only called those people he knew well enough to be able to speak with in nonspecific terms. Almost everyone pleaded with him to make known his having arrived in Cuba. "Please give out a press release or something," they said. "Otherwise the cops will continue harassing people here. They keep raiding houses in the middle of the night in the hope of catching you."

In response to their pleas, Williams held a press conference a few days later in the Prensa Latina Building; and the news of his arrival in Havana was soon being headlined in the United States.

The FBI apparently assumed his wife had escaped with him, because Mabel was able to fly from Canada to Mexico to Cuba via regular airlines without being bothered. Then, in mid-December, their two boys were taken to Cuba by some friends, thus ending four months of fear and flight for the family.

Because of the U.S. trade embargo there wasn't much in the way of gifts available for the boys, and they missed the cold weather back home, but that Christmas dinner in Havana was one of the happiest the Williams family had ever had.

Chapter Ten

TRUTH CRUSHED TO EARTH
SHALL RISE AGAIN

Soon after Williams arrived in Cuba he realized that things had changed considerably since his first visits there in 1960. As the most recent nation to adopt Socialism, it was attracting idealists and reformers from all over the world. The entire country seemed possessed by a vital mood, with everyone rushing about trying to build a new society. Many of the programs which he had seen being started the year before had been completed. The last vestiges of the *barrio* slums were gone. The children of even the poorest peasants were being educated at government expense. And the recent victory over the exile invaders at the Bay of Pigs appeared to have unified the people and given them a sense of confidence.

But Cuba was more than the center of revolutionary agitation in Latin America, it had also become a major battleground in the struggle between the different brands of Communism. Try as he did to avoid it, before long Williams found himself entangled in the snarl of contending factions.

Among the Whites with whom he became friendly was Cedric Belfrage, a British subject who had lived in the United States for years and was the editor of *The National Guardian,* a leftist weekly published in New York. Belfrage had come to Havana shortly after being deported from the States for alleged Communist affiliations. Mary, his American wife, had been a schoolteacher back home. They were both completely enthralled by the Revolution and frequently spoke about staying in Cuba for the rest of their lives.

After Williams had been in Havana for about two weeks—this was before his wife and boys arrived—he was invited to the Belfrage home for a party. It was a pleasant affair, attended by both Cubans and foreigners. The main topics of conversation were his escape from the FBI's dragnet and the struggle for Black equality in the United States.

A few days later he received a telegram from ICAP, the Cuban Institute for Friendship with Foreigners, saying that his presence was required at their office. Upon arriving there he found Cedric Belfrage and several other people who had been at his house, all of whom had been summoned by similar telegrams. Also in the waiting room was a middle-aged Puerto Rican Communist who had recently come to Cuba after having been deported from the United States. He attracted Williams' attention because he kept holding the newspaper he was reading in front of his face, almost as if hiding from the rest of them. After a few minutes they were ushered into an office in which were three top ICAP officials, including Raymond Cisneros, a member of the Cuban CP's Central Committee.

"Information has reached us that you people are criticizing the ICAP," one of the officials said. "We want you to know this is an agency of the government. Whoever condemns us attacks the Revolution itself, and risks being expelled from Cuba. If you are friends you will say what you dislike to our faces, not whisper behind our backs as you have been doing."

Williams was perplexed. "If that's the reason you have summoned these people," he asked, "why was I required to come here?"

"Look, Rob," Cedric Belfrage said, "it's obvious you were asked here because of attending that party at my house. A few of the guests may have been talking, and someone seems to be trying to make a big thing of it."

Becoming angry, Williams told the ICAP officials, "First of all, I didn't hear one word about your organization at Cedric's party. Secondly, although there is severe repression of Blacks in the U.S. South, I wasn't afraid to say what I wanted to down there, and I am not afraid to speak my mind here in Cuba either."

His directness seemed to surprise Cisneros and the others, and they said, "Now, now. Nobody is accusing you of anything. You are an honored guest in Cuba. We only asked you here in order to show you how ready we are to listen to criticism. That's all."

"If you want some criticism," he said, "then I'll be glad to tell you what I've heard. Even though this wasn't discussed at Cedric's house, in the short time since I've been here several people have complained to me about the ICAP. They say you are using the Revolution's funds to invite only retired old Communists to visit Cuba, while those revolutionary activists who aren't Party members are ignored. They charge that your organization has become little more than an exclusive social club for the aging Party functionaries of the world."

At this moment, as though on cue, the Puerto Rican Communist stood up. "We might as well quit kidding ourselves and confess," he moaned. "The truth is that all of us are in it up to here," and he gestured toward his throat. It was apparent to Williams that he was responsible for their having been summoned there.

Infuriated, he jumped to his feet and declared, "Let me assure you of one thing. I haven't had any personal criticisms of ICAP until this point, and when I do you won't have to wait for some slimy informer to tell you. I'll shout them to your faces long before anyone overhears me at a party. If this is the way you do things in Socialist Cuba, I don't belong in this place! I would rather go back to the United States in chains!"

Taken aback, Cisneros and the other officials hurriedly ended the meeting. The Puerto Rican left the room without raising his eyes, whatever accusations he was ready to make remaining stuck in his throat. It was Williams' initiation into one of the less inspiring aspects of the new situation which had developed in Cuba, and he didn't like it.

In the first year or two after the Revolution came to power there had been a campaign of tracking down enemies, he knew, but in those days the foe was those who had been party to the brutal repression of the Batista dictatorship: police torturers, gangsters, reactionary politicians, and so on. The Havana public trials of 1959, although used by the U.S. press to slander the Fidelistas, hadn't been aimed at critics or dissenters. What was now creeping into Cuban life was different, it was the imposition of political orthodoxy—informers, blacklists, and all. A situation similar to that of the Stalinist purges in the U.S.S.R. was on the verge of developing.

While constant U.S. attempts to overthrow Castro were primarily responsible for the fear and distrust which fueled this trend, Williams saw its leading exponents as being certain opportunistic elements in the Cuban and U.S. Communist Parties. Back in the summer of 1960 the Cuban CP had possessed little or no power. In those days Fidel was declaring, "The Revolution is neither Communist nor anti-Communist." His chief concern appeared to be to eliminate poverty and injustice, not to follow any particular ideology. It was the United States' cutting off of oil shipments in an attempt to force Cuba to abandon its nationalization of the plantation lands owned by large American corporations which had first caused Fidel to turn to the Russians.

With every shipload of Soviet oil arriving in Havana, the position of Cuba's Communists had grown stronger. This wasn't merely due to behind-the-scenes manipulation. Many Cubans spontaneously began to support the Party because they associated it with those who were helping their Revolution to survive.

Despite the assistance they were receiving from Russia and the other Communist countries, most Cubans still thought of their revolution as democratic. It was only in 1961, after the U.S.-sponsored Bay of Pigs invasion was defeated with the help of arms from the Socialist states, that Fidel publicly declared himself to be a believer in Marxism-Leninism. With Communist petroleum fueling its autos, Communist guns guarding its beaches, and Communist technicians helping keep its refineries and factories running, it was hardly surprising that Communist officials should rise to positions of power in Cuba's government.

Since they had been in close contact for years before the Revolution, the Cuban Communist Party called upon its American counterpart for help. Williams was told that the U.S. Party's Central Committee in New York was issuing letters of introduction to select comrades, especially those knowledgeable in propaganda and communications. By 1962 the possession of such a letter supposedly assured one an entry visa from the Cubans and a key job in a ministry in Havana.

In order to consolidate their position, the Communists seemed to be making it very difficult for anyone who wasn't allied with them to emigrate to Cuba. Friends of Williams' in the 26th of July Movement said it was only Fidel's personal intervention that had made it possible for him to gain asylum there.

Cedric Belfrage had been singled out as a target by several of the USCP members Williams met in Cuba. They warned him against being seen in Belfrage's company because he was a "British intelligence agent." Williams learned that he had, indeed, worked as a spy, but it was against the Axis powers during World War II. Not only had Belfrage publicly admitted this, he had written a book detailing his activities. In his book he told how he had grown disillusioned with Britain's Cold War policies and resigned his post. Williams' impression was that the USCP was really trying to discredit Cedric because, although a dedicated Socialist, he dared to hold independent views.

Although Williams had spoken to Fidel on several occasions during his 1960 visits, for the first few weeks of his 1961 exile in Cuba they hadn't met. One day at the Jose Martí Airport, they chanced to bump into each other in the corridor. "Well, Williams, how are you doing?" Castro asked.

"I'm doing just fine, Premier Castro," he answered, "and I'm really in debt to you and your people for helping me."

"You don't owe us anything," Castro said. "Helping men like you is our revolutionary duty." Then, as if having heard about the trouble following the party at Cedric Belfrage's, he turned to the woman next to him, one of the heads of the ICAP, and said, "Williams is a friend of ours. We don't want him to have any problems here in Cuba. Do you understand?" Turning back to Williams, he said, "I hope you'll excuse my not having seen you sooner. I've assigned Comandante Pinero to help you. Any time you need anything or want to contact me, just give him a call."

Though among the lesser-known leaders, Pinero was a man of considerable power. He held the office of assistant prime minister when Williams first met him, and later became one of the three directors of MINREX (the Ministry for Foreign Relations). The other two MINREX directors were Comandante Ozmany Cienfuegos and the foreign minister himself, Raúl Roa. Like Fidel and Che Guevara, Pinero always wore a U.S.-Army-type combat uniform and appeared to be in his late thirties or early forties. Unlike them, however, his photo was hardly ever displayed. Most people referred to him only as the "red beard." Williams was later told he was the head of the G-2.

Pinero had lived in the United States for several years, spoke fluent English, and was reputed to have fought alongside Fidel in the Sierra Maestra Mountains. He impressed Williams as sincere and well-meaning when they first met. He would go to great lengths to help so long as the only things Williams requested were for personal use. But every time he suggested doing something such as establishing a "Havana Information Center Against U.S. Racism," Pinero tried to discourage him.

"Williams," he said one day, "why don't you just relax and take it easy? Pretty soon there's going to be a workers' revolution in America—a Socialist revolution—and then you'll be able to go home without being arrested."

"I'm sorry to have to disagree with you, Comandante," Williams replied, "but I don't see the slightest possibility of a classic 'workers' revolution' in the United States. All that seems possible at this time is a Black uprising."

"No," Pinero declared, puffing on his cigar. "There can be no separate Black revolt. It will have to be a joint effort with the Whites because they constitute the vast majority of Americans."

"But the White workers aren't that oppressed in the United States," Williams insisted. "So long as they have jobs and can buy automobiles and homes, they've no real reason to rise up against the capitalists. Only those, like us Blacks, who are the victims of severe economic discrimination and racism, have the motivation to want to overthrow the system."

Pinero's answer to that was, "Since you aren't a Marxist-Leninist, you seem to be incapable of comprehending the contradictions of the U.S. economy."

As their debates continued, Pinero took a position Williams found very questionable. "Look at how the people of America are rallying to the Reverend King," he said. "Under his leadership Blacks and Whites are being united. Doesn't that show how wrong you are when you say a workers' revolution is impossible in the United States?"

"Reverend King is attracting so many White followers," Williams answered, "because he's leading our people away from revolution, not toward it."

Pinero considered this for a moment, then said, "You may be right, but the important thing is to organize Blacks and Whites and get them working for the same goals. Once you have accomplished that, you can educate the workers and get them to join the Communist Party, which will make the revolution."

Williams was surprised to hear what he considered a tired old line being repeated in Cuba. He knew that Fidel hadn't waited for the Cuban Communist Party to begin the revolution; he and his friends had gone out and started fighting Batista themselves. The

Cuban Communist Party leadership had, in fact, criticized him at first, labeling him a "bourgeois adventurer," and had only given its official endorsement to the Fidelistas in the last months when it looked as if they might win. Yet here was a Cuban leader, a co-mandante who himself had fought in the mountains, voicing ideas similar to those Williams had heard a decade earlier at leftist cocktail parties in New York.

"The U.S. Communist Party is never going to lead the revolution," he told Pinero, "because it's not a workers' party, it's just no good."

"You shouldn't get so excited," the comandante said. "If the USCP isn't what you'd like it to be, what you should do is follow the example of Doctor Du Bois: Join it and try to make it better."

"That's naïve," Williams said. "You can't get into bed with a bunch of sharks and cutthroats and reform them. Everyone knows the FBI has over a thousand agents among the ten thousand or so USCP members, and you can be certain they aren't rank and file; they're local and national leaders. It's better for Blacks not to have anything to do with that organization."

Williams soon came up with an idea which he insisted Pinero take to Fidel. "I know you are already broadcasting to the States," he told him, "but most of your programs are directed toward the U.S. public in general, not any specific segment of it. What I propose is that the Revolution provide me with radio facilities for a regular program aimed at Black America."

The idea for such a show had its genesis in Williams' child-hood. Back in Monroe in the 1930's when his father listened to the radio late at night he sometimes picked up speaking and singing in Spanish. Williams had assumed the broadcasts were from Mexico. It wasn't until he learned something about physics that he realized those programs were probably coming from Havana, the distance from Mexico to North Carolina being far too great for reception on a home radio such as theirs.

Then years later, one night in 1960 when Bob Taber of the Fair Play for Cuba Committee was visiting him in Monroe, Williams had tuned in Radio Havana, the Revolution's powerful long-wave station. "Bob," he'd said, "if the Cubans were to use some English in their long-wave programs, they'd be able to get through to millions of listeners in the United States who have ordinary home receivers."

Saying it sounded like a good idea, Taber had mentioned it to the Cubans on his next trip to Havana, but they hadn't done anything about it as yet.

Williams' experience with *The Crusader* had shown him how important it was to have a public platform. He hadn't been able to publish it since his escape, but now, if the Cubans were willing, through their radio he would once again be able to communicate with Blacks in the United States.

But Williams soon heard that Joseph North, the Havana correspondent of *The Worker,* was trying to persuade the Cubans to deny his request for a radio program. North was supposed to be an expert on the "Negro problem," and Williams was told that all English language broadcasts to the United States over Radio Havana had to be cleared by him. Since Williams was not only a Black, but had actually participated in the civil-rights struggle in the South, he assumed that his presence in Cuba was a threat to North's authority. As he believed that the group to which North belonged wanted to control communications between Cuba and the United States, the last thing he thought they would be interested in was someone who wasn't under their authority being given his own show.

Despite this, when Williams' request reached Fidel, he approved it and ordered that both long- and short-wave broadcast facilities should be provided. Williams then had to talk it over with Cesar Escalante, the brother of Anibal Escalante, the propaganda chief.

Escalante said, "Your radio program has been approved, but we still have to arrange the details with Ibarra and the other people who are setting up CMCA, the new English-language station." This immediately made Williams suspicious because the station Escalante was talking about was powered at only 11,000 watts and had a very limited range. In his request he had asked for permission to broadcast over Radio Progreso, which had a 50,000-watt output and could easily be heard in the United States.

Ibarra, the head of CMCA, was a Cuban who had lived in the States, where he had been affiliated with the Progressive Labor Party. When Williams went to see him, he asked, "Just what kind of program do you intend to produce?"

"I want it to be a combination-type show," Williams answered. "We'll play a lot of Afro-American jazz, the latest and hottest progressive stuff, the blues and good soul music, the kind you don't usually hear on the radio in the United States; and I'll intersperse my political commentary between the musical selections."

"Jazz?" Ibarra seemed astounded. "What you are talking about is decadent imperialist noise. If you want to play music, why not present some wholesome Cuban operatic selections?"

"Look," Williams said, "I'm not here to promote Cuban culture—there are other, more competent people whose job that is. What I want to do is contact my fellow Blacks in the United States, and I'm not going to reach them through Spanish renditions of Wagner, Vivaldi, or Tchaikovsky."

Ibarra acted as if he couldn't believe what he was hearing. "But don't you know there is a campaign presently under way against jazz?" he asked.

"My request to Fidel was for a one-hour show to be put on three times each week," Williams insisted, "and it was specifically to be based on jazz, not opera. He has given it his approval, so how can you object?"

"Oh, I don't object, not at all, certainly not if Fidel himself approves of it," Ibarra stammered. "My only reason for discussing it with you is because, as the director of this station, I'm responsible for whatever is broadcast."

"Don't worry," Williams declared. "You won't have anything to say about it. I, and I alone, will answer for what I do."

After stalling for a while, Ibarra gave in, and Williams began producing a thrice-weekly program which he called Radio Free Dixie. Having his own show was a great opportunity. Not only could he say what he pleased, he was able to experiment with the techniques of propaganda—something which had interested him for many years.

Racial discrimination and exploitation in the United States are possible, Williams felt, largely because the tens of millions of Blacks there, although many of them are angry, remain confused and disorganized. He wanted to try to find a way to focus their anger, and to urge them to join together and fight back. He didn't think that the usual political propaganda show could do this. A new and different form was required.

He sought out provocative music with the strong beats and melodies American Blacks could identify with. He used deep gut-sounds, featuring drums and basses, to try to develop a feeling akin to that found in the "Holy Roller" churches, where the congregations are so moved by music and chanting that powerful, normally suppressed emotions are released. Once the music had put the audience in a receptive frame of mind, the message was to be delivered. He also sought to create emotional effects by the use of the spoken word, almost as if it were a stirring sermon. But his topics, rather than being religious, were political in nature. His idea was that, if such a style of delivery could cause people to accept mystical and illogical ideas, a similarly evocative presentation dealing with the need to fight for their rights could also be effective.

The purpose of Radio Free Dixie wasn't entertainment or escapism; it was to agitate and educate its listeners. Williams felt that the best way to do this, especially when much of his intended audience had been denied a decent education, was to present his ideas simply and strongly, taking care not to become boring. The more significant the message the more important he felt it was to communicate in a simple, clear, and direct manner.

Mabel helped with the shows, as did an English-speaking Cuban girl who had recently returned to Havana after living in the United States for years. There were also several others who volunteered to help when they could, including an American from Boston, who substituted for Williams as announcer from time to time. Despite CMCA's limited range, the response exceeded Williams' expectations. Letters began to arrive almost as soon as he went on the air. Some included newspaper clippings about events in the States, while others provided details of stories that the Establishment press wasn't printing. He also received tapes made by various militant groups in America for him to broadcast so that they could be widely heard. There were neither sponsors nor censors to worry about.

What surprised Williams most of all was the letters from White Southerners who said they were happy someone had the courage to tell the truth about what was going on in the United States. He even received letters from White Navy and Air Force enlisted men and officers. A typical writer stated that, while he didn't agree with everything Williams was saying, the music was "real cool." Of course, there were also letters from people who denounced the show and claimed Williams was being "used by the

Communists." But even in many of these cases the writers admitted there was some truth in what he had to say about the plight of Blacks in the United States.

As Williams became increasingly familiar with the problems of producing a regular radio show, he tried refining his propaganda techniques. He seldom discussed international relations, only getting into that area when Cuba was being threatened. "The U.S. government says it's fighting Communism," he would tell his listeners, "and claims that's the only reason they're against Cuba. But in Cuba there is racial integration. In Cuba the police don't beat or kill Black people. And in Cuba everyone is given an equal chance for education and a job, no matter what color his skin happens to be. This is the type of government the rulers of the United States want to dupe Black Americans into helping them destroy. But we won't let them fool us."

His broadcasts soon triggered a severe reaction in the United States. A flood of speeches and newspaper editorials burst forth calling him a traitor. But the First Amendment to the Constitution protects the right of free speech, and Williams saw himself as exercising that right.

Criticism of Williams' radio show did not come from the United States alone. There were quite a few leftists in Cuba who questioned its content and style—and also its effectiveness.

When some of the U.S. Communist Party people in Havana suggested that CMCA drop Radio Free Dixie because only a small percentage of American Blacks were listening, and it was provoking many Whites in the South, Williams said, "I'm not running a popularity contest. If every Black in the United States was listening to my programs, there wouldn't be any need for them because that would mean we were so well organized we were already in a position to end racism. And if what I was saying didn't anger the racists, it would mean I had sold out to them. Since when does it make a person popular among the slave owners to tell the slaves to get up off their asses and fight for freedom?"

Shortly after Mabel and the boys arrived in Havana, Fidel reportedly told the G-2 officials, "The people of Cuba like Williams. If you let him alone in the streets they will protect him." As a result Williams' bodyguard and chauffeur were withdrawn, and from then on he was free to go anywhere he wished unescorted.

At about the same time, he and Mabel were moved out of

their apartment on the Malecon and given two adjoining rooms in the Hotel Riviera. Their boys started attending a special school outside of Havana where Spanish was taught to the thousands of foreign children living in Cuba. Among their classmates were orphans from the Algerian Liberation Struggle, the children of exiles from the regime which had taken over Brazil, and from various other places where right-wing forces had seized power. Bobby, the oldest Williams boy, proved to be very adept at learning new languages. He soon was speaking Spanish so fluently the Cubans said it was almost impossible to tell him from a native, and he was graduated at the top of his class.

In early 1962, after the Williamses had been living in the Hotel Riviera for a few months, the ICAP moved them to the Hotel Capri, another modern, high-rise structure built before the Revolution for the U.S. tourist trade. Williams had asked ICAP for one of the tens of thousands of vacant houses in Havana confiscated from those who had gone into exile, but they had said he would be more secure in a hotel. Although the ICAP paid for their rooms, when it came to food they really made things rough for Williams and his wife. They were given meal vouchers honored only in the hotel cafeteria which allowed them $.35 worth of food for breakfast, $1.50 for lunch, and $1.75 for dinner. The U.S. embargo on trade with Cuba had inflated prices to such a point that all they could get for breakfast was one cup of black coffee and one piece of toast. Meat was so expensive that lunch vouchers purchased only a Spam sandwich and a glass of fruit juice, and the allocation for supper barely bought a small plate of spaghetti.

What really angered Williams was the fact that he and Mabel were the only Blacks living in the hotel. He began to suspect that the ICAP had put them there in order to convince the foreign visitors who occupied most of the rooms that Cuba had done away with racism. Little did the dignitaries who daily saw him and his wife in the Capri's luxurious lobby know that they were being given hell in the food department. The ICAP officials had put them in a situation where they were eating as little as or less than the prisoners on a North Carolina chain gang.

Around this time, four Canadian women who were touring Cuba came to visit Williams. They were independent Socialists who had read about his case in the newspapers and had seen old copies of *The Crusader*. They asked what kind of income he had, he told them that, except for free room and board, he didn't have any. They were so outraged at hearing this that they raised several hundred pesos and handed them to him in the presence of some ICAP officials.

This appeared to embarrass the Cubans, because soon afterward a representative from *Bohemia* contacted Williams and said that the magazine would pay fifty pesos per article if he would write for it. Since he no longer had a car and chauffeur at his disposal and couldn't even afford eight cents for bus fare, he was forced to walk to the *Bohemia* office to deliver the pieces.

One of his first articles dealt with jazz, describing its African and slavery origins. "Jazz is the music of the Black people of America," he wrote, "and it's an insult to us to call it decadent. If you want to say it has been perverted by degenerate commercial elements, we can't object, but it's an affront to declare our music itself is bad." He went on to say that those Cubans who were against jazz were confusing it with "swing," a musical form promoted chiefly by Whites who called themselves "jazz musicians." Swing, he said, "borrows the superficial style of jazz, but not its emotional basis, resulting in sounds without real feeling. Like our blues, spirituals, and folk songs, true jazz comes from the tragic experience of the Black man in America."

His article was considered quite controversial because Blas Roca, one of the top Cuban Communist Party leaders, an old-style trade union organizer who once held a post in Batista's government, had just written a piece attacking jazz. His article had been along classic "Socialist realism" lines, and Williams felt that it had demonstrated an almost total lack of knowledge of popular music in the United States.

The publication of two such diametrically opposed points of view made the jazz question a political issue. Soon after Williams' article appeared, a delegation of young Cuban Communists came to his hotel and asked him to explain his position in greater detail. After he did so, several newspaper and magazine articles were published supporting his contentions.

Some of the young Communists then decided to arrange a jazz concert in Havana, and asked Williams to speak during the intermission. He said he would do so gladly, but couldn't help being skeptical about their chances of putting on such a show in the face of the Party's opposition. He found it hard to believe that such a simple matter had become a major issue, preoccupying people whose energies could have been better utilized in building the new state. To Williams' surprise, the young Communists got their jazz concert approved by the Party, and were able to put it on in a large Havana theater. Various classical and modern selections were performed, and crowds lined up for blocks to buy tickets.

The Cuban Party's campaign against jazz was dropped soon afterward; and the USCP group at CMCA swung over completely to the pro-jazz side. They began pushing jazz so hard, in fact, that Williams felt they were trying to make people sick of it. They soon started their own English-language jazz program on Radio CMCA. When Williams commented to Ibarra, the director of CMCA, "I thought you didn't want such 'decadent imperialist noise' on your station," he answered, "I still feel that way, but this broadcast is not for Cuba, it's for our listeners in the United States."

Since Williams wasn't on the CMCA payroll, he was free to come and go as he pleased. One day he chanced to walk into the station while the staff was having a meeting. A White USCP member named Harris Spencer was saying, "The American workers and the Cuban workers have international solidarity. If Cuba should be invaded by the imperialists, all we would have to do is appeal to the U.S. proletariat over the radio, and they would pour out into the streets. But we have to be careful not to alienate them by harping on the race issue."

"Harris," Williams said, cutting him off in the middle of a sentence, "how can you tell these people such nonsense? Did Cuba's broadcasts during the Bay of Pigs bring the American workers out into the streets? Did all those U.S. workers you're talking about stop the exile invaders on the beach?"

At this, one of the Cuban radio supervisors in the group shouted out, "Hell, no. We stopped them ourselves with our guns!" After the meeting broke up the supervisor told Williams, "I agree with you. The American workers aren't going to save us if we're attacked. We Cubans will have to rely on ourselves."

His attitude was shared by quite a few of the Communists Williams met in Cuba. Some were very sympathetic toward his ideas about organizing Blacks in the United States. When he told them about the problems he was having with his critics in Cuba, they apologetically said, "We want you to know that all of us are not alike." But moral support was the only thing they could give. Very few of these "Revolutionary Communists," as Williams came to call them, seemed to have much influence within the Party.

On the other hand, Williams came to refer to those who were giving him a hard time as "Bourgeois Communists" because, while denouncing the capitalists, he felt that their attitudes on many subjects, including Blacks, were almost indistinguishable from those of the U.S. middle class. Often when he would meet foreign leftists who had emigrated to Cuba, he'd ask them, "Why did you come here?" Those he classified as "Revolutionary Communists" usually answered, "To help build Socialism," but the "Bourgeois Communists" characteristically responded, "To enjoy Socialism." After doing the Party's work for years in their own countries, in Cuba they were being rewarded with good jobs, fine homes, private cars, invitations to banquets and receptions, and all-expense-paid tours of the other Socialist nations. Williams felt that what they were really doing was exploiting the suffering of those whose struggles had made the Cuban Revolution possible. Cutting through the clouds of jargon, he saw vanity, selfishness, and a tendency not to rock the boat as their underlying characteristics.

Quite a few of the members of the 26th of July Movement had managed to make the transition to Marxism after Cuba became dependent on Russian aid. Williams numbered most of them among the ranks of the "Revolutionary Communists" because they remained open-minded. For example, he had no trouble talking with them about whether or not Marx or Lenin had foreseen this or that contemporary problem. To the "Bourgeois Communists," however, any such discussion seemed to be sacrilege.

The "Revolutionary Communists" were for the encouragement of Cuban-type uprisings in other Latin American countries and approved of armed self-defense for Blacks, but the "Bourgeois Communists" tended to hedge on both of these issues. As Williams saw things, consciously or not, they were diluting the Revolution's initial militancy by constantly parroting the necessity for developing "Marxist-Leninist Working Class Solidarity." He considered such words fine when backed up by real deeds, but he knew from personal experience that they could all too easily become alternatives rather than spurs to action.

The activities of the "Bourgeois Communists" at CMCA became so objectionable that many of the *repatriados* (Cubans who had once lived in the United States) began referring to the station as "CM-CIA." When Williams first heard this, he thought they were joking. He discovered, however, that they were convinced the station was being used to transmit bad news about Cuba, and perhaps even secret messages, to the United States. He never found out if this was actually the case, but the more he listened the more he wondered what Harris Spencer and the rest of the USCP group were really trying to accomplish.

Sometimes Spencer or one of the other news commentators would broadcast such things as: "The lying imperialist press of the United States reports there are one thousand busses out of commission in Cuba because of the lack of spare parts due to the embargo and sabotage. Well, the imperialists are rotten liars. The truth is there are only eight hundred busses out of commission." Such a statement, rather than putting the lie to the U.S. press reports, intimated their only fault was in slightly overestimating the situation.

Then there was a show daily at 10:00 a.m. in which statements were made such as: "In the new Socialist Cuba of today, girls who once worked as domestics are being taught useful trades and now work in factories and as cabdrivers. They no longer are forced to perform domestic drudgery for the middle class. Soon the bourgeois system will be completely eliminated, and each woman will do her own housework."

"Who in the hell do you think is free to listen to the radio in the United States at 10:00 a.m.?" Williams asked the Cubans running the station. "If anybody hears this show, it'll be the middle-class housewives in Miami. How can you hope to make them sympathetic toward Cuba when all you do is tell them that if they lived here they wouldn't be able to hire anyone to run their washing machines and vacuum cleaners?"

The Cubans were trying to communicate with the U.S. public, just ninety miles away, in order to create sympathy for the Revolution. This was an unprecedented situation in which highly intelligent and persuasive techniques were required. Even if they were honest and sincere, Williams was convinced that the ineptness of the Party propagandists was both alienating progressive Americans and helping weaken the initial enthusiasm which had stimulated so many Blacks in the United States, including himself, to side with Cuba. He disagreed with their attempts to direct propaganda to the public in general. In America there were White workers, Black workers, Brown workers, Oriental workers, professionals, laborers, farmers, technicians. All with different problems and different outlooks. When the Cuban radio constantly repeated: "American workers are being exploited," Williams felt that it didn't mean a thing to listeners in the United States. Exploitation wasn't what most Blacks were complaining about. They would welcome being exploited alongside the White workers. What could a man care about being told, "The capitalists are extracting enormous profits from your labors and denying you a fair share," when he didn't have a job at all? It was stupid to aim the same message toward the employed and the unemployed alike.

Williams' suggestions evidently meant little to the USCP group at the radio station, because their only response was to attack him. He was criticized for not advocating Socialism in his broadcasts. Some comrades suggested that he be required to attend a Party school and study the theory of class struggle, while others complained about his not learning Spanish as most of them were doing.

"I'm not about to go to one of your schools," Williams told them, "because I'm not a Communist. And if the hypocritical things I see you people doing are typical of all Communists, I've no desire ever to become one. My work is Black Liberation in the United States, and the Cuban people are helping me only in order to show their support for our struggle. The least I can do in return is to devote all of my time and energy to that cause. Hell, you USCP guys have the time to take Spanish classes because you aren't making any revolutions!"

Another of their demands was that, like Fidel, Williams declare himself to be a Marxist-Leninist and encourage his Black listeners in the United States to do the same. "Yours is a class, not a race problem," they would insist. "Negroes are oppressed because they are workers, not because they are dark-skinned. The working class is not racist, and color prejudice will wither away once the capitalism which creates and maintains it is replaced by Socialism."

Williams' answer to their arguments was: "Marx was a smart man, but he didn't hold himself up as an expert on racism, and neither did Lenin. Why should I waste air time telling my people to join me in accepting theories they have never heard of by men whose names mean little or nothing to them? We don't require dialectical materialism to know how badly we are being treated. The only people American Blacks will follow are those who are doing something to help them break their chains."

Williams contended that the abolition of capitalism, by itself, wouldn't guarantee the end of racism because hatred of Blacks was too deeply embedded in the mentality of many Whites. After centuries of indoctrination, prejudice had become such an integral part of the "American Way of Life" that the White workers were teaching it to their children regardless of what the capitalists were advocating. And he felt that this would continue even if the Left came to power.

"Nobody claims Socialism can change people's thinking overnight," the USCP people would tell Williams in response to his arguments. "It will take some time."

"And what are we Blacks supposed to do while this is happening?" he would ask. "Shut up and wait?"

"You will have to be patient," they would say, "because it will require a period of reeducation."

"And who will design the Socialist United States' new school system?" he would demand. "Will the racist White working class be in charge of changing its own ideas?"

"Of course not," they would answer. "The educational system will be controlled by the enlightened elements of the new society led by the Communist Party."

"Isn't that the way it was supposed to happen in Russia and the other Socialist states?" Williams would retort. "Have the traditionally Jew-hating Russians eliminated all their anti-Semitism after nearly fifty years of Communist government? I can see the possibility of racism increasing rather than vanishing once the White working class is in power. If the United States became like Russia, or like you are trying to make Cuba, anyone who tried to protest against racism would be accused of being an 'enemy of the people,' because you would insist that what he was talking about couldn't possibly exist in a Socialist state."

"That isn't true," they would respond. "If someone were guilty of bad practices, of being a racist holdover from the past, you could always criticize him in Party meetings, the same way it's done in Russia."

"I've heard a lot about those meetings," Williams would say. "The only subjects discussed are those the chairman permits. Unpopular or controversial issues, such as the racism of the leadership itself, are ruled out of order. No, I don't care how good a government's intentions may be, I won't encourage my Black brothers to adopt a system which forbids its citizens from publicly asking for change."

It seemed really to disturb the "Bourgeois Communists" when Williams would say, "The U.S. economy is so complex and interdependent I'm afraid of what would happen if some of you people ever took over. It's one thing to crush the middle class in an underdeveloped nation, but if, as in Russia, you tried to replace every corporate executive and factory manager with someone whose only measure of competency was his loyalty to the Communist Party, it wouldn't be long before things got so badly screwed up you'd have to import goods from abroad in order to feed and clothe people."

Williams' concept of an ideal United States was one in which racism would be eliminated by enforced laws forbidding discrimination and by a thorough educational campaign; exploitation would be outlawed; military power would not be used to oppress other nations; industry and technology would be used to provide decent schools, housing, medicine, and jobs for all; and surplus capital would be used to help the underdeveloped nations of the world raise their levels of productivity and living standards. It wouldn't matter to him what such a system was called, so long as it achieved those things.

To the "Bourgeois Communists" his ideas were completely unacceptable. "Williams," they would say, "you are nothing but a naïve individualist. Your theories are no different from those of the Social Democrats. Your case is hopeless." What especially seemed to gall them was that, whenever Williams' name appeared in the press, the Cubans referred to him as a "revolutionary"— something they didn't call the American Communists.

One afternoon he encountered a Cuban acquaintance in the elevator. "I recently met a close friend of yours from the United States," the Cuban said. "He's a White Communist from California, and has been staying in this hotel."

"That's very strange," Williams said. "If he's such a good friend, why hasn't he contacted me?"

"Oh, he certainly is," the Cuban replied. "And when I said I was your friend too, he told me in confidence he'd fought at your side in North Carolina and helped you kidnap those two White people. He also told me, and of course I'll never repeat it to anyone, how you were compelled to rape a fourteen-year-old girl." Williams was so furious he could barely wait until the elevator reached the lobby. When it did, he rushed out and demanded the American's room number from the desk porter, but he already had checked out and left Cuba before Williams could get his hands on him. It turned out he'd only been in Havana three days, but in that short period had managed to repeat his "rape" story to dozens of people. He had told each person it was "confidential" information, which is undoubtedly the fastest way to spread a *bola,* or bouncing ball, as rumors are called by the Cubans.

Williams heard some time later that this same American was apprehended rifling the files of the Fair Play for Cuba Committee in New York. The Cubans were convinced he was a CIA agent. The incident illustrated how vulnerable many of the Party people were to infiltration by dogma-spouting enemy agents. They seemed to prefer FBI and CIA spies, who always agreed with them, Williams concluded, to independent revolutionaries who dared to question their doctrinaire views.

With each passing day, the "Bourgeois Communists" at the radio station made things more difficult for Williams. He began having trouble booking studio time for his show, and the recording facilities always seemed to be reserved for someone else. Then Harris Spencer and his group asked him to participate in a round-table program on "The Problems Faced by Afro-Americans from a Communist Point of View." When he declined, they put it on without him. Soon they were producing so many programs urging Black Americans to become Communists that some of Williams' listeners in the United States began to assume that he advocated it as well.

To make it clear that he wasn't to be identified with the

USCP, Williams went to Ibarra and said, "I'm quitting CMCA and, unless you let me broadcast by myself over Radio Progreso, I'm discontinuing my program altogether."

"But the listeners to Radio Progreso in the United States are used to hearing only Spanish," Ibarra protested. "If you do shows in English they may stop listening."

"That's no problem," Williams answered. "Just let me go on after your regular broadcast day ends at midnight. Your Spanish-speaking listeners in the United States will stay happy, while the people who want to hear my show will be able to do so."

After concluding that discussing his problems with Ibarra was getting him nowhere, Williams contacted Comandante Pinero. The moment Fidel heard about it, he declared that, unless the radio functionaries honored his original instructions to let Williams broadcast over both Radio Progreso and Radio Havana, he personally was going to come over and make them put him on the air.

A few days later Williams was called in to the Radio Havana offices by a Cuban Communist named Cardenas. "We've decided to permit you to broadcast on long-wave over Radio Progreso," he said, "but you've been denied short-wave facilities here. Radio Havana is the direct voice of the Cuban government and, since you refuse to let us exercise control over what you present in your program, we can't permit it to be broadcast over our official station."

"I don't understand your logic," Williams said. "Radio Progreso is also owned by the government. In fact, there isn't a radio or TV station in Cuba that the Revolution doesn't run. And Fidel himself said I could broadcast over Radio Havana."

"I don't give a damn what Fidel said," Cardenas retorted. "He's just one man and, in this instance, he has been overruled."

"If not even Premier Castro can decide who uses Radio Havana," Williams said, "I've no interest in it. Furthermore, this station reminds me of Mississippi. All the technicians and broadcasters working here are White, just as I would expect to see in a station in the U.S. South. I wouldn't want to be the only Black in the place." And he walked out.

Even though he was denied Radio Havana's short-wave facilities, being able to broadcast long-wave over 50,000-watt Radio Progreso enabled Williams' shows to reach a very large audience.

He began to receive letters from people as far away as Saskatche-
wan in Canada and the U.S. Midwest. And several of his shows
were recorded from the air and rebroadcast by the noncommercial
Pacifica FM stations in San Francisco, Los Angeles, and New
York.

Quite a few U.S. Blacks began to write him asking for help in
coming to Cuba to live. One from the Los Angeles area said he
had organized fifty Black families who wanted to emigrate. Williams decided not to respond to such letters because he sensed
that the trend in Cuban government circles was against encouraging non-Communist U.S. Blacks to come there. Also, he was hearing of more and more instances where those Black Americans who
had managed to get to Cuba were having problems with the authorities. If he answered the letters from U.S. Blacks who wanted
to come, he would have to advise them against it. Silence seemed
like the best response at the time.

With the increased range of Williams' broadcasts, the anger
of his U.S. critics grew. There was a bill unsuccessfully introduced
in Congress to deprive him of his citizenship. Each day the list of
politicians mentioned in the papers as denouncing him increased.
Such a well-known conservative as Senator Thomas Dodd of Connecticut demanded that something be done about his emissions. It
wasn't long before he began to receive letters from listeners in the
States saying that his broadcasts were being jammed by a beeping
noise. The source of this interference appeared to be a U.S. Navy
electronic surveillance ship anchored just outside of Havana Bay.
It sat there in full view, barely beyond Cuba's three-mile territorial
limit, monitoring whatever radio communications its highly sensi-
tive instruments could detect. The Cubans used to stand on the
Malecon and stare at it with hatred in their eyes. Williams marveled at how they managed to restrain themselves from blasting it
out of the water.

He assumed that the ship's primary mission wasn't to jam his
broadcasts, but the Navy brass apparently couldn't resist the opportunity to create a nuisance once his show began to draw fire in
Congress. What the interference implied was that the U.S. power
structure feared Radio Free Dixie more than it did the propaganda campaigns of the various Communist governments. At least
it wasn't making any attempts to jam their transmissions.

Shortly after Williams' thirty-seventh birthday, in early 1962, he was approached by several Cuban workers who ran a print shop for the National Institute for Agrarian Reform (INRA). One said he had worked as a printer in the United States before returning to Cuba after Fidel came to power. "I saw your *Crusader* magazine in New York," he said. "I've been talking to the workers in my shop, and we've decided that if you want to publish it here in Cuba we'll be proud to print it for you."

Williams gratefully accepted the offer. Not only did they print his newsletter, they also got their fellow workers at the INRA to donate the money for mailing it.

The first Cuban issue of *The Crusader* came out in April, 1962. On its front page was a cartoon which showed Williams and his family being protected by Castro. Across the sea in the United States stood a policeman holding a dog labeled "The FBI." Next to him were a hooded Klansman and a caricature of President Kennedy wearing a Nazi armband and brandishing a hangman's noose. Castro, who was offering a peace dove to the United States, was saying "STOP! No Racist allowed here!" and the headline under the cartoon declared "CUBA: TERRITORIO LIBRE DE AMERICA." On the masthead was a drawing of a medieval crusader in armor.

Williams began that first Cuban issue by saying, "It has truly been said that 'truth crushed to earth shall rise again!' True to this adage, the fighting little Crusader Newsletter returns to the vanguard of the liberation struggle. Yes, it yet lives to haunt those who thought they had destroyed it." He signed it "Robert F. Williams, Editor-IN-EXILE."

It wasn't long before he was visited by a G-2 agent who had acquired a copy of *The Crusader*. Waving it as he spoke, he said, "This paper of yours isn't being printed with government permission. We've been studying it and, all in all, it isn't bad, but we want to know how in the hell you've been getting it into the States?" Williams explained that, there being cargo ships going from Cuba to Canada, he was forwarding packages of several thousand copies each to friends in Toronto, who were then mailing them to people in the United States.

When word reached Fidel about *The Crusader,* he told Pinero to instruct the Party to help publish it. The Party officials suggested they could print it on their own presses, but Williams declined the offer, telling them, "The Cuban volunteers who print it now are doing fine. They are proud that something they're connected with is being sent to Blacks in the United States. I don't think it would be right for me to take it away from them. What I do need, though, is paper." The Party provided it; and he was soon able to send 30,000 to 40,000 copies to U.S. readers each month.

Williams' privately published newsletter proved as irritating to his critics in the Havana USCP group as did his uncensored radio program. They suggested that a Party editorial board be established for it. The board was to include several USCP writers, and each member, including Williams, would have only one vote. As this seemed like an obvious attempt to take control of the newsletter out of his hands, Williams refused to participate. "If the USCP people want to publish their own paper aimed at Black America," he told the Cubans, "I can't stop them, but I'm not about to let people whose primary goal isn't Black Liberation dictate *The Crusader*'s contents."

The "Bourgeois Communists" reacted to this by accusing him of attempting to create a "cult of the personality," the same charge Khrushchev had raised against Stalin. Williams considered it ludicrous for the same people who, only a few years earlier, had idolized the all-powerful Soviet dictator, to charge that he, a Black exile armed with little more than a typewriter, was following in Stalin's footsteps.

As the first anniversary of his arrival in Cuba neared, the attacks on Williams by his critics in Havana grew more extreme. In addition to his being a "rapist" and a proponent of the "cult of the personality," he heard that he was being labeled "schizophrenic." To respond to this he showed the Cubans a copy of his FBI WANTED poster, which a friend had taken from a police station in the United States and sent to him in Havana. "Isn't it interesting," he said, "that the comrades of the USCP are using the same terminology in criticizing me as does J. Edgar Hoover? Why don't you ask them where they got their information about my mental condition?" After that he heard no more such stories, but then something happened that really made him angry.

John, his younger son, was away at school in Santa Maria del Mar, about eighteen miles outside of the city, when he came down with a fever. Since his illness was highly contagious, he was taken to a hospital in Havana and placed in isolation. After a couple of

weeks, he improved enough to be released. A few hours after
Mabel left with John for the ride back to his school, she telephoned Williams at the hotel and said, "The doctor out here
thinks it would be better for him to spend a week at home with us
before rejoining his classmates. The only problem is that the am-
bulance that brought us has already left, and we've no way to get
back to Havana."

"Why don't you telephone the ICAP?" Williams suggested,
knowing they maintained a fleet of Cadillac limousines for the use
of foreign guests. But when she did so, the ICAP people said all of
their cars were tied up, and asked her why she didn't take a taxi.
When she answered that, had she the money for a taxi, she
wouldn't have called them in the first place, they told her to take
the bus. So she and their little boy, who was still weak from his
bout with the fever, were forced to walk over a mile through the
heat and dust out to the highway to catch a bus back to Havana.

A few days after this incident, Williams was visited by a government official who asked, "How much of an allowance are you
getting from ICAP and the Party?"

"All the ICAP is giving us is free room and just enough food
to stay alive," he answered, "and the only thing I'm getting from
the Party is some paper for my newsletter."

"But if nobody is giving you an allowance, where are you getting the cash to live on?" the official asked incredulously. After
Williams answered that his only source of spending money was
the fifty pesos he earned for each article he wrote for *Bohemia,* the
official notified Comandante Pinero, who insisted that they go to
Party headquarters immediately to straighten things out.

The functionaries at CCP headquarters disavowed responsibility, saying, "But we thought Williams was getting money from
the ICAP." And, when Pinero then took him to the ICAP offices,
the functionaries there declared they were innocent, saying, "Why
we were certain he was being supported by the Party!"

Unable to contain himself, Williams told Pinero about ICAP
having refused his wife and boy transportation. "That was a very
bad thing," Pinero said. "From now on you won't have to depend
on them. Fidel will see to it that the Party gives you a car of your
own, plus three hundred pesos per month allowance. And you
won't have to pay for the car's upkeep. Just take it to the Party garage, and they'll fill the gas tank and make repairs. We'll also pro-

vide money for the costs of mailing your newsletter from Canada to the United States. If there's anything else you need, please let me know. Fidel had no idea such things were happening."

Then Pinero took him aside and asked confidentially, "Williams, do you have a gun?" When he answered that he didn't, the Comandante said, "Well, we'd better get you one, just in case somebody here doesn't like you."

Williams chose a Czech .25-caliber automatic and a German P-38, a 9-mm Luger pistol similar to the one he had owned in Monroe. The P-38 was so bulky he kept it in the hotel, but all the rest of the time he was in Cuba he carried that Czech pistol under the handkerchief in his left hip pocket night and day. It was so small hardly anyone knew he was armed.

One day a journalist from the Polish News Agency's Havana Bureau came to Williams' hotel to interview him. After they had talked for a while, he said, "Mr. Williams, I want you to know how happy I am to meet you. This is the first time in my life I've ever spoken to a Trotskyite."

"A what?" Williams asked.

"A Trotskyite," he answered, an embarrassed look appearing on his face.

"And what makes you think I'm one of those?" Williams demanded. Blushing by now, he said, "Oh, I'm sorry. I'm truly sorry. But some American Communists came to our embassy recently and told us you're a follower of Trotsky."

"Well, I'm sorry, too," Williams said, "but I'm not a follower of his at all. You'll have to go somewhere else to meet one."

The Polish journalist apologized, and asked if they could continue with the interview anyway. From then on the Poles began inviting Williams to their embassy for various functions, and they enjoyed fairly cordial relations for the rest of his stay in Cuba. But the stories spread by his critics apparently succeeded in turning the rest of the eastern Europeans against him. Unlike the other Americans living in Havana, during his five years in Cuba Williams was never invited to receptions at the Russian, Czech, East German, Bulgarian, Hungarian, or Rumanian embassies.

Williams' support in Cuba continued to be primarily from the "Revolutionary Communists" and the members of the 26th of July Movement, headed by Fidel himself. This was evident when a group from the USCP approached Castro one day and said, "We don't understand why Williams is the only private person here who is permitted to have a radio program and newsletter." Fidel reportedly answered, "He is better qualified to judge what should be said to his people than is anyone else in Cuba. And that's the last I want to hear about this matter."

Williams suspected that Fidel backed him so strongly because there was a degree of similarity between what he was doing and Castro's own struggle. Before he took power in 1959, Fidel too had been criticized by the Communists for not being one of them, and he too had used the radio to urge his people to fight injustice.

The "Bourgeois Communists'" opposition hindered but didn't halt Williams' activities. The situation he now enjoyed was unique. Not only were the Cubans giving him sanctuary from the KKK and the FBI, they were providing a platform from which he could reach his Black brothers and sisters in the United States.

Although Fidel and the Revolution were the immediate cause, Williams attributed the ultimate responsibility for his unprecedented position to the U.S. power structure. First, the efforts by the racists to destroy the desegregation movement in Monroe had led him to become a full-time agitator. Then, the attempts to lynch him, culminating in the FBI's search for him, had led to his flight to Cuba. From his point of view, every time he had tried to obtain justice, those who rule America had presented him with the alternatives of (1) shutting up and becoming a "good nigger" or (2) being crushed. Instead he had chosen to stand up and fight. The repressive efforts of the racists had transformed him from an unknown Black in an obscure southern town into an international propagandist whose emissions were being read and heard by a small but growing number of people all across the United States.

And being in Cuba, in constant contact with leftists from many parts of the world, was also having its effect. Whereas in 1961 he had been concerned primarily with desegregation, in his first year of exile he began to consider the possibility of changing, rather than merely improving, the basic system of the United States. Robert Franklin Williams, the civil-rights and armed-self-defense leader, was becoming an advocate of revolution.

Chapter Eleven

"A PIG-HEADED SON OF A BITCH"

Back in 1962, Havana was occasionally rocked by loud blasts, as the anti-Castro underground attempted to demonstrate that it was still a potent force. In a particularly serious incident, an old car was filled with explosives and detonated on a crowded downtown street, inflicting many casualties among the passers-by. Furiously, Fidel went on television and announced: "Such terrorism will not be tolerated in Cuba. I am giving those responsible for this crime one last warning. If it ever happens again you won't be left alive long enough to plead for mercy!" Williams didn't know if his speech frightened off the terrorists or if they were captured, but after that he heard no more explosions in Havana.

In contrast to those committing acts of violence and sabotage, most of the "counterrevolutionaries," as the opponents of the regime were called, limited their dissent to criticizing the government. Williams was writing a new series of articles for *Bohemia* on the subject of U.S. Black history. They were widely read, and created a lot of friends for him among Cubans of both African and European ancestry. But his popularity also brought him into contact with quite a few people who opposed the Revolution. He was approached by strangers on the street, in cafes, and even at his hotel. After saying they had enjoyed his articles, they would proceed to unburden themselves of a seemingly endless list of complaints.

"We are telling you these things," they would say, "because we want you to know the truth about what is going on in Cuba— the terrible injustice which it is impossible for you to see for yourself." Most of these people were from the pre-Revolutionary middle class. Almost all claimed they had opposed the Batista dictatorship and supported the Revolution when it first came to power, but were now disillusioned. "We do not oppose Socialism in principle," some said, "and we know Fidel has helped the workers and the peasants, but that doesn't excuse the bad things being done."

One of their chief complaints was that many powerful government officials, having formerly been poor themselves, were purposely mistreating everyone who came from a well-to-do family. "They are more interested in getting revenge on us because we had money than they are in building a just society," was a common complaint.

Williams was surprised to find so many people of this type in Cuba. Hundreds of thousands had already left, and more were departing every day, but there was still a sizable number around. Some said that, despite having lost their stores and apartment buildings, they were trying their best to stay on because the Revolution had given Cuba a measure of self-respect which it had been denied for generations. For many, their personal inconveniences were somewhat compensated for by the pride of knowing that their tiny nation was defying the colossus to the north. It was obvious most weren't leaving Cuba because they were afraid to speak their minds. So long as they didn't actually do anything, Fidel had declared those in opposition could say what they wished.

The effectiveness of such criticism was limited, of course, by the fact that the government controlled all newspapers, radio and TV stations, and publishing houses. And certain complaints, such as those voiced in a classroom by a teacher to his pupils, could be considered criminal actions. Still, Williams doubted that during Batista's regime anyone would have dared to publicly criticize the government the way those who disagreed with the Revolution were doing now. It was true that many people left because they didn't want to live in a Socialist state. And there were also those who fled because they were certain the United States, unable to tolerate Communism ninety miles from its shores, would soon go to war against Cuba. But a large segment of the exiles left for the States because it was made so easy for them to do so.

Before 1959, emigration to the United States was under a strict quota system, and Cubans either needed sponsors to vouch for their support or to be wealthy enough to post a sizable cash bond. But once Uncle Sam began to try to topple the Castro regime, neither visas nor proof of financial stability were required; and the U.S. government paid relief money to the immigrants until they could be found jobs. Although some half million of

Cuba's eight million inhabitants had left the island, the Revolution still appeared to be enjoying the support of a majority of the population.

Several thousand of those who had left Cuba in the first years of the Revolution had returned. And Williams had personally met many people who, having become convinced Fidel was really eliminating the corruption of past regimes, had come back after living in the States for twenty years or more.

Another factor causing some people to leave was the U.S. embargo. Primarily an agricultural country, producing sugar and other cash crops for export, Cuba had imported almost all of its manufactures and a good part of its food—mostly from the States. But now that the flow of American products was completely cut off, the Revolution had to find other sources for everything from toilet paper to television tubes. The hundreds of thousands of U.S. cars and busses on the island were breaking down for lack of replacement parts. The newer buildings, designed without openable windows, were becoming almost unlivable as their air-conditioning equipment fell into disrepair. Small factories were being hurriedly improvised for the production of spark plugs, brake linings, carburetors, and nuts and bolts. Everywhere one went, the main topic of conversation was how to keep this or that American-made appliance running.

As a means of bringing Cuba to its knees, however, the embargo was a failure. While the Cubans didn't enjoy the rationing, long waiting lines, empty market shelves, and perpetual shortages, they accepted them as part of the price they had to pay for independence. Williams considered it the height of conceit for the United States to imagine that its refusal to sell the Cubans nylons and neckties would lead them to abandon their Revolution. The State Department's policy seemed to be based on the theory that, like narcotic addicts, those accustomed to the availability of American consumer goods could no longer exist without them.

Many of the Cubans who left because of the shortages were wealthy enough to have emigrated before Fidel came to power, but they apparently hadn't been disturbed enough to do so by the secret trials and sadistic murders of the Batista regime.

So long as they could watch the maudlin television shows relayed from Miami, they'd been able to avert their eyes from the suffering and oppression going on around them. Once the supply of Coca-Cola and Kotex dried up, however, they'd suddenly discovered that life in Cuba was unbearable. Fidel was permitting these people to leave because he considered the country better off without them, and Williams agreed wholeheartedly.

It soon became evident to Williams why so many discontented Cubans were approaching him. Having heard that he was being attacked by the "Bourgeois Communists," but defended by Fidel, they assumed that he possessed an inside line to the Cuban leader, and could help them with their problems. Several asked him to convey special requests to Castro, while a few went so far as to try to win him over to their side. Whenever they did this, Williams would clearly let them know where he stood, saying, "While I'm not sympathetic to certain elements in the Cuban and U.S. Communist Parties, I do support Fidel, the 26th of July Movement, and the Revolution as a whole."

"You don't understand," they would insist, "Fidel is no longer in control. The Communists are taking over, and will soon get rid of him. He is blindly handing Cuba to the Russians on a silver platter. The Revolution is being betrayed!"

Their words weren't completely lacking in substance. Williams had encountered dogmatists in the Cuban and U.S. Communist Parties who didn't consider Fidel their ideal head of state. They were always criticizing him for doing things on sentimental impulse, rather than for ideological reasons. Some even privately said they would be happy to see him replaced by a "true Communist." Also, Cuba, having broken with the United States only to find itself dependent on Russian guns and oil, did tend to give the impression that one form of foreign influence had merely been exchanged for another.

Despite these things, Williams thought Fidel was doing his best, and that he was still in charge. Whatever its shortcomings, the Revolution was making life better for Williams' kind of people—the poor farmers and workers. The embargo-produced shortages notwithstanding, jobs, housing, medical aid, and education were available for all regardless of color or economic class.

Williams reasoned that the very fact that those who opposed the government felt free to voice their complaints to someone like himself, a known supporter of the Revolution, demonstrated that life in Cuba was far freer than most Americans believed it to be. Fidel's permitting such criticism seemed to him to be a very healthy thing, which any true revolutionary should encourage. He didn't see how responsible leaders could work to better things if they silenced all those who tried to point out their deficiencies. No government he'd ever heard of had fallen by allowing its people to speak freely. On the contrary, he saw it as only when a system was weak and without real popular support that it fearfully tried to suppress all dissent.

Some of those who complained were totally against the Revolution. Others said that, while they still believed in Fidel, they opposed the Communists. Whatever their persuasion, by the end of the five years Williams spent in Cuba, almost all of them had gone into exile.

Not only was there far more sentiment against the Revolution now than during Williams' first visits, anti-American feeling had become really severe. Back in 1960, many Cubans had been confident that, once things calmed down, relations with the United States would improve. But by 1962 these same people were very angry and constantly cursed President Kennedy and the U.S. State Department. "Just because we try to run our own country, the Yankees cut off our oil and consumer goods," they would say, "but those bastards in Washington aren't content with trying to strangle us economically, they think they have the right to invade us as well."

Williams met many Cubans who had fought against the CIA-backed exile landing force at the Bay of Pigs in mid-April, 1961. They told him that the moment news of the invasion had reached Havana, tens of thousands of men, women, and teen-age children had rushed into the streets waving weapons. Commandeering trucks, busses, taxicabs, and private cars, they had hurried off to the front lines, which were only a few hours' drive from the capital. Some people were even seen weeping in the streets because they hadn't been able to get a ride to the battle zone.

There were so many civilian volunteers on the roads that the regular Armed Forces experienced difficulty moving into position. The enthusiasm wasn't limited to the civilians. Some Cuban Army officers told Williams that their casualties were far greater than necessary as a result of gung-ho troops' charging directly into the exiles' machine-gun fire.

The way Williams had seen the battle described in the U.S. press, it appeared as though the invaders bravely went down fighting. What he was told about it in Havana was far different. The exiles had been assured by the CIA that the tiny Cuban Air Force was already wiped out. But the Revolutionary Air Force was far from destroyed, and had bombed and sunk the exiles' ships, leaving them without antitank ammunition and fuel for their planes. Also, the exiles had been told that the Cuban people would rise up and join them the moment they hit the beach. But instead of being welcomed as liberators by cheering crowds, within a few hours of setting foot on Cuban soil they found themselves facing sixty thousand angry soldiers, militiamen, and armed civilians. Finally, the exiles had been promised that, should they require it, the U.S. Air Force, Navy, and Marines would come to their aid. Despite there being tens of thousands of U.S. troops waiting in ships just beyond Cuba's territorial waters and hundreds of planes loaded with bombs ready to take off from nearby aircraft carriers, when the exiles finally did call for help, none was forthcoming.

When the U.S. Navy declined to send in landing craft to rescue them from the beach, the invaders concluded that they had been taken for suckers. Rather than fight to the death, some 1,200 of the original 1,500-man force surrendered. The Battle of "Playa Giron," as the Cubans called it, organized, financed, and launched by the United States of America against a tiny nation with only 4 percent of its population, in less than seventy-two hours had ended in utter defeat.

What was probably the greatest surprise of the invaders' lives, next to the moment they realized the U.S. Marines weren't going to save them, occurred when Fidel put them on television. The moment they got in front of the cameras it appeared as if each prisoner was trying to out-apologize the next. They apparently couldn't believe the Fidelistas would let them live. Had their invasion been successful, it is highly probable that they would have mercilessly exterminated every supporter of the Revolution they could find.

Rather than putting the exiles up against the wall, Fidel demanded that the United States, having sent them to Cuba, pay ransom to get them back. To avoid the embarrassment of directly using government funds, during that summer of 1962 Robert Kennedy pressured major U.S. drug companies to donate the over $50 million in medical supplies required to buy the exiles back.

A soldier whom Williams had first met during his 1960 visits to Cuba came to see him at the hotel during the ransom negotiations. He was in tears, and said, "I want to ask you one question. I lost my best friend at Playa Giron—those exiles butchered him in front of my eyes. And now the government is getting ready to give them new clothes and send them back to the United States. I support Fidel. I support him with my life. But there are a lot of people I know who lost sons, and some say we ought to kill every one of those bastards. What should we do?"

"As a soldier," Williams told him, "it's your duty to accept the Revolution's policies, especially if you have confidence in it. Killing the prisoners won't bring back the dead, but the medicine Cuba gets in exchange for them will save the lives of a lot of people, especially mothers and babies. Anyway, I think you'd be playing into the hands of the U.S. government if you shot them. Kennedy would like nothing better than to try to make up for Playa Giron by going to the United Nations and accusing Cuba of mass murder."

By the fall of 1962 there was little chance of a small-scale invasion like Playa Giron being tried again. The Cuban Ministry of Revolutionary Armed Forces (MINFAR) had been modernized. Having several friends in the military, Williams was frequently taken on tours of their installations. Most of the regular troops were armed with new Belgian automatic rifles of the type standard for NATO forces. In addition to T-34's, they also had Russian heavy tanks. And the handful of U.S.-made T-33 jet trainers with which the Revolutionary Air Force had devastated the exiles' ships had been replaced by a significant force of modern Russian fighter planes and medium bombers.

Unlike the unorganized days of Playa Giron, when everyone had rushed wildly down to the beach and left Havana virtually unprotected, Cuba was now divided into specific defense zones with separate commands for western, central, and eastern sectors. At least twenty 5,000-man, "atomic age" divisions had been formed, each such unit possessing its own transportation and supply caches so that it could fight for a long time even if cut off from the rest of the country. One estimate Williams received was that, due to better training equipment and organization, the military potential now at Fidel's disposal was at least 500 percent greater than it had been back in 1961.

As it was known he had once been a U.S. Marine, the Cubans often asked Williams' opinion on their training camps and defense installations. Although both the regular army and the militia units he visited were in very high spirits, on several occasions he had to tell them that their procedures left much to be desired. A glaring example was the way the antiaircraft unit was laid out in the garden of the Hotel Nacional in Havana. The four guns in the battery were close together, and none was really dug-in, so that a hit on one would probably have knocked out the other three. Also, although helmets are a must for antiaircraft crews, who often have to stand out in the open and keep firing at planes diving right at them, the Cuban gun crews wore only berets. Most serious of all their errors, the ammunition for the antiaircraft guns was completely exposed. "You have to build reinforced underground magazines for your shells," Williams told the Cuban C.O. "Otherwise a near hit will set them off and blow this entire part of Havana sky high."

Another thing Williams commented on to the Cubans was the lack of discipline in many of their training camps. The atmosphere was very relaxed and the men seemed to enjoy their siestas. Williams agreed they shouldn't have the arbitrary and sadistic type of training to which he was subjected in the U.S. Marines at Camp Pendleton, but felt it was necessary to develop rapid response patterns and good coordination between the officers and their men. Great morale and dedication aren't enough, he observed. To stay alive, military actions have to be executed fast and well.

Williams saw lots of good soldiering by the Cubans, but he also saw fine men pushed aside because of politics. As in every other branch of government, the Communist Party was trying to gain control of the MINFAR. One of its tactics was the suppression of "Peking-oriented elements." Williams knew of several Cubans who had been sent to China to be trained as military specialists, but who had found themselves involuntarily discharged or given unimportant assignments upon their return. One Chinese-trained jet pilot was forced to be a telephone lineman. Since most of Cuba's arms and instructors came from Russia, the pro-Moscow elements in the MINFAR were finding it relatively easy to put themselves in the driver's seat. Some gave Williams the impression that they were more anti-Chinese than anti-imperialist.

One of the things that impressed him most about Cuba from
a military point of view was the distribution of guns to the hundreds of thousands of members of the People's Militia. This had
begun in 1959, when many of the U.S. weapons of Batista's forty-
thousand-man army were handed out by the victorious Fidelistas.
Then, following Washington's embargo on arms sales, vast quantities of Mauser rifles and other weapons captured by the Russians
from Germany at the end of World War II were sold to Cuba and
given to the *milicianos.* Although it bothered the "Bourgeois Communists" who, like many bureaucrats, were afraid of every
weapon not under their control, Williams was pleased to see so
many ordinary people armed in the streets. They were the same
poor workers and farmers who had been brutalized by Batista's
thug cops for years, but it was going to be very difficult for anyone
to mistreat them again, because now they had their own guns.

He could tell how much having weapons meant to the Cubans by the way they polished and decorated them. Their pistols
began to resemble a new art form as they tried to outdo each other
in tinting and engraving barrels and inlaying handles. To the man
who never before had a real voice in how he was governed, his
personal weapon was his ballot—it was his power.

As a reaction against the anti-Cuban position adopted by the
Organization of American States at Punte del Este, the Revolution
sponsored an Organization for Latin American Solidarity Conference in Havana. Although there were some White Americans
present who had come with a group of observers from the Canadian Peace Council, Williams was the only U.S. citizen invited to
address the meeting.

In his speech, which was broadcast by the Cuban radio and
TV, he said, "The symbol of Americanism to me is the sound of
the chains of my people being dragged. Yes, I can still hear the
echoes of those slave chains. If we had the opportunity to talk to
the American Indians of yesteryear, to the great chiefs like Thun-
der Cloud, Geronimo, and Sitting Bull, I wonder what message
they would have for us? They once faced a situation like the one
Cuba faces today. They believed in the goodness of the American,
in his treaties and sweet words. And we all know what happened
to them. No, our only answer to Punte del Este can be to prepare
our bullets and sharpen our machetes."

When he concluded, the conference delegates rose in a standing ovation. But that night several of the Canadian Peace Council and USCP people came to see him. "Williams," they said, "you missed a great opportunity today to strike a blow for peace. Instead, all you spoke about was violence and war. All of America, both North and South, was listening. Why didn't you try to appeal to the good intentions of the American masses?"

"How could I have spoken of something I know nothing about?" Williams asked. "If the American people have such good intentions, why didn't they protest what Batista was doing to the Cuban people in the past? And what makes you think they'll do anything to stop U.S. attacks on Cuba in the future?"

"Don't you understand?" they responded. "So long as Cuba is bulging with guns, the right-wing extremists can convince the American people that it threatens them? You should have spoken about the need for Cubans and Americans to peacefully settle their differences."

"Are you joking?" Williams asked. "Even the Blacks who live in the United States can't rely on the American people to protect them from being murdered by the racists. The Cubans being well armed is the only thing that has kept them from being destroyed."

At the same time the pacifists were admonishing Williams for telling the Cubans to keep up their guard, developments were taking place which threatened to thrust the world into an atomic war. During the summer of 1962 the number of Russian advisers in Cuba had increased rapidly; U.S. press estimates placed their total number at thirty thousand or higher. Although they all wore civilian clothes, it was obvious from their age range and other characteristics that most of them were soldiers. The unloading of weapons from Soviet ships was a common sight at the Havana docks. And there were lots of rumors circulating about the U.S.S.R. sending Cuba various types of missiles.

Blas Roca himself had pretty much given away the presence of missiles on the island when he made a public statement to the effect that Cuba had to be not only as strong as the United States, but even more powerful. He had also declared that, should Kennedy dare to launch another attack, the United States itself would be devastated. This was a clear indication that something new had been introduced into the situation, since no Cuban leader had ever made such a statement before.

As autumn approached, more and more reports circulated in

Havana about an impending invasion—this time to involve a force of many tens of thousands of exiles and mercenaries, and to be fully supported by U.S. air and sea power. As the tension increased, several of the USCP people who Williams felt had come to Cuba to "enjoy Socialism" started packing their bags and leaving for New York and other places far away from where the shooting might be.

Then, in October, the news finally broke that the United States had taken aerial photos of Soviet intermediate-range ballistic missile sites in Cuba. President Kennedy demanded that the rockets be withdrawn, placed the U.S. Armed Forces on alert, and threatened to search all ships, including Russian vessels, attempting to reach Cuba.

Instead of panicking, almost everyone Williams knew in Cuba—even confirmed "counterrevolutionaries"—began putting on a Militia or Army uniform. Some USCP members were also ready to fight to defend Cuban soil. It was the same sort of spirit that had seized the island during the "Playa Giron" invasion, Williams was told. All political differences were forgotten. *"Patria o Muerte!"* Fatherland or Death! was the rallying call.

As the details of the affair unfolded, Williams began to smell something fishy. The U.S. reconnaissance planes had been able to photograph the Soviet missile sites right out in the open. Seemingly no attempt had been made to hide them. It was as if the Russians wanted everyone to know the IRBM's were there. Secondly, although ballistic missiles require atomic warheads in order to be effective, Williams doubted that such warheads had been brought to Cuba. Knowing their independence and their willingness to die for their rights, the Russians weren't allowing the Cubans near the IRBM sites, and guarded them with their own troops. It seemed highly improbable they would risk placing atomic weapons on Cuban soil, where the Revolution might seize them. The entire business seemed more a flamboyant gesture than a serious act. But if Khrushchev was bluffing, Kennedy was calling his bluff, and a confrontation between the U.S. and the U.S.S.R. on the high seas seemed inevitable.

In the midst of the crisis Williams was visited by a G-2 agent, who told him, "We have received word the United States will invade tomorrow. The Revolution has built bomb shelters in the countryside where special-category people like yourself are supposed to go. If you want to pack your bags, transportation is waiting to take you out of Havana."

"No, thanks," Williams replied. "The Cuban people have sheltered me. If they are to be attacked, I prefer to fight at their side. If I'm to die, let it be on the beach with a rifle in my hands, not hiding in a bomb shelter."

Then he asked the G-2 agent, "How do you know for certain the invasion will take place tomorrow?"

"Russian Intelligence told us," he answered. "Thousands of U.S. Marines were seen boarding troopships in Florida today."

"I don't care what they told you," Williams said. "There isn't going to be any invasion tomorrow because the United States wouldn't dare try it without softening you up first. Before they land on the beach they will send over thousands of planes to try to knock out your Air Force, eliminate your antiaircraft and artillery batteries, block your transportation routes, and cut your communication lines. They probably know through their spies that Cuba now has Soviet ground-to-sea missiles capable of sinking a battleship thirty miles offshore. Until they eliminate them, an amphibious invasion would be suicidal. Also, until they bomb out the IRBM's they are complaining about, they can't be absolutely certain the cities of America won't be atom-blasted in retaliation. Believe me, before they try to invade, they will bombard for days. What Russian Intelligence has told you just isn't true." His words seemed to confuse the G-2 agent, who returned to his headquarters for more information.

That afternoon another secret policeman came to Williams' room. "There's a fellow a couple of floors down who claims you know him," he said. He then took Williams to a room which had an armed guard posted in front of it. They entered to find Cedric Belfrage sitting on the bed and looking very perturbed. "Hi, Rob," he said. "Will you please tell these people who I am? Mary and I hurried back to Cuba when we heard about the trouble, but the G-2 claims there isn't any record of our being invited, and have been holding us here in the hotel."

"Do you know him?" the G-2 agent asked.

"Yes," Williams answered. "He's a good guy."

Belfrage's enemies had apparently used the crisis situation to compromise his position with the Cubans. Soon afterward he and his wife left and went to live in Mexico.

When Williams heard over the radio from Miami that the Soviets had agreed to pull out their missiles, he couldn't believe it. "The State Department's propaganda experts have made up this story to demoralize the Cubans before an invasion takes place," was his first reaction. But then he tuned in Radio Moscow and heard the same news there. The Russians were announcing it as "a great victory for Socialism." Williams' disbelief changed to anger. It seemed to him that, just as Khrushchev had built up the hopes of the poor Blacks in Monroe by promising them an aid ship back in 1959, and then reneged so as not to offend the U.S. power structure, he now was betraying the Cuban people by giving in to Kennedy's blockade threat.

The next morning a group of U.S. "Bourgeois Communists" visited Williams. "Isn't Khrushchev wonderful?" they said. "He has saved us all."

"Wonderful?" Williams retorted. "I wouldn't call him that. He has sold Cuba down the river. He's nothing but a pigheaded son of a bitch!"

"You can't say that!" one of them said, astounded.

"I can say it, and I'll say it again. Khrushchev is a pigheaded son of a bitch! And you can go tell him I said it."

"No, no," the others protested. "We're grateful to Premier Khrushchev. If he hadn't agreed to pull out the missiles, there'd have been an atomic war. Millions of people would have been killed."

"If you're so afraid of dying," Williams shouted at them, "then why did you come here in the first place? Why don't you get the hell out of here and go back to the United States? Why do you eat the Cubans' food, goddamn it, if you aren't ready to risk death to defend them?" The USCP people seemed highly disturbed as they hurriedly left the room.

That evening a couple of G-2 agents paid Williams a visit. "What's wrong?" they asked.

"If you really want to know," he answered, "it's what's being done to Cuba by the Russians. The reason you're here is because the American Communists complained to you. I told them I think Khrushchev is a pigheaded son of a bitch, and I haven't changed my mind." One of the secret policemen started scratching his head. "I don't feel this way because of anything that has been done to me," Williams continued. "It's because Khrushchev has sold out to the United States behind Cuba's back."

At this the G-2 agent who was scratching his head pulled his chair closer and, in a low voice full of emotion, said, "Do you know what, Williams? I feel exactly the same way you do. And do you know what else? *El Caballo* [The Horse, the Cubans' nickname for Castro] feels the same way too. In fact, when he heard Khrushchev had made a deal with Kennedy to pull out the rockets without consulting us, he got so mad he kicked the door to his office right off its hinges!" The two secret police agents stood up and shook hands with Williams, saying, "We all feel the same way." Then they left.

The streets of Havana had been plastered with posters showing Soviet soldiers, jet pilots, tank and artillery crews—all with the caption: "Cuba Is Not Alone!" But the moment they realized what had happened, the Cubans began tearing them down. They had been prepared to fight to the death to defend their honor, only to find that their surrender had already been arranged.

As if embarrassed to be seen, the Russian advisers living in Williams' hotel began taking their meals in their rooms. A Cuban bank clerk told him that a Russian colonel he knew had come into the bank and stood with his back to the counter, saying, "I can't face you this morning. It's too humiliating." And Williams' boys told him that the Russian soldiers manning the antiaircraft missiles near their school at Santa Maria del Mar had stood with tears streaming down their faces as the U.S. jets swooped overhead. The Russian GI's wanted to fight, but apparently had orders not to open fire. As if they knew this, the American pilots were brazenly performing acrobatics at such low altitudes that their faces could be seen from the ground. Such provocative actions finally seemed too much for one of the few batteries of SAM ground-to-air missiles which the Russians permitted the Cubans to operate. They cut loose, blasting a U-2 spy plane out of the sky.

When it was announced that the Russians, to prove that the IRBM's had really been removed, had unilaterally agreed to open Cuba for inspection, Fidel refused to permit it. U Thant, the secretary-general of the United Nations, came to Havana to persuade him to change his mind. A friend of Williams' who witnessed their meeting said Fidel asked U Thant, "Under what authority do you come? Do you represent the United Nations? Are you a spokesman for the U.S.A.? Or is it the U.S.S.R. you speak for? And would you mind telling us what international law says that we, a sovereign nation, must open our territory to an imperialist aggressor for inspection?"

U Thant had answered, "It's not really a matter of international law. I'm asking you to do this for the sake of world peace."

"If it's a matter of preserving peace," Fidel retorted, "then you should have gone to Washington to ask the United States to stop organizing attacks against us. They are the real threateners of world peace. The only conditions under which we might consider permitting inspection would be if the U.S.A. allowed Cuba to inspect all of its military installations in turn." Since the United States wasn't about to do this, U Thant had to return to New York without success.

Kennedy's demand to inspect Cuba seemed to Williams an attempt to demonstrate that Fidel was merely another Soviet flunky. But Fidel wouldn't budge. "If the Soviet Union wants to remove its own weapons," he declared, "that's their business. But we and we alone will decide who can set foot on Cuban soil." Mikoyan, the Soviet deputy-premier, then flew to Havana. But even he was unable to sway Fidel, and the inspection never took place.

There have been conflicting stories as to why the Russians sent missiles to Cuba. Whether Kennedy would have risked war by stopping Soviet ships on the high seas. What would have happened had Khrushchev not given in. From what Williams could gather in Havana before, during, and after the crisis, this is what took place: Following the abortive invasion at "Playa Giron," certain that the United States couldn't afford the humiliation of defeat so close to its own shore, and that another, more powerful attack was coming, Fidel had asked Russia for a firm commitment to defend Cuba. The U.S.S.R., threatened by American IRBM's in Italy, Turkey, and other European nations, and not having its own rockets in similar proximity to the United States, saw an opportunity to make a grandstand play in the Cold War. Cuba's permitting the installation of Soviet IRBM's on its soil would throw the entire U.S. defense Establishment off balance. America's advantage in the balance of terror by having more ICBM's, strategic bombers, and missile-carrying atomic submarines than Russia could in this way be instantly overcome. Instead of expensive Soviet ICBM's having to travel thousands of miles over the North Pole, providing the Pentagon's radar with thirty minutes' advance warning time, cheap Russian IRBM's just ninety miles from Florida could devastate every city from Miami to New York almost before the Americans knew they were being launched.

This didn't mean having missiles in Cuba would have insured Russian victory in a nuclear war. Even had they launched a preemptive attack eliminating America's ICBM installations, a sufficient number of U.S. hydrogen bombs could have been delivered by other means to completely destroy the U.S.S.R. as well. But placing missiles in Cuba did provide Russia with a more credible deterrent against a U.S. attack than it already had, thus bettering its bargaining position.

Once the offer to supply missiles was made, and Cuba accepted, there was extensive debate in the Kremlin as to whether the IRBM's should be installed secretly or not. Even if the launching sites were expertly hidden, there was always the possibility the CIA's extensive spy network would ferret them out. There was also the danger that the Cubans, being a proud and emotional people, might become so angered at U.S. threats and insults that they themselves would announce they were defended by atomic weapons. The discovery of hidden missile sites in Cuba could be very dangerous because the logical assumption would be that a Russian surprise attack was imminent, which might lead the Americans to strike first. On the other hand, installing the IRBM's out in the open could be a clever move, as it would indicate the U.S.S.R.'s readiness to defend Cuba, rather than to launch a surprise attack on the United States.

The Russians must have also considered that the Americans would insist on the missiles being removed once they were discovered. The usual procedure in bargaining is to respond to a request with a counterrequest. If Washington didn't like the Soviet IRBM's in Cuba, Moscow could answer that it liked the U.S. missiles on its own borders even less. Although no public announcement of such a deal was made at the time, Kennedy quietly pulled out the American IRBM's in Turkey and Italy in return for Khrushchev's ordering the Russian missiles withdrawn from Cuba.

Another secret bargain Williams felt certain was made then was that, in return for Moscow's recalling the bulk of its thirty thousand soldiers from Cuba and trying to quiet the Revolution's agitation in the rest of Latin America, Washington would stop permitting exile raids from its territory and would see that a new invasion wasn't attempted. The proof that some such agreement was made later became quite evident. The United States subsequently began stopping the exile expeditions, confiscating the would-be raiders' boats and seizing their weapons. Reciprocally, the Cubans almost completely abandoned their once-dynamic program of supporting the guerrillas struggling to overthrow the dictatorships which protect U.S. interests in South and Central America.

Mao Tse-tung denounced Khrushchev's actions in the Cuban Missile Crisis as being "first adventurist, then capitulationist." Williams shared his feelings. He felt that the Russians had no right to play atomic chess with the Cubans as pawns. Rather than provocatively advancing their IRBM's, they could have demonstrated their support of the Revolution by simply declaring that they would consider an attack on Cuba tantamount to an attack on the U.S.S.R. The United States had assumed such a stance regarding West Berlin and South Korea. Even if the Russians thought they could gain by the missile ploy, the inherent danger far outweighed its possible advantages.

Not that such tactics were new. Williams had heard from acquaintances in Cuba that the U.S.S.R. had promised to help the Chinese develop atomic weapons back in 1957—only to break their word and pull out their technicians in 1960 when Mao refused to let Khrushchev order him around. Williams considered the worst consequence of Khrushchev's Cuban maneuver the demoralizing effect it would have on the hundreds of millions of oppressed people in the rest of the world. Cuba's defiance in the face of enormous U.S. military and economic power had inspired revolutionaries in many lands. It was a living demonstration that, if they would make the necessary sacrifices, the small nations could refuse to be subservient to the major powers. Non-Communists as well as Communists had admired the Cubans' courage in standing up against such great odds.

The Missile Crisis marked the high point of Russian prestige in Cuba and the beginning of its decline. Soviet oil, weapons, and other goods continued to be exchanged for Cuban sugar, tobacco, coffee, and nickel, but the Cuban man in the street's attitude had changed: He no longer saw Russia as a loyal ally, but just another

basically self-serving major power. The decline of Russian prestige
was accompanied by a lessening of the Cuban Communist Party's
popularity followed by a drop in influence of the USCP. Not that
there was a purge of Moscow-oriented Communists from positions of authority, but their ability to influence the Revolution's
policies diminished considerably.

Early in 1963, a group of U.S. Black militants contacted Williams with the idea of forming a new organization which could
help develop a revolutionary policy. They asked him to assist in
defining its basic concepts and to serve as chairman. It was called
the Revolutionary Action Movement (RAM), and its primary
function would be to establish and maintain contact among the
most militant elements of such groups as CORE, SNCC, the
NAACP, and the Black Muslims in order to develop a theoretical
base for what was coming to be called the "Black Liberation
Movement."

As chairman, Williams put out a call to militants throughout
the United States to form RAM chapters. The response was quick.
Groups were set up in a score of cities. At first RAM's goal was
limited to pressuring the U.S. government to enforce the guarantees of the Bill of Rights. Later the goal became "the end of racism
and oppression in the United States by whatever means necessary," clearly implying that force would be required.

Within a few years of its formation, dozens of RAM people
were arrested in various U.S. cities on bombing and murder-con-
spiracy charges. In New York a group led by a professional educa-
tor was accused of plotting everything from killing Roy Wilkins of
the NAACP to dynamiting department stores and the Brooklyn
Botanical Gardens. In each instance a Black police or FBI informer posing as a militant had infiltrated a RAM chapter and
testified to having overheard its members planning such deeds.

Williams claimed that all these cases were based on false testimony by *agents-provocateurs*. He denied that RAM advocated
assassination of its opponents, or that it believed in using terror
tactics against civilians. A corrupt system wasn't to be overthrown
by murdering its leaders, he contended; for, like the Hydra of
mythology, it could instantly grow two new heads for every one
destroyed. Nor would racism and oppression be ended by bombing crowds of shopping housewives. Such tactics could only result
in a wave of counterterror and the strengthening of hatred and in-

justice. "The charges against RAM," he declared, "are based upon nothing more than the nightmarish imaginings of the racist criminals who run the Justice Department and the various local police forces of the United States."

Following the 1962 Missile Crisis the declining prestige of the USCP in Cuba opened the door to certain other leftist elements, especially Progressive Labor (PL). In the summer of 1963, despite the U.S. State Department's ban on travel to Cuba, a touring group of young Americans, primarily under PL and Socialist Workers Party sponsorship, arrived in Havana. They were put up in the Hotel Riviera, and some of them soon began scandalizing the Cubans by their eccentric behavior. Williams didn't pay much attention to the various stories circulating about the Americans until a group of them came to see him. Following the Missile Crisis, he and his wife had been moved out of the Capri Hotel and into a comfortable home in the Miramar section of Havana. It was a two-bedroom dwelling, complete with furniture—one of the thousands of such houses taken over by the Revolution when their middle-class owners went into exile.

Williams welcomed the American young people, many of whom were college students, and asked them to sit down. They said they were visiting him to try to find out the truth about conditions in Cuba.

"How free is it here?" was their first question.

"So far as I am concerned," Williams answered, "it's far freer than the United States."

"Does that mean you can smoke pot without being arrested?" they asked. Several of them looked to him as if they might be using one kind of drug or another. Their hair was uncut, their eyes glassy and, although they weren't poor, they were wearing old and torn clothing, some even going barefoot.

"I don't know if you can smoke marijuana in Cuba or not," Williams answered, "since the subject has never been mentioned by anyone I've met here. The Revolution has more serious things to be concerned with."

"Suppose we want to dance in the streets of Havana. Will we be free to do that?" was their next question.

"I've seen Cubans doing it," Williams answered, "but only during carnivals and celebrations, when the streets are roped off. If you knew anything about the way the Cubans drive, you wouldn't ask such a question. You take your life in your hands just standing on the sidewalk here. Anyway, why would you want to dance in the streets when there are lots of dance halls available?"

"If this were really a free country," the young American leftists responded, "you could dance in the streets whenever you felt like it, or smoke pot, or do whatever you wanted to."

"And what about the rights of those who wanted to drive on those same streets?" Williams asked. "In exercising your freedom wouldn't you be depriving them of theirs?"

They then said, "We've heard the Revolution has been rounding up homosexuals and sending them to work camps. Is this true?" When he told them that, so far as he knew, it was, they declared, "It just isn't right. In a completely free country you must have complete sexual freedom too."

Although many of the young Americans held more conventional opinions, the activities of the eccentrics among them made a very bad impression on the Cubans. Some were extremely arrogant and belligerent, insisting on testing the political position of everyone they met. Others saw everything in Cuba as good and beautiful—even those things the Cubans themselves hated and wanted to get rid of. To these true-believers, if a country was Socialist, even its cesspools smelled like perfume. Then there were those who did such things as getting drunk and staggering around on the nineteenth-floor hotel window ledges, forcing the Cuban militia to get them down. Even though swimming on the beaches of Cuba after dark was banned because of the still-present danger of exile landings, some of the Americans insisted on doing it. One of them drowned one night in an unsupervised hotel pool.

Some of the antics of the youth group contributed to the suspicions Williams had long held about Progressive Labor. Among the PL leaders who had come to Monroe while he was still there were Jake and Milt Rosen. Then, in 1961, after he was forced to flee, they had sent their people into Union County and set up an organization to fill the vacuum left by his departure. Once they had established themselves, they started raising money from the Black domestics and other workers. One of Williams' former associates was appointed treasurer, but he had no real voice in how the funds were spent, and served only as a front for the PL leadership. The same tactic was used in establishing a local newspaper called

Freedom. A Monroe Black was the editor, but the PL organizers really ran it. At first they seemed to be doing good things, but it wasn't long before their tactics became increasingly arbitrary. They soon alienated most of Williams' people, who resented being manipulated; and the organization fell apart.

Among the members of the youth group that visited Cuba in 1963 was a Texan named Phillip Luce, the editor of *Challenge*, the Progressive Labor magazine. He came to Williams' house and showed him a magazine article he had written in which he supported Williams against an attack by a USCP spokesman who was criticizing him as being a "fanatic" and "extremist." Luce also said he had worked closely with Clark Foreman, who had been instrumental in getting the Emergency Civil Liberties Committee in New York to take on Williams' sit-in appeal after the NAACP had dropped it. Not only did Luce impress Williams as being sincere, he appeared more dedicated than most of the other PL people. But, soon after his return to the States from Cuba, Luce began to testify before various government agencies; and the leftists denounced him as a CIA agent.

That summer the brutal nature of U.S. racism resulted in the slaughter of several little Black girls when the Birmingham church they were praying in was bombed. Not that the murder of Blacks in Alabama or anywhere else in the United States was anything new. But this particular incident was so vicious—such an obvious attempt to terrorize the nonviolent desegregation movement—that it got worldwide publicity. Williams saw it as a sardonic commentary on the U.S. law-enforcement agencies that, while they pack the jails with those allegedly planning violence against the Establishment, they never seem able to discover who is responsible for murders and bombings *actually committed* against Blacks and the Left. And, when they are forced to put some KKK or other right-wing assassins on trial, racist and reactionary judges, prosecutors, and juries frequently either set them free or let them off with a slap on the wrist.

Angered by the Birmingham church bombing, Williams cabled several Black and Brown world leaders, asking them to make public statements against such acts. Among them were Sukarno of Indonesia, Nkrumah of Ghana, Ben Bella of Algeria, and Mao Tse-tung of China. He expected Sukarno to respond because there had already been demonstrations in his country against U.S. racism. Most of all, he thought Nkrumah would say something, because he had been a student in the States and knew about discrimination there from personal experience. Neither Sukarno, Nkrumah, nor Ben Bella, however, chose to make any kind of statement. Williams interpreted the unwillingness of those supposedly popular leaders to condemn the murder of Black children praying in church as a lack of a basic sense of humanity. Of all the world leaders he contacted, Chairman Mao was the last one he expected to be concerned about what was happening to Blacks in the United States.

Williams knew relatively little about China, and what sparse information he had didn't indicate that it had assumed a position against racism. He was happily surprised, therefore, when Chairman Mao came out with an unprecedented declaration of support for the struggle of Black Americans. Not only did he denounce the Birmingham murders, he stated that discrimination against Blacks in the United States was part of the worldwide system of capitalist oppression. And he also called upon the decent-minded White people of America to join in the fight to end racism.

Chairman Mao's statement took the Chinese embassy in Havana by surprise. The ambassador himself notified Williams of it by telephone before it was released to the press; and he then sent some of his diplomats to his house to read it to him in person.

"How did you communicate with Chairman Mao?" was the first thing the Chinese diplomats asked Williams. The idea that he had simply gone into the Cuban telegraph office and sent Mao a cable evidently hadn't occurred to them. Then they said that Chairman Mao had invited Williams and his wife to attend the October 1st National Day Celebration, the annual commemoration of the liberation of China from Chiang Kai-shek's rule in 1949.

A little over two years had passed since Williams and his wife had fled through the night from their house on Boyte Street. With the help of good friends in the United States, Canada, and Cuba, they had survived. Now they were being accorded an opportunity few Americans had been privileged to have.

One day toward the end of September, 1963, they drove outside of Havana to the José Martí airport, boarded a big TU-114 turbojet—the same type of plane in which Khrushchev had visited the United States—and took off on a journey to the other side of the world.

They were on their way to Peking.

Chapter Twelve

JOURNEYS TO THE EAST

Although the Soviet-built airliner in which they left Havana was comfortable, Williams and his wife found the twenty-one-hour nonstop flight to Moscow tiring. The late-September weather in the capital of the U.S.S.R. was rather cold, and they made good use of the heavy coats they had purchased before leaving Cuba.

As their itinerary called for a layover before going on to Peking, they checked into a hotel. The next morning they went sightseeing in one of the chauffeured limousines provided by Intourist, visiting the Kremlin, Lumumba University, and other places. One of the world's largest cities, they found Moscow cleaner and far less cluttered with billboards and commercial signs than New York and Detroit.

They observed that, while the stores were well stocked, they lacked the variety of goods seen in the States. The people on the streets were warmly dressed, and didn't seem disturbed at the sight of two Blacks riding in a chauffeured car. Since Williams didn't get to know many Russians during the short time he spent in Moscow, his impressions remained superficial.

After three days of sightseeing, he and his wife boarded an Aeroflot TU-104 twin-engined jet and took off for China. Although it was considerably faster than the TU-114 turboprop which had brought them from Cuba, its limited range necessitated two refueling stops while crossing Siberia. The total flying time required to travel the some six thousand miles from Moscow to Peking was only nine hours, but a storm over Mongolia forced them to spend the night at Irkutsk, a Soviet city on the shores of Lake Baikal.

The next morning, the weather having cleared, they were transferred to a British-built turboprop operated by the Chinese. On September 28th, six days after leaving Havana, they arrived in Peking.

Waiting to greet them at the airport was a large crowd, including many young people. There were quite a few other foreigners on the plane who had also been invited to the National Day Celebration. As each of them exited he was welcomed by representatives of the Chinese government's Peace Committee. Newspaper photographers and TV film crews busily covered the event, while a large band played in the background.

Most of the Chinese wore simple cotton suits with button-up tunic jackets and soft-brimmed caps. This Spartan style of dress, called the "national uniform," was introduced by Sun Yat-sen back in the days of the 1911 Revolution which overthrew the Empire. Dark blue was the most popular color, but browns, grays, and other hues were also worn.

What was most impressive about the welcome was the affection displayed toward the foreign guests, including Williams and his wife. The handshakes and smiles of the adults went far beyond mere polite formalities. And when the children, most of whom wore white shirts and red neckerchiefs, handed them flowers and gave the Young Pioneers' salute, the glow in their eyes showed how excited they were. Even the workmen at the airport stopped whatever they were doing to smile and wave.

As guests of the Peace Committee, Williams and his wife were given the full VIP treatment. A special room was placed at their disposal until the baggage was unloaded from the plane; they weren't required to go through either a customs or an immigration check; and a limousine was provided to take them to the Peking Hotel.

One of the first things Williams noticed about the hotel was that most of the other guests didn't bother to lock the doors when they went out of their rooms. When he remarked about this, an African diplomat who had been to China before said, "Nobody here would think of stealing from you. It just isn't done." Williams was incredulous at first, but soon saw it was true. One could leave valuables, even cash, lying out on the bed or the dresser, go away for hours, and return to find everything just as he had left it.

The Williams suite was the same one Doctor W. E. B. Du Bois had stayed in during his visit to China. It consisted of a large bedroom, a bath, and a small sitting room. Among the other guests in the hotel were Prince Sihanouk of Cambodia and the president of the Congo.

The Peking Hotel had been built before the "Liberation," as everyone in China called the Communists' coming to power in 1949. Like all other private establishments, it was now owned and operated by the state. New wings had been built, the rooms were simple and clean, and the service was excellent.

During his visit to China, Williams was to be far less impressed by the material aspects of what he saw than by the spirit of the people. In America he felt there was a tendency to evaluate life only in physical terms, to become obsessed with accumulating objects—large homes, supercharged cars, expensive clothing, jewelry, and so on. And he viewed this as one of the chief reasons U.S. society was in so much trouble. Too many Americans were deluding themselves by assuming that all their problems could be solved by things rather than by thinking.

This is not to say that the Chinese rejected all creature comforts, for they had a surprisingly large quantity of consumer goods in their stores. The variety of textiles, transistor radios, wrist watches, bicycles, typewriters, and other such products available in Peking far exceeded what Williams had seen in Moscow, and approached that to be found in New York. But the Chinese didn't seem preoccupied with things in and of themselves. The idea that man is primary, not secondary, appeared to permeate their society.

On the night of September 30th, the eve of National Day, Williams and his wife were invited to attend the banquet held in the Great Hall of the People, a large auditorium attached to the Peking Hotel. They entered the hall, which was decorated with two-story-high gold columns, to find a crowd of thousands of Chinese dignitaries and foreign guests already gathered. After a few minutes, the Army band struck up "The East Is Red," and the entire assemblage, which included Asian and African heads of state, turbaned Sikhs, Buddhist monks in saffron robes, Latin American revolutionaries, and western European diplomats, rose and applauded. Chairman Mao Tse-tung had arrived.

The first thing Mao did was to go around the banquet hall and personally greet every foreign guest. Meanwhile, a middle-aged Chinese woman, who had entered by another door, started welcoming the women. When she came to their table to say hello to Mabel, the interpreter introduced her, saying, "This is Chiang Ching."

"And what does she do?" Williams asked.

"Why she is Chairman Mao's wife," he said. Williams and his wife were embarrassed, but the friendly laughter of their hosts put them at ease.

Then Chairman Mao himself approached their table, and everyone stood up. Mao's wife stepped into line next to Mabel and put out her hand for him to shake. When he saw who she was, Mao pulled his hand back and said jokingly, "I don't have to welcome you. You're not one of the guests."

"Oh, yes," Chiang Ching said playfully, "I'm with the other women, and if you shake their hands, you'll have to shake mine, too." Everyone laughed, and the evening was off to a relaxed start.

When Williams was introduced, Chairman Mao said, "I'm very happy to see you here. I want you to know that the Chinese people support the struggle of our Black brothers in America." He was considerably taller than Williams had expected, being close to his own six feet and, although heavyset, wasn't fat. He appeared far younger than his seventy years, and his movements were those of a man in good physical condition. The most impressive thing about him was the aura of experience and sophistication which he radiated.

At nine the next morning Williams was taken to the top of the Tien An Men (The Gate of Heavenly Peace), the main entrance to the ancient Forbidden City, once the palace of China's emperors. The National Day Parade, due to begin at ten, was to involve half a million marchers. Most of the foreign guests were assigned to the regular reviewing stands, but Williams and his wife were led to the main rostrum to view the procession alongside various foreign heads of state and high Chinese officials. The president of North Korea and a leader from Pakistan were among the people flanking them.

Before the festivities began, they were taken to a reception room located behind the rostrum to meet Chairman Mao. He invited them to have tea, and then began to ask about the Black Liberation Movement in the United States, wanting to know how it was developing and what prospects Williams saw for it in the future. When he answered that he thought it would be a very long and difficult fight, Mao said, "You are quite young yet, and will have a lot of time in which to solve this problem. If you're impatient, then you're not really waging a revolutionary struggle, only reacting from emotion. It's not enough merely to lash out at injustice and oppression. A true revolutionary program must be planned and sustained, for its aim is to change society permanently." As they spoke, Mao kept laughing and joking and refilling Williams' cup of tea.

Although this first private talk with Chairman Mao lasted only a few minutes, it contrasted strongly with the meetings Williams had had with Fidel, who seldom asked him what he thought were serious questions. "We support the Black people in America," Fidel would say every time they met, but despite all the very real help he gave Williams, he never seemed more than moderately interested. Not only was Fidel only half Mao's age, and the Cuban Revolution in its infancy compared to China's, the contrast in their attitudes was due, Williams supposed, to the difference between being the leader of eight million and eight hundred million people.

The parade began at exactly 10:00 a.m. It was an impressive event, with more people streaming past the Tien An Men than Williams had ever seen before in one place. In contrast to the National Day parades of previous years, there were no military contingents. The jets and heavy tanks which had always been part of the display were being withheld to deaccentuate the role of machines. The power of the people was what was being featured.

Delegations from every facet of Chinese life paraded past: athletes, workers, professors, actors, dancers, farmers, doctors, miners, students, fishermen; row after row of smiling faces; millions of brightly colored flowers, streamers, flags, and balloons; examples of the latest in industrial and agricultural production; floats depicting scenes from feature films and stage plays; gymnasts forming human pyramids; and representatives of China's national minorities wearing their holiday dress. The only weapons shown were those of a battalion of Peoples' Militia: rifles, light mortars, machine guns, and bazookas.

At exactly 2:00 p.m. the procession ended. Chairman Mao posed for photographs with each of the guests on the main rostrum, and thanked them all for having come to China. Then Williams and his wife returned to the hotel to plan their itinerary for a tour of the country being arranged by the Peace Committee.

During the next five weeks they traveled several thousand miles by train, boat, bus, and jeep, going from the Korean Auton-

omous Region in the Northeast down through Wuhan and Shanghai to Canton in the South, visiting everything from steel mills to
communes.

Among the myths about the Chinese long fostered by the
communications media in the United States is that they are a cold,
unemotional people. "Inscrutable" was the word Williams re-
called from his childhood as most commonly used whenever
Orientals were referred to in popular novels, newspaper articles, or
"Fu Manchu" movies. But the more Chinese he met the more he
found this to be untrue. There was nothing hidden or reserved
about the students who greeted them at the countryside schools
they visited. They would rush out cheering and beating drums,
shake their hands, and say, "We support your struggle! We support your struggle!" Young and old alike would often sing "We
Shall Overcome" in Chinese.

Williams didn't consider "We Shall Overcome" a revolutionary song, for in the States it was most commonly associated with
Martin Luther King's pacifist desegregation movement. But hearing students sing it in remote regions of China, over ten thousand
miles away from the United States, helped convince him that
Chairman Mao's declaration of support for Black America was
more than a mere propaganda gesture for foreign consumption.

In a village in Mongolia Williams and his wife were the guests
of honor at the presentation of a new musical composition called
We Support Our Black Brothers in America. It was well performed
by the commune's symphony orchestra. The composer told them
he had been inspired to write it after reading Chairman Mao's
statement in response to Williams' telegram about the Birmingham church bombing. He was almost ecstatic at the idea that a
couple of Black Americans had actually been able to hear it. Since
one doesn't compose, arrange, and rehearse a symphonic work in
a week or two, it was obvious to Williams that it hadn't been done
merely for his benefit, but was a legitimate expression of the way
the composer and his countrymen felt.

At first Williams was puzzled as to why the Chinese, who live
so far away from the United States, should take such an interest in
the civil-rights struggle. One answer he found was that quite a few
of them either had relatives in the States or had lived there themselves. During his tour he often met Chinese born and educated in
the United States who had returned to their homeland. They well

knew what it was like to be discriminated against in housing, jobs, and other ways. Also, when the British, French, and other light-skinned Europeans had run the port cities of China, segregation and discrimination had been the rule. In one Shanghai Park a sign posted by the English had declared: "No Dogs or Chinese Permitted." The Chinese weren't voicing support for the U.S. civil-rights struggle as an abstract political ploy, but because they, like the Blacks, had been the victims of racism.

Not only were the Chinese friendly and hard-working, Williams found their honesty almost incredible. When he asked his guides where he could change some of his Cuban money, they first said, "But you are a guest. We will provide whatever you need." He insisted, saying he would feel more comfortable if he had some cash in his pocket, and finally persuaded them to take him to a bank where foreign currency could be exchanged. When they entered the bank, Williams could hardly believe his eyes. Stacks of bills were out in the open, piled on the tables and counter tops. Not a guard was in sight. While he was standing there gaping, a group of men entered with their arms loaded with bundles of bank notes; and he could see additional bundles stacked on the seats of their car parked across the street, unguarded and unlocked.

"You couldn't get away with it in the States," Williams commented to his interpreter. "I wouldn't dare go near a bank like this one back home. Why it would be robbed every five minutes."

"Don't worry," the interpreter said. "Nobody will touch that money. Things are very different here since the Liberation."

Williams saw similar scenes wherever he went, and they never failed to astound him. His entire life had been spent in an environment where the necessity for locks, bolts, fences, and armed guards was taken for granted.

"We know that our society is a true collective," Williams' interpreter said. "Taking state property would be stealing from ourselves. Theft is an offense against the entire community, and potential thieves know nobody will shelter or protect them. Even when they are successful, the moment they try to sell or display their ill-gotten gains the people seize them as enemies. The few policemen we have frequently spend more time protecting criminals from being punished by the crowd than in tracking them down."

Although they were still lacking in material things, the Chinese had such pride in their nation and themselves that, along with theft, vice seemed to have almost ceased to exist. Shanghai, which before the Liberation was called the "Sin City of the World," now appeared to be a model community. Most of the former criminal elements had been treated as victims of a bad society, not as "evil" persons. A great many of the prostitutes had been little more than slaves, having been sold to the proprietors of whorehouses when they were little children because their parents were so poor they couldn't feed them. Others had been forced to sell themselves into prostitution as adults when the shortage of jobs left no alternative. The Communists were able to rehabilitate both of these types very quickly. Once given proper job training, most of them leaped at the chance to assume more acceptable roles.

A third category of prostitute proved more difficult to deal with. There were a few whores whose personalities were so warped that they preferred working on their backs to operating a drill press or being a nursery-school teacher. This small minority was obligated to attend special live-in schools where they were subjected to reeducation courses, or what the Chinese proudly refer to as "brainwashing."

In the United States Williams had heard brainwashing described as some sort of fiendish manipulation of the mind which left its victims devoid of all will. What it really consisted of, however, seemed quite simple. The theory behind it was that ideas— such as the bourgeois ethic that the most desirable thing in life is to make as much money as possible and work as little as one can —are the result of years of being indoctrinated with selfish concepts. The Chinese, he found, view man as neither inherently good nor bad, but the product of what he is taught and the type of life he sees being led all around him. Therefore, to counteract the effects of a self-centered, personal-profit-oriented upbringing, they try to reeducate people to the benefits of cooperating for the common good.

It wasn't a quick process, and often required years of daily lectures, reading classes, and self-criticism groups. Experience had shown the Chinese that being patient is the only way to accomplish real change. "It is better to convince one person to join voluntarily in the construction of Socialism than to force ten thousand to do so against their will," they said whenever discussing the matter.

From a psychological point of view, hours, days, weeks, months, and years of inundating the mind with a particular point of view, while excluding all opinion which might contradict it, can be very effective. The every-man-for-himself-and-devil-take-the-hindmost thought patterns acquired by being raised in the pre-1949 Chinese environment were very persistent, and didn't change automatically just because new laws were enacted.

Williams had personal experience of how the U.S. Armed Forces, especially the Marines, practiced their own form of brainwashing. They specialized in harassing and beating young Americans—particularly those with some degree of independence and self-respect—until they were depersonalized and transformed into unquestioning killer-robots. And he considered the masters of thought manipulation to be the Madison Avenue advertising executives, whose television commercials were designed to create and maintain mass anxieties and insecurities. "Your breath smells," "You have B.O.," "Your head is aching," and "You have an upset stomach," were among the negative messages being ceaselessly pounded into the minds of tens of millions of people in order to make billions of dollars in profits. The American public was kept unsatisfied by constant reminders that only buying this or that product could alleviate their artificially induced needs.

Williams concluded that positive brainwashing, using psychological persuasion to rehabilitate prostitutes and criminals by opening their minds to the concept of working for rather than against their fellow men, was one of the most constructive innovations of the Chinese Revolution. Changing the form of society without changing the way men think wasn't enough. The battlefield of ideas was more important than the battlefield of guns.

Everywhere Williams went, something new was taking place. Swamps were being drained and deserts irrigated; dams and power-generating stations built to control floods and harness the power of the rivers; new railroads, highways, harbors, and airfields under construction and old ones modernized and enlarged; schools, hospitals, theaters, and libraries appearing across the land; the vast illiteracy which existed in China before 1949 almost eliminated; factories and cities springing up like mushrooms; and plans being drawn for even more construction. It was almost as if hundreds of millions of men and women had suddenly been transported to an inhospitable and previously uninhabited planet and

were trying overnight to transform it into a comfortable and productive place.

China had existed for many millenniums, but in the past
some 90 percent of its population had lived in less than a quarter
of its area—mainly the eastern coastal provinces. Until 1949, over
two-thirds of the arable land hadn't been turned by a plow. Now
the inland western regions (almost as large as the United States)
were being developed—along with the rest of the country.

When Williams toured the new villages in the West, he was
surprised to find many of the same consumer goods as in the department stores of Peking. He hadn't realized the Chinese were
producing modern appliances in sufficient quantities to supply
such remote areas. Farmers and shepherds out on the prairies
were wearing wristwatches and riding motorbikes. It was quite an
accomplishment, he felt, considering that less than fifteen years
earlier many Chinese peasants had been so poor that grandfather,
father, and son took turns wearing one patchwork suit of clothes
—two men huddling naked in the house while the third used the
clothes to labor in the fields. It reminded him of the "hot bed"
flophouses of Depression days in the United States, when louse-
infested cots were rented to the destitute around the clock—three
times a day on eight-hour shifts.

The average Chinese family didn't have a TV set, washing
machine, car, three-bedroom house or motor boat, and there
didn't seem to be even a remote chance of their getting such
things, but the famines and epidemics that once killed millions
had been eliminated. No one appeared to have to worry about a
job, food, clothing, or shelter, which was more than could be said
for tens of millions of poor Black, Brown, and White Americans.

The ignorance of China prevailing in the United States wasn't
shared by most other nations. Diplomats, journalists, businessmen, and athletic and cultural groups from every corner of the
earth were to be found there. While Americans were forbidden by
their government to set foot in "Red China," Canadian and
French tourists could be seen wandering about buying souvenirs
and snapping photos.

Williams became acquainted with people from Europe, Africa, Asia, and Latin America who were teaching at schools in Peking. He also met Rewi Alley, a journalist from New Zealand who
had been living in China for several years.

One of the most interesting of all the non-Chinese he came to know was Anna Louise Strong, the elderly American leftist writer. He and his wife were invited to her home in Peking's "Peace Compound," a residential area for foreign guests, on the occasion of her seventy-sixth birthday. She was a friend of Cedric Belfrage's, and wrote for his paper, *The National Guardian.* Williams had several talks with her about the Black Liberation Movement in the United States.

The anti-American propaganda in China was far milder than Williams had expected. Not speaking the language, much of what he could observe was restricted to illustrations on billboards and wall posters. The primary complaints against the United States appeared to be over its support of Chiang Kai-shek's regime on Formosa, and the growing American involvement in South Vietnam. Most billboards and posters dealt with domestic matters: exhorting the people to work harder, waste less, support the construction of Socialism, and so on.

The most serious problem then facing China appeared to be the damaging effect of Khrushchev's having pulled out thousands of his experts in 1961. The vast industrial complexes designed and run by the Russians were suddenly without either managers or operating plans. Chinese assistants with limited training had been forced to take over the critical positions vacated by Soviet technicians and engineers. Now, two years later, many areas of industry were still staggering from the blow. The withdrawal of Russian experts from China's new oil fields and refineries, plus a severe cut in petroleum shipments from the U.S.S.R., meant many trucks and busses had to be adapted to natural gas. Vehicles with large butane or propane tanks attached to their roofs were a common sight in Peking.

"Khrushchev called back his men," the Chinese told Williams, "because he looked upon our relationship as that of father and son, with the Russians being the father. But we insisted upon it being that between brothers and equals. After the Soviet technicians left, we discovered they had been charging us more for their goods than we would have had to pay the British and other capitalists for similar materials of higher quality. We also found that many of the things they were shipping to us could be manufactured less expensively right here in China. In fact, they had caused us to neglect certain areas of production in order to keep us dependent on them. The over-all nature of their aid, substantial and welcome though it was, seemed intended to maintain us as a primarily agricultural nation—a market for Russian manufactured goods."

The Chinese didn't tell Williams that they disliked the Russians. They spoke freely of how much the U.S.S.R. had helped them, especially in the years immediately following the Liberation. During the National Day Parade in Peking they had displayed portraits of Stalin alongside those of Marx, Engels, and Lenin. "When Stalin was in power," they said, "we had a good working relationship with Russia, but since Khrushchev and his revisionist clique have taken over, the Soviet Union has begun to degenerate as a Socialist nation. The Russians no longer want to lead the revolution, their only desire is to divide the world with the United States."

Another thing which seemed unusual to Williams was that wherever he went—to shipyards, factories, or farms—the Chinese kept asking him to tell them if he saw anything that had been done incorrectly. They seemed quite sincere about this, saying, "You come from a nation which is far advanced in technological matters. We know we must be making many mistakes. Please help us rectify our errors." But he didn't see many things to criticize. Their machinists were doing as well as any he'd known while working at the Ford, Cadillac, and Curtiss-Wright plants back home.

Williams' only major disagreement with the Chinese was over the future of the United States. He felt they had too much confidence in the American masses, being convinced they would soon "wake up to the folly of capitalism and create a Socialist state."

"I certainly hope you're right," Williams told them, "but I don't have that much confidence that the American people, especially the White workers, will do the right thing."

There were so many fascinating things to see in China that Williams could have gone on touring there for years, but after six weeks he decided to return to Havana. Although he had left his work in the hands of responsible friends, the energy and dedication of the Chinese kept reminding him how much there was still to be done. In answer to their hosts' unhappiness about their cutting short the trip, he and Mabel promised to return in later years to see the parts of the country they had missed.

As they were preparing to leave Peking for the return trip to Havana, Chou En-lai, China's foreign minister, invited Williams to come see him. A medium-sized man, Chou was a few years younger than Mao Tse-tung, and his face less rounded than Mao's. He spoke a fair English, Williams found, having traveled extensively in his youth and lived in France, Germany, England, and other countries. This made him one of the few top Chinese leaders to have a personal knowledge of life in the West.

Williams was impressed by Chou En-lai. He seemed very humble, was soft-spoken, and possessed a good sense of humor. Like Mao, he expressed interest in the race issue, and asked Williams, "What do you think China can do to support the Black people of America?"

Williams told Chou that in the future the Black Liberation Movement might need material assistance but that for the moment the moral support of the Chinese was more than enough. Chairman Mao's being the first head of state to condemn U.S. racist atrocities was a great contribution. The only thing Williams suggested was that the more people from the United States— Whites as well as Blacks—the Chinese could invite to see their country, the harder the capitalists would find it to maintain the climate of ignorance and fear they had created about China.

Williams had become disillusioned with the Soviet Union as the power that would help eliminate racism and exploitation. Not only Russia's policy in the Cuban missile crisis but her renunciation of support for wars of national liberation, it seemed to him, had let down the oppressed peoples of Africa, Asia, and Latin America, as well as the U.S. Black revolutionaries.

His China visit convinced Williams that Black America had an even more important ally than the U.S.S.R. It wasn't so much China's present condition that impressed him—for it was still emerging from dire poverty—it was the thinking and building going on there, the establishing of what he felt certain in the future would be the strongest nation on earth, that seized his imagination.

He could see the growing strength in the faces of the students in China's universities and in the hands of her farmers and factory workers. The United States seemed to him like a smug boxer, the champ at present, but becoming fat and sluggish. But China was like a youthful giant, gaining in strength every day, and already challenging the degenerating Uncle Sam. The U.S. leaders existed only for the present, their energies wasting away in trying to shore up corrupt regimes around the world; but the Chinese young people he met were working for the future. They were building their country as the base area for the liberation from poverty and oppression of the struggling masses of the rest of the world.

Returning to the pleasantly warm climate of Havana in mid-November, Williams wrote a series of articles about China for *Bohemia* and broadcast several interview tapes which he had made with young English-speaking Chinese at the Children's Palace in Shanghai. His favorable comments on China triggered a new rash of attacks in the U.S. press; and the anti-Peking "Bourgeois Communists" began to speak of him as a "Chinese-controlled Black Nationalist." But most of the Cubans he was friendly with were extremely interested in what he had seen in China. While they knew that there was a serious dispute between Moscow and Peking, they weren't certain as to its causes.

Copies of both *The Peking Review,* the official Chinese magazine, and *Moscow Times*, its Soviet counterpart, were available at several Havana newsstands; and each contained violent criticisms of the other's policies. The Cuban press, however, refused to take sides in the Sino-Soviet dispute or print the polemics of either nation. The only comment Fidel would make on the problem was to urge all Socialist countries to try to forget their differences. Despite their efforts to stay out of the controversy, the Cubans' almost total dependency upon the U.S.S.R. for oil and heavy industrial products was pushing them into the Soviet camp. A half-joking, half-serious saying going the rounds in Havana was: "Our hearts may be in Peking, but our stomachs are in Moscow."

It was a common practice for Cuban officials and political activists to display portraits of Fidel, Che, and other leaders on the walls of their homes and offices. To show their sympathy with both China and Russia, they had also put up pictures of Khrushchev and Mao. But when Williams returned from China, he saw that many of them had taken down their picture of Mao and removed the posters, books, and other articles of Chinese origin they had once proudly displayed on their desks. Instead of going along with what was obviously the "smart" thing to do, he unpacked a portrait of Mao which the Chinese leader had given him and hung it on the wall of his living room.

Shortly after returning from China to Cuba, Williams was listening to a live broadcast of President Kennedy's November, 1963, visit to Dallas, when the commentator announced that he had been shot. His first guess was that the extreme Right had done it. He didn't believe that the USCP had either the motive or the temerity to make such a move. He also rejected the possibility that the Fidelistas had killed JFK. They didn't like Lyndon Johnson at all, and it wasn't to their advantage to have him president. For the same reason, Williams discounted the chance of it being a Black Nationalist action. Not only was it improbable that Blacks could set up such a thing in Dallas, if there was anybody they didn't want in the White House it was a Texan. Despite the subsequent propaganda campaign to blame the crime on Lee Harvey Oswald as a lone aberrant individual, Williams remained convinced that it was done by the arch-reactionary wing of the U.S. power structure. As he saw it, they and they alone stood to gain by Kennedy's death, and Johnson's good fortune.

When the Cubans heard of Kennedy's assassination, many were saddened. Despite his having ordered the invasion at "Playa Giron," a lot of people in Havana had a grudging respect for the way Kennedy had called Khrushchev's bluff during the Missile Crisis. While he represented capitalism and imperialism to them as much as any one individual ever did, they realized that things could be worse. Some Cuban army officers told Williams, "This guy Johnson is one of those murderous Texas bastards. We know how they treat Mexicans where he comes from. He's not as intelligent as Kennedy was, and may try to do something violent against us."

Williams agreed with Malcolm X when he said Kennedy's assassination showed, "The chickens are coming home to roost." He saw Kennedy's authorization of the CIA-backed exile terror raids against Cuba, his development of above-the-law killer units like the Green Berets, and his failure to stop the KKK from murdering Blacks and civil-rights workers, as having helped to create the very atmosphere of hatred and violence which led to his own death. His assassination seemed to reaffirm the maxim that, when those responsible for enforcing the law fail to protect any one man, all men—no matter what color their skin or how high their station— are in danger.

As 1963 ended, Williams once again began having problems

with the "Bourgeois Communists." Their attacks had subsided after the Missile Crisis, but now they were regaining their old influence and renewed their campaign against him.

For example, the four people charged with helping Williams kidnap Mr. and Mrs. Stegall in Monroe were found guilty on February 28, 1964. Mae Mallory was sentenced to sixteen to twenty years in prison; Richard Crowder, eight to ten years; Harold Reape, five to seven; and John Lowery (the only White among the accused), three to five years. Outraged, Williams drew up a protest petition to present to the United Nations Commission on Human Rights in Paris. When he asked the Cubans to help him get signatures by circulating it through their trade unions, they said, "There are Cuban and American comrades who have offered to help with your petition, and we think you should let them do so."

"If you insist on my working with them, I will," Williams answered. "But I know the USCP isn't really interested in fighting racism in the United States."

Despite his objections, Harris Spencer and several others became part of the committee formed for the petition, and it wasn't long before half a million signatures had been collected. An Afro-Cuban woman trade-union official was to ship the petition to the United Nations in Paris after she returned from a short trip to Prague. As soon as she came back to Havana, Williams asked her, "When do you plan to mail it?"

"Oh," she answered, "didn't you know? It was sent by the other people on the committee some time ago. In fact I have already gotten a letter in response to it which seems a little strange."

The letter read something like this: "We have received your petition and are pleased to know that you are interested in avoiding miscarriages of justice in the United States. We, on the other hand, are interested in reestablishing justice in Cuba. We would, therefore, like to work with you in a campaign to secure the release of all political prisoners in Cuba and would appreciate your sending us a list of their names."

For a moment Williams couldn't understand why the United Nations Commission on Human Rights would write them anything like that. But then he looked at the letterhead and saw that it hadn't come from Paris at all, but from the "United States Association for the UN" in New York, which was a private group of

U.S. citizens—many of them quite wealthy—having no official connection with the United Nations.

When he asked the trade-union official who had mailed the package where he had gotten the wrong address, Williams was told that Harris Spencer was responsible. Spencer pleaded that he was innocent of any wrongdoing, and claimed that some other USCP member had assured him that the only way to petition the Human Rights Commission was through the United States Association for the UN. Neither Williams nor the Cuban trade unionists found Spencer's explanation acceptable, and several of them became so angry they began to talk about physically beating him.

The attacks against Williams soon became so vicious that complete strangers would stop him on the street and whisper, "The American Communists are working against you. They are telling our Party leaders you are a counterrevolutionary!" Several friends visited him in the hotel and said, "We never knew White American Communists believed in racial discrimination, but some of the things those USCP people are saying about you sound almost like they are prejudiced against Blacks."

Tired of beating around the bush, Williams decided to go directly to Blas Roca, the Cuban Communist leader. Ushered into his office at Party headquarters, he asked Roca point-blank, "I have been told that some of the American comrades say I'm a counterrevolutionary. Since you're an old Marxist-Leninist, and are considered one of the Party's top theoreticians, I would like to know just what your concept of a counterrevolutionary is."

Roca, a middle-aged mulatto, answered, "A man can sometimes be a counterrevolutionary without even knowing it."

"Oh," Williams said. "And how can that be?"

"I will give you a common example," Roca replied. "Suppose a man supports the government during the first stages of the Revolution, but then the leadership decides on a radical change in policy which he refuses to agree with. That would make him a counterrevolutionary, wouldn't it?"

"Do you mean to say that he would be a counterrevolutionary even if he didn't conduct any antigovernment activities?" Williams asked.

"Yes," Roca answered. "You can be a counterrevolutionary in your thoughts even if you engage in no physical opposition."

"In other words," Williams persisted, "aren't you saying that whoever fails to agree with the Party is an enemy of the people?"

"No, I am not saying anything like that," Roca replied.

"Well then," Williams continued, "what are you saying? Are we permitted no differences of opinion? Marx was a smart man, but are we expected to take his words as unimpeachable? Did human thought reach its ultimate development back in the nineteenth century, or is it possible for contemporary thinkers to discover new truths? And how can we ever know if there aren't better ways to build Socialism unless everyone has the right to express himself without being labeled a criminal? The government can make mistakes, can't it? What are you trying to do in Cuba, build a nation of thinkers, or bludgeon everyone into being flag-waving zombies?"

Following this barrage of questions, Blas Roca asked, "But Williams, why are you so critical? We have given you a house. We have given you a car. We let you broadcast on our radio and publish your paper here. What more do you want? Do you expect us to bring all twenty million Black Americans to Cuba and give them houses and cars? You know we don't have those kinds of resources."

Convinced Roca was trying to avoid a serious discussion, Williams decided to end the conversation. "Thank you very much for having given me this audience," he said. "I am sorry to have taken up so much of your time."

As he got up to leave, Roca's interpreter asked him, "Don't you have anything else to say?"

"No," he answered. "I have nothing more to say. Comrade Roca's answers were extremely informative."

In April, 1964, Williams received a telephone call from an American who was visiting Cuba. "Hello," he said. "My name is Allen Ginsberg. I have heard a lot about you back in New York, and would like to meet you and see what's on your mind." When he arrived at Williams' house, he said that he had been invited to Cuba by the cultural people in La Casa de las Americas. Williams hadn't read any of Ginsberg's poetry before leaving the United States, but knew that he was getting a lot of attention from the Establishment press.

After they had spoken for a while, Ginsberg said, "From reading *The Crusader* and from what I've heard, I expected you to be a skinny little bloodthirsty fanatic. I see now that my mental image was pretty far off, but I still can't agree with your advocacy of violence."

"If you don't believe in self-defense," Williams asked him, "are you, at least, involved in the desegregation movement?"

"Oh, I'm for freedom," Ginsberg answered. "I've been active in lots of demonstrations and picket lines for the right to smoke pot and be a homosexual."

"But what about civil rights?" Williams asked.

"That's not my bag right now," he answered. "We've got enough people doing that number. I am fighting for less popular causes—the right of everyone to do what they want to with their minds and their bodies. Potheads and homos should be allowed to have their kicks just like everybody else."

"My God," Williams thought to himself. "Are these the people we Blacks are supposed to join with in building a better world?" He had assumed that the preoccupation with drugs and sex of the PL student group was limited to a few aberrant individuals, but now it appeared evident that U.S. society as a whole was degenerating at an accelerating rate. And the Left seemed just as vulnerable to the general corruption as anyone else.

In the May–June, 1964, issue of *The Crusader,* Williams titled the lead article, USA: THE POTENTIAL OF A MINORITY REVOLUTION. The front page contained a cartoon showing a giant Black warrior labeled "Afro-American Revolt" setting fire to buildings and factories. Under the illustration was a caption reading, THE RACIST USA—THE TORCH OF RETRIBUTION! Among the points he discussed were the following:

". . . At the outset all revolutions are minority revolutions. In the early stages all revolutions have a very remote chance of succeeding. Revolutionaries display a propensity to accomplish the impossible. Is the Afro-American revolution to be an exception?

". . . Instead of the majority race extending brotherhood and justice   the fascist elements are arming . . . to liquidate us. It is becoming next to impossible for Negroes to conduct a 'peaceful' demonstration in America.

". . . Our people must prepare to wage an urban guerrilla war of self-defense. Self-defense develops to the stage wherein the source of evil and terror must be eliminated.

". . . The weapons of defense employed by Afro-American freedom fighters must consist of a poor man's arsenal. Gasoline fire bombs (Molotov cocktails), lye or acid bombs (made by injecting lye or acid in the metal ends of light bulbs) can be used extensively. During the night hours such weapons, thrown from rooftops, will make the streets impossible for racist cops to patrol. Hand grenades, bazookas, light mortars, rocket launchers, machine guns, and ammunition can be bought clandestinely from servicemen anxious to make a fast dollar. Freedom fighters in military camps can be contacted to give instructions on usage.

". . . Extensive sabotage is possible. Gas tanks on public vehicles can be choked up with sand. Sugar is also highly effective in gasoline lines. Long nails driven through boards and tacks with large heads are effective to slow the movement of traffic on congested roads at night. This can cause havoc on turnpikes. Derailing of trains causes panic. Explosive booby traps on police telephone boxes can be employed. High-powered sniper rifles are readily available. Armor-piercing bullets will penetrate oil storage tanks from a distance.

". . . Afro-Americans must remember that such a campaign of massive self-defense should not be based upon a lust for sadistical gratification. It cannot be a campaign for vengeance, however sweet and deserving vengeance may be. . . . It must not be anti-white, but anti-oppression and injustice. Uncle Toms should be as much a target as racist whites.

". . . If we truly seek freedom and human dignity we must be willing to pay for it in the fashion of the Algerians. Great multitudes of our people must be willing to fight and die in America's true cause and commitment to her Constitution, democratic principles, and the rights of man. . . ."

Williams concluded the issue by saying: "This year, 1964, is going to be a violent one. The storm will reach violent proportions by 1965, and the eye of the hurricane will hover over America by 1966. America is a house on fire—FREEDOM NOW!—or let it burn, let it burn. . . ."

The violent outbreak that wracked Harlem in the summer of 1964, soon after this issue of *The Crusader* was published, convinced Williams that, far from having lost contact with developments in the United States, his analysis of the situation was accurate. The USCP, however, used the occasion to publicly attack his advocacy of armed revolution. *The Worker* decried the arson and looting, and accused the Blacks involved of being thugs, troublemakers, and disturbers of the peace. It seemed to Williams as if they were picturing the police and businessmen as the heroes, and those ghetto dwellers who rebelled against them as the villains. The fact that TASS, the official Soviet news agency, immediately picked up *The Worker*'s criticisms and circulated them around the world indicated to Williams that the American Reds weren't acting on their own when they denounced him, but were obeying orders from Moscow. Like the *Reader's Digest*'s well-known practice of planting their own articles in small-town publications in order to reprint them as representing "public opinion," when TASS quoted *The Worker*, Williams felt it was really quoting itself.

In the summer of 1964, a Progressive-Labor-Party-sponsored student group somewhat similar to that of 1963 arrived in Havana. Once more the Cubans were treated to the sight of middle-class young Americans strutting around shoeless and unwashed, asking where they could get marijuana, and passing out from too much alcohol. The major difference between this group and the earlier one was that now there were a few Black Nationalists along. Led by a young New Yorker named Robert Collier, they, together with a few of the Whites, tried to give the group a militant orientation. The Collier faction had made a large BLACK LIBERATION FRONT banner, and they displayed it at the 26th of July Rally and the other public events they attended while in Cuba.

It wasn't long before trouble broke out between Collier's group and the rest of the Americans. One of the causes of friction was the charge that the PL organizers had restricted the number of Blacks invited to 10 percent of the group. They were supposed to have claimed this was necessary to keep the tour representative of the American population, but the Blacks charged that it was really being done to keep them from having any real voice.

The Cuban government was financing the trip, but Williams concluded that the White American leftists were running it in a rather highhanded manner. Their stated objective, to break down the U.S. State Department's ban on travel to Cuba, while worthy, wasn't the reason most of the Black militants had come along. Collier and his friends told Williams they were there to see just how ready Cuba and the other Socialist nations were to support the Black Liberation Movement in the United States, but they complained that the PL leaders were preventing them from contacting any important people in Havana.

As the friction between the two factions increased, a meeting was called to discuss "Solving the Race Problem Once Socialism Has Triumphed in the U.S.A." During it, one of the Black Nationalists asked the group, "In a Socialist United States would you White Marxists be willing to accept the election of a Black president?"

A PL leader answered, "Yes, but only if he is qualified."

"What do you mean, 'if'?" the Black demanded. "Isn't it assumed that whoever would be nominated from the Black community would be qualified? Isn't this the same type of garbage we are getting from the capitalists who say the only reason we don't have decent jobs is because, under their standards, we aren't 'qualified'? Here we haven't even gotten near to Socialism, and you have already figured out how you are going to deny us positions of leadership."

Then another of the young Blacks stood up and declared, "The only way we can cooperate with the Whites in the United States under Socialism is to have half of the Cabinet, Congress, and the Pentagon, Black."

In answer to this, a White girl said, "But, if the Blacks control 50 percent of the government, it wouldn't be fair to the Whites, who constitute almost 90 percent of the population."

"What difference would it make to you if the government were all Black?" he retorted. "You Marxists keep telling us it's wrong to look at things from a racial point of view, but here you are getting worried about having too many people with dark skins holding public office."

For Williams, the Black militants' real purpose in asking such rhetorical questions was to illustrate the PL leaders' hypocrisy in telling them that theirs was a class not a color problem, while they themselves set up restrictive quotas based on color.

Late one night Williams received a long-distance telephone call from the Black militants in the group, which was then off visiting the interior of Cuba. They had become angry with one of the White Americans, a sarcastic young man who they felt was really a racist at heart. "We got so pissed at that cat that we beat him up," they said. "Some of the guys think that we ought to kill him. We're calling you to ask if we should?"

Williams tried to persuade them not to do anything like that, saying, "First of all, it would be a serious insult to your Cuban hosts. Secondly, you would be playing into the hands of those Progressive Labor people who have been saying that Black Nationalists are just as bad as the KKK, and hate and want to murder all Whites." His arguments seemed to work—at least the White wasn't killed.

But the moment word of the beating reached the USCP clique in Havana, Williams heard that Mary Hart, an old U.S. Party member from Chicago, was telling everyone that he had personally instigated the trouble.

At a meeting the Americans had with Che Guevara, Robert Collier and the other Black militants asked him, "Why is it that, although one-third of Cuba's people are of direct African descent and another third have some African ancestry, you don't teach a single course in African history? Cuba is one of the few places in the world outside of Africa where our old religions and other cultural traditions have been preserved, but all that your schools offer are classes in European history."

When Che reportedly answered, "The Revolution is international; therefore we haven't felt the need to give African history any special consideration," some of the Blacks replied hotly, "Then the Revolution is practicing White chauvinism. We didn't think we would hear that kind of talk here of all places, and certainly not from you."

The exchange evidently bothered Che quite a bit because the Blacks told Williams that later in the day he sent word to them, saying, "I've been reconsidering your arguments. If you're willing, I'd like to meet alone with you."

When they heard about this, the PL organizers became upset. Until that moment they had been able to control all contacts between the students and the Cuban leadership. But they were powerless to do anything about the meeting.

The Blacks later said that Che told them, "The position I took yesterday was in error. I am contacting the University of Havana to ask that they add courses in African history to their curriculum. I see now that the problem of racism facing Blacks in the

United States is different from the questions facing the Whites. It's a mistake to lump everything together under the heading of the class conflict." He also said that there would be more direct contact established between the Cuban Revolution and Black Americans.

"If you really feel that way," one of the students asked him, "then what is your position concerning Robert Williams? Why is he having so much trouble down here?" Che responded that he didn't know many details, and promised to investigate.

When Williams heard about this, he assumed that, like the other Cuban leaders, Che was just pretending to want to help him. It was to be almost a year before he discovered his interest was sincere.

Shortly before they were due to return to the States, some of the Black militants told Williams they had become interested in going to school in the Soviet Union. When they asked if he would go with them to the Russian embassy in Havana to ask about getting scholarships, he declined, saying, "Your chances will be better without me."

When they returned after seeing the Russians, they were furious. "Williams, why didn't you tell us about those guys?" they demanded.

"If I had, you might have thought I was trying to prejudice you," he answered. "This way you found out for yourselves."

They told him the Soviet cultural attaché had answered their request for scholarships by saying that all such things had to be arranged under the official U.S.-U.S.S.R. exchange program. He had even suggested that they go back home and submit a request through the State Department. "Those Russians are really out of this world," they said. "That cat was talking to us like we were rich White guys. Man, if we had that kind of connection with the State Department, we wouldn't have to go to Moscow for anything."

Williams felt they were learning, as he had already learned, that the Russian leaders were far more interested in maintaining good relations with Washington than they were in helping the poor and the oppressed.

He didn't question the Russians' motivation, knowing that their fear of war was more than justified. They had suffered more than twenty million dead in World War II. Next to maintaining

an iron-fisted control over the central European states which functioned as buffers between them and Germany, their traditional
enemy, their chief interest was to avoid overirritating the United
States. They saw wars of national liberation as only strengthening
the hand of the "hawks" in the U.S. power structure who were
calling for an atomic war.

But, in the name of preserving peace, Williams felt the Russians were inadvertently helping to prolong the misery and exploitation of hundreds of millions of oppressed people around the
world. "The peace of the tyrant is not peace to the enslaved, who
dreams only of liberation," he was fond of saying. Having already
liberated themselves, he felt that the Russians were no longer
really interested in revolution. Russia's very success in rebuilding
her industry after the terrible damage inflicted by the Nazis, while
making any future attack upon her improbable, had changed her
leaders' point of view from that of dynamic proponents of change
to self-satisfied protectors of things-as-they-are. Khrushchev
wasn't one of those who made the Revolution; his was the next
generation, that of the functionaries who took it over. When such
men speak of revolution they almost always use the past tense,
and the only social changes they seem interested in are those
planned and administered by bureaucrats like themselves, Williams reflected.

The desire to avoid armed conflict with the United States
which Williams believed to be preoccupying the U.S.S.R. seemed
to be affecting the Cubans as well. The MINREX invited a sizable
group of American journalists to attend the 26th of July Celebration in 1964. Instead of primarily leftist newsmen, as had been the
practice since 1961, the Cubans were hosting twenty-six of the
U.S.'s leading columnists and international affairs experts, many
of whom, like Bob Considine of the Hearst papers and Al Burt of
the *Miami Herald*, were known as anti-Communists. Others in the
group included Max Lerner of the *New York Post*, Phillip Geyelin
of the *Wall Street Journal*, Art Hoppe of the *San Francisco Chronicle*, Dan Kurzman of the *Washington Post*, and Lyle Stuart of *The
Independent*. Williams wasn't concerned with their politics. He
considered it highly intelligent of the MINREX to realize that the
best way to counteract the absurd rumors and horror tales about
Cuba being circulated in the States was to let widely read and re-
spected American columnists come over and see things for them-

selves. What bothered him was that there wasn't a single Black writer among them.

A few Black newsmen had been invited, but all were from very conservative publications, and they had declined to come. Williams surmised that they feared their White advertisers wouldn't like it. Informing the Black public about a country which has openly defied the United States doesn't help sell cars, whiskey, skin lightener, or hair straightener.

Those militant Black journalists, like William Worthy and Hubert Muhammed, who did want to come to Cuba, were neither invited nor allowed to enter, even though they offered to pay their own way. Williams knew this because several of them had telephoned and cabled to ask his help in having the MINREX issue them visas. Some had even gone all the way to Prague to try to get admitted to Cuba, only to be turned down.

When Williams asked the Cubans about this, they told him: "We can't let Americans we don't know enter our country just because they're Black. We have to be careful about those fellows. After all, everyone knows that the CIA's using Blacks to try to infiltrate the Socialist countries."

"And what about the hundreds of American Whites to whom you give visas?" Williams asked. "Do you think the CIA has only Black agents?"

He subsequently discovered that Comandante Pinero, his liaison with Fidel, was in charge of the MINREX Visa Department, and was rejecting the visa applications of all Americans who weren't approved by the USCP. The only exceptions took place when (as in the case of the U.S. journalists) Raúl Roa, the Foreign Minister, or some other leader, personally intervened.

Following the Missile Crisis, several Black reporters had been given visas in 1963, but with the resurgence of the Moscow-oriented faction in 1964 non-USCP-aligned Blacks appeared to be once again unwelcome.

The American journalists had been in Cuba less than two weeks, but their dispatches were already appearing in the U.S. press. With a few exceptions, they were reporting that, despite many serious problems, the Cuban people were still supporting the Revolution. For a short while it appeared as though a new, less hostile, period in Cuban-U.S. relations might be in the offing. But U.S. foreign policy was soon to take a new turn.

The first Williams heard of the August, 1964, U.S. raids against Hanoi and Haiphong was late at night when the radio from Miami carried President Lyndon B. Johnson's speech in which he said he had ordered the bombing because the North Vietnamese had attacked American warships in the Gulf of Tonkin. His action didn't surprise Williams. Having lived in the South, and having been threatened all his life with brutality and lynching by the racists, he saw it as typical for the U.S. government to drop bombs on colored people who refused to surrender to its threats. It also seemed to be a standard part of the "American Way of Life" for LBJ to justify bombing a tiny nation lacking the capability to strike back at U.S. cities by pretending that the victim was the aggressor.

The next morning, when they heard about the air raids, the Cuban people were furious. The visiting U.S. reporters were advised by the MINREX to stay inside their hotel until the situation clarified. Mass rallies were held in Havana and other cities to demonstrate Cuba's sympathy with the people of Vietnam. The honeymoon was over. Most of the American journalists cut short their visit and returned to the States within the next few days.

What especially disturbed the Cubans was that, for the first time in history, the U.S.S.R. had permitted the United States to bomb a Socialist state. "What would the Russians have done if those planes had hit Warsaw or Prague instead of Hanoi?" people asked. "Is an attack on a brown-skinned Socialist nation in Asia any less an aggression than an attack on a light-skinned one in Europe?" What concerned them most of all was the thought that, if able to get away with bombing Hanoi, LBJ might be tempted to blast Havana next. Williams expected that the Russians would at least make a show of force by shipping five or six hundred MIG interceptors and pilots to Hanoi, and was chagrined when they refused to make the sort of commitment which would deter the Americans from repeating their attack.

With things going as they were in Cuba, he was delighted when the Chinese once again invited him to attend their National Day Celebration. This time not only were he and his wife to be their guests, John and Bobby, their two boys, were to accompany them on the trip.

As in 1963, they flew from Havana to Moscow, and from there to Peking. The Chinese provided a camera crew to film Wil-

liams as he traveled throughout their country; and after he left
they produced a thirty-minute documentary motion picture about
his visit.

During two months spent touring the country he observed
such great changes that it was hard to believe only a year had
passed. Not one of the thousands of trucks and busses he saw had
the natural-gas tanks on their roofs which had been so common
back in 1963. His guide had told him the year before about rich
new oil deposits having been discovered in the western regions,
but he had assumed it would take four or five years to develop
them. Only twelve months later, the flow of Chinese-produced oil
from the interior seemed already to have made up for the cutoff of
Soviet petroleum imports. Chinese-designed and manufactured
trucks and autos were in extensive use, the factories under construction a year earlier were in operation, and new projects were
being built. The pace of growth was, if anything, even greater than
before.

At the National Day Celebration in Peking, however, there
appeared to be far fewer foreign guests than in 1963. The same
friendly and enthusiastic atmosphere prevailed, but the increasingly violent Sino-Soviet dispute was obviously manifesting itself.
In some cases, Williams thought, the dignitaries of countries dependent on the U.S.S.R. may have declined to attend lest they
offend the Russians; while, in other instances, the Chinese may
not have extended invitations to those they felt to be too closely
allied to the Soviet side.

Williams' two boys, who by now were twelve and fourteen,
were fascinated by China. They liked it so much that they asked if
they could get scholarships to go to school there. When the Chinese said it would be fine, Williams and his wife agreed to let John
and Bobby remain in Peking after they returned to Havana. They
wanted them to get as much education as they desired and, from
what they had seen of the Chinese educational system, the schools
there seemed to be as good as those anywhere in the world. Both
boys were already fluent in Spanish, and this would give them a
chance to learn Chinese as well. And, anticipating that he might
have more problems in Cuba, Williams thought it would be easier
to leave for somewhere else if there were only himself and his wife
to worry about.

Among the events which took place while he was in China

was the November, 1964, victory of Lyndon Johnson over Barry Goldwater. It was the first U.S. presidential election Williams had been unable to vote in since becoming twenty-one, but he didn't feel left out. He had come to believe that the entire thing was a farce. The public-relations image of Johnson as a liberal trying to save the world from Goldwater, a warmongering super-rightist, impressed him as being so much hogwash. The underlying contradictions of American society, especially the racist nature of its power structure, would continue to worsen no matter which party controlled the Administration, he felt.

Another development occurring while Williams was in Peking was Khrushchev's exit from power. Many of the foreign diplomats, especially the western Europeans, seemed far more elated about it than did the Chinese. One official told him, "Khrushchev's being fired means very little, because those taking his place are of the same stripe as he was. He has been relieved only because too many of his adventuristic schemes failed. We don't expect his replacement to result in any changes, except for the worse."

The most significant event to take place that winter was the detonation of China's first atomic bomb. When the news was announced in Peking, crowds ran through the streets singing, chanting, and beating drums. It was like a holiday celebration. "Russia's reneging on her agreement to provide us with atomic weapons was a blessing in disguise," a Chinese physicist told Williams. "It encouraged us to approach the problem in our own way. Now the world knows we will be able to defend ourselves without having to ask anyone else's permission." For the first time in history, a colored nation had the A-bomb.

As they prepared to return to Havana, Williams and his wife were approached by representatives of the North Vietnamese government. "The war is going very badly for the Yankees' puppets in the South," they said. "We believe that to save face the United States is contemplating a new attack against our country. We are, therefore, planning a conference in our capital city of men and women from all over the world who wish to show their solidarity with the people of Vietnam. It would give us great pleasure if you and your wife would attend."

A few days later, Williams and his wife were aboard a Chinese airliner flying toward Hanoi.

NEITHER A CAPITALIST NOR A SOCIALIST UNCLE TOM

Among those aboard the Hanoi-bound plane was Anna Louise Strong, who had been invited to attend the peace conference along with several other Americans living in China. One of them, Sidney Rittenberg, a writer for Radio Peking, told Williams he had been a trade unionist in the United States and had started working with the Chinese Communists back in 1947 when Mao was still in Yenan. Another, Frank Coe, said he was an economist.

A few of the passengers had expressed apprehension that the U.S. Air Force might try to shoot down the plane because it was carrying Americans who were friendly to North Vietnam. There was an audible sigh of relief when, after several hours in flight, they began circling the Hanoi airport.

From the air the signs of war were evident. Antiaircraft batteries surrounded the runways, and sandbagged revetments sheltered the planes on the ground. Landing without incident, they were given a friendly reception, then driven to quarters in the center of the city.

There were networks of trenches and air raid shelters throughout Hanoi. New U.S. attacks had been expected ever since the bombings following the Tonkin Gulf incident of the past August. Preparations for a possible land invasion were also under way. Late at night the roar of trucks and tanks and the muffled padding of sneaker-clad soldiers running could be heard in the streets.

In the rural areas which Williams was to visit during the next three weeks the Vietnamese peasants seemed considerably less well off than did their Chinese counterparts. He saw none of the tractors and harvesters which were already in wide use in China.

Almost everything was being done manually, the spade and the hoe constituting the basic farm implements. It sickened him to think that a nation as powerful as the United States was threatening such poor people—many of whom, lacking even a mule, had to pull their wooden plows by hand.

Back home, he knew, the Johnson Administration's propagandists were claiming that the challenge posed by the North Vietnamese couldn't be countered without full-scale air raids. The thousands of American troops, millions of tons of bombs, and billions of dollars in weapons already expended in South Vietnam weren't enough. Unless Hanoi surrendered to Washington's demands and stopped supporting the National Liberation Front, North Vietnam's cities, factories, farms, and roads were to be blasted into extinction.

Along with the other delegates to the peace conference, Williams and his wife attended a banquet at the Presidential Palace in Hanoi, where they were seated next to Premier Ho Chi Minh. As it was close to Ho's birthday and that of Anna Louise Strong as well, a large cake had been prepared for both of them. When the waiter brought it to their table, Ho asked him to sit down and join them. He then stood up and began cutting the cake himself, giving the waiter the first piece before serving the guests.

Sitting at Ho's side was an eleven-year-old Vietnamese farm boy who had been severely injured when the U.S. Air Force bombed his school. The sight of the child's eyes peering out from a livid mass of scar tissue seared itself deeply into Williams' memory.

Ho, who spoke English quite well, told his dinner guests that he had invited the disfigured boy to come live with him at the Presidential Palace. By treating the boy as if he were his own son, he said that he was trying to prepare his people to withstand the worst the United States had to offer. To the Vietnamese, such horribly maimed victims of American air power, rather than embarrassing objects to be hidden from sight, were being publicly honored as living examples of the sacrifices they would have to be willing to make if they wished to continue opposing the United States.

When Williams asked Ho about his life, the North Vietnamese premier said that he had done a lot of wandering about when he was young, working at such jobs as assisting Escoffier, the world-famous French chef, and swabbing decks on a merchant ship. "Everywhere I traveled in my youth," he said, "I saw that the same man was responsible for evil. He was behind the misery in Asia, in Africa, in Latin America, and in the United States. He was the same all over the world; and today he is trying to crush our people in South Vietnam."

Asked if he was a Communist back in 1919 when he went to the Versailles Conference to plead for independence for his country, Ho answered, "I hadn't yet become one then. My only idea was to help liberate my people from the French colonialists. I lived in the United States for some time back in the early 1920's, hoping your country would help us in our struggle. Even after I became a Communist, I still thought the United States was on the side of the oppressed peoples of the world. When we were fighting together against the Japanese, the Americans kept saying they would support us, but once the war ended they let us be enslaved again. And now they have become even worse oppressors than the French were."

One of the most interesting things Ho told Williams was that he had attended some of Marcus Garvey's rallies in Harlem back in the twenties. Garvey, one of the first Black Nationalists, had led a "Back to Africa" movement which attracted quite a few followers and gave many Blacks an awareness of themselves as a people.

"Listening to Marcus Garvey speak," Ho said, "made me realize the only way we Vietnamese would be free was by organizing ourselves. He inspired me to leave the comforts of life in the United States and return home to fight. During the more than a quarter century which it took us to throw out the French, I often thought of his words."

When the peace conference convened, Williams was asked to make a speech. He assumed that the delegates from the U.S.S.R. and the other nations which he felt were under "Bourgeois Communist" influence expected him to give a standard polemic about how the "valiant American working class" supported the peace movement. But what he did was deliver what he believed to be one of the first Black Nationalist speeches ever heard by that type of international audience.

In essence, Williams declared that the United States was a racist nation which was practicing genocide against the Black and

Brown peoples of the world. "The American Indians were the Yankee's first victims," he said. "They were forced into 'strategic hamlets' a century ago, just as the people of South Vietnam are now being herded into barbed-wire enclosures." He ended his address by predicting that each year to come would witness not only a greater fight against U.S. imperialism throughout the world, but would see more and more resistance to oppression within the United States.

At the conclusion of his speech, which got only a lukewarm response from several of the delegations on the floor, the Vietnamese workers, peasants, and students crowding the galleries applauded loudly. "Those are the masses," Williams' interpreter said. "They are cheering you because they know very well about racism. Under the French we had the same White chauvinism here that Blacks are suffering from in America. Some of our more bourgeois elements don't understand this as well as do our working people."

A few days later Williams' hosts asked if he would like to interview a U.S. Navy pilot shot down during the August bombing raids on Hanoi and Haiphong. The American was brought to his place that evening. His North Vietnamese guards thought he might be dangerous, and offered to watch him while they spoke, but Williams asked them to wait outside.

The prisoner's name was Everett Alvarez. He was of Mexican-American descent from California and the first U.S. pilot to be shot down over North Vietnam.

"I was near the coast when my plane got hit," he told Williams. "There was a big bump. It started shaking and went into a spin. When I pressed the ejection button something must have knocked me out because the next thing I knew I was in the water with my parachute all around me. Then I looked up and saw three small boats full of Vietnamese. The men in them had rifles and machine guns, and I was sure they were going to open fire. Instead of shooting, one of them started making some kind of gestures which I didn't understand. Then the guy next to him raised his machine gun. At the last moment I realized they wanted me to surrender my sidearm. Not until I took off my automatic and handed it up to them did they pull me out of the water."

Alvarez said he had been only slightly wounded and had since recovered from his injuries. After they had spoken for a while he suddenly seemed to realize that, although he and Williams were both Americans, their situations were quite different.

"Hey," he asked, "how did you get here, anyway?" When Williams answered that he'd flown to Hanoi from Havana via Moscow and Peking, Alvarez looked at him as if he were joking. "And how come they have given you such a fancy place to stay?" was his next question.

"They are treating me nicely," Williams answered, "because I came here as a friend, not to kill women and children like you did."

"We didn't mean to kill any civilians," Alvarez protested. "Our orders were to bomb only military targets. If some innocent people got hit accidentally, well, war is war."

"War?" Williams asked him. "What kind of war is it when the United States bombs a country so tiny most Americans never even heard of it? Isn't war something Congress is supposed to declare? Haven't Americans always claimed that the Japanese attack on Pearl Harbor was criminal because it was made without a declaration of war? The United States hasn't been attacked by North Vietnam. Sending you over here was in violation of both the U.S. Constitution and all international law."

"Look," Alvarez said, "those things have nothing to do with me. These people are fighting our allies down South. If the president ordered the U.S. Navy to blast them, who was I to disagree? It was my duty."

"If a North Vietnamese pilot bombed Los Angeles, slaughtering women and children, and was then shot down, what do you think the people there would do to him?" Williams asked.

"I guess they would lynch him," Alvarez replied.

"You bet they would lynch him. And they would be right, because he would be a murderer, not a prisoner of war. You can consider yourself goddamn lucky the Vietnamese haven't hung you. They have every reason in the world to do so. What I can't understand is why you, a Mexican-American, would volunteer to drop bombs on Brown-skinned Asians. Don't you realize you're working for the same White racists who are pushing around your own people in Texas, Arizona, and New Mexico?"

"Oh, I don't think we Mexican-Americans have it so bad in the States," Alvarez replied.

"Stop putting yourself on," Williams told him. "We both

know very well that the Chicanos have been getting screwed for more than a hundred years. Most of your people are fruit-pickers and laborers, and are treated as badly as we Blacks. If you want to defend democracy, why don't you fight for a better life back in the United States?" His words seemed to penetrate, because Alvarez said that once he got back to California he planned to resign from the Navy and become involved in the civil-rights movement. Williams had the impression he really meant it.

Alvarez kept hinting he thought Williams might have been sent to see him by the U.S. government. He was absolutely certain he would be freed in the near future, but hundreds of other shot-down American aviators were subsequently to join him in captivity.

The question that kept coming up in Williams' discussions with the North Vietnamese was, "Why are there so many Black soldiers in the U.S. forces which are attacking our people?" His response was that he considered most Blacks in the United States to be semislaves who'd been drafted into the military by force. "Those of us who do volunteer," he added, "usually do so only because our lives as civilians are so miserable that being a soldier is the only way we can think of to raise our standard of living."

At the request of representatives of Radio Hanoi, Williams taped an interview on this subject. In it, he asked: "Isn't it shameful for Black Americans to be in Vietnam killing other colored men on behalf of Yankee imperialism? And wouldn't Black GI's be serving themselves far better by being back home defending their wives, sisters, and mothers from being raped and brutalized by the racists?"

Ho Chi Minh provided his private railroad car for the trip from Hanoi to the Chinese border. Having come from a family of railroad men, Williams enjoyed traveling by train. Unlike the United States, which switched almost entirely to diesels years ago, the Chinese were still using a lot of steam locomotives. There were extensive sections of double track. Passing through the industrial sections of cities, many so new he hadn't yet heard of them, Williams saw mile after mile of factories lining the right of way.

The entire route from Hanoi to Peking was crowded with trains heading south. Freight cars loaded with trucks, tanks, artillery, steel, oil, and every sort of Chinese product passed night and day. While Lyndon Baines Johnson was pouring American troops into South Vietnam, Mao Tse-tung was rushing supplies to North Vietnam to help repulse the impending onslaught.

After almost a week the Williamses arrived in Peking. Williams was anxious to get back to Havana because he'd heard that his adversaries in the USCP there were making a new effort to undermine his position. During his absence someone had surreptitiously switched the Radio Free Dixie broadcasts from 50,000-watt Radio Progreso to a tiny 1000-watt transmitter. This only became known to Williams as a result of receiving letters from U.S. listeners, who said that his broadcasts had become very faint; and he later discovered that they were being beamed from outside of the Cuban capital.

Bidding farewell to John and Bobby, who had already learned several words of Chinese, Williams and his wife left Peking aboard a TU-104 jet. Representatives from both the Chinese and Cuban embassies were waiting when they landed in Moscow. They suggested that, before leaving the airport, they reconfirm their flight to Havana. But the Russian ticket agent said she could find no record of their having reservations. "All flights from Moscow direct to Havana are booked solid," she said. "The best thing for you would be to fly from here to Prague, and then take the flight from there to Cuba."

"That's impossible," the Cuban official accompanying Williams told her. "The Prague to Havana flight has to refuel in Gander, Newfoundland. Mr. Williams is wanted by the FBI, and can't risk setting foot in Canada, even in transit. If he takes that flight the Canadian police might turn him over to the Americans."

Then the representative from the Chinese embassy asked the Aeroflot ticket agent, "Wouldn't it be possible for Mr. Williams to wait a few days? How far in advance are the flights to Havana sold out?"

"It isn't certain," she answered, "maybe a month, maybe two. I'm afraid there are just no seats available on Moscow-Havana flights in the foreseeable future."

At the Cuban's insistence, the ticket agent telephoned the office of Aeroflot's director, but the answer was the same: "Mr. Williams will have to go via Prague."

Finally, the Cuban said, "Since you don't have any empty seats, we'll make some available ourselves. Several of our embassy personnel hold confirmed reservations on tomorrow's plane, and we're going to pull two of them off and give their tickets to Mr. and Mrs. Williams." The Russians had no choice but to let them on the flight.

When they boarded the plane the next day, there were at least a dozen empty seats. And Williams was later told by some Canadians who took the Prague-Havana flight that, when they stopped to refuel at Gander, the Royal Canadian Mounted Police had come aboard and searched the plane as if they expected to find someone. Although it was impossible to know for certain, the incident appeared to Williams to have been an attempt by the Soviet authorities to deliver him to the FBI.

By January, 1965, the Moscow-oriented elements in Cuba had gained the ascendancy. The new Party line was to denounce everything that smelled even faintly Chinese. Having just returned from his second trip to Peking, Williams found himself a prime target for harassment and accusations. The Cuban post office began returning many of the letters sent to him from friends in the United States with "No Longer in Cuba" stamped on them. Telephone callers from the States trying to reach him found themselves connected with a stranger who asked, "What do you want to tell Williams? I am taking all of his messages." And a rumor began circulating that Fidel had said, "Williams is getting too big for his pants. We are going to have to cut him down to size."

Williams wasn't surprised when he chanced to meet some Latin American friends and one exclaimed, "What are you doing here? Four months ago some Mexican journalists wanted to interview you, but when we telephoned, nobody answered. The MINREX told us you were out of the country, but the Prensa Latina news agency said you were on the Isle of Pines. What's going on?" Since in those days saying someone was "on the Isle of Pines" meant that he or she was in the prison located there, they were surprised to find him freely walking the streets. As he hadn't been out of the country at the time, Williams presumed that the story was part of a campaign by certain factions in the Cuban government to cut him off from his foreign contacts.

It was around this time that the chairman of the Communist Party in Havana called him into his office and declared, "Williams, we want you to know that the Revolution doesn't support Black Nationalism. We believe in integration, in White and Black workers struggling together to change capitalism into Socialism.

Only in this way can there be an end to discrimination. Black Nationalism is just another form of racism. Cuba has solved her race problem, but if we went along with your ideas about Black self-determination in the United States, it wouldn't be long before somebody would start demanding that our Oriente Province should become a separate Black state as well, and we are not going to let that happen."

Williams felt that he'd discovered one of the keys to his problem: The Party was afraid of Black Nationalist concepts spreading to the more than one-third of the Cuban population of African ancestry. This wasn't because they really suspected the Afro-Cubans of harboring separatist sentiments, the island being far too small for anyone to seriously consider dividing it. Instead, Williams believed that the Havana Communist Party, which was predominantly White, knew that, compared to the Black and mixed elements in the central and eastern areas, it enjoyed a disproportionately large voice in the government, and feared that an awakening of Black self-consciousness might lead to demands for a more equitable distribution of power.

The first few months of 1965 witnessed several events of great significance: Around-the-clock bombing raids were launched against North Vietnam. The U.S. Marines swarmed ashore to suppress an uprising in the Dominican Republic. And Malcolm X was assassinated in an auditorium in Harlem.

LBJ's actions against North Vietnam and the Dominican Republic infuriated the Cuban masses. Thousands volunteered to go to Hanoi and Santo Domingo to fight against the U.S. forces. The North Vietnamese, however, said that they had no shortage of manpower, so Cuba's assistance was limited to sending them plasma, clothing, sugar, and other commodities. In the case of Santo Domingo, despite the popular willingness to help, the Cuban government wasn't about to engage the United States on a foreign battlefield, and the revolution there was quickly suppressed.

The murder of Malcolm X, while not having a great impact on the Cubans (most of whom knew very little about him), saddened Williams deeply. He had lost a friend and one of his first supporters. He felt that Malcolm X was struck down just as he was making a significant transition. His visit to Africa and the Middle East had opened a new vista in his thinking—the possibil-

ity of a union between Black Americans and their African brothers. He had realized that the Black Liberation Movement in the
United States was an integral part of the world revolutionary
movement against racism and capitalism. This realization, and his
growing influence, had made Malcolm a threat to the U.S. power
structure. Williams had no idea who specifically ordered him
killed, but the circumstances surrounding his death—the lack of
police protection plus the ambiguities involved in the apprehension and trial of his alleged assassins—appeared to him to be
strangely similar to those involved in the earlier murder of President Kennedy.

On a Friday morning in April, 1965, an agent of the secret
police came to Williams' house and said, "Comandante Guevara
has asked us to get in touch with you. If you are free late tomorrow afternoon, he would like you to drop by his office for a talk."

Che's office was located in one of the high-rise office buildings facing the Plaza of the Revolution in southwest Havana. It
was approaching sunset when the G-2 agent took Williams there.
The square was almost empty. A few Cuban Army officers were in
the lobby of the building, but otherwise it appeared deserted.
They took the elevator up and entered a reception room to find
Che's personal guards, a couple of Afro-Cubans, sitting there.
When the G-2 agent told one of the guards who Williams was, he
went into the inner office to announce him. Then he came out and
said that he should enter.

The first thing Che did after Williams accepted his offer to be
seated was to start pacing up and down as though something were
bothering him. He had taken off his cartridge belt and wrapped it
around his holstered .45-caliber automatic and placed it on the
desk. As usual, Williams was carrying his little Czech .25-caliber
pistol in his hip pocket, but, since he was considered a friend, nobody had tried to search or disarm him.

Pointing to a copy of *Hoy,* the official Cuban Communist
Party newspaper, Che asked, "Williams, have you seen today's
paper?" When he answered that he hadn't Che said, "There is an
editorial in it supporting the Reverend Martin Luther King. The
Party is praising his policy of nonviolence. They say it is the only
correct way for you Blacks to behave, but I disagree, and so do a
lot of other people in the Revolution." Throwing the paper down
on his desk with an expression of disgust, he said, "No, I don't

agree with this at all. The only way to achieve freedom is to answer the violence of oppression with the violence of liberation."

Suddenly changing the subject, he said, "I have been wanting
to talk with you for a long time. Do you know that when I was in
New York visiting the United Nations headquarters, I met some
people from Harlem, and the first thing they asked me was why
the Revolution wasn't giving you more support? Also, when I was
in Africa, several people there asked me the same thing. It embarrassed me because I had to tell all of them I really didn't know
what your problems were. Why haven't you ever come to see me
about these things?"

"I have never brought my troubles to you," Williams answered, "because Fidel said Comandante Pinero was responsible
for helping me."

Che looked at him for a long moment, then asked very forcefully, "Are you absolutely certain you have never tried to contact
me?" As he returned to this question several times during the next
hour or two of their conversation, Williams sensed that Che felt
someone was trying to isolate him by interfering with his lines of
communication. The sunset landscape was visible through the
office window. It looked out on the empty Plaza of the Revolution,
divided by the long shadow of the José Martí Monument. The
darkening walls of the room and the stillness of the deserted government building all heightened Williams' suspicion that Che was
becoming a man alone.

In response to his question, "What can Cuba do to help the
Black Liberation struggle in the United States?" Williams told
Che of his various plans. Che was enthusiastic and promised to get
Williams the backing required. "I have to leave Havana for a
meeting in the interior with the other leaders," he said, "but I will
be back in one month's time. When I return I will personally telephone you to arrange a second meeting in order to continue our
discussion. Meanwhile, I am assigning Captain Aragones, my personal aide, to help you. He will get in touch in two or three days at
the most. Don't worry, your troubles here will soon be over."

Night had fallen by the time Williams left Che's office and
was driven back to his house by the G-2 agent. He waited several
days to hear from Captain Aragones. Finally, after more than a
week, he telephoned G-2 headquarters and asked to speak to him,

but was told that the captain had unexpectedly been required to leave town.

Soon afterward, various things began happening to everyone who had been part of Che's personal entourage. Officers known to be loyal to him were demoted or shipped off to the provinces. His name ceased to be mentioned in the press. And a Chilean artist who had been painting a mural in his office building was told that the half-finished work was being abandoned.

First one month, then two, went by, but Che didn't return. During the second month after his disappearance, agents of the G-2, men who said the "red beard," meaning Comandante Pinero, had sent them, began to ask Williams questions. "Fidel knows Che promised to help you," they said. "We have been ordered to find out exactly what he was going to do and see that it gets done. So why don't you tell us what you were planning?" Sensing that they were trying to find out how much Che had told him about the differences he was having with the others in the leadership and fearing that he had met with some foul play, Williams pretended ignorance. "Oh, that Che is just a liar like everybody else here," he answered. "I didn't believe anything he said and don't even remember what he was talking about. He is no different from the rest of your leaders—all talk and no action."

His response didn't satisfy them, and they continued to try to pry information from him during the remainder of his residence in Cuba.

The following October, when Fidel announced that Che had voluntarily resigned all of his positions in the Revolution and left Cuba to work for Socialism elsewhere, Williams was extremely skeptical. What made him doubt just how willingly Che had departed was the fact that the letter of resignation he was supposed to have written was dated only a day or two after their meeting. He found it hard to believe that Che would have assured him that he would be back in one month unless he really meant it. He was known as a man who planned things well in advance and held to his word once given. If Che actually had written that letter, Williams was certain it must have been under some sort of pressure, and certainly long after the date which appeared on it.

It was more than a year later that Williams chanced to see Captain Aragones. He was getting gas for his car at the Party's

service station when Aragones drove up to the next pump. At first
Williams didn't recognize him. He was no longer in uniform, his
bodyguards were gone, and he was in a small Volkswagen instead
of the large Oldsmobile he had previously driven. His name was
no longer listed on the Central Committee, and it was rumored
that he had been discharged from the military.

When Aragones noticed Williams looking at him, he appeared to become apprehensive. Throwing up his hands in a gesture of futility, he drove away without waiting for the attendant to
give him gas. It seemed evident to Williams that everyone who
had ever worked for Che was out of favor with those who controlled Cuba.

In August, 1965, the Black ghetto of Watts, California, exploded. Williams' prediction of such outbursts, published fourteen
months earlier in *The Crusader,* had become prophetic. Watts not
only traumatized the American business community, it marked
the beginning of a new era in race relations in the United States.
As Williams saw it, the old days of the "cringing nigger" were
over. Black America was striking back.

He didn't view what happened in Watts as an act of revolution, which requires consciousness and direction, but saw it as an
outbreak of rebellious violence. He perceived those who looted
stores and burned buildings as reacting against decades of police
brutality, intolerable housing, bloodsucking finance companies,
and a hate-filled White society which discriminates against all minorities. Had the uprising been planned or directed, the violence
would have been much worse than it was, and the damage inflicted upon commercial property far greater. Watts was rather, he
felt, a spontaneous, chaotic explosion of desperation, a half-blind
striking out at everything and anything which had come to represent the tormentor. Its significance was in showing Black Americans that, unarmed and unorganized though they were, they could
still resist the power structure and inflict tens of millions of dollars
of damage upon it.

While it was true that he had predicted outbreaks of the
Watts type, Williams considered the outcry against him raised by
such men as Senator Thomas Dodd of Connecticut and Fred
Schwartz of the Christian Anti-Communist Crusade, who charged
that he had planned and directed the entire affair, as being ridiculous. He knew that no amount of printed or broadcast words can

motivate unarmed people to go up against police guns unless they are already so frustrated they don't know what else to do. While it was the beating of some Blacks by the Los Angeles police that apparently triggered the Watts outburst, Williams saw police brutality as only one aspect of a savage society. He didn't believe that sadistic cops, reprehensible though they were, would be allowed to exist unless their actions were approved by those who control the system. Their employers were the businessmen, civic groups, fraternal organizations, churches, chambers of commerce, and political parties who run the United States. Therefore, the Blacks who vilified and stoned them were, though perhaps only half-consciously, lashing out at the totality of the Establishment—not just at the police.

Also, Williams felt that Watts was more than an isolated event. With wars of national liberation breaking out all over the world, it appeared inevitable to him that Black Americans would rebel as well. The expectations of humanity were rising, and that included Black humanity in the United States. Not only was Watts symptomatic of the resentment building throughout the ghettos, he thought, but it demonstrated how incompetent the U.S. power structure is in meeting the needs of large segments of the population, and how vicious it becomes when challenged. The dragnet arrests of over four thousand Blacks, the shooting of more than eight hundred, and the killing of almost fifty, without a single incident of a policeman being shot or seriously injured by the rioters, demonstrated the readiness of the power structure to drown in blood any and all uprisings. But the mass arrests and shootings in Watts, rather than intimidating the Blacks of the United States, angered them, and led to the hundreds of similar acts of rebellion which subsequently took place elsewhere in the nation.

One of the things that seemed to outrage American liberals was the looting which characterized outbursts such as Watts. Williams referred to such phenomena as "people-ization"—the violent end product of years of being urged to desire the unattainable. He summed it all up: Although the United States is the wealthiest nation in the history of the world, tens of millions of its citizens lack the bare minimum necessary to stay alive. Malnutrition and death from starvation are so widespread that they are openly acknowledged even by U.S. government commissions. And, for every child that dies because its parents are unable to earn a living wage, dozens more spend their stunted, disease-ridden lives in almost constant hunger. As these children grow up, they see their poverty surrounded by incredible wealth. Everywhere they go they are tempted by shop windows, billboard advertisements, television commercials. At night they lie dreaming about the consumer goods which are constantly dangled before their eyes. Williams wondered if Americans with good jobs and money for their needs and luxuries can imagine what it feels like to walk past showrooms filled with new cars, household appliances, and expensive furniture; to pass supermarkets bulging with fancy foods; and then to go home to an unheated, rat- and cockroach-infested tenement. He doubted that those who so easily condemned the rioters had ever had to eat a meal of beans and stale bread while gagging from the stench of a broken toilet, then sit and stare at an antique television set which showed nothing but the glamorous, carefree existences of the very rich or those who enjoy a high living standard.

The U.S. advertising industry boasts that it offers freedom of choice. But to those Americans so poor they can't make any selections the net effect of advertising is to goad them mercilessly. Little wonder, then, that when the emotional dam breaks and years of pent-up frustrations are suddenly released, the ghetto dweller recklessly rushes out into the streets to seize those things that have been denied him for so long. The "people-izers" of Watts and other places had been so urged to possess the consumer goods of which America has such surplus that they were willing to risk a police bullet in the back just to grasp a pair of new shoes or a bottle of beer. And, once the glass of the store windows was broken and inhibitions shed, whatever they couldn't carry away to their miserable hovels, the rebels burned.

Of course, not all of those who rebelled did so for lack of consumer goods. Many who took to the streets had jobs, and a large percentage came from the educated and middle-class segments of the Black population. Williams felt their uprising was motivated primarily by anger over being humiliated and emasculated by a racist society.

It was interesting to observe the Cubans' reaction to Watts and the uprisings which followed in Harlem, Rochester, Birmingham, and other cities. Most people Williams knew in Havana were completely flabbergasted. Although they had been talking for years about resistance to racism, they apparently hadn't believed that the Blacks were capable of taking such dramatic and widespread action. Shocked though many of the Cubans were, they cheered the spirit behind Watts as the beginning of what would some day become a popular revolution in the United States.

The Cuban Communist Party, however, was very critical of Watts. Williams heard its spokesmen complain: "Such events will widen the division between White and Black workers, and make it all the more difficult to create a true Marxist-Leninist society in America."

In response he told them: "After a century during which they haven't lifted a finger to help us, we Blacks would be stupid to delay our struggle just for the sake of some mythical unity we are supposed to develop with the Whites. We have begun to fight, and we will continue our resistance to racist tyranny, no matter who is offended. Those Whites who have turned away from us because of Watts are the worst sort of fair-weather friends. We are better off alone than with such undependable allies."

Williams felt that the stories in the U.S. press about the Cubans having supplied guns and money to the Blacks in the ghetto uprisings were so much nonsense. If they had offered him money, he would have readily accepted it. But the most they ever said they would give him was $200 per month with which to buy American phonograph records and news publications needed for the preparation of his Radio Free Dixie broadcasts. Not even this small amount of money ever got to Williams. Despite the Party's approval, there were always delays, and the money never reached him.

He knew it was possible that the Cubans were supporting Blacks other than himself, but had no knowledge of it. So far as he was concerned, if anyone was getting significant amounts of cash from them, it was only because they were the sort that the "Bourgeois Communists" could manipulate for their own ends. The same was true for weapons.

When a group of CIA agents was apprehended, a large quantity of sabotage equipment was confiscated from them by the G-2. The weapons they had brought to Cuba included highly sophisticated incendiary devices. Enclosed in packs of cigarettes, they were said to be so powerful that one of them could burn right through the reinforced concrete floor of a modern apartment or

office building. But when Williams suggested that it would be po-
etic justice for such destructive things to be sent back to the
United States for use by Black freedom fighters, the Cubans flatly
refused.

Such incidents convinced him that, if Black Americans were
ever to turn to revolutionary violence, they would have to do it on
their own. There were millions of guns in private hands in the
United States. When the time came to defend themselves on a nationwide scale, they would stockpile legal weapons purchased in
gunshops and department stores, acquire illegal arms from un-
scrupulous dealers and money-hungry military men, steal materials from arsenals and warehouses, and manufacture various types
of war articles in their own secret workshops. There wouldn't be
any need to wait for armaments to be sent from anywhere else.

In the fall of 1965, soon after Fidel announced publicly that
Che had resigned his posts and left Cuba, Williams discovered
that someone had printed a counterfeit version of *The Crusader*.
This became known when several copies of the forgery, having
been sent to wrong addresses, were returned to him by the Cuban
Post Office.

The phony "Special Edition of October, 1965" had been prepared with great skill. It was an almost exact copy of one of the
real issues, using the same masthead, typography, and journalistic
style. Williams later found out that, in addition to English, it was
published in French and Spanish. It had been sent to almost everyone on his mailing list, especially subscribers in India and Africa. As it contained articles supposedly written by him, which
both severely attacked the Soviet Union and criticized Chairman
Mao's theory of revolutionary warfare, it was obviously intended
to get Williams thrown out of Cuba.

When he realized what had happened, Williams tried to get
the Cubans to help him make a worldwide announcement revealing the forgery. He went to the home of Armando Hart, who at
that time was the secretary general of the Communist Party and
the minister of education, and had a long talk with his wife. She
told him she would take the matter up with the Central Committee
and suggested that they could broadcast a denunciation of the
false issue over Radio Havana.

Since this wasn't done, and the Party didn't see fit to contact
him further about the matter, Williams assumed that, even if they

didn't publish it themselves, they weren't interested in helping him counteract the incorrect impression it gave of his position. That false *Crusader* might have been put out by the CIA, by anti-Peking elements in the Cuban or U.S. Communist Parties, or by someone else. Its authorship remains a mystery.

As 1965 drew to a close, Williams began seriously to consider leaving Cuba. Although the Cuban people themselves were still supporting him—he wanted for nothing in the way of personal comforts—there was almost constant interference with his radio broadcasts and newsletter. He was convinced that he would soon have to find some place else from which to conduct his work.

He had attempted to go to Ghana, but a letter to Shirley Graham, the wife of Dr. W. E. B. Du Bois, who was close to President Kwame Nkrumah, asking for her help in getting invited there, had gone unanswered. He had also attempted to visit Sweden after being invited to give a series of lectures by some university students. The Cuban government, however, kept stalling on his request for an exit visa, claiming, among other things, that it would be too dangerous for him to go to western Europe because the CIA might try to assassinate him if he did.

One day, in a conversation with some foreign visitors, Williams said that he wouldn't mind living in Canada. Shortly afterward an American woman who had been present told him she had discussed his case with an official at the Canadian consulate. "He suggested you had a good chance of getting a visa," she said. "So why don't you go see him?"

At the consulate, a clerk asked Williams to wait out on the veranda. After a few minutes a man approached and suggested they take a walk in the garden. From his accent and what he said, Williams gathered that he was from the United States—possibly a representative of the U.S. State Department disguised as a Canadian diplomat.

"Do you like being in exile?" was the first thing he asked. When Williams assured him that he didn't, and had only left the United States to escape unjust imprisonment, the "Canadian" said, "You know, Canada isn't necessarily the best place for you. There is a possibility that under the proper circumstances you could return to the States."

"Do you mean I could go back without being arrested?" Williams asked.

"That would depend on several things," he answered. "First of all, we understand your sons are living in Peking. It would be a demonstration of good faith on your part if you brought them home with you and announced that you didn't see any reason why American Blacks should look to Red China for inspiration."

"They can come home if they want to," Williams answered, "but I'm not about to order them to leave China. They are getting a good education there, which is something I couldn't afford to give them in the States. Also, I believe there are some very important things we Blacks can learn from China. I am not going to denounce a country which has been good to me."

"There is another condition," the supposed-Canadian diplomat said as they continued to walk in the consulate garden. "The U.S. government would want some commitment as to the activities you'd engage in upon your return."

"I just plan to live a normal life, like anyone else," Williams answered. "I want to devote my time to writing."

"Come now," he said, "we know what sort of man you are. You wouldn't be satisfied to stay out of the fight for civil rights, would you? All that we want is your promise to work with the Reverend Martin Luther King or one of his associates. If you give your word that you will limit yourself to nonviolence, there is a good chance the kidnapping indictment against you will be forgotten."

"I'm sorry," Williams answered, "but I'm not a pacifist, and doubt I could ever be one. If anybody attacks me, I will defend myself. I will not be a hypocrite and tell my fellow Blacks to let themselves be brutalized."

"It's completely up to you," the "Canadian" said. "All you have to do is disassociate yourself from China and promise to work with Reverend King's people. Otherwise your chances of getting into either the United States or Canada are pretty slim. We know your situation here in Cuba is becoming more difficult every day. The Party people aren't very sympathetic toward you, are they?"

Not only was he familiar with Williams' problems with the "Bourgeois Communists," he then proceeded to tell him certain things which only someone intimately connected with the Cuban G-2, Comandante Pinero's organization, could have known.

Every time Williams had tried to help some Black Americans

visit Cuba, the G-2 had asked him to present his request in writing, detailing everything he knew about each person for whom he wanted a visa. They claimed this was necessary for security reasons. They also said that Fidel himself was interested in receiving written reports concerning the various Black Nationalist and militant organizations Williams was in contact with, and what they were planning for the future. Assuming that Fidel wanted to know these things in order to help him, Williams had done as the G-2 agents asked.

He was most unpleasantly surprised, therefore, when this "Canadian," a complete stranger, proceeded to exhibit an intimate knowledge of his plans, said they were doomed to failure, and advised him to cease thinking along such lines! He was so familiar with the details of Williams' confidential reports to the Cuban G-2 that he had to be in possession of copies of them. Williams was forced to conclude that, instead of delivering them to Fidel, the Cuban intelligence agents were making his plans available to a U.S.-oriented foreign government. As a consequence, they had to be falling into the hands of the CIA as well. What seems like the most probable reason that something like this was being done is that some sort of secret deal to curtail Williams' activities had been arranged between certain elements in the Cuban and U.S. governments.

During the debate on a bill aimed at making it a crime for American citizens to broadcast anti-U.S. propaganda from Communist countries—one of several unsuccessful attempts—a member of Congress had said it was doubtful Cuba could be persuaded to stop Williams' radio shows so long as the United States continued to allow the exiles to conduct raids against the island. By 1965 Cuba's chief concern was no longer to spread revolutionary ideas throughout the western hemisphere, but only to be left alone to solve her various internal problems. It was, therefore, certainly within the realm of possibility that an arrangement had been made to mute him in exchange for Washington's stopping the exiles.

But, if this were indeed the case, Williams felt that it wouldn't have made a very good impression to let it be known that the Revolution had grown so timid it was afraid to let a Black freedom fighter continue broadcasting to his brothers in the United States. Instead, a clandestine approach appeared to have been decided upon. As Williams saw it, his old enemies in the USCP had been joined by the pragmatists who had taken control of much of the Cuban government, and they were cooperating in a campaign of lies, trickery, and sabotage aimed at stopping his radio show and the publication of his newsletter. As one USCP stalwart at the radio station had put it, "Just remember, Fidel is way up there at the top and you are way down here at the bottom; and there are a lot of us in between who can mess you up very badly without him ever hearing about it."

Williams would have liked to return to the States. He felt that he had learned a great deal during the four years of his exile which could be of use back home. Also, being able to observe the latest developments in the Black Liberation Movement at first hand appealed to him. He saw the situation in Cuba as degenerating—the revolutionary dynamic being replaced by Party elitism. The conditions posed for returning home, however, were impossible to accept. He did not intend either to denounce China or embrace the Reverend King's pacifism.

The First Tri-Continental Conference, a convening of revolutionaries from Africa, Asia, and Latin America, took place in Havana in January, 1966, but Williams wasn't invited to attend. A day or so after it began, he was visited by a group of delegates from various African nations. "Brother Williams," they asked, "why are you boycotting our meeting? Comandante Ozmany Cienfuegos, the conference secretary, told us you refused to pick up the invitation waiting for you at the reception desk."

"Do you really believe that?" he asked.

"Of course we do," they said. "Why should a leader of the Cuban government lie about something like that?"

"Let's go over to the Habana Libre Hotel, where the conference is taking place," Williams answered, "and I'll show you who is lying."

At the reception desk, he asked the woman on duty if she had an invitation for him. After searching unsuccessfully through all of her files, she suggested he go to Comandante Cienfuegos' office and ask for it there. When they got to his office, Cienfuegos said that Williams' credentials had been misplaced. "Just wait outside here a few minutes," he said, obviously upset at the presence of the African delegates, "and I will have a new set of papers prepared for you at once."

Williams received his observer's credentials. Then the Africans suggested that, to avoid such situations in the future, he draft a resolution asking the conference to recognize that Black America, although not geographically a part of Africa, Asia, or Latin America, be considered an oppressed nation. This would guarantee that Williams or other Black American revolutionaries would be invited to any future meetings. The Africans then told him to ask the South African delegation to propose his resolution to the conference for a vote. "We are trying to organize both the Black and White members of our working class to oppose capitalism," the South Africans said in response. "Therefore we oppose recognizing American Blacks as a separate class of oppressed people. That would be a form of Black racism." And they refused to help.

The South Africans' negative response startled Williams, but, when he investigated the make-up of their delegation, he found that the Blacks in it were taking orders from two Moscow-oriented White Communists.

The same situation seemed to exist in many African delegations; the Angolans and others also refused to present Williams' resolution because they considered it to be "racist." When a Black delegate from Jamaica heard about it, however, he said, "We would be happy to support our brothers in America." What was surprising to Williams was that he wasn't known to be a Communist and appeared rather middle-class and conservative in his outlook.

Once the word got around that Jamaica was backing it, the delegates from Indonesia and Venezuela said they would sponsor the resolution as well. The South Africans, Angolans, and Cubans opposed it, and an Afro-Cuban trade union leader vainly tried to have the wording changed. Instead of calling for support for "Black America's struggle against racism," he wanted it to appeal for "A struggle by all American workers against capitalism." Despite hours of wrangling and hair splitting in committee, when it came up before the full conference it was adopted.

But the Cuban delegation was in charge of preparing translations, and various delegates began complaining that their versions of the passed resolution had been altered without authorization. As a result of the protests, the Cubans made even more changes, and the entire thing became completely confused. There were at least three different versions of the resolution being circulated.

At the same time, the pro-Soviet elements in the African delegations reportedly started spreading the word that, "If you want Cuban or Russian help for your liberation movements, you shouldn't be seen speaking to that Williams fellow." Some African delegates even approached Williams and said outright: "If you weren't so friendly with the Chinese you wouldn't be having so many problems."

At the conclusion of that 1966 Tri-Continental Conference, Fidel gave a private dinner for certain key Latin Americans in the Polynesio Restaurant of the Habana Libre Hotel. Deciding it might be a good opportunity to speak to the Cuban premier, Williams walked up to the guards at the door and showed them his observer's credentials. Not knowing that he was having trouble with the Party, they let him enter. In a moment, he found himself face to face with Fidel, who was sitting in a booth with some Mexican delegates.

When the prime minister saw Williams approaching, he stood up and started shaking his hand. "Fidel," Williams said out loud, "please excuse my barging in like this, but I have been asking for a meeting with you for a long time without success. I want you to know that my work here in Cuba is being sabotaged."

The restaurant suddenly became so quiet all that could be heard was the sound of breathing. Fidel was visibly embarrassed at being told in front of a large number of foreign guests that someone whom Cuba was supposed to be supporting was having serious difficulties.

Williams hadn't intended to shame him, but feared that if he'd tried to take him off to the side to discuss things in private, Pinero and the others would have been able to separate them before he could say anything. Thinking that it might be the last chance he would have, he had blurted out his complaint.

Looking around the restaurant, Williams realized that almost the entire Cuban cabinet was there. As his eyes contacted those of Ozmany Cienfuegos and the others, they looked away. Not one nodded or made any sort of friendly greeting. Then Fidel broke the silence.

"Williams," he said, "you are mistaken. Comandante Vallejo is taking care of your problems. You have nothing to worry about."

"I'm sorry," Williams answered, "but I don't even know who Comandante Vallejo is."

At this, Fidel turned toward a white-bearded man in uniform at the next table and said, "There he is. Hasn't he been helping you?"

"I don't want to disagree with you, Fidel," Williams said. "I have seen that man at many public events, but have never been introduced to him." Vallejo, as he found out later, had served in the U.S. Armed Forces during World War II, then joined Fidel in the Sierra Maestra, and was now his personal physician and translator.

After being pointed out, Vallejo shouted, "Hey, Williams. Come over here to my table. I want to talk to you." He was obviously trying to get him away from Fidel, who then said, "Vallejo, give Williams your office and home telephone numbers so he can always get in touch with you. I definitely want to see him. Do you understand?"

At this, several of the Cuban officials who had been giving Williams a bad time became visibly agitated. He assumed they were frightened that he would now be able to tell Fidel about the way they were interfering with his work and spreading lies about him.

When Williams went over to his table, Fidel's physician said, "The only reason I haven't seen you before is that Pinero has been able to handle all your requests."

"That isn't true," Williams answered. "I haven't been able to get an appointment with him for weeks."

"All the same," Vallejo insisted, "we are aware of your problems and are trying to work things out for you."

"How can you know what is bothering me?" Williams asked.

"We know," Vallejo said, "because Mrs. Dodd and Mrs. Brown have been keeping us informed."

The women he was referring to were USCP members living in Havana. Clara Dodd was the daughter of a former U.S. State Department official. Both she and her husband, Alfred Stern, who had made a small fortune as a real-estate developer in Levittown-type housing developments, had fled the United States in 1957 after being named as Soviet spies by Boris Morros, a FBI informer who worked as a music director on Hollywood "B" films. She was now connected with the Casa de las Americas literary circle, while her husband was helping the Cubans develop prefabricated housing. The other woman Vallejo had mentioned, Phyllis Brown, was a friend of hers.

"How can Dodd and Brown be informing you about my problems?" Williams demanded. "Those people aren't interested in Black Liberation. So why would you ask them about me?"

"But we thought they were working with you," he said.

"Hell no!" Williams answered. "If you want to know what I am doing, why don't you ask me about it?"

"If that's the case," Vallejo answered, "I promise to come see you right away."

A few days later, he showed up at Williams' house and said, "We understand you aren't getting along with the American Communists living here in Cuba."

"That's true," Williams answered. "They are telling everyone I am a Black Muslim, a Black racist, a Black Fascist, and a Trotskyite."

Glancing up at the autographed photo of Chairman Mao on the living-room wall, Vallejo said, "And they accuse you of being pro-Chinese, too, don't they?"

"Yes," Williams answered, "but in that instance they are telling the truth. I am pro-Chinese, and I don't mind anyone knowing it."

Vallejo assured him that Fidel would make certain his show would go back to being broadcast by Radio Progreso's high-powered transmitter and would be handled by Radio Havana's shortwave sender as well. Then he said, "Fidel is out of town at the moment. He will come and have a long talk with you himself in a couple of days." But several postponements followed, and, until Williams finally left Cuba, Fidel never did get around to see him.

Among those invited to the first Tri-Continental Conference was a Tanzanian journalist named D. H. Mansur. A balding, medium-sized man in his thirties, he appeared to be of mixed Arab-African descent. Williams had first met him the year before with a group of his countrymen who were establishing diplomatic relations between Cuba and their newly independent nation, the former British East African colony of Tanganyika. On that occasion Mansur told Williams of having been to Moscow and suggested he might well be appointed the first Tanzanian ambassador to Havana. On this, his second visit, he was being given the full VIP treatment and was staying at the Hotel Capri. Williams' first impression of Mansur was that he was a sincere revolutionary. He was very friendly, and said he could arrange an interview with almost any high Cuban official other than Fidel.

Following the conclusion of the conference, Mansur told Williams that he expected to go to New York to take care of some diplomatic matters at the United Nations. "Exactly when will you be going?" Williams asked. "I have $1,550 in U.S. dollars which I want to send to certain people active in the Black Liberation struggle in the States. Do you think you can help me do so?"

"I'm not certain just when I will be going," Mansur answered, "but our Tanzanian chief of secret police, who is here incognito on a special mission, will be leaving for the United States in two or three days, and I'm sure he will deliver the money for you."

On the night before the Tanzanian was to leave for New York, Williams prepared an envelope containing the money and a letter written in code. Mansur accepted it from him in the lobby of the Habana Libre Hotel, and took it upstairs to the other man's room.

After Williams had been waiting about fifteen minutes for his return, Mansur reappeared on the other side of the lobby in the company of Comandante Pinero. Between them was the Tanzanian who was supposed to take the package to the United States. When he caught up with him the next day, and Mansur said Pinero was a good friend of his, Williams began to have second thoughts about having given him the money, but it was too late to do anything.

During the days that followed, Mansur told Williams he had served as a guide and translator for Ozmany Cienfuegos and the other Cuban leaders who had visited Tanzania. "Did you know that the Cubans and the Russians are trying to make trouble between the island of Zanzibar and the mainland government in Dar es Salaam?" he asked. "They are doing this in order to break the union between the two parts of the country. Once Zanzibar is independent they plan to set up a base on the island from which to take over all of East Africa."

Among the other stories Williams was told by Mansur was one about the Cubans being responsible for a lot of trouble in

Leopoldville. "They sent a group of their Black soldiers there disguised as Congolese," he said. "They operated from a secret base inside Tanzania, and were supposed to help the U.S.S.R. better its position in central Africa. The CIA found out about it, however, and most of the Cubans were wiped out."

The gist of Mansur's various tales was that the Cubans and the Russians were arming and training "Moscow-oriented" Africans, not primarily to fight the imperialists, but to oppose those nationalist revolutionaries who refused to place themselves under the control of the U.S.S.R.

"Why have you turned against the Cubans?" Williams finally asked him. "You were so enthusiastic about them when I first met you last year."

"I decided they were no good," Mansur answered, "because I found out they are only using Blacks as their puppets. They have an Afro-Cuban as their ambassador in Dar es Salaam, but he has to take orders from the first secretary, who is White. This shows they are racists."

While some of what the Tanzanian said seemed to make sense, the more Williams got to know him the less he liked him. Mansur was broadcasting to Africa over Radio Havana and often laughed openly at how he was making anti-Communist statements which, since they didn't speak Swahili, the Cubans had no way of understanding. He also said that the director of Radio Havana had secretly asked him if he would work for them in counteracting the Chinese influence in East Africa.

Mansur's relationships with the Cuban workers in his hotel repelled Williams. On one occasion, he struck a waiter in the face because he hadn't been served fast enough; and then had the Party force the waiter to apologize. He also demanded that the director of the hotel provide him with a prostitute. When told that prostitution had been abolished by the Revolution, Mansur said it was a lie and boasted that any Cuban woman would sleep with him for money. He told Williams he had informed the officials of the Party that he wanted one of the chorus girls from the night club at the Capri, and that they had compelled her to submit to his demands in order to pacify him.

"Why do they let you get away with such behavior?" Williams had asked. "I've never known a guest of the Cubans to act so shamefully."

"I can do anything I wish to here," Mansur had answered, "because I know things about certain leaders of the Revolution, especially what they are doing in Africa."

Williams' misgivings about having entrusted Mansur with the money and coded message grew so great that he telephoned his friends in New York to see if they had received it. Learning that they hadn't, he confronted Mansur and demanded to know what had happened. "Maybe our chief of secret police didn't go directly to New York," he answered. "He might have stopped off in Mexico City or Washington en route."

After waiting a week, Williams telephoned New York again, this time checking to see if the man had arrived at the United Nations. When told he hadn't, he cabled an inquiry to Minister Babu, a Tanzanian leader whom he had met in China. Babu responded quickly, saying that D. H. Mansur had no official position whatsoever in Dar es Salaam. Williams realized he had been taken for a sucker!

When he went to Mansur's apartment and showed him the cable from Minister Babu, the supposed diplomat broke down. "Shoot me, please shoot me," he wept. "I promise to get your money back. The Cuban Party will give it to me. Please don't inform President Nyerere, or the Tanzanians will kill my wife and children. Oh, please."

"Look," Williams said. "I don't give a damn about you. I want the return of our money and the coded message in that letter. What have you done with it?"

"It is gone, gone," Mansur wailed. "I gave your letter to a Cuban government official."

"Tell me his name," Williams demanded. "If that's all you have done, then there is a good chance I can get it back. The Cubans have no reason to interfere with my sending money to our people in the United States."

"No, no," Mansur said. "I think the man I gave it to was working for the CIA. It is gone."

Then Mansur began to plead with Williams to go with him to the Reuters and Associated Press correspondents in Havana. "I will write out a complete confession in front of them of how I have betrayed your trust," he said.

It suddenly dawned on Williams that he might be scheming to get him to state in front of U.S. and British newsmen that he

had tried to send money and coded instructions to Blacks in the
States. By doing so, Mansur could try to cook up a sensational
story linking the Black Liberation Movement and foreign interests, with Williams as some sort of subversive go-between. Disgusted, he turned on his heel and walked out of Mansur's hotel
room.

Once word of what he had done started getting around, various people approached Williams with other complaints about
Mansur. An African woman, the wife of a diplomat, said he had
tried to bribe her and some Cuban friends into taking him to Havana night clubs where lesbians were supposed to congregate.
Flaunting a roll of bills, he had bragged about how much money
he could make if he could get some photographs showing that
such things still existed in Cuba. "I was able to force the Angolans
to leave Dar es Salaam by publishing photos of them in bad places
there," she quoted him as saying.

Williams then learned that Mansur had requested permission
to leave Havana. Despite his services being essential to the setting
up of broadcasts to East Africa, the Party sent him off on a trip to
the interior of Cuba.

While the Tanzanian was away from Havana, Williams met a
Congolese woman who was looking for him. "I have certain confidential communiqués for Mansur to take to Dar es Salaam," she
said. "They are vital for the underground forces operating in the
Congo." But when Williams told her what Mansur had done to
him, and the secrets he was openly revealing, she was horrified.
After a long discussion, she said, "It has always been a mystery to
us how the imperialists discovered the presence of Black Cuban
soldiers in the Congo. It is obvious now that Mansur is the missing
link we have been searching for. He must be the one who betrayed
us and caused so many brave freedom fighters to be slaughtered."

Upon hearing this, Williams telephoned Comandante Vallejo
and said it was imperative he come to his house at once. When he
arrived, Williams told him about the entire Mansur affair, and
how the Congolese woman was certain he had informed on the
Cubans who were wiped out in Africa. Vallejo was so excited he
almost ran out of the house, saying, "I am going directly to Fidel.
This matter must be investigated at once."

The next night, at 12:30 a.m., two G-2 agents Williams had
never seen before appeared at his front door. "Tell us everything

you told Comandante Vallejo," they demanded belligerently. When he asked whose office they came from, they answered that the "red beard" had sent them.

"Well you can just go back to Pinero and tell him I don't deal with crooks," Williams said. "Anything I have to say I will say to Fidel."

"We don't have to stay here and be insulted by you," one of them retorted. "Mansur is a good revolutionary and a friend of Cuba's. His only problem is that he talks a little too much." As they left, Williams overheard him say to the other agent, "That Williams had better watch out. He is going to get messed up."

The next day, Mansur was suddenly flown out of Cuba to London. Despite repeated attempts to reach Fidel, including telephone calls to the offices of President Dorticos and Celia Sanchez, Fidel's secretary, Williams wasn't able to get to see him. With Vallejo also refusing to answer his calls, he was completely cut off from the upper echelons of the government. The only officials he could reach were minor functionaries from Pinero's office, who laughed and tried to shrug off the affair as a joke.

Since Ozmany Cienfuegos had been Mansur's sponsor in Cuba, and Vallejo had obviously gone to Pinero with his story, Williams concluded that the three of them were working together in the matter. Mansur himself had said that, if Williams wanted any special favors in Cuba, he would be advised to become friendly with Cienfuegos. "His power is on the rise," Mansur had said, "while Fidel's is declining."

Mansur had also said there were certain people in Cuba who wouldn't hesitate to kill Williams if he became too much of a problem for them. Convinced that Comandantes Cienfuegos, Vallejo, and Pinero were against him, Williams felt that the time had come to leave.

The place where he felt he could be most effective was Hanoi. By this time U.S. bombers were attacking North Vietnam around the clock, and hundreds of thousands of American soldiers were being poured into the South to try to crush all resistance to the Saigon regime. But Williams felt that the propaganda emanating from Hanoi left much to be desired. So he contacted their representatives in Havana and volunteered to go there to help in preparing radio broadcasts and publications aimed at Black GI's fighting in South Vietnam.

Although they were then turning down the offers of White USCP people who wanted to work in Hanoi, the North Vietnamese told Williams he would be most welcome. And they agreed that his wife could accompany him.

He then contacted the Chinese and asked if they could stop off in Peking en route to Hanoi in order to visit their sons. "China is your home," the ambassador answered. "You may visit our country whenever you wish, and stay as long as you like."

Williams felt that this really took the wind out of the sails of his enemies in Havana. The Cubans couldn't very well refuse to let him go to North Vietnam without making themselves look bad. And those of his critics who were saying that he had become "homesick" because he wanted to return to the United States had to swallow their words.

Some months prior to his departure, he stopped his Radio Free Dixie broadcasts, and ceased publishing *The Crusader.* The Cubans, as if to demonstrate he was still welcome to remain in their country, began to provide all sorts of unsolicited favors: They renovated his house and increased his living stipend from three hundred to four hundred pesos per month. But, to put the lie to those who said he was "enjoying Socialism," Williams refused to accept his allowance for the last three months he was there.

Shortly before leaving Cuba, he was invited to Clara Dodd's house to meet Leo Huberman, the editor of *The Monthly Review,* a USCP theoretical journal published in New York. When Huberman asked, "Rob, have you been getting any help from White Americans?" Clara Dodd cut in and said, "Oh, he doesn't want any help. He is a Black Nationalist and doesn't believe in working with us."

"That's what she says," Williams retorted, "but, if you want to know the truth, White Americans have always supported our movement. They have been sending me contributions and helping distribute my newsletter in Canada and the United States for years. I have no objections at all to cooperating with them, so long as they don't try to tell us what to do."

Although she had always been friendly, and had often told him how much she supported the Black Liberation Movement, Williams now was convinced that Clara Dodd was also among those spreading lies about him. It seemed to him that there was hardly anyone he could trust.

As the date set for his departure approached, three Cuban men came to see Williams. They weren't among the well-known leaders of the government but were dedicated revolutionaries who had fought with Fidel in the mountains almost from the beginning. "We have learned that you plan to leave Cuba," one said. "And it makes us very sad. We know you have been having problems with certain people here, but won't you please change your mind and stay?"

"I'm sorry," Williams answered, "but I'm not a Cuban citizen, and don't want to get involved in the internal contradictions of the Revolution. It would be better if I left."

"We know our nation is not as revolutionary as it once was," the Cuban said. "We are struggling to get it back on the right path again. If you leave, it will weaken our position. The Cuban people like you. Fidel is also sympathetic toward your work. The problem is that he is surrounded by people who are misinforming him. Even we can't get to see him any more."

It was hard to do, but Williams had to refuse. "My only concern is Black Liberation in the United States," he told them. "I know the Cuban people support us, and we American Blacks are all for you in return. I could stay on here indefinitely if I were willing to let the 'Bourgeois Communists' order me around, but I didn't refuse to be a capitalist Uncle Tom just to become a Socialist one. I must go where I can work unhindered."

At this, one of the Cubans said, "But how will we ever be able to explain to our children why a Black revolutionary from the United States was unable to live here? The fact that you had to leave will be a shameful blot on our record. Please don't do this to us."

Williams explained in detail some of the incidents leading to his decision to leave. When he heard about such things as the Mansur affair, one of the three Cubans said, "Williams, you are right in deciding to go. The situation here is dangerous for you; others have been given much more trouble for far less. The problem we face is our own. We must work to solve it ourselves. It isn't fair to ask you to forgo doing everything in your power for your people just so you can help us."

His argument appeared to be accepted by the other two, and the three of them left after shaking hands and telling Williams how much they hoped he and other Black Americans would some day be able to again look upon Cuba as a truly revolutionary land.

The five years he'd spent in Cuba had been valuable. They had taught him that there are people of all colors who sympathize with the struggle of the Blacks in the United States and are ready to give everything, including their lives, to help them.

But he had learned too that the feelings of the people of a nation are not all that matters when it comes to international affairs. What a man is ready to do as an individual, and what he does when representing the state, can be radically different. So long as Cuba's leaders believed the only way for their nation to survive was to avoid seriously irritating Washington, there was no hope of their giving anything but lip service to the Black Liberation Movement in America.

Continuing to use the slogans of revolution long after all real efforts at radical change have been abandoned has been the general rule throughout history. In the latter part of the eighteenth century, "The American Way of Life" struck fear into the hearts of the kings and emperors who ruled Europe because it represented the first large-scale success of the then-revolutionary bourgeoisie in overthrowing feudalism. Two hundred years later, even though it had come to stand for the most oppressive system plaguing mankind, the leaders of the United States still engaged in polemics about "spreading democracy" throughout the world. The leaders of the U.S.S.R. as well, decades after having eliminated the revolutionary tendencies within their country, continued to urge their people to work for the "goals of the Revolution" of 1917. And this almost unavoidable tendency of revolutionaries, once in power, to become first pragmatists, then conservatives, and, finally, reactionaries, had affected Cuba.

As Williams saw it, the Cuban leadership couldn't afford to announce openly that it had ceased to actively support revolution in the rest of the Western Hemisphere. Once told their sacrifices were not required to help the oppressed, the Cuban people might demand that their leaders be replaced by men who would resume revolutionary struggle. Or if they, too, had lost the will to fight, they might insist upon their state being run by efficient technicians who would assure them as high a living standard as possible. Not wanting to lose power to either revolution or consumer-oriented elements, the Cuban leadership was doing everything it could to maintain the illusion that it was still dedicated to revolt in the

Americas. *"Viva la Revolución!"* remained the slogan, but it had become only an empty catch phrase so far as Williams was concerned.

Williams reflected that the transformation of romantically idealistic Cuba into another bureaucratized state had necessitated the isolating and weakening of popular individuals such as Che and Fidel. The existence of charismatic leaders is always a threat to the bureaucrat.

Che's example of devoting his leisure time working as an unpaid laborer in the fields and factories was disturbing to those who believed that the only way to run a country is by the carrot and the stick—police terror for those who try to think for themselves and material incentives for those who follow orders. When he spoke about building a society whose members would work together without thought of cash reward, where people would take pride in what they were doing for others, not in how much they were able to acquire for themselves, Che was challenging the basic world view of the "Bourgeois Communists." The faceless organization man can't control things so long as there are leaders who can appeal directly to the altruism of the masses.

Fidel, as well, was disliked by many of the political hacks and executives. They would speak about him being "irrational," which he certainly was by their standards. "He is a megalomaniac and does things on impulse rather than for the best interests of the Party," was a statement Williams heard voiced by Party stalwarts on more than one occasion.

Many bureaucrats were convinced that Socialism couldn't be built by individuals, but only through the development of a strong "collective." The chief advocate of this school of thought was Anibal Escalante, the director of information. There were quite a few Party functionaries who spoke more about him than they did about Fidel. He represented their type of man: the political opportunist who is sycophantic toward those from whom he takes orders or can derive advantage, and is indifferent or abusive toward those whom he doesn't think can do him any good.

The poor farmers and workers, on the other hand, were Fidel and Che's strongest supporters. Even if they sometimes made mistakes, the workers excused them because they had confidence in their dedication to the national welfare. "Fidel is honest. He tries to help us every way he can," was what they would say even when some major setback occurred. They wanted human leaders whom they could see and touch, not anonymous officeholders who issued endless decrees in multiple copies.

It wasn't that the "Bourgeois Communists" were afraid of the masses. Some of them were skilled public speakers capable of going out and stirring crowds almost as well as Fidel. It was just that they viewed leadership as an elite fraternity of those clever enough to get the people to dance to their tune, and did everything they could to elevate themselves above the general population. Fidel's wearing a beard and refusing to discard his fatigue uniform was a gesture of asceticism. He was renouncing any personal reward so long as a single man, woman, or child had to go without. Both he and Che had been born into the bourgeoisie but had chosen to reject their families' wealth. All too many of the Party functionaries, however, seemed to have turned to Communism for selfish reasons and wanted only to get for themselves the benefits previously enjoyed by the ruling class.

They saw no need to dirty their hands working with the people, whom they tended to look on as sheep, with themselves as the shepherds. Rather than trying to gain the respect of the masses, the Escalante faction, and others of like inclination, spent their time consolidating their positions. By placing their followers in strategic positions throughout the Party and government, they thought they could cause the nation to follow whatever policies they chose.

Due to their efforts, Fidel had become increasingly insulated. In the name of caution, they urged him to stop walking about openly in the crowded streets of Havana as he had done during the first years of the Revolution. The almost daily face-to-face contacts which had helped him keep his fingers on the pulse of the Cuban people ceased. By 1966, a heavy guard surrounded him wherever he went, clearing the sidewalks whenever he left his car to visit someone. Just as only those "safe niggers" who won't do or say anything disturbing are selected by the U.S. president's advisers to visit the White House, so Vallejo, Cienfuegos, Pinero, and others screened the Cuban workers who were allowed to speak to Fidel.

By preventing those with serious grievances against the Party from getting through to him, they both protected themselves and helped weaken his position with the people. So long as his popularity was necessary to help them control the country, they continued to swear allegiance to Fidel, but there was no doubt in Williams' mind that they would try to get rid of him once they felt strong enough to run the place by themselves.

Cuba wasn't immune from the back-stabbing, head-chopping, and assassinations that have characterized societies in flux from the French Revolution of the late 1700's through the Russian Revolution of 1917 to the Kennedy-killing United States of the 1960's. Black Americans had a great deal to learn by observing and analyzing the power plays taking place in other lands, and Williams saw it as inevitable that they, too, would be torn by internal conflicts. Differing backgrounds and interests already divided them into a multitude of contending factions, and they were constantly being tricked into wasting their energies tearing at each other's throats, instead of joining forces against their common foe.

Williams was told by friends that his enemies in the USCP clique in Havana were telling the North Vietnamese that, since he was an "anti-Communist" and a "Black racist," permitting him to go to Hanoi would alienate many Whites in the United States and weaken the peace movement. The North Vietnamese had invited him to a small reception at their embassy the day before he was to leave, but their ambassador called at the last moment and said, "I'm sorry, but because of the danger from the U.S. bombings, we have decided it would be inadvisable for you to go to Hanoi at this time." When he suggested that things might be better at some later date, Williams said, "As I have to stop off in Peking to see my two boys, anyway, I might as well wait there until your government feels I can continue on to Hanoi."

Since he and his wife already had their visas and air tickets, there was little anyone could do to stop their departure short of having them placed under arrest. Still, just before they left, the Cuban airlines people called and suggested that they fly to Peking via Prague, the plane to Moscow being delayed. Williams reminded them that he couldn't do that because of the possibility of being taken off the plane by the Mounties when it landed to refuel at Gander, Newfoundland. "What I would prefer," he said, "would be to take the Iberia Airlines flight from Havana to Madrid, and from there on to Peking via Pakistan."

"What?" the Cubans asked. "Do you mean to say you'd rather fly to a reactionary country like Spain than go via the Soviet Union? Do you trust Franco more than you do our Russian comrades?"

"I know that the U.S.S.R.'s leaders are hostile toward me," Williams answered, "whereas, while Spain may be Fascist, it hasn't been denouncing me in its press." This apparently so embarrassed the Cubans that they contacted the Russians and got them to guarantee that Williams would be allowed to transit their territory without any problems. So he and his wife decided to take the risk and fly via Moscow.

Having told the Cubans that they planned to return in six months, they left most of their personal possessions in Havana; taking with them only a portable typewriter, a phonograph, and some jazz and rock records. On July 17, 1966, almost five years after arriving there as a hunted fugitive, Robert Franklin Williams left Cuba to join his sons in China. That nation, he was soon to discover, was in the midst of one of the most far-sweeping debates in human history: The Great Proletarian Cultural Revolution.

Chapter Fourteen

TO SERVE THE PEOPLE

Moscow is far different in July than in December. Instead of the dark, heavy clothing which the sub-Arctic weather necessitates most of the year, the men don short-sleeved shirts and the women walk about in gaily colored print dresses. The expressions on peoples' faces, as well, are summery; the pale faces and frozen scowls of the winter months being replaced by sun tans and smiles.

As on their two earlier trips, Williams and his wife stopped in the Soviet capital for a few days. The U.S.S.R.'s rapidly improving relations with the United States were evidenced by the presence in their hotel alone of over three hundred American tourists. The fact that the U.S. Armed Forces were bombarding North Vietnam didn't prevent the Russian government from welcoming U.S.-State-Department-authorized exchange students and scientists. But, despite Williams' impression that the Kremlin was doing everything in its power to please Washington, the Soviets honored the guarantee they had given the Cubans, and he was permitted to continue his flight to China without difficulty.

Upon landing in Peking, Williams and his wife were once again welcomed by representatives of the Peace Committee. Uncertain as to the length of their stay, they moved into temporary hotel quarters, where they were soon joined by their sons.

In the almost two years since they had seen the boys, both had grown several inches. Bobby, at sixteen, was taller than his father's six feet, while John at fourteen, was almost as large. They were attending a secondary school located on the outskirts of the city. During their first year they had been required to learn to read, write, and speak Chinese, a complex language involving sounds and accents far different from those of English, and were now sufficiently fluent in Mandarin, the most widely used dialect, to take courses in mathematics, history, and other subjects alongside the regular students. Although they had been a bit lonely at first, once the language barrier was overcome they had made quite a few friends among their Chinese classmates.

Their unusual experiences of the past five years—the clash with the racists back home, having to flee the United States, adjusting to life in Havana, and then having to readjust to being alone in Peking—didn't appear to have daunted the boys. If anything, they seemed more intelligent and mature than one might have expected. Via books and periodicals, they were keeping well informed on U.S. developments and demonstrated a good current knowledge of the Black Liberation Movement there. Their father and mother were extremely proud of them.

One of the first things Williams did after arriving in China was draft a long letter to Fidel Castro. In its twenty-six pages he explained his decision to leave Cuba, stating, in part: ". . . I support the Cuban Revolution and am grateful for the hospitality and friendship that the Cuban people have shown me. . . . I bring this matter to your attention so that you may deal personally with it, or place it into the hands of the people so that they may know about . . . those persons who are supposed to be leaders of the Cuban Revolution, people like Comandantes Vallejo, Pinero, and Ozmany . . . who are either outright thieves and crooks themselves, or who keep company with and give aid and comfort to . . . enemies of the Cuban people and revolutionaries throughout the world.

"I am doing this completely on my own initiative . . . I feel a personal obligation . . . to the Cuban Revolution and the Cuban people, and I hope that I will be more fortunate in reaching you than I was in the more than four years that I resided in Cuba."

When Williams presented this letter to the Cuban embassy in Peking in early September, 1966, they refused to accept it. He then sent a copy to Premier Castro via the mails. After a long wait, receiving no response, and considering it his duty to Cuba to do everything possible to bring out the facts of the situation, he sent copies of it to key revolutionaries and journalists throughout the world.

Some time later, friends of his who had visited Havana after his departure wrote that the Cubans were now publishing *The Crusader* themselves. At first Williams assumed they were only distributing leftover copies of back issues, but then a friend in the

United States forwarded a new copy he had received in the mail. The moment he saw it Williams concluded that someone in the Cuban government was actually forging his publication.

Like the counterfeit "Special Edition of October 1965," this one copied *The Crusader* format and style exactly. The reason Williams was certain it was being printed by the Cuban authorities was that it bore the postal meter stamp used for all official mail. The lead article was a strong attack on the Chinese. He viewed it as an obvious attempt to offend his hosts and thus make it difficult for him to remain in Peking.

When he showed the Chinese a copy of this forgery, they told him that many similar things were being done. Several faked issues of *The Peking Review* and other official Chinese publications were also known to be in circulation. They didn't say outright that the Cubans or the Russians were guilty—only that "certain elements on the international level" were thought to be responsible.

Both to counter such tactics and to get back into contact with his supporters in the United States, Williams decided to resume publishing *The Crusader* himself. The Peace Committee arranged for the printing and mailing facilities, and the first Peking issue came out in October, 1966. Approximately 5,000 copies were shipped in bulk to various people in the States who Williams knew would distribute them. His master mailing list had been left behind in Cuba, but a copy was available in Canada, and when it reached China, he was once again able to deal directly with individual subscribers. On the masthead, instead of a knight in armor, he used a drawing of a crossed torch and a machine gun. *The Crusader* was now clearly revolutionary.

The next issue (January, 1967) was 6,000 copies, the following one jumped to 8,000, and each subsequent edition increased about 2,000 copies until circulation reached almost 30,000. As it had been in Cuba, it was the sole private journal being published in China. Although Williams knew that their position on many issues differed from his, despite their paying for *The Crusader* to be printed and airmailed throughout the world, the Chinese made no attempt to dictate its contents.

The Peace Committee also told him that, if he desired, the facilities of Radio Peking could be placed at his disposal, but he chose not to reinstitute Radio Free Dixie. Red China's transmit-ters were more than powerful enough to reach the United States but, because of the great distance involved, it would have been possible to broadcast only on shortwave frequencies. Since most of the people he wanted to reach lacked shortwave receivers, Williams decided that his time would be better spent writing.

In addition to printing and mailing *The Crusader,* the Peace Committee provided him with their standard cash allowance for exiles. A car, chauffeur, and interpreter were available for his use. And if he felt the need for additional funds, he had only to ask. All in all, so long as he was forced to remain outside of the United States, he couldn't imagine a more congenial working situation.

When the Chinese consider a person their friend they do everything they can to help him. Had they come to the conclusion that they no longer wished to assist Williams—rather than try to surreptitiously sabotage his work—they would have asked him to leave their country. This was a clear-cut position which he found preferable to the indirection of those he felt had opposed him in Cuba.

On the eve of the October 1, 1966, National Day Celebration, the representatives of the Peace Committee told Williams, "If you wish to do so, we would be honored if you gave a speech from the top of the Tien An Men before the parade."

The following morning, with Chairman Mao standing at his side, he addressed the one and a half million people assembled in front of the Gate of Heavenly Peace. As Williams spoke, a Chinese interpreter translated his speech and both of their voices boomed out over the loudspeakers.

Mao's expression was serious. When Williams concluded, he said, "Thank you," in quite good English and gave him an autographed copy of the "little red book," a selection of his best-known sayings. He was showing the world in the clearest possible terms China's commitment to Black America.

Following the introductory speeches, the National Day parade began. As in 1964, with the exception of a militia unit, there were no military contingents. The display of slogans supporting the Great Chinese Proletarian Cultural Revolution was an innovation, as was the behavior of the marchers. Although Chairman Mao made a point of standing on the rostrum during most of the procession, there were moments during the several-hour-long event when he normally retired to the reception rooms to relax and sip a cup of tea. But today, unlike previous parades, the marchers were refusing to pass the Gate of Heavenly Peace without seeing him. Every time a new group of demonstrators drew abreast of the main reviewing stand, they would stop marching and begin chanting his name, holding up the rest of the parade until he came outside and waved at them. Many had traveled thousands of miles to get to Peking, and did not intend to return to their communes in the hinterland without having seen Chairman Mao.

The Great Chinese Proletarian Cultural Revolution had begun in the schools. A student at the University of Peking started it by pasting up a wall poster criticizing the dictatorial tendencies of certain administrators. When the bureaucrats lashed out at him for questioning their judgment, a woman teacher had come to his defense. When she, too, was attacked, Chairman Mao Tse-tung himself interceded on her behalf. Mao's declaration of the right of the people to criticize even the highest officials released a vast reservoir of discontent. Evidently there were functionaries who had permitted themselves to become overly concerned with possessions and power; and the masses had grown dissatisfied with such leaders.

Led by the Red Guards, millions of young people began to tear down the pillars upon which they felt the selfishness of the past was being re-enshrined. Within a few short months the whole of China, one-fifth of the entire human race, was plunged into a philosophical debate without equal in history. Williams analyzed the controversy this way:

Although fragmented into a multitude of factions, for want of better terms the two primary schools of thought contending in the Cultural Revolution could be described as "democratic idealism" versus "limited pragmatism." From the limited pragmatist point of view, most men are incapable of governing themselves; and, in the absence of strict rulers, nations either break down into anarchy or are taken over by war lords and demagogues.

Limited pragmatists see revolutions as taking place only when a large enough number of people become so discontented with the failure of those in power to satisfy their minimal needs that they lose their fear of death and rise up. Once a feudal or capitalist system has been replaced by Socialism, they believe the revolution will subside. In the eyes of these "practical revolutionaries" (as the limited pragmatists like to refer to themselves), once the means of production have been taken out of private hands, all attempts to continue to agitate for change are a threat.

Convinced that the basic attitudes of the masses can't be altered except by long years of reeducation, they view the old system of more-pay-for-more-work as the only really dependable way to get people to do anything. Altruism, dedication, freedom, justice, and all other such ideals are seen as crowd-pleasing terms to be mouthed in public, but discounted in practice. What they really depend upon to maintain themselves in power are fear, selfishness, and lethargy, which they believe are inherent to the nature of man.

Seeing society as composed of either the leaders or the led, they strive to secure positions which provide the benefits due those in command. "If the individual citizen is motivated only by what he can get for himself," they reason, "then why shouldn't those who devote their lives to organizing people be compensated with the best the system has to offer?" Continuing in this direction, they next question why someone who is working for the public good should permit his decisions to be open to criticism from below. Since, in the opinion of the limited pragmatist, man lives by bread alone, whoever dares to question the wisdom of those whose organizational skills maintain an adequate supply of food must be either an "aberrant" or a "counterrevolutionary."

The discontent of the Chinese young people and masses, however, was not the result of a shortage of jobs, food, clothing, or shelter. What fueled the nationwide explosion of criticism was the fact that limited pragmatism, while based upon much that is valid, is an inadequate philosophy for satisfying man's most human need: the realization of his imagination.

The limited pragmatist stops thinking once he has devised a minimal solution to satisfy immediate needs. The democratic idealist, however, keeps envisioning better ways of doing things and is not content until he has developed those relationships which utilize the inherent potential of a situation to its fullest. The limited pragmatist, consciously or not, tends to become the preserver of things-as-they-are. The democratic idealist strives continually to realize things-as-they-could-be for the best interest of the most people. Historically, the idealist is the innovator, the creator, and the inspirer, while the pragmatist is the copyist, the exploiter, and the functionary.

Williams had been inspired by visionaries like Dr. W. E. B. Du Bois, who created the NAACP because they dreamed of an organized and powerful Black America, but he felt administrators like Roy Wilkins had taken it over and, in order to keep their jobs, tried to make the dream nonthreatening to the White liberal Establishment. Dreams, however, are difficult to "civilize" without being vitiated in the process.

The difficulties of changing basic relationships in China were compounded by the tendency of people long accustomed to being buffeted by foreign invasion and civil strife to prize authoritarianism and established ways of doing things. Because of this, Chairman Mao had always looked to the young people, those least indoctrinated in the old traditions, to lead in the revolutionary struggle. The youth of China were in the forefront of the armed battle against Chiang Kai-shek's forces and the Japanese. Their children formed the cadres which spread the new political-economic system throughout the nation after the 1949 Liberation. And their grandchildren were now striving through the Red Guard to eliminate the remnants of bourgeois culture and replace them with revolutionary ideals.

As the months went by and the Great Chinese Proletarian Cultural Revolution gained momentum, the young people closed down many universities and technical institutions. Some students established committees to develop new curriculums in their schools, while others went out to study and work with the peasants and laborers.

They weren't saying higher education as a whole was a waste of time, but they did insist that all education must help to change society, rather than just provide one with the means of earning more money and becoming a member of a privileged elite.

Along with the positive aspects of the student ferment, things sometimes went too far—the baby being thrown out with the bath water. Those educators who maintained it was necessary for universities to teach the basic academic courses often came under severe criticism. Many things which represented the past, even priceless relics of China's cultural heritage, were destroyed along with that which warranted discard.

Each day wall posters appeared on more buildings. And the paste on the new slogans and criticisms often hadn't dried before they were covered by even newer declarations. It was a common

sight to see wall announcements next to one another both attacking and defending a given person or position. Rival factions
waving banners and beating drums demonstrated in the streets.
Giant rallies were held by the young people, and even Chairman
Mao and other top leaders such as Lin Piao, Liu Shao-chi, and
Chou En-lai participated in them. Street-corner crowds were agitated by students and members of the Red Guard at all hours of
the day and night.

Sometimes the debates got out of hand. Mobs ran through
the streets hounding those they felt guilty of having placed self-in-
terest above serving the people. On several occasions, those wearing Western-style clothing, such as tight trousers, short dresses, or
high-heeled shoes, became targets of public harassment. There
were numerous instances when rival factions resorted to everything from fist fights to deadly armed clashes. But following their
denunciation by Chairman Mao and other leaders, the violent
outbreaks largely ceased. Some of the other extreme practices of
the Cultural Revolution were more persistent. During one period
it was common to see people wearing large dunce caps being led
through the streets or driven in trucks to appear before "Struggle
Meetings," where their critics listed the charges against them.

The best proof that the country wasn't totally disrupted was
that at the height of the Cultural Revolution Williams and his wife
were able to travel far from Peking without experiencing any
problems.

During a visit to Shanghai, the largest city in China, they had
a long talk with a young man who was a member of his factory's
Revolutionary Committee. "After the students got things stirred
up," he said, "we workers joined in. I was one of the first to publicly criticize the bad policies of certain of the Party officials at our
factory. As a result, they called me a counterrevolutionary and ordered me out of the Militia. Guided by the thought of Chairman
Mao, I refused to be silenced, and before long the other workers
came over to my side. The functionaries couldn't run the plant
without our cooperation, and we eventually established a Revolutionary Committee and took over the administration ourselves.
Today we, the workers, make the decisions. Our motto is 'Serve
the People,' and production has increased."

Based on Williams' experiences in the United States and

Cuba, the idea of workers being able not only to criticize management, but actually to take over their factories, seemed incredible. As he visited city after city across China, however, he saw that it was true. In some establishments the employees were so dedicated to increasing production they put in overtime hours without pay; and there were several places where they slept next to their machines so they could begin work the first thing in the morning.

There was even greater acceptance of the new movement in the countryside. Touring Shansi Province, Williams and his wife went to the Wu Xiang Mountains, where they visited the Da jai Commune. The people there had transformed hundreds of square miles of once barren mountainside into highly productive farmland by carefully terracing the slopes and carrying fertile soil up from the valleys below. Each terrace was reinforced with stone walls to prevent erosion, reservoirs had been erected on the mountaintops, and an intricate irrigation system carried the water to each field. The farmers of the Da jai Commune, caught up by the new spirit of selflessness, had refused to accept any aid from the central government. Using little else besides their hands, they had accomplished this almost superhuman feat completely on their own.

Their hard work and intelligent planning produced one of the largest corn crops in China, and there was so much surplus remaining after they delivered the required portion to the state that the commune treasury was bulging. The farmers were eligible to receive enough money to buy many of the luxury items available but, instead of rewarding themselves with material things, each and every member of the commune declined to take more than a minimal share of his profit. Instead, the funds were being used by the Revolutionary Committee to make the commune more productive and to help the central government develop the entire nation.

Several of the older people of the commune tearfully told Williams how miserable their lives had been before 1959. Pride shone from their faces as they said that being able to give as much as they could to help build Socialism brought them great happiness.

In addition to growing corn and other crops, the members of the commune were mining their own iron ore, smelting it in small open-hearth furnaces which they had built, manufacturing light farm machines, and even making hand grenades and other weapons for their militia.

In an emergency, they were prepared not only to supply themselves with food and the other basic necessities, but also to defend their part of the country militarily. Williams was told that Chairman Mao was encouraging this both as a precaution against U.S. attack and in order to hasten the building of a nation so vast that attempting to regulate it completely from one central point hindered rather than helped its development. China was emerging as a constellation of thousands of communal cells, each as self-governing and economically independent as possible, but all co-operating and contributing to the national interest.

Williams felt that the strength of China's Socialist system was really shown when criticism began to be directed against even such powerful national figures as Liu Shao-chi, the theoretical leader of the Party. Although he wasn't mentioned by name, the streets of Peking were soon covered with wall posters denouncing "China's Khrushchev," which everyone knew meant Liu. He defended himself vehemently, but was eventually deposed. The fact that such a battle within the highest circles of state didn't result in a civil war or bloody purge was unprecedented. "How many other nations," Williams thought, "the U.S.A. and the U.S.S.R. included, could have survived such a debate?"

Since he had said that not even the highest official should be above criticism, a powerful movement against Chairman Mao himself soon came into being. Among those who openly criticized him were some of the members of the "Druzhba Group." This was an organization primarily composed of foreigners—propagandists, teachers, and specialists who were working for the Chinese. Many of them lived in the Druzhba Compound, a special residence area on the outskirts of Peking originally built for Russian technicians. Soon after the Cultural Revolution started sweeping the country, they had formed a Revolutionary Committee and begun criticizing various policies and leaders, printing their own literature and putting up wall posters.

Some of the Americans in the Druzhba Group pressured Williams to attend their meetings, but he declined. His experience in Cuba had taught him the dangers of a guest's taking sides in the domestic quarrels of his hosts. The Druzhba people insisted that

any foreigner who refused to participate in the Great Chinese Proletarian Cultural Revolution was either a "reactionary" or practicing "bourgeois irresponsibility." But, at the same time they felt
free to criticize the Chinese, they seemed to assume that, as foreigners, they were immune from criticism.

Williams' refusal to join them led several of the Druzhba people to start attacking him. They also disliked his telling the Chinese that the American people as a whole were racists. They had
been maintaining that most Americans were free of racism, and
that its existence was due solely to the efforts of the capitalists.

Williams didn't fear the charges leveled against him by these
critics because he was confident the Chinese were too wise to be
swayed by unsubstantiated accusations. "China is quite capable of
solving its own problems and needs no foreign intervention," was
his position.

China's policy toward oppressed peoples seemed as nearly
correct as Williams could hope for. The Chinese had pledged
themselves to support all nations and groups struggling for self-determination, without requiring that they accept Communism first.
Williams saw this as the only attitude a true friend could take. Demanding that someone swear allegiance to you before you'll help
him is really exploiting his dilemma. Genuine help should have no
strings attached. Black Americans needed assistance, but only so
long as accepting it didn't merely re-enslave them to a different
master. He had been happy to accept the help of the Cubans—
until they began to attach conditions. He had also seen how the
Russians demanded that those they aided must follow their dic-
tates. Williams concluded that Mao's teachings were a differen-
tiating factor.

The more Williams learned of Mao's ideas, the more impressed he became with their obvious logic. He soon began sending copies of the "little red book" to friends in the United States.
He was not suggesting that Black Americans blindly adopt Mao's
ideas, but he hoped they would help Black Americans develop
their own revolutionary philosophy. He felt that Mao's statement
that man's primary reason for existence is to serve his fellow men
is one that few decent persons could dispute.

In February, 1967, Williams and his wife were given an apartment in the Peace Compound, a residential area which had been
part of the Italian embassy before the Liberation. It consisted of

two large bedrooms, a dining room, and a living room. There was no kitchen; meals for all the compound's tenants were prepared in a central facility operated by the Chinese. There were also servants who cleaned and serviced the entire complex. Among their neighbors were Anna Louise Strong and Rewi Alley, a writer from New Zealand.

Like Williams, neither Strong nor Alley participated directly in the Cultural Revolution. They never joined the Druzhba Group, several of whose members were eventually imprisoned. The details of that case, which included arrests of such "old China hands" as Sidney Rittenberg, were obscure. What little was revealed indicated that the Chinese became convinced they were part of a Moscow-oriented conspiracy against Chairman Mao.

The spring and summer of 1967 saw increasing resistance to the U.S. power structure both at home and abroad. At home, the flames of Black rebellion swept city after city. The story of Watts was repeated in the ghettos of Newark, Detroit, and other cities. Their appeals for jobs and justice falling on deaf ears, the slum dwellers again were smashing and burning. Thousands of police and soldiers, armed with tanks, machine guns, helicopters, and gas, were unleashed to try to crush the rising tide of protest. Factories were shut down. The streets filled with garbage. Mail went undelivered. America's Black slaves were rebelling in a hundred places at once.

In South Vietnam, too, the struggle against the U.S. forces and their allies was accelerating. And in North Vietnam a technologically underdeveloped nation a fraction its size was fighting the North American behemoth to a standstill. The Pentagon was dropping more bombs on the Southeast Asian jungles than had been dropped on Nazi Germany. Billions of U.S. taxpayers' dollars were being spent, hundreds of U.S. aircraft were falling in flames, and thousands of U.S. soldiers were being wounded and killed, but victory was not in sight.

In the May, 1967, issue of *The Crusader,* Williams urged Black GI's to stop slaughtering their Asian brothers. He suggested that, if they had to kill to protect freedom, they turn on their real oppressors and enemies. "America is the Black man's battleground" was his theme. And he described some of the ways in which U.S. Blacks could effectively defend themselves against the brutality of the racist Establishment.

Williams' words caused President Lyndon Johnson angrily to ask the U.S. Post Office to investigate *The Crusader's* "content and mailability." As a result, Postmaster General Lawrence F. O'Brien ordered it banned from the mails. LBJ's indignation brought on a rash of newspaper headlines and editorials portraying Williams as a bloodthirsty maniac spouting race war.

The American Civil Liberties Union went to court in his behalf. They protested that banning a publication from the mails without first legally proving it contained statements of a criminal nature violated the First Amendment of the Constitution. Williams circumvented the Post Office's seizures by airmailing copies to American subscribers in plain sealed envelopes without return addresses. It was impossible for the authorities to check millions of individual letters, and many copies of *The Crusader* got through. The ban applied only to the May, 1967, issue, and subsequent editions were delivered without difficulty.

When reports that Che Guevara was in the mountains of Bolivia began to appear in the press in the summer of 1967, Williams felt he was in great danger. He was convinced Che had been forced to leave Cuba, despite all the official declarations from Havana that he had voluntarily chosen to carry the torch of revolution around the world. Che's campaign against selfishness, his attempt to inspire the Cuban people to work for idealistic satisfaction rather than merely for wages, had run into a lot of resistance. Also Moscow was opposing wars of national liberation in Latin America and looked upon independent-minded Communists like Che as dangerous enemies.

With these considerations in mind, Williams wrote in the mid-1967 issue of *The Crusader*: "If the Cubans know where Che is, then so does the CIA, and he'd better get the hell out of there because his life isn't worth a plugged nickel."

Two months later the world learned of Che's death at the hands of the CIA. Williams mourned him as a great revolutionary who had died fighting for the liberation of mankind.

Perhaps inspired by Che's martyrdom, Williams began planning to return home. He knew he risked imprisonment, but he felt it was no longer possible to stay away from what he saw as the main field of battle.

From a legal point of view, the kidnapping charge against him was weak. His four co-defendants had been freed in 1965 when the North Carolina Court of Appeals threw out their conviction. Its grounds were that the Union County jury selection system discriminated against Blacks. They had been reindicted, but in almost two years no attempt had been made to extradite them after they left the state to live in New York.

In the December, 1967, issue of *The Crusader,* Williams called upon his supporters to prepare to welcome him back with such an outcry that his fate—whatever it was to be—could not be hidden. In the event he was seized and forced to stand trial, he called for a "Monroe Court-in" protest crusade. During the months that followed, he wrote to North Carolina officials to try to determine how much bond he would have to post, the particulars of the charges, and other details of the situation which would await him upon his return. His personal safety no longer seemed paramount; the racist injustice of America had to be unmasked before the eyes of the world.

In March, 1968, he wrote a pamphlet titled *Listen, Brother!* (World View Publishers, New York, 1968) addressed directly to the tens of thousands of Black Americans fighting in South Vietnam. In it he said:

". . . The man wiped out the Aborigine brothers. He wiped out the Maori brothers. He wiped out the American Indians, and all of this was done in the name of Christianity and democracy. The man wiped out all the dark brothers he could, and now he sicks us on each other to further accomplish his genocidal designs. Brother, colored people are sure enough being used against themselves by the devil. Brother, it's getting time for some change. It's getting time for us to stand and put a hurting on our real enemy. What has a barefoot peasant in Vietnam ever done to you? How is he a threat to your democracy? You are a threat to yourself and should be shuffled off to the crazy house if you believe that you've got any democracy to lose, let alone defend. Brother, colored is colored and you know that Charlie has always been against that. The man is snowing you. He claims that it is a case of Communism, pure and simple. Brother, was your great-great-grandmother a Communist? Is your mother a Communist? Were the four little girls in the Birmingham Sunday School Communists? Is this why they were hated and butchered? Brother, isn't it about time you started questioning Whitey's motives?

". . . The man kicks your mother's ass, trains you like a nigger-biting vicious police dog, arms you with his latest shit, and sends you 10,000 miles to terrorize other innocent and defenseless colored women and children. Brothers, what kind of fools are we?"

At the end of March, 1968, a group of Black organizations held a conference in Detroit to establish The Republic of New Africa, a nation whose borders would encompass the states of Alabama, Georgia, Louisiana, Mississippi, and South Carolina. Despite his having lived in exile for almost seven years, the Detroit Conference elected Williams their first chief of state.

When informed of their decision, he sent the following:

NOTE OF APPRECIATION:

I wish to express my deep gratitude to the brothers and sisters who have elected me president of *THE REPUBLIC OF NEW AFRICA* (U.S.A.) and to all the brothers and sisters who have given me a vote of confidence in my mode and motive of struggle for Black liberation. My heart goes out to the brothers of the Black Panthers, SNCC, Mau Mau and to all those resolutely striving to reclaim the dignity of downtrodden Black humanity. I shall never cease striving to prove worthy of the great trust you have invested in me. It is my fervent and determined hope that I shall walk among you again soon.

Williams saw the motivation for establishing The Republic of New Africa as twofold: First, many Black Americans had become convinced of the futility of begging for integration. They no longer wished to live next door to those who despised them. Nor did they want to become an equal part of a decadent society. They were recoiling in revulsion from a system so insane that its only response to the complaints of the poor and the exploited was to enlarge its police forces and brutally suppress all dissent.

Second, Black America had yet to be compensated for the evil it was subjected to during centuries of slavery. The post-Civil War promise of "forty acres and a mule" for every former slave had never been kept. The Germans had been forced to pay damages to the Jews, Poles, Russians, French, and others whom the Nazis enslaved and exterminated. Giving America's Blacks five Deep-South states—its roads, buildings, and factories had been built by Black hands—would hardly begin to make up for what they had endured both before and since Emancipation. The twenty million or more Blacks in the United States constituted a people greater in number than most of the member states of the United Nations. To Williams, it was quite logical for them to have their own country. He did not appear overly concerned by the problems inherent in realizing such a plan in the United States.

In April, 1968, the Reverend Martin Luther King was assassinated. While the United States and other Western nations voiced shock, the news was received without much comment in Peking. In Williams' eyes, King had been a Nobel-Prize-winning tightrope walker between the aspirations of the Blacks and the demands of their racist oppressors. But when rank-and-file pressure became so great that he could no longer both remain a leader and be invited to the White House to shake hands with LBJ, he had finally taken a truly courageous stand. Williams surmised that the rulers of Washington, having no use for a Black who dared call for a halt to their infamy in Vietnam, had him murdered and then used the FBI and the courts to make certain the truth about him would never be revealed.

As Williams saw it: Mao Tse-tung, Ho Chi Minh, and Fidel Castro all had dreams. With gun in hand, they made them reality. But Martin Luther King's attempt to realize his dream by turning the other cheek got him only a bullet in the neck. The only law the racist-capitalist-imperialists of the United States knew was force. And whoever chose to serve the people by challenging the power structure either had to defend himself or die.

Chapter Fifteen

AFRICA

To revitalize his contacts with the Black Liberation Movement in the United States and sympathetic elements in other countries, Williams sought to travel outside of China. In late 1967, friends arranged an invitation for him to lecture at Uppsala University in Stockholm, but pressure from the U.S. government caused the Swedes to deny him an entry visa. Then, in early 1968, he was also denied admittance to France.

Rather than having a negative effect, these rebuffs led to a meaningful alternative: He decided to visit Africa, especially Tanzania.

Located on the east coast of Africa just south of the equator, Tanzania is almost as large as Texas and has more than twelve million inhabitants. Before World War I, it was a German colony known as Deutsches Ost-Afrika. Following the Kaiser's defeat, it was taken over by the British and called Tanganyika. Then, in 1964, soon after Tanganyika had achieved independence, an uprising overthrew the British-appointed Sultanate on the nearby island of Zanzibar, and the two former colonies merged to form Tanzania, the first really independent Black nation in Africa. Within its borders are 19,000-foot Mount Kilimanjaro, the Serengeti Game Preserve, Lake Victoria, and other natural wonders of the world. Its capital city, Dar es Salaam, has one of the finest ports on the Indian Ocean. It is also the headquarters for the Liberation Committee of the Organization for African Unity (OAU), which is struggling to overthrow the regimes in Mozambique, Rhodesia, South Africa, and the other parts of Africa still under White minority or colonial domination.

Williams' interest in visiting Africa was manifold. First, he wanted to see his ancestral homeland. He felt that walking on African soil and getting to know its people might help him understand his cultural heritage. Then, he wanted to explore the possibilities of developing close long-term ties between African and Black American revolutionaries.

He had learned that the Tanzanians, to encourage foreign visitors, were permitting their consulates to issue tourist visas without first checking on each applicant with the Foreign Ministry in Dar es Salaam. So, wary by now of bringing attention to himself by using diplomatic channels, he went to the Tanzanian consulate in Peking and received a standard tourist permit. Then, acquiring an Alien Travel Document from his hosts, he left China by air, traveling via Cairo, Addis Ababa, and Nairobi to arrive in Dar es Salaam in early May, 1968. Mabel, who had remained in Peking with the boys, was to join him as soon as she could.

Williams' image of African life had gone through several changes. As a child he'd had the usual White-media concepts implanted in his brain and thought of Africa as a jungled continent, teeming with crocodiles, elephants, and lions, and inhabited by half-naked ferocious savages, many of them cannibals. Later, at Johnson C. Smith College in Charlotte, he met some African students, and his ideas changed drastically. In addition to similar skin pigmentation, he and they seemed much alike. The African students were trying to achieve a higher living standard through education. They were quite properly dressed, intelligent, and literate. Later Williams learned that they weren't really typical of the population. Being hypersensitive to the "bare-assed nigger" image of Africans held by most Americans, and coming from the middle and upper economic and social classes, they went out of their way to emphasize the more technologically advanced aspects of life in their homelands. So the impressions he got from them, though far more realistic than the Tarzan movies, were not entirely accurate.

The third change in his image of Africa took place during his years in Cuba and China, where he became friendly with a large circle of diplomats and revolutionaries. Through such people as Minister Babu, he had come to realize that Africa was neither an uncivilized jungle nor a middle-class suburbia. It was, instead, a vast continent with hundreds of millions of inhabitants encompassing thousands of different societies and languages and a multitude of nations. Rather than being mostly malarial lowlands, a great part of Africa consisted of high-altitude grassy plateaus with year-round temperate climate. Some cities, like Nairobi, had the same skyscrapers and autos as many Western capitals. Others, like

Dar es Salaam, while not quite as flashy in their architecture, possessed modern factories and dock facilities.

During both his six-month 1968 visit and a second trip to Africa in 1969, Williams was to learn a great deal more. But his stay in Tanzania had barely begun when an event took place which forcefully reminded him of the vicious nature of life back in the United States.

Shortly before noon on June 4, 1968, he was standing in front of the U.S. Information Service Library in Dar es Salaam, having gone there to see the type of books being offered to the people of Africa, when an East Indian came running out of the bank across the street shouting, "Bobby Kennedy's just been shot! The radio says that he's just been shot!" He then ran into the USIS Library to confirm the story, but emerged saying they knew nothing about it.

Recalling that there was a Reuters teletype receiver in the lobby of the nearby Kilimanjaro Hotel, Williams went there. A large crowd was gathered around the teletype, discussing the dispatches that Bobby Kennedy had been shot in Los Angeles at the very moment of his victory in the California primary election. As news of his grave condition circulated, many of those in the hotel lobby expressed shock and disbelief. Williams overheard several Europeans declaring, "It's awful that such a wealthy and powerful nation can be so violent. The United States is a threat to the whole world. How can they explain this? American society has totally degenerated. It's the end," and so on.

A couple of Black Americans who were with the Peace Corps turned to him and asked if he was from the United States. "Yes, I am," Williams answered, "but I don't live there right now."

"I just can't believe this has happened; I'm stunned," one said.

"The death of any man, White or Black, is a tragedy," Williams responded, "but I'm surprised that you, a Black, should be shocked by someone being shot down in the United States. They've been slaughtering our people there for four hundred years, haven't they? Didn't they recently murder President Kennedy? And Medgar Evers? And Malcolm X? And Reverend King? And countless others who were less famous? So why should Senator Kennedy's being shot come as such a surprise?"

Bobby Kennedy's death was especially disturbing to the Tanzanians because he had recently visited Dar es Salaam as part of a tour of East Africa and was very popular there. In recent years he had also built up a considerable following among U.S. Blacks by coming out publicly for desegregation. Still, Williams had always considered him the worst sort of hypocrite. His antagonism dated back to 1961 when Williams felt that Kennedy had first refused to answer the Monroe Blacks' pleas for help, then joined with the racists in an attempt to crush them. Both he and JFK had, in Williams' opinion, permitted and encouraged the development of the very immorality and violence which had finally devoured them.

As he saw it, had the Kennedys used their wealth and power to fight for justice and a decent life for all, the forces of reaction might still have struck them down, but they would have died heroes, and those who had hired their murderers would have felt the wrath of the American people. But the many compromises they had made in order to gain the White House, such as the deal Williams believed they had made with the KKK in North Carolina, prevented them, he felt, from taking a stand until it was too late. The liberal who profits from and participates in international and domestic repression, and then (alarmed by the resulting popular unrest) expediently switches and demagogically criticizes his reactionary partners isn't murdered; he has committed suicide.

One of the most interesting things Williams discovered about Dar es Salaam was that its population combined several quite different human types: the native Blacks were intermingled with White Europeans, Brown East Indians, and light-Brown to Black Arabs. This wasn't a phenomenon limited to the Tanzanian capital. The mixing of peoples from various parts of the Indian Ocean, which stretches from Malaysia westward to the Middle East and then southward to the Cape of Good Hope, had been going on for thousands of years. And European traders and colonial conquerors had been present in the area for centuries. Nairobi, Lusaka, and the other East African metropolitan centers all had mixed populations.

But outside the cities the Africa of ten thousand years ago prevailed. There the vast majority of the inhabitants were Black, lived in tribal villages, and lacked almost every technological convenience. Modern transportation, communications, education, housing, industry, agriculture, and medicine didn't exist for the average man. Centuries of colonialism, while witnessing the con-

struction of a very few railroads and highways for the extraction
of natural resources, had left most of Africa poorer and less organized than it was before the Europeans shot their way into control of it. Even in Black-ruled Tanzania, large sectors of the economy were controlled either by Whites or East Indians. The Whites
ran the major companies, while the East Indians and some Arabs
monopolized the medium and small businesses. In reaction to this
situation, the governments of Kenya, Zambia, and other newly independent African nations were tending toward "Africanization"
of many businesses. Thousands of non-Black merchants, mostly
Indians, were having their enterprises either partially or completely taken over by the state.

There were extreme differences and problems within the
Black population as well, the ties of tribalism being far deeper
than Williams had anticipated. Ancient antagonisms and resent-
ments still plagued most African governments, and few politicians
were able to achieve or hold important posts unless their tribe was
powerful.

The idea of national or all-African, rather than merely tribal,
welfare was just beginning to emerge. It had taken a great leader
like President Julius Nyerere to get the various tribes together so
they could win their fight for independence and bring Tanzania
into existence. In contrast, the civil war between the Ibo tribesmen
of Biafra and the Yorubas of Nigeria, in which millions died, had
demonstrated all too tragically the problems of tribal rivalry
which still persisted.

On top of its tribal differences, Africa was severely split along
class lines. The tiny Tanzanian middle class of mostly European-
and American-educated Black professionals and businessmen impressed Williams as being more Uncle Tomish than the worst of
the Black bourgeoisie in the United States. Many of them seemed
concerned only with emulating and taking the place of the White
colonialists. When a poor African was waiting in line in an airport
or store, and a White or a well-dressed Black was behind him, the
Black clerk or official would often tell the poor man to step aside
while he waited on the wealthy person first. The bad habits of decades of colonial rule hadn't vanished in five or six short years of
independence; almost everyone in the country with a profession
had been trained under the old system. The efforts of militants like
Nyerere and others were slowly changing this situation, but Wil-

liams felt that, so long as the mines, oil fields, power plants, and
other basic industries of even such independent nations as Tanzania were largely European-controlled, building a decent society
there would remain an uphill struggle.

Despite its vast wealth, the United States seldom provided
the underdeveloped nations with a steel mill, truck or auto factory, shipyard, or any of the other elements of heavy industry. It
remained for China, itself only just emerging from the Dark Ages,
to build the first major textile mill in all of Black Africa. Up until
the completion of the Chinese-built "Friendship" mill in Dar es
Salaam in 1968, hundreds of millions of Africans, despite ex-
porting both cotton and wool, had to wear clothing woven in
other continents. The capitalists weren't interested in helping the
colored peoples of the world achieve economic independence;
they preferred to keep them as suppliers of raw materials and con-
sumers of manufactured goods. On the other hand, the Chinese
and the other Socialist nations were offering to help the newly
emerging states develop their heavy industry and natural resources because they believed that doing so would both gain them
allies and hasten the end of capitalism.

One of the most meaningful parts of Williams' trip was getting to know revolutionaries from Mozambique, Angola, Rhodesia, South Africa, and the other areas which were still under the
heel of the colonialists. Representatives of ZAPU, FRELIMO,
ANC, and the other guerrilla groups, most of whom belonged to
the Liberation Committee of the Organization for African Unity,
discussed their activities with him and were very enthusiastic
about developing ties with Black revolutionaries in the United
States.

In addition to mounting armed attacks against the racist regimes controlling their homelands, they were conducting campaigns to mobilize ever-larger numbers of their people. Both from
Tanzanian territory and from clandestine locations inside their
own countries, they were beaming revolutionary propaganda messages over the radio, circulating pamphlets, and sending out agitators.

The governments opposing them were using tanks, jet aircraft, napalm, and other modern weapons—almost all supplied by
the United States—to try to stamp out the sparks of rebellion. Despite the widespread terror and repression, "relocation" concen-

tration camps, detention without trial, and firing squads of the Nazilike regimes in South Africa, Angola, and other areas, Williams saw the forces of liberation as slowly but steadily growing larger and stronger.

The freedom fighters of Black Africa were also becoming more internationally minded. Some of them told Williams they were paying a great deal of attention to U.S. events and felt that Black Americans might be able to help them significantly. "While few of us ever had the opportunity to handle a weapon before commencing our battle against the colonialists," they said, "most U.S. Blacks have been brought up surrounded by guns. Perhaps your people in America could send some military experts here to help train their African brothers?"

Their suggestion seemed to Williams to have merit. Not only was there at least a shotgun or .22-caliber rifle in most rural Black homes in the United States, hundreds of thousands of Blacks had been given military training by Uncle Sam. Rather than have them remain dependent upon White military instructors—in 1968 the Canadians were training the Tanzanian Army—Black American vets might be able to assist their African brothers.

But he felt that the initiative for such aid would have to come from the Africans—and that it would be unwise for anyone to try to go there and insist that they accept unsolicited advice.

Military technicians weren't the only kind required. They also discussed such things as encouraging Black American doctors to take their vacations in Africa, where they could work to help their people, rather than wasting money lounging around resorts and gambling casinos in an attempt to equal the decadence of the White bourgeoisie.

Williams' wife joined him in Dar es Salaam in July. She had flown from Peking via the same commercial air routes he had used.

The possibility of being a target for CIA assassination while in Africa had occurred to Williams, but he had decided to chance it, thinking that the United States wouldn't be anxious enough to kill him to risk offending the Tanzanians. He had noticed several Blacks who looked like secret policemen tailing him soon after his arrival in Dar es Salaam. Also, he'd been told by informed friends that the United States had tried to pressure the Tanzanians into throwing him out, but President Nyerere had refused to treat him differently from any other tourist. In order to help speed the development of his country, Nyerere had made many compromises with the capitalists, but when it came to barring a Black American political refugee, he apparently drew the line.

In order to meet people more easily, Williams rented a motorcycle, and began going off on excursions into the countryside. Traffic on the Tanzanian roads being relatively sparse, he felt that traveling by motorcycle would make it difficult for anyone to follow him without being seen. His longest trip was from Dar es Salaam to Lusaka, the capital of neighboring Zambia. It was along a makeshift highway called Hell's Run, a one-thousand-mile route, which he negotiated both ways in about a week.

Hell's Run had been built as a result of the seizure of power in Rhodesia by the Ian Smith regime. Located in the center of Africa, and dependent upon oil imports to operate its rich copper mines, once the White minority took over in Rhodesia, landlocked Zambia found itself in deep trouble. There was no easy route to either get fuel in or copper out without dealing with the racists. A solution was found by hacking out a roadway to Dar es Salaam through the jungles, mountains, and swamps.

Many of the same capitalist regimes, such as the United States, which had large investments in Rhodesia, wanted to maintain the flow of copper from Zambia. As a result, they helped the Tanzanians and the Zambians to maintain the Hell's Run: U.S. Air Force C-130 Hercules transports could be seen every day flying bulldozers inland from Dar es Salaam; some 1,500 Canadian, British, and U.S. semitrailer trucks and tankers were constantly on the move, hauling oil in and copper out; and the Italians were building a pipeline.

Traveling along such a road by motorcycle was an unforgettable experience. Besides having to constantly dodge giant trucks on what was in many places little more than a cow trail, Williams had been warned that in some areas there was danger of running into an elephant or a lion. He spent as little time as possible resting along the way in those regions, driving all night when there was no safe place available to sleep.

Of all his experiences in Africa, the most impressive took place one evening in the countryside near Dar es Salaam. As he sped along the main highway on his motorcycle, Williams heard drums beating off in the bush. Slowing down, he discovered the

sound was coming from a village a little way off the road. On the
spur of the moment, he stopped and walked over to the native set-
tlement. The villagers were dancing in a circle around a group of
men beating on large wooden drums. They appeared undisturbed
by his presence, and laughed and smiled in friendly greeting.

Although he had learned a few words of Swahili, which is a
combination of Arabic and certain African languages, Williams
wasn't able to speak it well enough to learn the nature of the
event. Despite the lack of verbal communication, he felt a strong
kinship with the villagers because of the underlying similarities between their music and dance rhythms and those of Black America.
Being able to stand there under the African night sky, surrounded
by the sights and sounds of his brothers and sisters enjoying life as
their people had during the millenniums before they were dragged
across the seas to slavery in the New World, gave him a sense of a
common bond which all of his reading in Black history had failed
to convey.

He hadn't felt this common heritage with the bourgeois Africans, most of whom were straining to reject their village heritage
and replace it with the trappings of European and U.S. culture.
But here he felt completely at home. The superficial and dishonest
had no place with these people; they had yet to become de-Afri-
canized like those who had migrated to the cities.

It wasn't the first time Williams had sensed a kinship among
Blacks. Mingling with the peasants and workers of African descent in Cuba, hearing the rhythm of their music and watching
them dance, he had felt underlying similarities, and realized that
things like music and dance movements transcend national and
language differences. Despite centuries of separation, those of African origin—whether they lived in U.S. ghettos or Cuba's mountains—so long as they hadn't been culturally disinherited by mimicking their oppressors, seemed to him to share certain primal life
rhythms and emotions. They were "soul brothers."

At the same time he was gaining an awareness of the spiritual
values of African life, Williams realized it was necessary to be
wary of confusing the superficial aspects of culture with its inner
meanings. Merely speaking Swahili or other African languages,
wearing a "natural" hair style, and sporting African-style clothing
wouldn't give one an African soul. He felt that many American
Blacks who affected such trappings were using them as a form of

escape from the necessity to strive for equality and justice. It was
the positive values of Africanism that should be encouraged—
such as honesty, dignity, bravery, and cooperation. The more
Blacks throughout the world came to understand that they shared
a common heritage, the easier it would be for them to unite and
fight together for their common goals, he thought.

Williams visited the recently built University of Dar es Salaam. A beautiful and impressive campus located in the hills near
the sea to the north of the city, it was perhaps the only educational
institution in the world having parts which had been donated by
both the United States and China. On its faculty were both American and eastern European instructors. Once they learned who
Williams was, the students at the university invited Williams to
speak there on several occasions. He also participated in a demonstration held by the Tanzanian Association for National Unity
(TANU) and the University Revolutionary Front at the U.S. embassy in Dar es Salaam on July 20, 1968.

Hundreds of young people massed in front of the bank building that housed the embassy and loudly protested America's presence in Vietnam. Their posters ranged from Che's famous statement, "We must make two, three, many Vietnams," to "Ameri-
cani Vampiri" (Swahili for "Americans are vampires"). A group of
them entered the building and delivered a seven-point note of protest to the American ambassador. According to their leader, the
U.S. ambassador had invited them to tea. "We responded," he
told the crowd, "by telling him: 'Mr. Ambassador, how can you
offer us tea when your hands are dripping with the blood of the
people of Vietnam? We don't want to drink with you until you get
out of Asia and the other parts of the world where your armies are
killing our colored brothers.' "

For a group of Blacks not only to protest U.S. policy but to
refuse to have tea with a White ambassador was something quite
new and different for Africa.

As in China, Williams saw the youth of Africa as the vanguard of forces working for revolutionary change. He felt it be-
hooved the young people of Black America to establish contacts
with their African counterparts so they might assist one another.

In contrast to the rising tide of self-awareness and desire for
independence on the part of Africans, he sensed a growing danger
posed by the technologically advanced powers who were seeking

to control the continent. The West was striving for influence among the African nations—but only to ravage their vast natural resources, he felt, not to benefit the people. Mechanization and automation, plus population surpluses in Europe and the United States, were making the people of Africa an annoying problem, rather than an inexpensive labor source, as they had been in the past. He had no doubt that, if the contemporary imperialists could have their way, they wouldn't object to the Blacks of Africa being exterminated en masse—so long as the gold, diamonds, copper, uranium, oil, and other treasures were left intact. Human beings— especially ones who insist on controlling their own nations—only get in the way of bulldozers, automatic mining machines, and drilling apparatus.

Williams saw the international battle for the Congo and its mines as presaging this trend. He felt that genocidal conflicts such as the civil war in Nigeria were secretly welcomed by the exploiters. Competition for the rich oil fields of the breakaway Ibo areas were what led England, France, the United States, and Russia as well, to supply modern arms to the combatants.

In addition to the race among imperialists to control Africa's mineral deposits, he saw a mighty struggle for political position taking place between the U.S.S.R. and China. The Russians had made their greatest gains in the Moslem nations north of the Sahara. From Algiers to Cairo to Damascus, Soviet-built weapons, machinery, and factories were in evidence; and with them had come Russian advisers, technicians, and political influence. The Chinese, on the other hand, had achieved their major successes in the sub-Saharan areas, especially East Africa. They had supplied Tanzania with tanks and other arms, were operating a joint Chinese-Tanzanian sea transportation line with regular sailings between Dar es Salaam and Shanghai, and were building a billion-dollar railway from Tanzania inland to the mines of Zambia.

A significant difference between Chinese aid and that of other nations was that China lent money to the underdeveloped African states interest-free. Everyone else, including Russia, demanded interest on their loans.

With so many divergent elements vying for power, Williams saw the future bringing large-scale violent confrontations. Of one thing he was certain: the racist regimes in Rhodesia, Mozambique, Angola, and the Union of South Africa would eventually be overwhelmed by the forces of Black Liberation. Africa's revolutionaries were on the move, and they wouldn't be turned back until the entire continent was free.

Not only was Williams able to establish important links with African revolutionaries, he was visited by representatives from many militant U.S. organizations. Hardly a day went by without someone flying in to see him from New York, Detroit, Chicago, or elsewhere. The U.S. State Department's ban on travel to China had made it difficult for him to have visitors there, but in Tanzania there was no such problem.

Although he had seriously contemplated staying in Dar es Salaam and establishing a Black Liberation Movement Information Center—even going so far as to inquire about buying or renting a house there—Williams suddenly decided to return to China. He had learned that the Tanzanian government did not plan to renew the six-month tourist visa he had used to enter the country. In October, 1968, he and Mabel boarded a Chinese ocean liner bound for Shanghai. Just prior to doing so, apparently to facilitate his long-planned homecoming, he visited the U.S. consulate in Dar es Salaam, where he asked for a passport, but was issued one valid only for return to the United States.

On May Day, 1969, he once again stood atop the Gate of Heavenly Peace in Peking. There, both Mao Tse-tung and Lin Piao autographed his copy of the "little red book."

Then, on the night before their final departure from China, Williams and his wife were the guests of Premier Chou En-lai at a farewell banquet in the Great Hall of the People. Chou asked if he wasn't afraid of being murdered or jailed once he got to the United States, and Williams expressed his hope that the American government would be more interested in what he had to say than in silencing him. Chou seemed somewhat skeptical of his chances, but said he hoped Williams would be able to work for better relations between the peoples of China and the United States.

No matter what was about to happen to him, Robert Franklin Williams' eight long years of exile had come to an end. He was going home.

Chapter Sixteen

THE THREE-PART PROGRAM

As he prepared to return home, Williams mulled over the outlook for racial and political change. In his eight years of exile, many things had changed in the United States—for better and for worse. On the positive side, there was a new spirit of militancy among Blacks. The pacifist concepts of the Reverend Martin Luther King, Jr., had almost received a death blow when he was struck down. Blacks had joined forces with Browns and Whites to elect Black public officials in many areas. They had begun to protect their leaders from racist assassinations. Throughout the nation a movement to the Left was in evidence.

But the years of his exile, it seemed to Williams, had also witnessed an unprecedented resurgence of racism and political repression. The sympathetic attitude toward Blacks of the Kennedy Administration—hypocritical though Williams thought it was— had resulted in some constructive programs. But after JFK's death lesser men had brought them to a halt. Johnson's occupancy of the White House—begun when Kennedy was murdered, punctuated by the assassination of Malcolm X, characterized by sending hundreds of thousands of troops into Vietnam, and ending shortly after the assassinations of the Reverend King and Robert Kennedy—had seen the United States transformed into one of the most despised nations since Hitler's Germany. And the coming to power of Richard Nixon—who quickly revealed himself as an irresponsible mediocrity, Williams felt—was aggravating the violent internal convulsions of the capitalist system.

Apparently incapable of curbing their appetites for power and profit, and unwilling to institute the reforms needed to eliminate a vast and growing mountain of social ills, the U.S. rulers seemed to Williams to be attempting to cover up their contradictions by increasingly severe acts of repression. Support of dictatorships overseas and Ku Klux Klan lynchings at home no longer sufficing to intimidate people, they had abandoned all pretense and were openly engaging in military aggression and police-state terror.

First Black militants, then dissenters of all colors, were being murdered with impunity by uniformed dupes and assassins instigated by vicious demagogues in high office. No-knock search warrants and no-warrant arrest laws, the denial of bail to those not yet tried, hand-picked grand juries and hanging judges were evidence to Williams of a national trend toward Fascism. The entire Bill of Rights, from freedom of speech to equality before the law, was under the most severe attack in its history—not by "subversives" or foreign troops but by all too many of the local, state, and federal officials pledged to defend it. The injustice long visited upon Black Americans was now being unleashed upon everyone who dared question the profits and privileges of the power structure. As he saw it, the United States as a whole was being "niggerfied."

The Ronald Reagans openly proclaimed their position on "bloodbaths." The Nixons and Agnews called upon "patriots" to band together to help rid society of "bums" and "rotten apples." But the rulers of America weren't maintaining computerized name files and concentration camps only for political dissenters. Technology and automation making Black labor less and less necessary, and Black demands for justice and equality threatening profits, the power structure was accelerating its repression against Blacks as a people.

There was less and less willingness on the part of White wage earners—themselves increasingly impoverished by inflation and a faltering economy—to pay taxes to provide subsistence for the growing millions of unemployed and unemployables. Fewer and fewer voices were being raised against the police when they used brutality in the name of "law and order" to silence those who protested the lack of jobs and social justice.

It was becoming increasingly evident to Williams that something had to change. Either the moribund capitalist system would be discarded by the people, whose needs it was no longer fulfilling, or (as happened in Nazi Germany) those who benefited from its inequities would try to keep it alive by exterminating millions of "undesirables" and feeding it with their blood. And that element of American society which was poorest, illest, least educated, and most troublesome was obviously the "niggers."

But killing "niggers" in the old way by denying them adequate food, medicine, and housing was too slow, he reflected, and doing it with lynch ropes, clubs, and bullets had become obsolete. More modern techniques were being devised. Police forces were stockpiling various military-type weapons. Financed by Congress and guided by the FBI and CIA, "Special Weapons and Tactics" squads were being trained by Armed Forces experts in cordoning off and assaulting urban areas.

Having already used dum-dum bullets and searing gases forbidden by international convention, the domestic counterparts of those defoliating and incinerating Vietnam were planning to use napalm to "pacify" the Black ghettos of the United States as well.

The "purification" by fire of social "plague spots" and the murdering of vast numbers of people for political, economic, religious, and other reasons had been going on for centuries. And America's brutal past and present-day indiscriminate shooting and killing of both Blacks and Whites during domestic disturbances indicated that the Nazi "final solution" policy for Europe's Jews presented an irresistible temptation to the US. power structure for getting rid of America's Blacks. Williams didn't doubt that it was the objective. The only question was: When?

Williams felt that U.S. degeneration into a Hitlerian state had to be stopped. All true patriots would have to unite against the forces of repression, and Blacks, having been enslaved and oppressed for so long, should be in the forefront of that resistance. Everything Williams had learned at home and abroad indicated to him that Black America would of necessity develop a Three-Part Program involving: (1) *organization,* (2) *struggle,* and (3) *defense.*

Organization, essential to all other resistance activities, would necessitate: (a) strengthening and invigorating already established organizations and (b) creating and maintaining new organizations. Blacks would have to put aside their differences of the past. Almost every established group could make a positive contribution —some by continuing to press for civil rights, others by trying to provide Blacks with higher education and well-paying jobs, still others by arming for self-defense. Completely new organizations would bring together the isolated and alienated majority of

Blacks. Affinity groups of all types—from teen-age social clubs to political discussion circles—would be brought into existence, and membership in them encouraged. The talents of Blacks in every aspect of contemporary society would be harnessed. Those with professional expertise would establish liaisons both within and between their disciplines, and strive to interest and assist young people in sharing their knowledge.

Whatever other groups he might join, everyone would be encouraged to take an interest in the affairs of his immediate area. Through organization of *neighborhood committees,* the vast majority of Blacks would be involved. The individual would be in contact with his *neighborhood committee* so that it could help him as well as enlist his aid when needed for the good of the area. Each *neighborhood committee* would develop contacts with city, county, state, and national units, thus providing a vast structure of self-help units throughout the United States.

Whatever the specific focus of a given organization might be, its primary program would be aimed at stimulating *cooperation* and *education.*

Cooperation among Blacks has been discouraged for centuries. First, the slave dealers made certain that captives belonging to the same tribe or language group were separated lest they join in revolt. And it was common practice to sever husbands from wives, and parents from their children. The plantation owners' ideal slave was an isolated, cowed, and powerless individual, and they ruthlessly crushed whoever attempted to be otherwise.

In modern times several factors, especially the lack of employment, plus the widespread practice of refusing welfare payments for children in households where an able-bodied male inhabits the premises, serve to drive fathers away from their families. And many of those Blacks who do manage to get decent jobs are seduced by the bourgeois ethics of avarice and individualism, and, as a result, become even more alienated.

Because of this, every organization would have to encourage its members to work together. Once having learned to cooperate in matters of local interest, they could undertake more far-reaching efforts.

Education would be an essential aspect of every group's activities. Reading material and lectures which help develop Black self-awareness and pride would be vitally important. The very fact that so many Blacks lack decent schooling would make the acquiring of all types of knowledge (especially reading—the key to educating one's self) a primary concern. Those who already understood the nature of capitalist society would educate their fellows to the desirability of radical change. Preaching revolution to people who have not yet begun to understand its necessity is futile, in Williams' opinion. The true revolutionary is a teacher and a guide of men—not a terrorizer and stampeder of cattle.

Struggle, part two of the Three-Part Program, would have two basic aspects: *policy* and *tactics.* Policy would not be dictated by any one person or group, but would arise from a dynamic interaction. More and better communication between Black organizations and individuals would be developed. Those who in the past had been Uncle Toms would not be automatically excluded, for changing times change men, and many of yesterday's "house niggers" would become dedicated radicals.

Due to the multitude of divergent elements which make up Black America, a collective leadership would probably be the best way to coordinate efforts. Egoism, the ethic of the oppressor, would have to be strenuously avoided. As always, the power structure would try to kill off, compromise, or buy out Black leadership. But Blacks, learning how to protect themselves against such tactics, would put the shoe on the other foot by taking advantage of every available opportunity to infiltrate the system. Having sympathizers inside the camp of the oppressors would be of critical importance.

Struggle wouldn't be delayed until organization was complete, but would be undertaken at the same time. People are encouraged to join a movement when they see that it is really trying to accomplish something. While the specifics of struggle policy would be worked out by collective endeavor, its broad goals would be (1) *human rights,* (2) *self-determination,* and (3) *revolutionary social change.*

Human rights would require continuing the fight to eliminate discrimination and injustice on all levels. But Blacks would also struggle for more than merely being equally exploited and misled alongside White Americans.

Self-determination is particularly important because the years since Abolition have shown that, no matter how sympathetic Whites as individuals may be, the underlying profit-at-any-cost orientation of the capitalist system leads Whites as a whole to take advantage of Blacks and other minorities whenever possible. Blacks should strive to govern their own communities and take steps to provide themselves with police protection, health care, and other things which are inadequate or denied them.

The objectives of *struggle* would soon go beyond *human rights* and *self-determination. Revolutionary social change* would become the long-term goal. Working for the first two goals would inevitably revolutionize the situation, since capitalism has shown itself to be so prone to economic and moral collapse. A new way of life, including Socialist ownership, would come, but its exact form would remain for the people themselves to work out.

In determining their struggle policies Blacks would strive to universalize their goals, to discover those ideals which appealed not only to themselves but to Brown, Oriental, Indian, and oppressed White Americans as well.

Tactics would be divided into two basic categories: *economic* and *political.* Boycotts, selective-buying, strikes, slowdowns, sit-ins, wade-ins—everything already attempted would be evaluated and used again wherever applicable. Properly organized, the purchasing power of twenty-two million Blacks would either insure the profits of those companies which conducted themselves in a decent manner, or produce bankrupting losses for those that maintained discriminatory policies.

Another aspect of *economic struggle* would be voluntary taxation. Through income, purchasing, property, and other taxes, the Blacks of America already involuntarily contribute a vast sum to help maintain the very system that exploits and represses them. If only what is spent in the ghettos on narcotics, whiskey, and cigarettes went to support the Black Liberation Movement instead, it would have more funds at its disposal than anyone except the U.S. government itself.

Political struggle tactics would involve continuing to press for the election of both Black and anti-racist non-Black candidates. They would also use all the stratagems in the political book: joining forces with other interest groups, lobbying, conducting letter-writing and propaganda campaigns, circulating petitions, voting in blocs, and whatever else would contribute to the achievement of the Blacks' goals.

Defense, the third aspect of the Three-Part Program, would be developed simultaneously with *organization* and *struggle*. To protect person and family, millions of Blacks would exercise their rights under the Constitution to possess a pistol or rifle. But harsh experience has shown that the individual who relies solely upon his own efforts will be surrounded, outnumbered, and crushed. It would be imperative, therefore, that all residents of a given area unite their defense efforts. This would be done through the *neighborhood committees*, which would form separate defense units. Each local *defense unit* then would coordinate strategy with its counterparts throughout the district, town, or city. Thus, when racists attempted to assault individual Blacks, they would be forced to contend with the Black population as a whole.

But static community defense would not be enough if the power structure persisted in its present course, because whenever the Blacks repulsed the violence of the KKK, Minutemen, or other racists, they could expect that police, National Guard, Army, Air Force, Marine, and Navy units would be brought into action.

It was at this point that Williams' projection of what would come in the United States became extremely apocalyptic. He envisioned that, once major military attacks were launched, the Black *defense units* would not only resist them frontally. Units beyond the immediate battle zone would interfere with their attacker's communications, cut his transportation lines, threaten his flanks and rear, and do everything else possible to cause him to falter in his onslaught. Williams was certain that the U.S. power structure wouldn't stop its violence against Blacks even after they had shown their readiness and capability to defend their communities. The Pentagon's Vietnam-trained experts could be expected to declare entire urban ghettos, such as Harlem or Watts, "free-fire zones."

To discourage the annihilation of their communities, Williams theorized, Blacks would have to develop what the U.S. power structure calls a "credible deterrent." Just as the international balance of power is a result of possession by both East and West of intercontinental ballistic missiles, so Black Americans would carry defense to its ultimate by organizing the means of visiting mass destruction upon their enemies. The first means of "massive retaliation" or (should the prospect of genocidal attack become imminent) "pre-emptive first strike," would be the ordinary house match. All of its ships, aircraft, tanks, radar, missiles, and anti-missiles together couldn't defend the United States against this weapon, for those who would wield it are already inside the fortress. Blacks are within arm's length of the oil fields, mines, factories, dams, and power plants that provide the life force of capitalism. A few matches lit at the right times and places could do greater damage than anything short of an atomic holocaust.

To make their deterrent credible, Blacks would develop the ability to execute simultaneous, widespread, and repeated acts of destruction. Secret, squad-size *attack units* of revolutionaries would spring up all over the United States. Composed of anywhere from three to seven members, and maintaining a high level of discipline, they would engage in the second phase of popular resistance: *acts of revolutionary violence.* The first phase, *rebellious outbursts,* such as Watts, was largely over.

The authorities, of course, would attempt to infiltrate both the *defense* and *attack units.* The horde of police, FBI, and CIA spies would necessitate utilizing every counterintelligence technique available. Friends trained in informing and infiltrating by Uncle Sam could be helpful to Blacks. The power structure must have such Blacks, but it can never be certain of their true loyalties.

Security could be increased by applying the tactics developed by the ancient Chinese triad secret societies or of the cell-pyramid structure used by contemporary underground organizations.

The modus operandi of the *attack units* would be to avoid open battle, to hit and run, to destroy without being destroyed, to emerge from darkness, strike without warning, and vanish into the night.

Williams felt certain the escalation of repression, to which Blacks would respond with revolutionary violence, would result in a garrison state. The barbed wire, sentries, helicopter patrols, midnight searches, and identity checks characteristic of nations in the throes of civil unrest were already to be seen across the United States.

But the arrival of a totalitarian state—concentration camps and all—would serve only to radicalize more people, for it would show even middle-of-the-road Whites that those who controlled the nation were ready to eliminate everyone's constitutional rights before they would permit Blacks to have theirs.

The Black masses, finding themselves faced with extermination, would increase their resistance until it was transformed into the final phase of resistance: *revolutionary civil war*. No longer would the fighting be concentrated in the ghettos; the centers of industry, military, and the government would be the primary battlefields. The small *attack units* would merge into company, regiment, and army-size fighting groups. The secret war would become open battle. The enemy's forces would be pinned down and diverted by commando actions throughout the nation. Fields and forests would be put to the torch. Friends in the Armed Forces would assist in the seizure of arsenals. And not even the thousands of atomic weapons stockpiled through the nation would be safe from appropriation. A war with no fronts, with combat taking place simultaneously in a thousand hot spots, would ravage America.

Repercussions of the conflict would be felt throughout the world, Williams foresaw. Competitor nations would seize the opportunity to tear off chunks of the crumbling U.S. empire. And the withdrawal of overseas U.S. military forces to face the civil war at home would lead to the triumph of national liberation movements in Africa, Asia, and Latin America.

Williams recognized the possibility of defeat of the U.S. revolutionaries, but he felt that, even so, the injury to the nation would be total: cities destroyed, industry ruined, famine and epidemic sweeping the land, and the long-term effects of atomic, chemical, and bacteriological weapons rendering vast areas uninhabitable for years. Nationally and internationally, the capitalist system would receive its death blow. Uncle Sam would be a gutted hulk, the imbecile-derelict of the nations, a giant with brain and body consumed by the diseases of racism and greed.

Chapter Seventeen

STRANGE HOMECOMING

Our policy should be to encourage those Black revolutionaries in a position to do so to join the police, National Guard, Army, Navy, Air Force, Marines, FBI, CIA, State Department, etc.; to strive for positions of responsibility in major corporations; and to do everything else possible to learn about and gain control of the keys to power. Discretion as to one's militancy will, of course, often be necessary in such situations.

—Robert Franklin Williams
Dar es Salaam, July, 1968

Leaving China in mid-1969, Williams went to Africa once again. In August of that year he sent Mabel and the boys home to the United States, and in September he boarded a jet in Dar es Salaam bound for Cairo, London, and Detroit. Moments after landing at London's Heathrow Airport he was taken into custody. Claiming to be looking for "firearms and ammunition" which they said the FBI had told them he'd be trying to smuggle into the United States, the British police searched his person and luggage. While they failed to find anything, he was taken to spend the night in Pentonville Prison.

Williams assumed that he was being jailed only until the next morning's flight to Detroit, but instead he was held incommunicado for two days. On the third day, word having somehow gotten out, three representatives of the Black Panther Party of England came to Pentonville to visit him. As they left they warned the warden: "We're going to free our brother, either peacefully or by force. It's up to you to decide."

The following day groups of West Indians, Africans, Asians, and White British liberals began demonstrating in front of the prison.

Williams was then told by the prison authorities that his detention was due to a combination of factors: TWA's refusal to fly him to Detroit, and the British government's decision that he was an "unadmittable alien." He was to be deported. Two representatives of the airline then appeared and said they couldn't honor his air ticket because of the fear that he might hijack the plane. His quip, that he'd already been every place that people hijack planes to, apparently failed to amuse them. He was taken back to Heathrow to be placed on the next jet to Cairo—his last stop before having arrived in London. There he asked the TWA representatives if they didn't fear that he would now hijack the Cairo flight and force it to fly to Detroit, instead. While they were trying to decide if he was serious, an airfield service truck rammed the jet. The aircraft was damaged so badly that it couldn't take off; and Williams was returned to Pentonville.

While all this was happening, he had begun a total fast, refusing even water so long as he was held prisoner.

On the fifth day he was once again returned to Heathrow. There, with a dozen or more policemen lined up in the corridor, he was told by a representative of the British Foreign Office that they had been authorized to use force if he refused to board the Cairo flight. "The only way I'll enter that plane is either dead or unconscious," he responded. At this, the diplomat telephoned his superiors, and they ordered Williams taken back to prison.

His detention had become the subject of headlines and editorial comment around the world. British members of Parliament were criticizing their government's actions on television; the American Civil Liberties Union was preparing to sue TWA for breach of contract for refusing to honor his ticket; and his associates in the Republic of New Africa were supposedly planning to declare war and initiate military action against England—something which, while appreciating the sentiment, Williams considered premature at best.

Finally, on the sixth day, with protest demonstrations taking place in front of the U.S. embassy in London—some Black Panthers actually got into the embassy grounds and confronted American officials—TWA announced that it would fly Williams to Detroit after all. On Saturday, September 13, 1969, almost exactly eight years after having fled his hometown in North Carolina, he boarded a jet in London to return to the United States.

But what had become a bizarre spectacle wasn't yet over. To compound the scenario, which Williams was certain had been written by the CIA, instead of permitting him to board a normal flight, TWA provided a special plane. Except for his lawyer and himself, it carried no other passengers. With a full complement of stewardesses at his call, and at an estimated cost of $20,000 to the airline, Robert Franklin Williams was flown across the Atlantic in an empty jetliner.

To cap the entire incident, just before takeoff a Black in African-style dress entered the plane and introduced himself as a TWA vice president. He went to great lengths to try to convince Williams that his employer was the "most liberal" of airlines, having "more Black pilots and stewardesses than any other U.S. company." He said that he hoped Williams would be more considerate of TWA now that he knew how "progressive" they were. Being asked to embrace those whom he felt had just caused him to spend a week in jail seemed to Williams the height of absurdity.

Waiting for the plane in Detroit were hundreds of Williams' supporters, journalists, radio and TV camera crews, and the FBI. Before he could speak to anyone, two FBI agents placed him under arrest and hustled him off to the Federal Building. The sight of a tall bearded Black wearing dark sunglasses, and attired in a Chinese "national uniform," flashed onto the screens of tens of millions of TV sets across the nation. The "Crusader" had come home.

No sooner was Williams taken before the judge than a series of events began which were to puzzle and concern many of his most ardent supporters. First, instead of being imprisoned, he was released on a relatively low bond of some $11,000. Then, although Michigan's Governor Milliken ordered him extradited to North Carolina to stand trial on the 1961 kidnapping charge, the authorities proceeded so slowly in handling his appeal that more than two years later it was still pending. This was in marked contrast to the haste with which Black militants such as Bobby Seale and Angela Davis had been extradited.

In March, 1970, Williams testified in a closed-door session before the Internal Security Sub-Committee of the Senate Judiciary Committee, the group headed by Mississippi's Senator Eastland.

Then, in mid-1970, Williams and his wife drove to New York City and told acquaintances there that they had permission to go to Canada for a vacation. The government's granting such a privilege to a person under indictment for kidnapping was unusual.

The net effect of these things was to cause disillusionment among many of those who had hoped that Williams was going to rally and unite Black revolutionaries in the United States. This impression was added to by his resigning from the Republic of New Africa, as well as disassociating himself from several of his oldest friends both at home and abroad.

Then, in February, 1971, the *New York Times* published a guest editorial by Williams. It was illustrated with a large photograph of him shaking hands with Chairman Mao Tse-tung. The position he took was so moderate and conciliatory that it was difficult to believe the founder of *The Crusader* had written it. Rather than calling out "KILL, BABY, KILL," as he had a few years previously from Peking, he was asking the United States to grant China "understanding and recognition."

Although Williams may have viewed his editorial simply as an effort to encourage friendlier relations between the United States and China, it appeared to this writer to be part of the State Department's campaign to assuage the Chinese during the then-current invasion of Laos. Publishing a piece complimentary to China by an American long known for his support of that nation, and doing so in the most prestigious U.S. newspaper, seemed an unmistakable attempt to signal Peking that Washington didn't mean to attack it.

Williams was cast in the role, not of anticapitalist firebrand, but of moderate international diplomat; and the ideas expressed in his article differed very little from those then being tendered by President Nixon.

As if to cement the opinions of those who had become convinced that he had reached an accommodation with the U.S. government, it was revealed that Williams had joined the staff of the Center for Chinese Studies at the University of Michigan, and he had also become the recipient of a grant from the Ford Foundation. The first chairman of the Revolutionary Action Movement, several of whose members were serving prison terms, had apparently become acceptable to the Establishment's academic and cultural circles.

The true meaning of the events following Williams' home-coming remains obscure. A number of his former followers have concluded that, in return for both publicly criticizing Cuba, as he has done in various interviews, and abandoning the call for revolution which characterized his emissions from Cuba and China, he has been rewarded by those whom he previously considered his mortal enemies. Others have more kindly assumed that he has grown tired of struggling for revolutionary social change—and has retired from the Crusade. Williams himself has done or said little to dispel these opinions. He continues to give lectures to student groups in the Midwest, but what he has to say, while considered anathema a decade ago, today fails to engender the ire of editorial writers and politicians.

It is evident that the U.S. legal system is dealing with him in a manner far different from what he expected. Instead of finding himself on trial in the Union County Courthouse, with a crowd of ten thousand of his sympathizers demonstrating outside, he has been presented with a very difficult choice: He still faces the possibility of extradition and imprisonment in the South, while at the same time he has been given what he sought in vain for so many years—a good job, prestige, and recognition in the pages of the *New York Times*. The methods for dealing with those who challenge the "American Way of Life" aren't always limited to bullets and direct bribes. Many dissidents who have stood up to threats without flinching have been subtly compromised by being given well-paying positions within the system.

Williams himself warned of this when he declared in the March, 1968, edition of *The Crusader:* ". . . The man is attempting to buy off as many Uncle Tom 'Revolutionaries' necessary to confuse, demoralize and wreck the Black revolution. We must avoid falling prey to the vain words of ambitious Black men in the sinister employ of satanic white savage oppressors. . . . The international liquidationists of racist and imperialist America's power structure have infiltrated the Marxist movement, the revolutionary movement, the Black Nationalist movement and everything else that constitutes a potential threat. . . . They are endeavoring to curb our growing militancy by feigning adherence to Marxist and humanist principles."

As of this writing, it is impossible to determine whether or not Robert Franklin Williams may have been predicting his own future. One thing is certain, the fiery utterances he hurled at the United States from Havana and Peking aren't being heard. But while the strident polemics of *The Crusader* are no longer causing alarm in the White House and the halls of Congress, and while the gut-level sounds of Radio Free Dixie have faded into silence, the concepts which were voiced in them have not vanished at all. The idea of armed self-defense on the part of oppressed minorities, and of a revolution aimed at overthrowing the system which controls the United States, is spreading. Although sporadic, and still lacking in organization and know-how, many of the activities described in the Three-Part Program are nevertheless taking place.

Robert Franklin Williams didn't invent the antagonisms which threaten America's existence, he reacted to them. And his participation or lack of it will not be the determining factor in the future of this nation. The crusader may or may not have laid down his shield, but the crusade for justice and equality throughout the world goes on.